LONGMAN LINGUISTICS LIBRARY

A HISTORY OF ENGLISH PHONOLOGY

Andrew Linn,
 Cambridge 1997

General editors
R. H. Robins, *University of London,*
Martin Harris, *University of Manchester*
Geoffrey Horrocks, *University of Cambridge*

A Short History of Linguistics
Third Edition
R. H. ROBINS

Text and Context
Explorations in the Semantics and Pragmatics of Discourse
TEUN A. VAN DIJK

Introduction to Text Linguistics
ROBERT DE BEAUGRANDE
AND WOLFGANG ULRICH
DRESSLER

Psycholinguistics
Language, Mind, and World
DANNY D. STEINBERG

Principles of Pragmatics
GEOFFREY LEECH

Generative Grammar
GEOFFREY HORROCKS

The English Verb
Second Edition
F. R. PALMER

A History of American English
J. L. DILLARD

English Historical Syntax
Verbal Constructions
DAVID DENISON

Pidgin and Creole Languages
SUZANNE ROMAINE

A History of English Phonology
CHARLES JONES

Generative and Non-linear Phonology
JACQUES DURAND

Modality and the English Modals
Second Edition
F. R. PALMER

Semiotics and Linguistics
YISHI TOBIN

Multilingualism in the British Isles I: The Older Mother Tongues and Europe
EDITED BY SAFDER ALLADINA
AND VIV EDWARDS

Multilingualism in the British Isles II: Africa, The Middle East and Asia
EDITED BY SAFDER ALLANDINA
AND VIV EDWARDS

Dialects of English
Studies in Grammatical Variation
EDITED BY PETER TRUDGILL AND
J. K. CHAMBERS

Introduction to Bilingualism
CHARLOTTE HOFFMANN

Verb and Noun Number in English:
A Functional Explanation
WALLIS REID

English in Africa
JOSEF SCHMIED

Linguistic Theory
The Discourse of Fundamental Works
ROBERT DE BEAUGRANDE

General Linguistics
An Introductory Survey
Fourth Edition
R. H. ROBINS

Historical Linguistics
Problems and Perspectives
EDITED BY C. JONES

A History of Linguistics Vol. I
The Eastern Traditions of Linguistics
EDITED BY GIULIO LEPSCHY

A History of Linguistics Vol II
Classical and Medieval Linguistics
EDITED BY GIULIO LEPSCHY

Aspect in the English Verb
Process and Result in Language
YISHAI TOBIN

The Meaning of Syntax
A Study in the Adjectives of English
CONNOR FERRIS

Latin American Spanish
JOHN M. LIPSKI

A Linguistic History of Italian
MARTIN MAIDEN

Modern Arabic
Structures, Functions and Varieties
CLIVE HOLES

A History of English Phonology

Charles Jones

LONGMAN
LONDON AND NEW YORK

Longman Group Limited,
Longman House, Burnt Mill, Harlow,
Essex CM20 2JE, England
and Associated Companies throughout the world.

Published in the United States of America
by Longman Inc., New York

First published 1989
Second impression 1994

British Library Cataloguing in Publication Data

Jones, Charles, *1939–*
A history of English phonology. –
(Longman linguistics library).
1. English language, to 1988. Phonological
system
I. Title
421'.5'09
ISBN 0-582-04054-X CSD
ISBN 0-582-29156-9 PPR

Library of Congress Cataloging in Publication Data

Jones, Charles, 1939–
A history of English phonology.

(Longman linguistics library)
Bibliography: p.
Includes index.
1. English language – Phonology. I. Title
II. Series.
PE1133.J6   1989   421'.5   88-13610
ISBN 0-582-04054-X
ISBN 0-582-29156-9 (pbk.)

Set in Linotron 202 10/11pt Times

Produced by Longman Singapore Publishers (Pte) Ltd.
Printed in Singapore.

Contents

Preface

Even given that one has taught a subject area to what seems to be innumerable bands of patient undergraduates over an inordinately long period of time, it is only when one comes to attempt to write about it in overview that one realizes both the immensity of the task and comes to appreciate what must have been the extraordinary labours of earlier writers. Even a review of the monuments of traditional nineteenth- and twentieth-century scholarship in English historical phonology would be in itself a daunting enough exercise and we can now only marvel at the industry, foresight and imagination of many of those writers who, in addition to the theoretical problems involved in constructing a framework within which to present their data, had the massive task of collecting much of that data for themselves at first hand. Paradoxically, their success in both enterprises has perhaps come to have a stultifying effect on subsequent writers. When one reads much of the modern literature relating to historical English phonology which has been produced in the last thirty or so years, one is continually struck by the extent to which it relies upon both the actual data collection and the descriptive nomenclature of the earliest writers: over and over again we find the same instances cited and terminology utilized, until it appears that the handbooks themselves have somehow come to have a status in their own right both for source and descriptive materials.

That there is a general reluctance to return to the 'raw materials' is understandable enough given their complexity and vast extent, but it seems to the writer that, at least up to a point, many of our views concerning what we mean by phonological innovation and death are still largely fashioned within the boundaries of a paradigm which was constructed over eighty years ago. We are clearly a very long way from the time when a complete rewrite of the phonological history of English can be contemplated – indeed, one becomes ever more pessimistic about the prospect of such a project and others like it given the decline in funds available for postgraduate Arts research, a decline which threatens not only future research activity but the very teaching of many areas within English studies themselves. This book certainly does not attempt to produce any major rethink on phonological change, far less does it claim to provide anything like an exhaustive coverage of all recorded types of sound change dealt with in the handbooks.

What it does attempt, however, is to view historical phonological change as an ongoing, recurrent process; it sees like events occurring at all periods, a phenomenon which is disguised, we shall claim, by too great a reliance upon certain characteristics of the scholarly tradition. Expressed in the most simplistic terms, we shall in effect argue that those innovations arrived at by speakers of the English language many hundreds of years ago are not in principle unlike those that can be seen to be happening today. Phonological mutations are, on the whole, not to be regarded as unique, novel, once only events. Speakers appear to present to speech sound materials a limited set of evaluative and decoding perceptions, together with what would seem to be a finite number of innovation producing stratagems in response to their interpretation. Yet we shall continue to stress that, tempting though such a 'globalist' view of phonological change might be, this interpretation may itself be a direct product of the kinds of data selected for presentation in traditional handbooks. As a balance, we shall stress the fact that phonological change is often 'messy' and responsive to a highly tuned ability to perceive fine phonetic detail of a type which, by definition, rarely has the opportunity to surface in historical data sources.

I should like to thank all my colleagues and friends who have been tolerant of my pesterings and various misguided enthusiasms while I was writing this book, notably Lars Malmberg, Ann Squires, Gary Underwood and Ian Hancock. I am also indebted to Ann Squires for her inspired suggestion of the illustration which forms the cover of this book. My wife showed remarkable patience with what was becoming an increasingly temperamental author. Perhaps we can now both return to looking after our Soay sheep with fewer distractions.

School of English
University of Durham
March 1988

Acknowledgements

We are grateful to the following for permission to reproduce copyright material:

Edinburgh University Library for a table from p. 44 of *The Works of William Bullokar*, Vol. 3, *The Booke at Large* (1580). We are unable to trace the copyright owner of a table by Christopher Cooper from a page facing p. 22 of *The English Teacher* (1687) appearing in *English Historical Linguistics 1500–1800*, Vol. 175, edited by R.C. Alston (Scolar Press 1969) and would appreciate any information which would enable us to do so.

FOR

PAUL EDWARDS

Ofersæ bið broðor Eadmund for unrihtlic hringnimende
(*Fragmens Wappingensis*)

Chapter 1

Aims, methods and models

1.1 Aims

The idea that somehow a language, like a nation or even a literature, can be said to have a history, is one which we should perhaps not be too ready to accept uncritically. Even the most cursory review of the extensive literature on language change (lexical, syntactical and phonological) reveals a scholarly tradition where both linguistic innovation and destruction are treated as though they operate within the frame of reference of one of the most widely recognizable characteristics of the description of political and social temporal mutation – a set of established and delimited 'periods' or epochs. Although by no means accepted by all social and political historians, there exists a widespread view which sees possible the identification of a periodic, episodic structure for human events and activities, within which one can identify whole sets of shared and identifying features characteristic of a particular episode: thus there are Mayan, Roman, Byzantine, Khmer, Ottoman, Marxist, Surrealist, post-Structural and a myriad other dynastic sets. Alongside such a concept of history runs that which sees possible the identification of specific events, actual occurrences which can be more or less specifically dated and which are often treated as focal points, culminations of sequences of individual 'happenings' which are themselves more or less motivated or directed: thus we have the Norman Conquest, the Roanoke settlement, the Anglo-Saxon invasions, and so on. For many years past, the study of language change through time has followed a model of history showing such characteristics, language innovation and death being viewed as period typical and often quite transparently linked with identifiable social and political events. For many of the features typifying the transition from Old to Middle English causal explanation was looked for in the events of the Norman Conquest, the 'inventiveness' of the syntax and vocabulary of the sixteenth and seventeenth centuries was laid at the door of an expanding overseas Empire, while the 'rational' nature of the grammar of English in the eighteenth century was viewed as a consequence of the Augustan social and literary mode.

Such a view of language change as language history sees language itself divided up in a periodic, episodic fashion very often on the basis of criteria which are themselves non-linguistic in nature: thus we have Continental English, Old English, Middle English, early Modern English, Old High German, Middle High German, Old Norse and so on. Each of these periods is characterizable in terms of some set of epoch appropriate changes, such as *i-umlaut*, the loss of inflexions, the *Great Vowel Shift* and the like. Most typical of this standpoint is its tendency to see language change as comprising a very large set of largely unrelated individual events (each with their own set of causations or lack of them), all itemized with a unique nomenclature of a more or less metaphorical type, such as *Breaking, Smoothing, Retraction, vowel shifts, umlauts* and *ablauts*. Such event-descriptive waters were especially muddied by the highly compartmentalized nature of the scholarly tradition itself which, for cultural and often idiosyncratic reasons, produced a situation whereby individual periods came to be the research territory of separate scholars and schools where there was little or no inclination to enquire into the chosen realm of other workers. As a result, the tradition of English and other historical linguistics is often bedevilled by the proliferation of descriptive nomenclature and by a failure to relate phenomena in one often ad hocly delimited period with others, no matter how transparently similar, uncovered by other writers in their separate research domains.

In one sense the treatment given to phonological change in this volume will be ahistorical. While we shall not set out to be paradigm-shattering in any significant sense and will indeed largely set our materials within the very periodic framework we have just found cause to criticize, utilizing at the same time much of the event-specific nomenclature to be found in the traditional literature, we shall nevertheless make a concerted attempt to see phonological innovation in a wider context, emphasizing wherever possible the shared, common features of such change throughout the entire temporal span of the language. We shall attempt to demonstrate that a great deal of what goes for phonological change is, in fact, non-period-specific and that many of the processes we shall investigate are liable to occur at any point in the temporal continuum. The types of phonological 'events' and processes which are said to be typical of the modern language are just as likely to be found, we shall argue, in the language's earliest recorded materials and to recur thereafter. Such an approach to phonological change will argue against anything catastrophically new occurring in that area of the grammar over such a relatively short chronological span as the last thirteen hundred or so years and a cornerstone of such a viewpoint will be that many phonological realizations are constrained as well as conditioned by the ways in which speakers' perceptions of the properties of sounds, in the broadest possible sense, are structured. More specifically, much of the discussion in the pages which follow will centre around the ways in which language users 'know about', have constructed models for the shape of the stressed vowel and those elements to its right within its syllable domain. For instance, one of our major concerns will be to show that innovations to the shape of this vowel space are not of an unconstrained kind throughout the history of the language, but can be a function of the phonetic nature of those elements which 'close' the syllable. Very generally, a stressed vowel precedent to segments which are themselves relatively highly vowel-like will provide the language user with a perception of an overall vowel-level heightening throughout the syllable, a vowel-level prominence adding which can be achieved through a number of separate stratagems. We shall, no matter how tentatively, even go so far as to suggest that language users will respond in determinate ways to certain phonological combinations and that such a response is based, at least in part, upon preconceptions as to some 'ideal' set of configurations appropriate to certain kinds of phonological structures.

Such a 'like-context/like-response' model for phonological mutation can only be clearly demonstrated when a number of theoretical conditions are met. In the first place, we shall require to provide considerable motivation for any claim that phonological innovation and death can result from an attempt by speakers, however metaphorically we might express it, to achieve some preferred (perceptual) target or end. Secondly, if we intend to argue that phonological mutation is not an open-ended affair but perhaps limited to a very small number of operations, then we shall quickly see that some kind of rather different kind of descriptive model from that typically expressed in most language 'histories' will have to be to some extent engaged. Indeed, we shall on many occasions have cause to notice how the shared nature as well as affecting context of many of the phonological novelties we shall come across at different temporal moments has generally been concealed as a result of the limitations of the theoretical apparatus traditionally used in their description.

However, even though our inclination will be to view phonological change as recurrent, even directed and perhaps also largely predictable in its general nature, we shall still provide (wherever practical) as much period-specific and local descriptive detail as possible for the sets of events we shall isolate for discussion; and that description will be set out in a fashion which will be very familiar to the reader of the scholarly tradition. But by a careful (and it might be argued, too selective) sampling of the major events in the historical phonology of the English language, we shall at the same time attempt to convince the reader that what are often described as innovations unique, say, to Middle English, can in fact – if we are prepared to accept certain theoretical assumptions – be regarded as 'repetitions', 're-enactments' of very similar kinds of processes recorded many hundreds of years earlier and which are themselves found active at many moments in the language's future record.

1.2 Method

While very conscious of the inherent dangers of oversimplifying both the phonological processes involved and the data selected to illustrate them, and all the while sensitive to the fact that there are a great many phenomena which will not readily fit into the pattern which we shall be utilizing, we shall attempt to view the historical phonology of English as though it were a set of repeated, recurrent and, indeed, ongoing operations. The kinds of operations we shall centre upon and which can be followed from chapter to chapter across the temporal spectrum and through the nomenclature maze, include *vowel durational increase, diphthongization, monophthongization*, and *vowel shifting*. Further, we shall attempt to show that even delimiting the set of possible phonological processes to a group like the above is over generous; it being possible to view apparently contradictory operations such as, say, diphthongization and monophthongization as closely related or even identical, provided we are prepared to accept arguments for a more highly structured type of descriptive theoretical model. Likewise, we shall see that the triggering contexts for vowel durational increase and diphthongization are very often extremely alike, suggesting that we are perhaps (despite the nomenclature) in the presence of a single perceived operation rather than two, mutually contrastive ones. However, it is perhaps our concern with the nature of the *syllable* and its structural order which, although leading us into the most complex theoretical issues, will enable us to make some powerful, all embracing statements concerning the inter-relatedness of phonological processes traditionally seen as disparate. We shall claim in many places that speakers introduce innovative phonological processes either to preserve or establish what they see to be some kind of cannonical, preferred perceptual shape for that suprasegmental entity.

However, before we give too strong an impression that we shall be entirely globalist in our treatment of the historical phonological events in the English language, it is well to stress at this point that we shall at all times emphasize the 'patchy', incomplete nature of the operations we shall describe and we shall wherever possible make reference to diffusion phenomena and the social and other factors which condition them.

1.3 Model

In the majority of instances in the chapters which follow we shall present our historical data and the changes, alternations they undergo in terms of a very traditional (mainly articulatory) phonetic framework, utilizing a straightforward and non-controversial transcription. However, although this will enable us to relate most of what we say to the standard handbooks, it will nevertheless continually expose the shortcomings of such a framework both in description and explanation. Certainly, it will quickly become clear that minimalist models of the kind generally found in 'history of the language' handbooks will force us into an extremely fragmented view of the processes of phonological change and, if we are to justify our claim that such change is recurrent, non-period specific and of a relatively unitary nature, then we shall require the services of a model which has a considerably greater degree of structural organization and complexity. But it is clearly impossible in a short introductory section such as this to provide an exhaustive description of what will probably be for most readers an unfamiliar theoretical framework. Although we shall attempt to portray some of the more salient points of our phonological hypothesis in the remainder of this section, we shall regularly set out further detail of particular aspects of the model at appropriate places in subsequent chapters. The actual model to which reference is being made is usually known as *Dependency Phonology*, and a full treatment can be found of it in Anderson and Jones (1974 and 1977), Durand (1984) with additions in Anderson and Ewen (1987).

One of the central tenets of this and other recent hypotheses lies in the way it regards phonetic segments as *relatively contrastive* in terms of their level of prominence or observability. Segments such as [t], [m], [l] and [u], for instance, are graded with respect to each other to the extent to which they are prominent in a particular observable characteristic. That characteristic is their inherent *vowel-ness*, or the extent to which they share the articulatory and especially the acoustic signatures of vowel sounds. Transparently, a segment like [u] is highly vowel-ful, but it has been the claim of many modern phoneticians and phonologists that other segments in the phonological inventory can be seen as having more or less prominent features of vowel-ness as well (Hooper 1972; Lass 1984 : sect. 8.3.3). Sonorants like [l], [m] and [r] are notably vowel prominent, while voiceless obstruents such as [p], [t] are free of any vowel characteristic altogether and are vowel-non-prominent or consonantal. A model like this sees the entire phonetic segment inventory as arrangeable along a scale or hierarchy of relative vowel prominence – the *sonority hierarchy*, a simplified version of which is shown in Figure 1.1. Segments at either extreme of that scale

FIG. 1.1   sonority hierarchy 1

C		V
non-vowel-like: consonantal	————————————	vowels

are seen as full (V) or empty (C) in their vowel-ness attribute, those between being 'mixed' or complex with respect to these two parameters. Very informally, we might express this pure/(internally) mixed segment composition notion as in Figure 1.2. There we see a scale whose left to right movement is

FIG. 1.2   sonority hierarchy 2

| C |	| C|v|	| C | V |	|c| V |	| V |
1	2	3	4	5

characterized by a step by step 'contamination' by vowel-ness quality or, alternatively, where consonantalness is systematically being suppressed: numerals correspond to voiceless obstruents, voiced obstruents, voiced fricatives, continuant sonorants and 'pure' vowels respectively.

Vowels segments themselves can likewise be viewed as mapped against a set of parameters, with 'pure' elements at the parameter edges, 'mixed' in intermediate positions. We might consider the vowel space as represented by a triangle (see Fig. 1.3), at whose points are three pure vowel characteristics, *palatality*, *labiality*,

FIG. 1.3   Palatality [i] 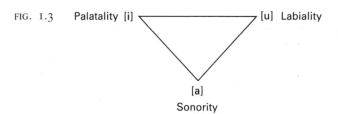 [u] Labiality

[a]

Sonority

and *sonority*. These characteristics can be defined according to
both articulatory and acoustic criteria, *palatality* being associated
with highness and frontness (the vowel [i]), *labiality* with low pitch
and relative backness (the vowel [u]), while *sonority* is associated
with a very open oral tract and a pitch characteristic which is
relatively low (the vowel [a]). Such pure, primary or simple
parametric elements can combine to form sets of mixed or complex
vowel configurations, much in the way we suggested above that
segments like [l] and [m] represented mixtures of V and C elements.
The vowel complexes show varying levels of prominence of the
parametric vowels to each other, in a fashion which we might very
informally express in Figure 1.4. In this way, segments such as [e],

FIG. 1.4   the internal structure of vowel segments

| a | | a |i| | a | i | |a| i | | i |
SON   SON pal   SON PAL   son PAL   PAL
[a]   [æ]   [ɛ]   [e]   [i]
           | a |u| | a | u | |a| u | | u |
           SON lab   SON LAB   son LAB   LAB
           [ɒ]   [ɔ]   [o]   [u]

[ɛ] [o] and [ɔ] can be seen as (internal) complexes of the various
pure vowel elements, differing vowel qualities (height and backness) being a reflection of the relative prominence of one or other
of the pure elements over the other in the complex construction.
Complex mixes involving the pure palatal and labial segments
[i] and [u] – segments such as [ü] – can also be achieved, while
mixtures of already internally mixed segments such as [o] and
[e], producing [œ] are possible as well within the terms of reference of this framework, and fuller details can be found on
pp. 88–9 below.

We shall see too just how useful the notion of relative vowel
level prominence between segments can be when we come to
consider those phonological units larger than segment size such as
the *syllable*. Although we shall investigate the nature of this unit
in some detail in section 3.5 below, it is clear even at this point
how the structure of syllables depends upon some *central*, peak

element, surrounded by other phonetic segments which are relatively less vowel-like in their composition than is the peak (Lass 1984: sect 10.3.5). Thus, in a syllable such as [kræmp] '*cramp*', we can see how movement away from the syllable centre peak [æ] involves a relative decline (through [m] to [p] and [r] to [k]) in the vowel-ness levels of the individual segments as expressed on the *sonority hierarchy*. Again, as we shall have cause to observe in our section on *vowel harmony* (sect. 2.5 ff) and *syllabicity shifting* (sect. 2.4.5), syllables may also show prominence differentials between vowel components. Thus, in an item such as [hæpɪ] '*happy*', the [ɪ] syllable two vowel is less prominent (more weakly stressed) than the [æ] of syllable one, while in an item like [gou] '*go*' with a stressed vowel area comprising two 'halves', it is the former half [o] which is perceived as the relatively more pronounced.

But the full significance of such informally and metaphorically expressed concepts for the nature of general phonological processes, especially as these relate to phonological change, as well as their fuller explication must wait for later chapters.

Chapter 2

The Early English period: the beginnings to the thirteenth century

2.1 The nature of the data

The kinds and variety of evidence available to us make any attempt to provide a detailed account of the phonology of the earliest period of the English language an extremely difficult and tentative exercise. Although there is a surprisingly large amount of extant manuscript material from the eighth to the thirteenth centuries, its usefulness as evidence for matters phonological and phonetic is severely constrained by a number of different factors. In the first place, we have to rely for almost our entire knowledge of the language's phonology during this episode upon the testimony of orthographic representations. For the whole of the 600-year period which is the topic of this chapter, we have almost no information concerning the pronunciation habits of its language users other than the orthographic notations used to represent them. Although we shall see that there is one possible important exception, for the most part there is no direct comment provided during this epoch upon the idiosyncracies of its pronunciation system of the type we commonly find several hundred years later.

Worse still, although there survive several extensive texts known to have been composed by speakers from different regional localities, any regionalisms they might have been expected to show in the form of novel spelling representations do not regularly materialize. One reason for this appears to stem from the fact that, for much of the period, many scribes were predisposed to utilize what was for all intents and purposes a kind of inter-regional spelling 'standard'. They regularly wrote using a fixed, conventional orthographic representation based upon the spelling habits of the prestigious West Saxon dialect of the ninth and tenth centuries. The near universal use of this almost invariant orthog-

raphy throughout the earlier part of our period serves to suppress
a great deal of the evidence for phonological diversity which
might otherwise have surfaced to show innovation produced by
both temporal and regional influences (Campbell 1959: sects
1–21; Ker 1957: pp. xxxiii–xxxvi). Indeed, during most of the
period covered by the eighth to the thirteenth century we are
confronted by an orthographic standardization not unlike that we
find in Modern English printing practice, where (albeit with a few
trivial exceptions) the same set of spelling conventions is
regarded as equally suitable for the representation of Englishes
as phonologically disparate as those of California and West
Africa.

However, the Old English picture is not quite one of unrelieved
spelling uniformity and texts showing some orthographic variation
do survive especially from the very beginning and later parts of the
period. These show sufficient levels of spelling innovation and
inconsistency to provide at least a limited insight into the nature
of contemporary phonological phenomena. Consider, as examples,
the following four short passages, selected from parallel renderings
of chapter xiii, verses 26–8 of St Mark's Gospel.

Ðonne geseoð hi (hig) mannes sunu cumendne on ge-nipum (ge-
nypum) mid mycelum mægene 7 wuldre. þonne sent he his englas 7
hi (hig) gaderiað his gecorenan of feower windum of eorþan
heanesse (heahnysse) oþ heofenes heahnesse. Leorniað an bigspell
(bygspell) be þam fic-treowe. Ðonne his twi (twig) bið mearu 7 leaf
beoð acennede ge witon þ sumor is gehende.

Ðanne ge-syeð hyo mannes suna cumende on ge-nipum mid
mycelen maigne 7 wuldre. Ðanne sent he his ængles 7 hyo gaderieð
his ge-corene of feower winden of eorden heahnysse oð heofenes
heahnysse. Leorniað an byspell be þam fictreow. Ðanne his twi
beoð mare 7 leaf beoð akenned ge witen þæt sumer is gehende.

ðonne geseas sunu monnes cymmende on wolcnum mið mægne
miclo 7 wuldre. 7 ða sendas englas his 7 gesomniað ða gecoreno his
of feower windum from hrof eardes wið to heannise heofnes. from
ficbeame ðonne leornas gie bispell mið-ðy uutedlice twigge his nesc
bið 7 acenda biðon wutas gie þte on neh sie sumer

ðonne giseað suno monnes cymende of wolcum mid mædgne micle
7 wuldre. ðonne sendes engles his 7 gesomnas ða gicornu his from
feower windum from hrofe eorðo wið to heonisse heofnes. from
ficbeom ðonne liornige bispell miððy wutudlice telgu his hnisca
bioðon 7 acende bioðon leof wutas ge þte neh se sumor.

The first two passages above are taken respectively from MS Corpus Christi Cambridge 40 and Bodley Hatton 30 and represent

samples of West Saxon-type orthography from around the beginning of the eleventh and the middle thirteenth centuries (Skeat 1871–87). The second pair represent regional spelling conventions utilized by what are assumed to be scribes with Northern dialectal speech characteristics; they, as their 'stilted' syntactic serial order suggests, are the product of glosses – word-by-word renderings – of the Latin texts of the *Lindisfarne* and *Rushworth* gospels, and date from around the middle of the tenth century. Table 2.1 isolates a few of the spelling variants to be found in these brief samples and tentatively relates them to the very general kinds of phonological alternations they might be said to indicate. Taken very much at their face value, the shapes in column 1 point at least to the possibility that, for whatever sets of reasons, speakers could alternate [o] with [æ]/[a], [e]/[ɛ] with [æ], and [ɪ] with whatever is represented by ⟨y⟩; although – especially in the last instances – we must always be willing to accept the possibility that some orthographic contrasts are purely conventional and have no significance at least for phonological contrast.

TABLE 2.1

Vowels	Vowel contrasts		Consonantal contrasts	Syllable contrasts
	Vowels	Diphthongs		
(a) ⟨genypum⟩ ⟨nipum⟩	(a)	(a) ⟨seað⟩ ⟨seoð⟩ ⟨syeð⟩	(a) ⟨eorþan⟩ ⟨eorden⟩	⟨mægene⟩ ⟨maigne⟩ ⟨mægen⟩
⟨bispell⟩ ⟨byspell⟩		(b) ⟨leornas⟩ ⟨liornige⟩	(b) ⟨heahnysse⟩ ⟨heanisse⟩	
(b) ⟨þonne⟩ ⟨þanne⟩		⟨bioðon⟩ ⟨beoð⟩ ⟨bið⟩	⟨bigspell⟩ ⟨byspell⟩	
(c) ⟨englas⟩ ⟨ængles⟩		(c) ⟨mægene⟩ ⟨maigne⟩	⟨twigge⟩ ⟨twi⟩	
(d) ⟨cumendne⟩ ⟨cymmende⟩			⟨hnisca⟩ ⟨nesc⟩	
I	2		3	4

Column 2 forms illustrate what would seem to be mono-phthongal/diphthongal alternants (⟨bið⟩/⟨beoð⟩; ⟨mægene⟩/⟨maigne⟩) and to suggest that the diphthongs themselves may well be of different types. Those in column 3 seem even less ambiguously to point to genuine consonantal segment variation, notably in the continuancy contrast between [ð]/[d], as well as the apparent deletion of whatever is intended by the symbols ⟨h⟩ and ⟨g⟩ word internally and finally. Lastly, the column 4 shapes suggest phonetic alternation involving a discrepancy in syllable composition and structure; one where the same item appears to be treated as if it could be interpreted as a tri-syllabic {mæg}{en}{e} or one of two disyllabic versions, {maig}{ne} or {mæg}{en}.

But we have to stress that all such conclusions concerning the nature of phonological alternations in this early kind of English are obviously extremely crude and simplistic. Any credence we should wish to accord them requires to be supported and reinforced by evidence from other kinds of sources; such sources might include the testimony of subsequent historical development or the compatibility of an individual alternation with what are recognized to be the features characteristic of general and ongoing phonological processes. One particular touchstone we shall appeal to on many occasions for endorsement and verification for innovations which are otherwise supported only by general orthographic data is the invaluable evidence of a scribe known as Orm, enshrined in an extensive thirteenth-century manuscript eponymously entitled the *Ormulum*. This scribe provides us with what are fairly direct indications of approximate graphic/phonological correspondence, a type of evidence which is more often associated with the grammarians and phoneticians of the sixteenth and later centuries. Orm furnishes us with what might be described as a limited, primitive phonetic alphabet; he consistently uses symbolic conventions to denote particular phonological characteristics of his language, notably stressed vowel duration, and he often both adapts conventional symbols and invents new ones to highlight the phonetic idiosyncracies of segments which would otherwise be left unspecified in his normal orthographic inventory. The following is a fairly representative sample of Orm's orthographic inventiveness (Dickens and Wilson 1954: p. 84, ll. 54–60):

Loke he wel þatt hêt write swa, forr he ne maȝȝ nohht elless Onn Ennglissh writenn rihht te word, þatt wite he wel to soþe Annd ȝiff mann wile witenn whi icc hafe don þiss dede, Whi icc till Ennglissh hafe wennd Ḡoddspelles hallȝe lare; Icc hafe itt don forrþi þatt all

Crisstene follkess berrhless Iss lanḡ uppo þatt an, þatt te33
Godspelles hall3he lare wiþþ fulle mahhte foll3e rihht þurrh þohht,
þurrh word, þurrh dede.

Although we shall have the opportunity to discuss some of the
scribe's idiosyncracies in more detail below, we might note here
his use of geminate consonantal symbols to indicate, it seems,
the relative shortness of the precedent vowel space (⟨þatt⟩,
⟨rihht⟩); his invention of new and modification of extant symbols
such as ⟨ḡ⟩/⟨Ḡ⟩, ⟨3h⟩ and ⟨33⟩ to denote in turn the voiced
obstruent [g], the voiceless velar fricative [x], and the non-syllabic [i]
segment in diphthongal vowel space – ⟨ma33⟩, [mæi]/[mai] 'may'.
We should note too his use of special vowel diacritics like ˆ and
(at other places in the text) ′ (Napier 1889; Heald 1965; Harlow
1959; Ker 1957: pp. xxxiii–xxxvi).

Historical phonologists have traditionally turned to another
source whereby the more general characteristics of the phonology
of the earliest English can be inferred; contrast can be made
between the orthographic representations in Old English manuscripts and those which appear in materials recording other early
cognate Germanic family languages, notably Old Saxon, Old High
German, Crimean Gothic and the temporarily later 'Old' Frisian
(Jeffers and Lehiste 1979; Haas 1969). Consider the selection of
forms in Table 2.2. The (a) types there appear to show that the
Old English items have come to have effaced intervocalic segments
represented by the symbols ⟨g⟩, ⟨h⟩ as well as those bilabial nasals

TABLE 2.2

(a)				
OS	⟨slahan⟩	WS	⟨slean⟩	'to kill'
	⟨regin⟩		⟨ren⟩	'rain'
OHG	⟨samfto⟩		⟨softe⟩	'soft'
	⟨fimf⟩		⟨fif⟩	'five'

(b)			
OHG	⟨land⟩	⟨land⟩	'land'
	⟨lengi⟩	⟨leng⟩	'long'
	⟨ahto⟩	⟨eaht⟩	'eight'
	⟨kneht⟩	⟨cneoht⟩	'boy'
	⟨erl⟩	⟨eorl⟩	'earl'

(c)			
Gothic	⟨badi⟩	⟨bedd⟩	'bed'
	⟨fani⟩	⟨fenn⟩	'fen'

which have immediately to their right some voiceless fricative [f]
segment. That the Old English vowel space in such items (unlike
those of the Old Saxon and Old High German stressed syllable
context) is durationally *long* may be, we could speculate, the
direct result of such a segment lost. The (b) examples on the other
hand, seem unequivocally to show three Old English items with
some kind of *diphthongal* stressed vowel space, compared with
what the spelling suggests are the monophthongs of the equivalent
Old High German items. Evidence like this points at least
circumstantially to some kind of [e] → [eo] vowel change, a
diphthongization, vowel space 'splitting up' process apparently
blocked by a following nasal, but provoked by a right contiguous
[r], or whatever ⟨h⟩ may be said to represent phonetically in Old
English. Again, the instances under (c) apparently suggest a
contrast between an [a] and [e]/[ɛ] stressed vowel space, superficially
associated with the presence or absence of the [i] vowel in the second
syllable. But all such evidence is at best provisional and heavily
reliant upon assumptions concerning chronological precedence.

Yet perhaps we should not be over-anxious to discount the
phonological implications of even the highly regularized
orthography of the majority of the earliest English scribes. There
is evidence to suggest that such writers were educated in an Irish,
Celtic tradition of orthographic representation (Daunt 1939; Ker
1957: pp. lvi–lx), a tradition which we have good reason to believe
was based upon a sophisticated understanding of the general
workings of both phonetics and phonology (Ó'Cuív 1973; Robins
1967: pp. 66–93). Consider, as an instance, some of the statements
to be found in the seventh-century *Scholar's Primer*, the *Aurnicept
na n-Éces* of Cenn Faeled (Calder 1917); the orthographic practice
of placing an ⟨h⟩ symbol after, for instance, a [b] obstruent as a
means of indicating consonantal aspiration is there described
(Calder 1917: p. 33) as:

> It increases *b* till it acquires the forces of *p*. . . . i.e. *b* with
> aspiration is put for *p*, so that *h* increases it, for *p* is the aspiration
> of the Gael.

while we find vocalic segments characterized (Calder 1917: p. 29)
in such terms as:

> What are the peculiar, proper, common and improper of the word
> vowel? Easy. Peculiar to it is voice path, since it finds voice by
> itself. Proper to it, they express a voice, for it expresses itself.
> Common to it, i.e. voice foundation, for it is the foundation of the
> words.

and the description of syllable shape we find in the *Scholar's Primer* (Calder 1917: p. 95) is one which is echoed, as we shall see in several places in the chapters which follow, in the kinds of view held by many modern phonologists:

> How far does a syllable extend to its greatest and least? The greatest number of letters that can make up a meaningful syllable is five. The smallest limit is a syllable of one letter and that can make up a word, . . . such as *á* '*a mountain*', . . . *o*, '*an ear*'; and ⟨I⟩ Column Cill's '*island*' (*Iona*). The syllable reaches its greatest length with five letters, i.e. ⟨bracht⟩, '*fat*', ⟨tracht⟩, '*strand*', ⟨drucht⟩, '*dew*', ⟨scalp⟩ '*gap*'.

Scribes trained in a tradition like this must be assumed to have had some conscious knowledge of the workings of the sound system of their language and how it could most appropriately be represented orthographically. We should perhaps therefore not draw back too hastily from treating with respect such orthographic cues as they provide for the phonetic peculiarities of their contemporary speech.

2.2 Vowel lengthening processes in Old English: lexical and derived length in Old English

Much like its modern counterpart, the phonology of the earliest English shows a vowel inventory maintaining a contrast between durationally long and short stressed vowel segments; thus ⟨dæȝ⟩ [dæj] '*day*', but ⟨dæd⟩ [dæːd] '*deed*'; ⟨nefa⟩ [nɛvə] '*nephew*' but ⟨hēr⟩ [heer] '*here*'; ⟨spinel⟩ [spinəl] '*spindle*' but ⟨hwīl⟩ [hwiil] '*time*'; ⟨dohter⟩ [dɔxtər] '*daughter*' but ⟨fōt⟩ [foot] '*foot*'; ⟨þurst⟩ [θurst] '*thirst*' but ⟨hūs⟩ [huus] '*house*'. The relative durational contrast in items like these was one which speakers had no way of predicting, the length of the vowels having to be specified in the language's lexicon as being arbitrarily long or short. However, there are situations where durational contrast can be contextually triggered, introduced into a language's phonology through the agency of other processes which at first sight have no obvious connection with stressed vowel length. We shall try to show in this section that some of the long vowel sequences which are to be found in the Old English phonological inventory were introduced in this way, although for speakers of Old English the original contextual trigger for the length contrast may have itself come to be no longer obvious and the long vowel sequences come to be treated as lexical, non-predictable. At the same time we shall show that during the Old English period proper several contextually provoked vowel lengthening processes were in operation and that they were productive for most speakers of that language.

Let us begin by considering some of the mechanisms whereby new long vowels might be introduced into a language's phonological inventory. One fairly well-documented means by which this might occur arises when, for some reason or another, speakers 'lose', 'delete' or 'efface' a consonantal segment which originally stood between two vowel sounds. That is, a sequence like vowel + consonant + vowel is converted, through consonantal deletion, into one where we find vowel + Ø + vowel. A good example of just such a process can be found in the history of French phonology. Compare the Latin forms in Table 2.3 with their Old

TABLE 2.3

Latin	Old French	Modern French	
⟨bataculare⟩	⟨baailler⟩	⟨băiller⟩	'to yawn'
⟨gradalem⟩	⟨graal⟩		'cup'
⟨adaptas⟩	⟨aates⟩		'suitable'
⟨sigillum⟩	⟨seel⟩	⟨sceau⟩	'seal'

French (ninth-century) equivalents. The Old French examples clearly show that two vocalic elements which were originally in distinct syllables and separated by an intervening consonantal element (in Table 2.3 cases [t], [d], and [g]) are, on the loss or deletion of that element, brought together and treated as a long vowel within the domain of a single syllable beat, thus [gradal+em] → [graal+em] → [graal]. In this way (and we are not for the moment concerned with the reasons for the loss of the consonantal element) new long vowels are created: there is a sequential repetition of what were originally two separated vowels of the same quality (height, backness, roundness). However, it is interesting to notice that even when the vowels originally separated by a consonantal element are not of an identical quality, on the loss of the intervocalic element a long vowel still very often results, consider Table 2.4. While examples (1) and (2) with *long* stressed vowels illustrate, on the loss of the intervocalic consonant, a new diphthongal syllabic element [üε], [äi], those like (3) and (4) with an original short stressed vowel demonstrate in Modern French a new durationally extended vowel segment subsequent to the consonantal loss; i.e. there has been an assimilation of the two originally disparate vocalic elements which results in two vowels

TABLE 2.4

Latin	Old French	Modern French	
(1) ⟨crūdelem⟩		[krüɛl]	'cruel'
(2) ⟨nātīvum⟩		[näif]	'naif'
(3) ⟨fagina⟩		[fɛɛn]	'fâine'
(4) ⟨aetatem⟩	⟨edage⟩	[aaʒ]	'âge'
	⟨eage⟩		
	⟨aage⟩		

with identical height, backness and roundness characteristics differentiated only by the fact that one is the more prominent by virtue of its taking the syllable beat or peak; the value of one of the contrasting vowel elements has come to be generalized across the entire vowel space (de Chene 1979: p. 90).

A process rather like this seems to have been operative probably at the very beginning of the Old English period, although there is some evidence that it was a feature of later Old English phonology as well. If we compare West Saxon forms with their non-English Germanic language 'counterparts', we can see that a change seems to have occurred whereby an intervocalic [x] could come to be effaced resulting, apparently, in a durational increase in the vowel immediately preceding it. Consider the data in Table 2.5, where we follow the custom of most editors in inserting a ⟨-⟩ over those vowels which are said to show relative durational length increase. (Wright 1925: sect. 148; Sievers and Brunner 1941: sect. 130; Campbell 1959: sect. 240 ff). There is, of course, rarely anything in the West Saxon spelling system to show that the first element of the new diphthongs produced by the [x] deletion was durationally

TABLE 2.5

	Non-English Germanic	West Saxon Old English	
OS/OHG	⟨slahan⟩	⟨slēan⟩	'to kill'
OS/OHG	⟨aha⟩	⟨ēa⟩	'water'
OS/OHG	⟨fliohan⟩	⟨flēon⟩	'to flee'
	⟨fliehan⟩		
OS/OHG	⟨thwahan⟩	⟨þwēan⟩	'to wash'
	⟨dwahan⟩		
OS/OHG	⟨lahan⟩	⟨lēan⟩	'to blame'

long. We can usually only infer this to be a fact from the subsequent
historical behaviour of such vowels and from spelling evidence from
later periods. But let us for the moment follow the majority opinion
and assume that the forms in the right hand column are something
like [fleeən], [æǽa] etc. Finally, consider the instances in Table 2.6
where we can see the possibility of the deletion of a voiceless velar
fricative [x] immediately preceding a consonantal segment which is
voiced. Here again, loss of [x] and increased duration of the
immediately preceding vowel appear to be intimately connected,
although it is interesting to notice that both the fricative deletion
and vowel lengthening are resisted when the post [x] consonantal
segment is *voiceless*, cf. ⟨pliht⟩ '*danger*', ⟨plihtlic⟩ '*dangerous*';
⟨niht⟩ '*after night*, ⟨nihtlic⟩ '*nightly*'. That the lengthening process is
still productive in late (tenth-century) Northumbrian is perhaps
evidenced by the following alternant spelling forms from the gloss
to the *Lindisfarne Gospels*: ⟨tēar⟩/⟨tæher⟩/⟨teher⟩ '*tear*'
(*lacrima*) and ⟨ēar⟩/⟨æhher⟩/⟨eher⟩ '*ear*' (Campbell 1959:
sect. 224).

TABLE 2.6

	Non-English Germantic	Old English	
Gothic	⟨þwahl⟩	⟨ðhuehl⟩	'*washing*'
OHG	⟨dwahal⟩	⟨thuachl⟩	
		⟨þwēal⟩	
OS	⟨stehli⟩	⟨stȳle⟩	'*steel*'
OHG	⟨stahal⟩		
		⟨pleoh⟩/⟨plēolic⟩	'*danger(ous)*'
		⟨eoh⟩/⟨ēored⟩	'*horse/cavalry*'

2.2.1 Compensatory lengthening

Although differing somewhat in detail, standard handbook
treatments of the above lengthening phenomenon tend to view it
as a two stage process. Firstly, for some set of reasons rarely set
out, there is said to occur the loss of the post-stressed vowel or
intervocalic [x] segment. Secondly, and consequentially, such a loss
is compensated for by an increase in the duration of the preceding
stressed vowel. The implication is that the effacement of one
segment within a word compels speakers somehow to adjust its
internal structure to 'make up for' such a loss; the stressed vowel

space comes to be extended to fill out the gap left by the deleted fricative. Such a model would suggest that speakers have intuitions concerning the internal, ideal, preferred segmental composition of higher phonological entities like syllables. Loss of a segment of one type provokes a gain in a segment of another. This is clearly a complicated theoretical area and is one to which we shall return several times below.

2.2.2 Lengthenings in more general fricative contexts

The data in Table 2.7 suggest that for West Saxon Old English (and, as we shall see, other dialects as well) post-vocalic segment effacement was not confined to the voiceless velar [x] fricative, but could involve other fricative segments as well, notably the voiced alveolar [ʒ] and palatal [ǰ] types (both generally orthographically realized as ⟨g⟩). The 'consequence' of such an effacement results once more, apparently, in an increase in the durational value of the precedent stressed vowel. The stressed vowels in the column 3 items of Table 2.7 are generally accepted as being durationally long. That this process was an occasional feature of even the earliest

TABLE 2.7

	Non-English Germanic		West Saxon Old English	
OS Gothic OHG	⟨regin⟩ ⟨rign⟩ ⟨regan⟩	'rain'	⟨regn⟩	⟨rēn⟩
OHG ON	⟨wagan⟩ ⟨vagn⟩	'cart'	⟨wægn⟩ ⟨wægen⟩	⟨wǣn⟩
OHG	⟨magetin⟩	'girl'	⟨mægden⟩	⟨mǣden⟩
OS OHG	⟨þegan⟩ ⟨degan⟩	'warrior'	⟨þegn⟩	⟨þēn⟩
Gothic OHG	⟨fraihan⟩ ⟨fragen⟩	'to ask'	⟨frignan⟩	⟨frīnan⟩
OS OHG	⟨angegin⟩ ⟨ingagan⟩	'against'	⟨ongeagn⟩ ⟨ongegen⟩	⟨ongēan⟩ ⟨ongān⟩ ⟨ongēn⟩
	1		2	3

Old English can be seen from the occurrence of forms like ⟨snegl⟩/⟨snēl⟩ 'snail'; ⟨sigdi⟩ and ⟨brigdels⟩ for the later ⟨sīðe⟩ 'scythe' and ⟨brīdel⟩ 'bridle' in the earliest glosses and textual fragments (Campbell 1959: sects 243, 267; Wright 1925: sect. 146).

We might add credence to the generality of such a phenomenon by pointing to a rather similar kind of process in the history of Classical Latin where the voiced dental fricative ([z]) when it immediately preceded another voiced obstruent such as [d] was apparently deleted with a concomitant 'compensatory' lengthening of its precedent stressed vowel – cf. the data in Table 2.8. Yet we find short stressed vowels contiguous with undeleted [z] when its following consonant is voiceless in items such as ⟨dispono⟩ 'I arrange', ⟨distribuo⟩ 'I divide' and ⟨distineo⟩ 'I hold' (deChene 1979: p. 66).

TABLE 2.8

Pre-historic form		Classical form	
*[ni-zd-o-s]	'nest'	[niidus]	⟨nīdus⟩
*[si-zd-ō]	'I sit'	[siido]	⟨sīdo⟩
*[fidez-li-a]	'faith'	[fideelia]	⟨fidēlia⟩

We have been arguing thus far in favour of a phonological change whereby fricatives have become deleted post-vocalically with a stimultaneous or certainly resultant *compensatory lengthening* of the stressed vowel before them, such that [VFricC]→[VC] (fricative deletion)→[VVC] (compensatory stressed vowel lengthening). Can we perhaps offer another kind of explanation which would enable us to surmount the rather difficult matter of explaining away the original fricative 'loss'? DeChene (1979) has argued that in cases like [rejn] → [reen] and the others listed above in Table 2.7 we are, in fact, dealing with *segment substitution* rather than segment loss and that there is no need to make reference to compensatory lengthening at all. We have already proposed in Chapter 1 that there appears to exist a hierarchy between phonetic segments relating to their degree of vocalicness or vowel-like-ness. We saw how sonorant consonants like [r] and [l] were high up on such a hierarchy and also that fricative consonants, especially when voiced, had prominent vocalic characteristics as well. What might therefore be suggested is happening in cases like [rejn] → [reen] is that the relatively vowel-like fricative [j] is perceived as belonging to the stressed vowel space proper. That is, the item is perceived not as [r + vowel + fric + n] but as [r + vowel₁ + vowel₂ + n] where vowel₂ is the 'vocalized' fricative. We shall show at several places below that such fricative → non-syllabic vowel transformations are relatively common: cf. the Middle English change whereby Old English ⟨dæʒ⟩ [dæj] → ⟨dai⟩ [dæi] (pp: 149–50). Perhaps Old English Kentish and late Northumbrian spellings like ⟨maiden⟩ for West Saxon ⟨mæʒden⟩ provide direct evidence for the kind of vocalization process we have been describing.

However, and we shall refer to it only in passing, there is also orthographic evidence to suggest that the [ǰ] fricative, far from being perceived as a non-syllabic vowel, could actually on occasion remain intact and produce *diphthongization* in the vowel space before it. Consider the spellings in the late Northumbrian (tenth-century) gloss to the *Lindisfarne Gospels* where we find manifestations like ⟨gefraign-⟩, ⟨gefreign-⟩ *'ask'*, ⟨heig⟩ *'hay'*, ⟨ðeign⟩ *'lord'* alongside ⟨gefrægn⟩, ⟨heg⟩ and ⟨ðegn⟩. Perhaps we might treat such spellings as early examples of the Middle English version of the diphthong producing innovation of *Breaking*, a process we shall discuss in sect. 3.4.2. If they are indeed that then we shall have to consider the extent to which changes like pre-fricative diphthongization and voiced fricative vocalization are phonologically related or at least to be considered as alternative perceptual stratagems to a particular phonetic trigger.

2.2.3 Stressed vowel lengthening in nasal sonorant contexts

We have been putting forward the proposal, in the arguments set out in the last part of the previous section (following deChene 1979) that vowel length extension can arise through the combination of a stressed vowel segment with a following voiced fricative element, the latter coming to be perceived as equivalent to a non-syllabic vocalic segment: i.e. as the second 'half' of the stressed vowel space. Lengthening has in this way arisen from segment-type substitution rather than through any need to compensate for the loss of a consonantal element in the structure of the lexical item. However, we shall see that this type of hypothesis for derived vowel length becomes very strained when we attempt to apply it to some of the best documented processes whereby the phonology of Old English came to acquire certain of its long vowels. One of the most frequently discussed features of the phonology of that language relates to the means by which it came by, in its pre-historic period, some of its [ii], [oo] and [uu] vowels. Essentially, it has been argued, these long vowels arose from a contextually triggered change as a result of which their short equivalents were lengthened in a pre-nasal context, where the nasal itself was immediately followed by a voiceless fricative at a point of articulation shared by, or very close to, that of the nasal itself. The affecting contexts were thus

(1) the velar nasal [ŋ] combined with the voiceless velar fricative [x]

(2) the bilabial nasal [m] in combination with the voiceless bilabial fricative [β] or perhaps the labio-dental fricative [f]

(3) the alveolar dental nasal [n] with either the inter-dental fricative [θ] or the dental fricative [s].

Consonantal clusters of this type where place of articulation is shared by two segments but whose manner of articulation characteristic (i.e. sonorant, obstruent) is not, are called *homorganic*. Consider the data in Table 2.9 which represent a few of the many cases exhaustively cited by Campbell 1959: sect. 121; Wright 1925: sects 113, 61, 97; Nielsen 1981: sects 73, 145; Sievers

TABLE 2.9 Pre-English homorganic lengthening 1

| | | | West Saxon | |
	Non-English Germanic		Old English	
(1)	[a]		[ɔɔ]	
OHG	⟨hansa⟩	'troop'	[hɔɔs]	⟨hōs⟩
OHG	⟨amsala⟩	'blackbird'	[ɔɔslə]	⟨ōsle⟩
OHG	⟨andar⟩	'other'	[ɔɔðər]	⟨ōþer⟩
OHG	⟨samfto⟩	'soft'	[sɔɔftə]	⟨sōfte⟩
(2)	[i]		[ii]	
OHG	⟨fimf⟩	'five'	[fiif]	⟨fīf⟩
OHG	⟨hrind⟩	'cattle'	[hriiðər]	⟨hrīþer⟩
OHG	⟨sind⟩	'journey'	[siið]	⟨sīþ⟩
(3)	[u]		[uu]	
OHG	⟨gund⟩	'war'	[guuθ]	⟨gūþ⟩
OHG	⟨mund⟩	'mouth'	[muuθ]	⟨mūþ⟩
OHG	⟨sund⟩	'south'	[suuθ]	⟨sūþ⟩
	1		2	

and Brunner 1941: sect. 80; Anm.1, 51–2. Column 1 forms generally evidence a short [a], [i] or [u] vowel immediately preceding consonantal clusters like [ns], [nθ], [ms], [mf]/[mβ] (although in OHG some of the non-nasal fricatives have subsequently become obstruents, cf. ⟨ander⟩, ⟨hrind⟩ and ⟨sind⟩). The Old English forms show what appear to be two innovations: (a) loss of the nasal initial element in the post-vocalic clusters and (b) lengthening of the stressed vowel. (For the later Old English change whereby [aa] → [ɔɔ] in the examples under (1) see pp. 130–32.)

That a similar process affected short [i], [a] and [u] in the environment of velar nasal initial [ŋx] clusters may be deduced from the examples in Table 2.10. Here again column 2 forms illustrate innovative vowel length while column 3 items show contexts where, for reasons that need not concern us here, the nasal segments have been preserved. Clearly, we could argue that the additional stressed vowel length is the result of compensatory lengthening brought about by the loss of the nasal segment (from whatever provocation) at the end of the first syllable. We could even argue that nasal deletion is predictable to occur in proximity to a *continuant* consonant like [x], and fail before *non-continuants* like [k] and [g] in cases like ⟨þencan⟩ and ⟨geþungen⟩. But it is still not at

TABLE 2.10 Pre-English homorganic lengthening 2

*Postulated Germanic or Non-English Germanic			Old English	
(1)	[a]		[ɔɔ]	
OHG	*[θaŋx-] ⟨denchan⟩	'to think'	⟨þōhte⟩ 'he thought'	⟨þencan⟩ 'to think'
(2)	[i]		[ee]	
	*[θiŋx-]	'to thrive'	⟨þēon⟩	⟨geþungen⟩ 'have thrived'
(3)	[u]		[uu]	
	*[θuŋx-]	'to seem'	⟨þūhte⟩ 'it seemed'	⟨þyncan⟩
	1		2	3

all obvious why such contexts should have such an effect on contiguous nasal elements.

Alternatively, is it possible to suggest that the long vowel forms arise by some kind of vocalization of the nasal initial segment in the consonantal cluster after the fashion of our proposals above for changes like [reɪ̯n]→ [reen]? While we will show in our discussion on pp. 236–47 that vocalization of sonorants like [l] and [r] is a commonplace in the historical phonology of English and other languages, it is not so easy to point to cases involving a similiar process with nasal sonorants. However, deChene (1979: p. 75) cites just one such occurrence from the phonology of Polish (Rubach 1977) where 'a nasalized labial semivowel appears as a regular alternant of /n/ . . . following a mid vowel and before a fricative. Thus we have *wstega* [fstɛŋga]/festeng + a/"ribbon", but wstazka [fstɔ̃w̌žka]/fsteng + ek + a/"*ribbon*, diminutive"'. The [g] of the second form has been palatalized to [ž], by the *e* of the *ek* suffix, the [ŋ] becomes vocalized to [w] retaining its nasalization [~] feature, a characteristic which then spreads to the preceding vowel which has been rounded before it. Notice, too, how this vocalization only operates when the segment following the nasal is a continuant, as is the case with our ⟨þōhte⟩/⟨þencan⟩ instances in Table 2.10. However, parallel examples are not easy to come by and this – together with some of the data we shall discuss immediately below – might lead us to look for another explanation for such phenomena.

2.2.4 Lengthening in nasal and non-nasal sonorant contexts: Late Old English *homorganic lengthening*

In our attempts to account for the above innovatory vowel lengthening rules we mentioned the importance of the nature of the segment immediately following the nasal. That its shape is crucial to the operation of that lengthening process was clear when we noted that lengthening of the stressed vowel would only occur when that post-nasal segment was a *fricative*, i.e. when the affecting clusters are [mf], [ms], [ns], [nθ], but not when the segment immediately following the nasal is an obstruent, as in [mb], [nd], [nt]. That this is indeed the case can be seen from the developmental pathway taken in early North Germanic languages by [mp], [nt], and [ŋk] clusters, where – rather than acting as a trigger for vowel lengthening – the nasal is itself apparently replaced by an obstruent sharing its place of articulation: nasalization is taken out of the construction altogether. Compare Old Icelandic forms like ⟨kapp⟩ '*struggle*', ⟨batt⟩ '*bound*' and ⟨drekk⟩ '*to drink*' with their Modern German parallels ⟨kampf⟩, ⟨bant⟩, ⟨trinken⟩.

One reason for raising this point relates to another important vowel lengthening process which occurred late in the Old English period. In this change stressed vowels tended to gain in durational value when they preceded nasal and other sonorant initial clusters not unlike those which caused vowel lengthening in the pre-historic period described above in Tables 2.9 and 2.10. Like these last, the affecting late Old English clusters show *homorganicity*, i.e. the two elements comprising the cluster share articulatory place. However, unlike earlier affecting clusters where the post-nasal segment was some kind of fricative, some of the Old English lengthening contexts can also show post-nasal elements of a more general kind, including obstruents like [b] and [d], as well as sonorants like [r] and [l]. Thus, rather than [mβ], [mf], [ns], [nθ] shapes, we find lengthening triggers like [mb] and [nd] and [nl]. Again, this late Old English change is not constrained to operate before nasal initial clusters only, but will operate even before those initiated by [r] and [l]. Critically, however, the increase in vowel length which comes about *does not result in any deletion of the poststressed vowel sonorant element*, so that reference to either compensatory lengthening or sonorant vocalization would appear to be ruled out as explanations for the increase in stressed vowel duration.

Late Old English *homorganic lengthening* is a process which raises issues both of a theoretical and descriptive kind. Let us begin by providing a brief (albeit overgeneralized) account of its principal manifestations although we shall see that there are some important constraints upon the change which we shall have to treat separately. At some date in the late Old English period short stressed vowels had their duration increased before sonorant initial consonantal clusters whose elements shared an approximate place of articulatory gesture. These clusters are usually cited as:

[nd], [ŋg], [mb], [ld], [rd], and perhaps [rn].

A full list of instances can be found in most handbooks and we shall only cite a few here (see Berndt 1960: pp. 18–20; Mossé 1952: sect. 18, p. 16; Campbell 1959: sect. 283, p. 120; Wright 1925: sect. 143, pp. 70–1; Wyld 1927: sects 113–14, pp. 67–70; Luick 1964: sect. 268). The items in Table 2.11, on the basis of evidence we shall consider below, are generally considered to show new long stressed vowels in the late Old English period. The existence of some blanks in this display generally means that, as a result of other phonological processes, a particular vowel is not to be found in a given context. Thus, the lack of [ɔ] and [ɛ] vowels in pre-nasal contexts is accountable for by the prior operation of mid

TABLE 2.11 Late Old English homorganic lengthening

	[aa]	[ɔɔ]	[uu]	[ii]	[ɛɛ]
-[ld]	⟨bald⟩	⟨fold⟩	⟨sculde⟩	⟨cild⟩	⟨feld⟩
	⟨cald⟩	⟨gold⟩	⟨sculdor⟩	⟨milde⟩	⟨sheld⟩
		⟨sold⟩		⟨wilde⟩	⟨ȝeldan⟩
-[mb]	⟨camb⟩		⟨cumb⟩	⟨climb⟩	
	⟨clamb⟩		⟨dumb⟩		
	⟨lamb⟩				
	⟨wamb⟩				
-[nd]	⟨band⟩		⟨bunden⟩	⟨binden⟩	⟨ende⟩
	⟨hand⟩		⟨fund⟩	⟨blind⟩	⟨senden⟩
	⟨land⟩		⟨grund⟩	⟨find⟩	
			⟨hund⟩	⟨wind⟩	
-[ŋg]	⟨lang⟩		⟨ȝung⟩	⟨singen⟩	⟨geng⟩
	⟨sang⟩			⟨þing⟩	⟨streng⟩
	⟨strang⟩				
-[rd]		⟨bord⟩			⟨ȝerd⟩
		⟨ford⟩			⟨swerd⟩
		⟨hord⟩			
		⟨word⟩			
		⟨sword⟩			
-[rn]		⟨corn⟩	⟨bourne⟩		⟨ernen⟩
		⟨morn⟩	⟨murnen⟩		⟨fern⟩
					⟨lern⟩
-[rl]					⟨erl⟩
					⟨cerl⟩

vowel raising before [m] and [n] such that, for example, [fɔnd-] →
[fund-].

2.2.5 The reconstruction of vowel length

How are we to know that the vowels in contexts like those described
above have been lengthened, and at what date did such a
lengthening actually take place? West Saxon scribes provide little
in the way of indication of vowel length either by double vowel
symbol spelling or by diacritic marking (but see Heald 1965;
Harlow 1959; Ker 1957: xxxiii–xxxvi). We generally have to fall
back upon the evidence provided by spelling from a much later

date than that in Old English manuscripts or to assume the existence of lengthening in particular environments where it is a prerequisite for other, length-sensitive changes such as the *English vowel shift* of the fifteenth and sixteenth centuries. For example, items like ⟨cild⟩ and ⟨grund⟩ are generally held to have shown *short* stressed vowels in West Saxon Old English. Yet these words appear, by the sixteenth century, as [čaɪld] and [graund] – that is, with [aɪ] and [au] diphthongs resulting from an application of the *English vowel shift* affecting *long* vowels like [ii] and [uu]. We must therefore assume that before the operation of the vowel shift, the stressed vowels in these words had become lengthened. It is interesting to note, however, that items such as ⟨lamb⟩, ⟨hond⟩, ⟨fern⟩ and ⟨dumb⟩ still show *short* vowels in Modern English and have not been subject to this same vowel shift change. Either we are wrong in our assertion that their stressed vowels were lengthened in late Old English before their homorganic clusters or that they were only sporadically so or that they were shortened again at some date before the vowel shift. The picture, as we shall see, is rather a complex one.

Certainly the testimony provided by the spelling evidence in Middle English is anything but unambiguous. By the fourteenth century in the works of authors such as Chaucer, Wycliff and Gower we find spellings suggesting that *homorganic lengthening* had indeed occurred: ⟨ybounde⟩; ⟨bowndyn⟩; ⟨boond⟩; ⟨feeldes⟩; ⟨feild⟩; ⟨field⟩; ⟨foord⟩; ⟨fourde⟩, where the digraph spellings point at least to the existence of a 'complex' (long or diphthongal) stressed vowel space. However, we are just as likely (in fact, more so) to come across forms like ⟨bund⟩; ⟨bond⟩; ⟨feld⟩; ⟨ford⟩ where there is no orthographic suggestion of lengthening. ⟨ii⟩ spellings for possible long high front vowels are particularly rare. Yet there is one manuscript which does tend to lend consistent orthographic support for the lengthening of short vowels before homorganic clusters. The author of the *Ormulum* (c. 1200) devised, as we have already noted above, a spelling system which seems to differentiate regularly between short and long vowels. Shortness is indicated by writing a double consonant symbol following the vowel in question, while a vowel immediately followed by a single consonantal symbol is generally to be thought of as being long, although there are exceptions to and complications within this system which we need not enter into here (Napier 1889). Columns 2 and 4 in Table 2.12 clearly show the general principle of the *Ormulum's* spelling system for short and non-derived long vowels. What then, will a spelling system like this tell us about the relative length of stressed vowels before sonorant initial

TABLE 2.12 Stressed vowel length in the *Ormulum*

Old English	Ormulum		Old English	Ormulum	
Short vowels			*Long vowels*		
High Front					
⟨fyllan⟩	⟨fillen⟩	*'fill'*	⟨fȳlan⟩	⟨filenn⟩	*'defile'*
⟨sittan⟩	⟨sitten⟩	*'sit'*	⟨tīd⟩	⟨tid⟩	*'time'*
⟨bryd⟩	⟨bridd⟩	*'bird'*	⟨brīd⟩	⟨brid⟩	*'bride'*
⟨gylt⟩	⟨gillte⟩	*'guilt'*	⟨hwīl⟩	⟨whil⟩	*'while'*
Mid Front					
⟨werc⟩	⟨werrc⟩	*'work'*	⟨sǣcan⟩	⟨sekenn⟩	*'seek'*
⟨wencel⟩	⟨wennchell⟩		⟨wēpan⟩	⟨wepenn⟩	*'weep'*
		'child'			
High Back					
⟨full⟩	⟨full⟩	*'full'*	⟨fūl⟩	⟨fule⟩	*'foul'*
⟨murcnian⟩	⟨murrcenn⟩		⟨hūs⟩	⟨hus⟩	*'house'*
		'to murmur'			
⟨þurh⟩	⟨þurrh⟩	*'through'*			
Mid Back					
⟨godcundnes⟩	⟨goddcundness⟩				
		'divinity'	⟨gōd⟩	⟨god⟩	*'good'*
⟨geþoht⟩	⟨þohht⟩	*'thought'*			
			⟨cōm⟩	⟨cóme⟩	*'he came'*
Low					
⟨mann⟩	⟨mann⟩	*'man'*	⟨rǣd⟩	⟨ræd⟩	*'advice'*
⟨ran⟩	⟨rann⟩	*'he ran'*			
			⟨dǣl⟩	⟨dæl⟩	*'part'*
⟨dæʒ⟩	⟨daʒʒ⟩	*'day'*			
1	2		3	4	

(homorganic) clusters like [ld], [mb], [nd], [ŋg], [rn], [rl] and [rd]? The spellings in Table 2.13 from the *Ormulum* are illustrative. While we should think of the data there as providing only a very impressionistic view of the *Ormulum* materials it seems reasonably clear that vowel lengthening (signalled – under (1) – by a single graph after the stressed vowel) does indeed appear to have occurred in our environment. This spelling system even shows that all elements in the cluster must be voiced since we find unlengthened vowel representations in items like ⟨funnt⟩ *'font'*, ⟨þinnkenn⟩ *'to think'* and ⟨strennkenn⟩ *'to sprinkle'*. However, it also very clear that this lengthening process is very 'patchy', since the items under (2)

TABLE 2.13 Homorganic lengthening in the *Ormulum*

-[ld]	-[mb]	-[nd]	-[ŋg]	-[rn]	-[rl]	-[rd]
(1)						
ald	camb	grund	gang	corn	cherl	hird
gold	climben	hand	lang	hirne		hord
child	crumb	land	sang	ærn		ferd
hald	dumb	fend	þingenn			ord
shild	lamb	kinde	strengenn			swerd
	wambe	findenn	strang			ærd
		sendenn				
(2)						
shillde		unnderr	lannge	steornne	derrling	
nollde		stunnd	brinngenn		barrliȝ	
shullder		annd	ganngenn			
		sinndenn				
		biȝonndenn				

show double consonantal graphs where long vowels might be expected via *homorganic lengthening*. [nd] clusters seem particularly open to 'exceptional' behaviour in this respect. Even more puzzling is the fact that some of the items represented as having long vowels in our table apparently do not undergo the later diphthongization of the *English vowel shift* – cf. ⟨crumb⟩ and ⟨hirde⟩ – suggesting that their stressed vowels may have become shortened again or never have been lengthened in those dialects principally affected by the fifteenth-century change. While we merely note it here, we shall have more to say concerning this 'patchy', 'exception'-ful nature of phonological operations at various places below (see especially sects. 5.2.1 and 5.2.2).

2.2.6 The date of the *homorganic lengthening* process

We shall return to some of the other interesting aspects of this late Old English change as manifested in the spellings of the *Ormulum* – cf. spellings like ⟨cild⟩ but ⟨cilldre⟩ '*children*', ⟨lamb⟩ but ⟨lammbre⟩ '*lambs*', and ⟨grund⟩ but ⟨grunndwall⟩ '*foundation*'. In the meanwhile, let us spend a little time discussing a possible date for this important vowel-lengthening rule. Campbell (1959) says the change 'certainly belongs to the Old English period' (sect. 283, p. 120); Sievers and Brunner (1941) speculate 'Etwa im 9. Jahrhundert' (sect. 137.3, p. 118); Jordan (1974) confidently asserts that the change occurred 'In the second half of the eighth and the first half of the ninth centuries' (sect. 22, p. 43), while Wright (1925) tells us that 'it is impossible to ascertain the date at which the lengthenings took place and whether they took place in all dialects at the same time' (sect. 143, p. 70). In general, even those authors who offer positive dating proposals rarely provide any concrete evidence for their assertions.

We have already pointed out that in general the Old English spelling system does not appear to have any developed mechanism to show stressed vowel-length contrasts. However, there may be an exception to this state of affairs in the practice of the scribe (or scribes) who provided the Old English interlinear gloss to the *Lindisfarne Gospels*. The language of this gloss is Northumbrian of the tenth century and shows many non-West Saxon features both in spelling and in syntax/morphology. Although we shall not be making categorical claims in what follows, since much more research is required, we shall suggest that the scribe of this gloss indicated vowel length by two means: (a) doubling the vowel graph, (b) the placing of an acute accent mark $\langle\,'\,\rangle$ over the lengthened vowel. Now we must assert from the outset that neither of these devices is used completely consistently: there is a great deal of variation which is either indicative of the scribe's erratic vowel-length marking habits or that vowel length itself was a variable or a patchy feature of the phonology of his language.

Let us begin by looking at spellings which in classical West Saxon show lexical long stressed vowels (data are taken from the *Index Verborum, The Anglo-Saxon Gloss*, Book 2, ed. Ross and Stanley, 1962). We find instances like the following – with numerical occurrence in brackets: $\langle$tid$\rangle$ (26×): $\langle$tíd$\rangle$ (89×); $\langle$lar$\rangle$ (6×): $\langle$lár$\rangle$ (10×); $\langle$ric$\rangle$ (25×): $\langle$ríc$\rangle$ (99×); $\langle$nu$\rangle$ (26×): $\langle$nú$\rangle$ (31×): $\langle$nu$^u\rangle$ (2×): $\langle$núu$\rangle$ (1×): $\langle$nú$^u\rangle$ (2×); $\langle$gast$\rangle$ (42×): $\langle$gaast$\rangle$ (27×): $\langle$gáast$\rangle$ (1×): $\langle$gást$\rangle$ (9×). Again while we find $\langle$scíp$\rangle$ (4×) and $\langle$scip$\rangle$ (1×) for 'sheep', there are no accented forms whatsoever for $\langle$scip$\rangle$ 'ship' with its lexical short vowel. In general, short vowels are not represented by digraph spellings nor are they accented, as can be seen from spellings like $\langle$fader$\rangle$, $\langle$dæȝ$\rangle$ and $\langle$wæter$\rangle$ (Clemoes 1952).

We do not wish to claim, we must stress, that the graph duplication and the accent placement are infallible guides to vowel length in the manuscript (cf. spellings like $\langle$úndæd$\rangle$ and $\langle$stan$\rangle$ (31×); $\langle$stán$\rangle$ (5×), OE $\langle$stān$\rangle$), nevertheless the usage is perhaps significant enough to enable us to draw some conclusions about the length of stressed vowels preceding homorganic clusters in this tenth-century text. Consider the items in Table 2.14. Numerals after forms denote frequency of occurrence in the *Index Verborum*. There are no instances of either double graph

TABLE 2.14 Homorganic lengthening in the gloss to the *Lindisfarne Gospels*

-[ld]	-[mb]	-[nd]	-[ŋg]	-[rn]	-[rd]
⟨gold⟩ 4	⟨lombe⟩ 1	⟨uind⟩ 1	⟨long⟩ 11	⟨corn⟩ 8	⟨word⟩ 101
⟨góld⟩ 1	⟨wombe⟩ 1	⟨uind⟩ 1	⟨lóng⟩ 1	⟨córn⟩ 1	⟨wórd⟩ 6
	⟨clumbe⟩ 1				⟨oordes⟩ 1
⟨sald⟩ 70		⟨fand⟩ 5	⟨strong⟩ 2	⟨morgen⟩ 5	
⟨sálde⟩ 1		⟨fánd⟩ 1	⟨stróng⟩ 1	⟨mérne⟩ 1	⟨sword⟩ 9
⟨sáldon⟩ 1					⟨swórd⟩ 1
		⟨blind⟩ 1	⟨ðing⟩ 5	⟨domern⟩ 1	
⟨f'gu^{u}lde⟩ 1		⟨blínd⟩ 3	⟨ðing⟩ 1		
				⟨motérn⟩ 1	
⟨ald⟩ 20		⟨lond⟩ 32			
⟨áld⟩ 3		⟨lónd⟩ 16		⟨carcérn⟩ 1	
⟨haald⟩ 1					
		⟨grund⟩ 2		⟨ðórn⟩ 1	
		⟨grúnd⟩ 1			
		⟨uu^{u}nden⟩ 1			

or accented vowels in the context of [rl] clusters. If indeed the accented vowels represent length, then it is interesting to see that a great many stressed vowels before homorganic clusters are so marked in this gloss. The scribe's marking is far from consistent and this may merely represent his random orthographic habits and have no phonological significance. On the other hand we might speculate that the lengthening rule was highly novel, and therefore perhaps optional at this date. Mossé (1952) notes that 'In Northern English there was no lengthening before *-nd*, *-mb*; we have the following with short vowels, *find(e)*, *bind(e)*, *clim.*' While our data in Table 2.14 suggests that this is true for vowels before [mb] clusters, ⟨ ́ ⟩ marks are used quite extensively in [nd] contexts in this Northumbrian dialect. It is worth bearing in mind too that these data from the *Lindisfarne Gospels* appear to confirm the 'patchy' nature of the *homorganic lengthening* rule that was clear from the *Ormulum* materials.

Since it has implications for many subsequent proposals we shall make for the motivation behind alternations for stressed vowels in pre-sonorant consonant environments in general, let us briefly examine what might be some of the causes for the perception by language users of increased vowel durational prominence in the context of [mb], [rd] cluster types. Two points must be borne in mind. Firstly, there is no loss, with the vowel lengthening, of the sonorant element in these clusters unlike the [gans] → [gɔɔs] cases listed above in Table 2.9, so it appears as though we are not dealing with sonorant 'vocalization'. Secondly, the lengthening only occurs in these cases when the second element of the cluster is voiced – recall the *Ormulum* spellings showing short stressed vowels in items like ⟨þinnkenn⟩. Some recent experimental research might enable use to cast at least a little light on the question and even enable us to retain the hypothesis that vocalization is indeed involved.

It is possible to measure precisely the amount of time taken in the production of phonetic segments in natural speech situations, especially as regards vowels and sonorants. An interesting experiment carried out by Raphael (1972) measured the relative durational length of vowel and nasal segments in words like *bend/bent, pint/pined, mount/mound* and *stunt/stunned*, i.e. cases where there is a stressed vocalic element followed by a nasal initial homorganic cluster whose second element was either voiced or voiceless – [nd]/[nt]. The relative durational length of the vowel/nasal elements in such forms was measured in milliseconds (m/secs), and results like the following were obtained:

	100 m/s	50 m/s			150 m/s	200 m/s	
b/	ε	/	n	/t b/	ε	/	n /d

It is clear that when the cluster ends in a voiced segment not only is the stressed vowel's length markedly increased, but *the length of the nasal sonorant grows by a factor of four times*: we end up with a long vowel + long nasal output. Perhaps we might therefore look upon late Old English *homorganic lengthening* not so much as a vowel-lengthening rule, but as a vowel/ nasal-lengthening process, a suggestion first proposed by Luick (1964: sect. 268, Anm. 4, pp. 245–6).

However, this fact is also interesting in view of our earlier remarks on the vocalization of [ǰ] in the [ðeǰn] → [ðeen] change. Given that nasal sonorants are relatively high on the vocalic hierarchy, the appearance of an extended nasal signal immediately following the stressed vowel might induce speakers to reinterpret the 'first half' of that long nasal as belonging to the vowel space proper. We might therefore tentatively suggest that a sequence like [bɛnnd] is somehow re-interpreted as [bɛ+*non-syllabic vowel*+nd], with resultant reinforcing of the stressed vowel's duration and simultaneous retention of the nasal sonorant.

Two important points emerge from this brief discussion of stressed vowel lengthening phenomena in the early English period which have implications for many other innovations in the historical phonology of the language. In the first place, if it is indeed the case that when, for whatever reason, a segment to the right of the stressed vowel is lost from the syllable, with the consequence that the stressed vowel's duration becomes increased to (metaphorically) fill in that lost element, then it would seem that language users have intuitions concerning the overall shapes of syllables. If syllable shape is compromized by segment loss, then some of our data have suggested that it could be restored through increasing stressed vowel length in 'compensation'. The importance of speakers' perceptions of syllable structure for phonological innovation will figure largely in many places below, notably in sections 3.2.1, 3.5, 4.5 and 5.3.3.

Secondly, those segments to the right of the stressed vowel which we have shown to have affected its durational quantity are of a rather limited phonetic set – they are fricatives like [x] or [j] or sonorant consonants like [r], [l] or [m], [n]. Such segments we have observed above (see pp. 5–6) to be relatively highly positioned on the *sonority scale*, and are therefore relatively vowel-like in their internal composition. Even those elements with which they combine in length provoking contexts were, we observed, almost always voiced - they too seemed required to show some level of vowel prominence in their internal make up. Again we shall see in the next section and in many other places in this book (notably sect 3.4.1–3.4.6) that stressed vowels are especially susceptible to mutation in just such relatively highly vowel-like environments throughout the history of the language.

Finally, we might think of the phenomenon of increased vowel duration as one mechanism whereby the stressed vowel can be made to become more observationally prominent: it can be seen as a means of highlighting or spotlighting the vowel space in the syllable. But as we shall see in the immediately following sections, vowel lengthening is not the only highlighting device available to speakers in such pre-sonorant/fricative contexts – stressed vowel diphthongization is, we shall argue, another as is manipulation of vowel height.

2.3 Diphthongization processes in Old English

We shall devote this section to an investigation of one of the best documented sets of changes undergone by stressed vowels in the Old English period. Indeed, one reason why we shall spend such a considerable effort in describing these Old English changes is that they are of a type which occurs over and over again in the history of the English language, one indeed which is still observable (as we shall see) in the phonology of many dialects today. The process we shall be concerned with involves a change whereby speakers come to produce a diphthongal vowel shape in a context where previously a steady state monophthong was realized. Consider, as an example, the pronunciations in various Modern English dialects for the items 'feel' and 'fear' presented in Table 2.15 Clearly,

TABLE 2.15

Dialect A	Dialect B	
[fil]	[fiʌl]	
	[fiəl]	'feel'
[fir]	[fiʌr]	
	[fiər]	'fear'

speakers of dialect B show a vowel space which has a transitional movement, a trajectory from a high position to one which is low or central – [iʌ], [iə]. Dialect A, on the other hand, manifests a vowel space which is constant or fixed. The precise dialectal provenance of this alternation need not concern us here (although both types are to be found among Scottish and Northern British English speakers) but it would appear that for some varieties of the modern language when the stressed vowel space is immediately followed by a sonorant consonant like [r] or [l] (and we omit phonetic detail for the moment) then speakers appear to split that vowel space into two 'halves', the second of which shows a height/backness characteristic contrasting with that of the first. Such contrasts or 'splits' in the vowel space are usually referred to as *diphthongs* (Stampe 1972: pp. 106 ff; Lass 1984: pp. 135 ff). We shall show that not only is a process like this one of the most common in almost every period of the language's history, but that its appearance at a very early point in that history serves to set it apart at a very early stage from many other Germanic language types.

This Old English diphthong-producing process is not a simple one, but to outline its main characteristics and sequence of operation, let us look at some carefully selected examples involving the front vowels [i], [e] and [a] as they occur in Old English immediately preceding the sonorant consonants [r] and [l] and contrast them (see Table 2.16) with the way they are manifested in similar contexts in other early Germanic languages like Gothic

TABLE 2.16

Non-English Germanic		Old English	
		Early Old English	West Saxon
[i]		[iu]	[eo]
Gothic ⟨lirnojan⟩ *'to learn'*		Bede ⟨uuiurthit⟩	⟨leornian⟩
[e]		[eu]	[eo]
OHG ⟨erda⟩ *'earth'*			⟨eorþe⟩
[a]		[æu]	[æa]
OHG ⟨barn⟩ ⟨all⟩ ⟨alt⟩	*'child'* *'all'* *'old'*	Urswick Cross ⟨bæurn⟩	⟨bearn⟩ ⟨eall⟩ ⟨eald⟩
1		2	3

and Old High German. A number of interesting points emerge from these rather complex data:

(1) A comparison of columns 1 and 2/3 shows clearly that the phonology of Old English as a whole is characterized by the appearance of what the *spelling* suggests are diphthongal vowel shapes like ⟨iu⟩, ⟨eo⟩, ⟨æu⟩ and ⟨ea⟩ where the Gothic and Old High German examples show monophthongal ⟨i⟩, ⟨e⟩ and ⟨a⟩.

(2) Column 2 spellings, predating those of 3, show that when this new diphthongal element was realized in place of the stressed monophthongal vowel its first 'half' retained the original vowel shape, while the second 'new' element had a high, back configuration: [u] – cf. ⟨barn⟩/⟨bæurn⟩.

(3) The column 3 diphthongs found in West Saxon dialect texts show, however, a different second half element from this [u] in column 2 and represent the result of a later change which appears to have affected diphthongs in general. Let us consider the mid

vowel [e] as an example. The following changes appear to have
taken place:

PRE-OE		EARLY OE		WS
[e]	→	[eu]	→	[eo]

(although there are no examples of an [eu] diphthong before [r]/[l]
in the extant early Old English corpus, we can fairly safely assume
that such a stage occurred, both on the analogy of the high and
low vowel behaviour as well as from the presence of ⟨eu⟩ spellings
in very similar kinds of contexts).

The West Saxon spellings in Table 2.16 strongly suggest that the
new [u] glide vowel element was lowered to [o], thus causing it to
agree in height with the original (now first half of the diphthong)
preceding stressed vowel. That is, we no longer see a vowel
trajectory involving both a change in backness and height, but one
where only a backness shift occurs:

	FRONT	BACK			FRONT	BACK
HIGH		u	→	HIGH		
MID	e			MID	e	o

However, the low vowel examples look rather puzzling. The
spelling forms suggest that we have a development something like:
[æu]→[ea]⟨ea⟩. Our argument immediately above, however, would
suggest that in fact something like [æu] → [æa] occurred, where the
second half of the vowel space has been lowered to reflect the
height of the stressed first half [æ]. That a pronunciation like [æa] is
indeed what occurred is evidenced by such early ⟨æa⟩ for later
⟨ea⟩ spellings as ⟨aethiliæardi⟩, ⟨balthhæardi⟩ (Samuels 1952:
p. 25) and ⟨þæah⟩ for ⟨þeah⟩ (Campbell 1959: sect. 135), as well
as ⟨ȝeræafte⟩ compared with ⟨ȝereafian⟩ in the later Vespasian
Psalter: ⟨ea⟩ would therefore appear to have been an orthographic
convention for the representation of the diphthong [æa].

(4) Our instance in column 2 of [i] → [iu] shows the expected
realization of the high, back segment before [r] where, since both
vowels share the same degree of highness, there is no requirement
for any further modification to the height of the second half element
in the vowel space. Nevertheless, and we shall discuss this in more
detail below, the ⟨leornian⟩ spelling in column 3 suggests that
the new [iu] diphthong 'fell together' or 'collapsed' with [eo]
at some, perhaps later, date. Consider again some other pertinent
data, as in Table 2.17. Here again we can see that where the

TABLE 2.17 Diphthongization in velar fricative contexts

Non-English Germanic		Old English	
		Early OE	West Saxon
OHG ⟨lihti⟩	'light'		⟨leoht⟩
OHG ⟨ehu-⟩ ⟨kneht⟩	'horse' 'boy'	⟨Eumer⟩	⟨eoh⟩ ⟨cneoht⟩
OHG ⟨ahto⟩ ⟨sah⟩	'eight' 'he saw'		⟨eaht⟩ ⟨seah⟩
I		2	3

Germanic examples have a vowel space filled by a single vowel type, those in Old English show one divided into two parts, i.e. they manifest diphthongs. Consider first the ⟨Eumer⟩ instance in column 2 which reflects what seems to be a personal name of a murderer mentioned in Bede's *Ecclesiastical History of the English People* (Colgrave and Mynore 1969: p. 164): '*uenit. . . .sicarius uocabulo Eumer*'. This name appears to be composed of two elements ⟨eoh⟩ '*a horse*' and ⟨mer⟩ (?⟨mære⟩'*great*') (Campbell 1959: sect. 348.5). The last segment of ⟨eoh⟩ has, for reasons which need not concern us here, been deleted. Such a form, when compared with the OHG ⟨ehu-⟩, would suggest that the [e] vowel space has been split into two parts, the latter a high and back [u] before a consonantal segment which on this occasion is not the sonorant [r] or [l], but some sound represented by the symbol ⟨h⟩. Notice again that the [eu] diphthong so produced has been second-element height adjusted to realize [eo] in later Old English. We can perhaps postulate a similar process for the other front vowels whereby they too diphthongized to [iu] and [æu], the latter height adjusted to [æa]. Once again, too, the new diphthongal [iu] can show 'collapse' with [eo], so that [liuxt] → [leoxt].

As this last example shows, many scholars hold that the sound represented by the ⟨h⟩ graph was the voiceless velar fricative [x], a sound now absent from many varieties of Modern English, although still to be found in some Scottish and Irish pronunciations for the symbols ⟨gh⟩ and ⟨ch⟩ in words such as ⟨loch⟩

[lɔx], ⟨bought⟩ [bɔxt] and ⟨daughter⟩ [dɔxtər]. We shall see below that this [x] was not only a fairly common feature of the general phonology of English until the sixteenth century but was one which regularly affected the length and monophthongal status of stressed vowels in its vicinity as it still does to this day in many of those dialects which retain it. The mechanism for diphthong formation illustrated in Tables 2.16 and 2.17 affects West Saxon short *front* vowels only and might be summarized in a preliminary fashion in Table 2.18. Such a diphthongization process is generally referred to as *Breaking* or *Fracture* and we shall proceed to look in some detail at the way it is manifested in the various dialectal regions of Old English.

TABLE 2.18 *Breaking*

[u] *Vowel insertion*	*Second element height adjustment*
[i] → [iu]	→ [iu]
[e] → [eu]	→ [eo]
[æ] → [æu]	→ [æa]

2.3.1 Old English *Breaking*

In this section we shall present a fairly detailed examination of the ways in which this diphthongization process shows itself in the various environments which trigger it. We do this not merely because it is interesting in its own right or because Old English *Breaking* is a major early English phonological process, but because it highlights many of the descriptive and theoretical difficulties we shall encounter when considering later, related changes. Immediately we begin to look more closely at this diphthongization we see that the very general description which we have so far provided for it is grossly inadequate. There are, in fact, many peculiarities associated with the process which will make its description rather complex. In the first place, its dialectal manifestations are rather elaborate. Secondly, individual vowels appear to react rather differently to separate aspects of the affecting context: for instance, it would appear that the high vowel [i] fails to undergo Old English *Breaking* when in the immediate vicinity of [l], while it will do so quite regularly in the environment of [r] and [x]. Thirdly, the affecting contexts themselves are not homogeneous in the consequence they produce. For instance, the velar fricative [x] is a 'strong' context for diphthong production, while the sonorants [r] and [l] – although sometimes capable of producing the same result while standing alone – almost always appear to require 'reinforcement' by a following consonantal element.

Let us examine, in 2.3.1(1), (2) and (3) below, the ways in which respectively the short low, mid and high front vowels ([æ], [e] and [i]) behave in *Breaking* environments.

2.3.1(1) Stressed low front vowels: [æ] preceding [r] and [l] contexts

The data in Table 2.19 show the various manifestations in the earliest English of the slightly palatal [æ] vowel peak in a syllable which is terminated by an [r] initial cluster. The stressed vowel spellings in column 1, 2 and 4 items appear to suggest a monophthongal vowel space. The West Saxon dialectal forms clearly stand out from the others with their graphic ⟨ea⟩ in stressed vowel position, a symbol combination which, we suggested above, denotes the diphthong [æa]. The examples we have quoted suggest that this diphthongization only occurs when the [r] sonorant is followed by another consonant or shows a geminate spelling (whatever that may signify phonetically). In other words, the stressed vowel [æ] has to its immediate right a syllable-terminating consonantal cluster initiated by a sonorant [r]. All regional dialects of Old English appear to show this [æ]

TABLE 2.19

Non-English	English		
	early OE	WS	Northumbrian
[a]	[æ]	[æa]	[æ]
	⟨uarm⟩	⟨wearm⟩		'knife'
	⟨uarras⟩	⟨wearras⟩		'hard skin'
	⟨sparuua⟩	⟨spearwa⟩		'leg calf'
	⟨arc⟩	⟨earc⟩		'the Ark'
OHG				
⟨arm⟩		⟨earm⟩		'arm'
⟨hard⟩		⟨heard⟩		'hard'
⟨barn⟩		⟨bearn⟩	⟨barn⟩	'child'
⟨warp⟩		⟨wearp⟩	⟨warp⟩	'he threw'
⟨maruh⟩		⟨mearh⟩		'mare'
⟨maruk⟩		⟨mearc⟩		'boundary'
⟨haruc⟩		⟨hearh⟩		'temple'
I	2	3	4	

→ [æa] change in such an environment, with the exception – as our data in column 4 show – of Northumbrian texts, especially those of an early date, where [æ] persists. However, by the tenth century in this dialect (e.g. in texts like the *Lindisfarne Gospels* and the *Durham Ritual* glosses) some diphthongal forms are also evidenced. Early West Saxon documents are extremely rare, but the items in column 2 of Table 2.19 are taken from the *Parker Chronicle* (Smith 1964: p. 13) – which seems to preserve some early spellings – as well as from some early West Saxon *Charters* (Sweet 1885). There are some very important constraints too upon the pre-[l] diphthongizing process (see Table 2.20). Firstly, it is regionally restricted to West Saxon and Kentish. Other

TABLE 2.20 [æ] preceding [l] contexts

Non-English		Old English		
	early WS	WS	non-WS	
[a]	[æ]	[æa]	[æ]	
(1)				
OHG				
⟨all⟩	⟨alle⟩	⟨eall⟩	⟨all⟩	*'all'*
Gothic/OS				
⟨haldan⟩	⟨haldan⟩	⟨healdan⟩	⟨haldan⟩	*'to hold'*
OHG/OS				
⟨ald⟩	⟨alda⟩	⟨eald⟩	⟨ald⟩	*'old'*
OHG				
⟨kalt⟩		⟨ceald⟩		*'cold'*
OHG				
⟨halp⟩		⟨healp⟩		*'he helped'*
(2)				
OS				
⟨wal⟩		⟨weall⟩		*'wall'*
OHG				
⟨halla⟩		⟨heall⟩		*'hall'*
OHG				
⟨fallan⟩		⟨feallan⟩		*'to fall'*
(3)				
OHG				
⟨wal⟩		⟨hwæl⟩		*'whale'*
OHG				
⟨smal⟩		⟨smæl⟩		*'small'*
		⟨Ælfred⟩		*'Alfred'*
		⟨Ælmihtig⟩		*'Almighty'*

dialects show a monophthongal vowel space in this context. Secondly, the stressed vowel space once again undergoes a split only when the affecting sonorant is itself the first member of a consonantal cluster like [ld] or [lp] (those under (1)) or is geminate (those under (2)) – i.e. the space immediately following the vowel must contain two separate segments, either [ld]/[lp] or one which is 'lengthened' (geminate), [ll]. That is, what is important is both the *size* of the affecting environment: i.e. it must contain two rather than one or three segments (cf. [lfr] in ⟨Ælfred⟩ where there is no [æ] → [æa] diphthongization) as well as the *nature* of the segments which comprise it i.e. [lp] and not [lm] – cf. the undiphthongized [æ] vowel in ⟨Ælmihtig⟩. The domain of the former constraint lies, as we shall see on several occasions below, in the composition of the supra-segmental structure known as the *syllable*; the overall structural characteristics of this entity seem to play a very important role in determining whether the stressed vowel space can be simple (monophthongal) or complex (long or diphthongal).

2.3.1(2) [æ] preceding [x] contexts

The examples in column 2 of Table 2.21 clearly show that the diphthongization process was operative regardless of whether the following fricative was single/short or one of a cluster. Thus ⟨seah⟩ and ⟨eahta⟩. Indeed the voiceless fricative context seems to be the 'strongest' of the *Breaking* triggers, admits of very few constraints

TABLE 2.21

Non-English	Old English	
	West Saxon	
[a]	[æa]	
Gothic		
⟨mahts⟩	⟨meaht⟩	*'might'*
OHG		
⟨ahto⟩	⟨eahta⟩	*'eight'*
OHG		
⟨sah⟩	⟨seah⟩	*'he saw'*
OHG		
⟨hlahter⟩	⟨hleahtor⟩	*'laughter'*
OHG		
⟨fahs⟩	⟨feax⟩	*'hair'*
1	2	

upon its operation and seems to be regularly found in all regional dialects.

2.3.1(3) Mid front vowels: [e] preceding [r] contexts

Notice again that, as with the examples under 2.3.1(1) and (2), the data in Table 2.22 suggest that the diphthongization only appears to occur when the triggering [r] context is itself part of a consonantal cluster; the *Breaking* is again somehow sensitive to the total number of consonantal segments present to the right of the stressed vowel (see below pp 45–6). Such diphthongization of [e] → [eo] in a pre-[r] context is one of the most common types and figures prominently in most Old English regional dialects.

TABLE 2.22

Non-English	Old English	
[e]	[eo]	
OHG		
〈erda〉	〈eorþe〉	'earth'
OS		
〈herta〉	〈heorte〉	'heart'
OHG		
〈werden〉	〈weorþan〉	'to become'
OS		
〈erl〉	〈eorl〉	'earl'
OS		
〈swerd〉	〈sweord〉	'sword'

2.3.1(4) [e] preceding [l] and [x] contexts

Unlike its behaviour in the immediate vicinity of [r] sonorants, the diphthongization of [e] in [l] contexts is severely constrained (see Table 2.23). Most of the available evidence suggests that the stressed vowel space is 'split up', made contrastive, only when the sonorant [l] is the first member of a cluster whose second element is either [x] or [k], i.e. some kind of back segment. Thus, we fail to find any diphthongal vowel space in items such as 〈delfan〉 'to dig', 〈helpan〉 'to help', 〈helm〉 'helmet', 〈elm〉 'elm tree', 〈elnung〉 'comfort' and 〈sweltan〉 'to die' (even though clusters like [lp] and [lf] regularly appear to trigger the diphthongization of [æ] → [æa] – 〈healf〉, 〈healp〉). It is difficult to see any motivation for a constraint like this. At the same time, [l] on its own does not seem to be a sufficiently strong trigger to provoke the split up of the stressed vowel space before it. An [eo] shape in its vicinity only seems especially likely when the [l] is itself tied to another *Breaking*

TABLE 2.23

Non-English	Old English	
[e]	[eo]	
OHG ⟨elaho⟩	⟨eolh⟩	'elk'
OHG ⟨melkan⟩	⟨meolcan⟩	'to milk'
OHG ⟨scelh⟩	⟨sceolh⟩	'wry'

triggering segment – [x]. The situation is even more complex when we come across spellings such as ⟨seolcan⟩ and ⟨seolf⟩ which appear to contradict our last assertion that the diphthongization of [e] is confined to contexts like [lx]. We might wish to treat such forms as exceptions or as generalizations of a limited rule process to a wider environment and the latter would not be too difficult to accept in the case of ⟨seolf⟩ where the post-[l] segment is, like [x], a fricative. Many scholars (Campbell 1959: sect. 146; Sievers and Brunner 1941: sect. 85, footnote 7) believe that the *Breaking* of [e] is a genuine process in such cases only when the consonant *preceding* the stressed vowel is [s] – ⟨seolf⟩. However, no phonetic/phonological rationale for such an assertion is ever provided.

Consider the items in Table 2.24 below, where again, column 3

TABLE 2.24 [e] preceding [x] contexts

Non-English	Old English			
	early OE	WS	late WS	Kentish
	[eo]	[eu]	[eo]	[io]
OHG ⟨kneht⟩		⟨cneoht⟩	⟨cnieht⟩	⟨cnioht⟩	'boy'
OHG ⟨fehtan⟩		⟨feohtan⟩	⟨fieht⟩	⟨fioht⟩	'to fight'
OHG ⟨sehs⟩		⟨seox⟩	⟨siex⟩		'six'
OS ⟨ehu-⟩	⟨Eumer⟩	⟨eoh⟩			'horse'
1	2	3	4	5	

forms show the powerful diphthongizing effect of [x] either as a single segment or as the first member of a cluster. That the process initially involved the splitting of the stressed vowel space into two halves, the second of which was [u], can be seen from the ⟨Eumer⟩ instance already discussed on page 37 above. In fact, the surface realization of this *Breaking*-produced [eo] diphthong is rather infrequent since it is very often subject to mutation through the operation of subsequent phonological processes, as can be seen from the examples in column 4 where it has been altered to whatever is represented by ⟨ie⟩ in late West Saxon, or in the column 5 instances, 'collapsed' with [io] (Sievers and Brunner 1941: sect. 86, footnote).

2.3.1(5) High short front vowels: [i] preceding [r] contexts

The kinds of diphthongal realizations which we find for front high (pure palatal) [i] vowels in all *Breaking* contexts are particularly diverse (see Table 2.25). We have already discussed, for example, the ⟨uuiurthit⟩ case suggestive of a vowel space divided into halves like [iu], and have shown how this new diphthong had its second element lowered, precipitating a 'collapse' or merger with the [eo] diphthong.

2.3.1(6) [i] preceding [x] contexts

Again, dialectal realizations of *Breaking* of [i] in this context are rather complex. Both Kentish and Northumbrian texts show what appears to be lowering (unrounding) in the second half of the diphthong in such forms as ⟨Piahtred⟩ (cf. ⟨Piohtas⟩); ⟨fiah⟩ '*money*' (cf. ⟨feoh⟩) and ⟨Wiaht⟩ (cf. ⟨Wioht⟩). This effect extends also to those [eo] diphthongs produced through other phonological processes – ⟨wiarald⟩ '*world*' (cf. ⟨weorold⟩) and ⟨bebiade⟩ '*I command*' (cf. ⟨bebeode⟩) (Campbell 1959: sect. 280; Sievers and Brunner 1941: sect. 86.3) (see Table 2.26). Alternant diphthongal outputs in this affecting context like [iu]/[io]/[eo]/[ia] might suggest that for contemporary language users certain vowel contrasts were seen as more 'viable' than others. Even at this early point in our discussion we might tentatively suggest that a diphthongal stressed vowel space contrast involving the pure palatal and labial [iu] segments was somehow not as readily perceivable as one like, say, [eo] or [ia]. At several places below we shall apparently find evidence to infer that complex diphthongal vowel space is subject to alteration based upon considerations of maximalization of the vocalic contrast between the two halves of its structure (see sect. 5.3.1; Lass and Anderson 1975: pp. 209–12; Campbell 1959: sects 293–5).

TABLE 2.25

Non-English		Old English		
	early OE	WS	late WS	
[i](/[e])	[iu]	[io]	[eo]	
OHG				
⟨hirti⟩		⟨hiorde⟩	⟨heorde⟩	*'shepherd'*
OHG				
⟨irri⟩		⟨iorre⟩	⟨eorre⟩	*'anger'*
Gothic				
⟨lirnojan⟩		⟨liornian⟩	⟨leornian⟩	*'to learn'*
OS				
⟨berht⟩		⟨biorht⟩	⟨beorht⟩	*'bright'*
	⟨uuiurthit⟩			

TABLE 2.26

Non-English	Old English	
	West Saxon	
[i]	[io]	
Gothic		
⟨tihhojan⟩	⟨tiohhian⟩	*'to consider'*
Gothic		
⟨mihst⟩	⟨miox⟩/⟨meox⟩	*'dung'*
	⟨Wioht⟩	*'Isle of Wight'*
	⟨Piohtas⟩	
	⟨Peohtas⟩	*'Picts'*

2.3.1(7) [i] preceding [l] contexts
There appears to be no evidence for the diphthongization of short high vowels in this context; cf. such forms as ⟨gefilde⟩ *'plain'*, ⟨scilling⟩ *'shilling'* and ⟨wilde⟩ *'wild'*.

2.3.2 *Breaking* of long stressed vowels
Although the spelling system of West Saxon manuscripts strongly suggests that what were durationally long front monophthongs underwent a diphthongization process much like that affecting their short counterparts, their range of *Breaking* operations is far more constrained both dialectally and phonologically while at the same

time there are serious problems as to the interpretation of the
phonetic value of the diphthongization of long vowels in general.
Consider the data in Table 2.27. Diphthongization in this particular
context is especially problematic and we cannot deal with its
detailed difficulties here, but a few points are worth noting. Firstly,
the diphthongization of long vowel inputs appears to be constrained
to occur only in pre-[x] contexts, the process tending not to
occur when they are contiguous with [r] and [l] sonorants either when
these stand alone or act as the first elements in clusters. Is there
some kind of constraint upon the appearance in the language of
syllables which have a {stressed vowel + non-syllabic vowel + [r]/[l] +
consonant} configuration? If there is, it might reinforce our earlier
tentative suggestion that the presence or absence of the
diphthongization of the vowel space could itself be sensitive to
speakers' perceptions as to what they thought to be the appropriate
shapes of syllables. We shall address this kind of question in some
detail in our section devoted to Middle English *open syllable
lengthening* (3.2).

TABLE 2.27

Non-English	Old English	
	West Saxon	.
[aa]/[ii]/[ee]	?[ææa]/[eeo]	
Gothic ⟨nēhs⟩ OS/OHG ⟨nāh⟩	⟨nēah⟩	'near'
OHG ⟨līhti⟩ ⟨wīh⟩ ⟨līh⟩ ⟨fīhala⟩	⟨lēoht⟩ ⟨wēoh⟩ ⟨lēoh⟩ ⟨fēol⟩	'light' 'error' 'lie' 'file'

The question mark before the phonetic value of the diphthongal
West Saxon outputs in Table 2.27 expresses our uncertainty
concerning what might have been the actual surface realization of
long vowel *Breaking* in that language. As we have seen earlier,
the Old English vowel inventory shows a long and short
monophthong distinction (e.g. [ii] versus [i]) as well as a
monophthongal/diphthongal one (e.g. [i]/[ii] versus [io]). But does it

also manifest a long versus short diphthongal contrast, say [æǣa] alternating with [æa] of the type we questioningly suggested to be the output of the West Saxon *Breaking* of long vowel inputs? It does seem to be the case, for example, that the subsequent development of those vowels derived from short and long diphthongs was quite distinct, suggesting that Old English speakers treated them as separate, identifiable outputs. For instance, short diphthongs tend to undergo later processes appropriate for short monophthongs; likewise, there are many cases where what should be long diphthongs (both derived and lexical) take the same historical route as that of long monophthongs. For example, we shall see in Chapter 4 that the 'descendants' of the long diphthongs produced by OE *Breaking* and OE lexical long vowels both undergo the *English vowel shift*. On the other hand, the derivatives of lexical Old English short vowels as well as short *Breaking* diphthongs tend not to so do. Nevertheless, some scholars (notably Lass and Anderson 1975: pp. 79 ff) argue that although West Saxon speakers recognized that the rules of their phonology could produce sequences like [æa] and [æǣa], the latter were not 'permitted' to appear at the level of pronunciation and were conflated with short [æa] shapes. We shall return to this problem of constraints on vowel configurations in syllables (especially when in conjunction with certain consonantal elements) at several points in later parts of this book.

2.3.3 Causes of this diphthongization in pre-[x], [r], [l] contexts

From the earliest philological descriptions, *Breaking* has been treated as arising from a purely mechanical set of articulatory factors. Since the only vowels which can act as input to the process are front, and since the most common triggering context is [x] – a back, velar fricative – it has been argued that the muscular transitional movement from a front position to one which is raised and back, involves the (incidental) production of a vowel sound intermediate between the two extreme horizontal positions; what had been a juxtaposition of two horizontally discrete segments becomes one where there is a vocalic trajectory continuum. Before it can achieve the position appropriate for the realization of the raised, back [x] fricative (so such a model argues) the tongue, starting from a fronted placement, has to pass through a position whereby a vowel sound like [u] can be produced. The implication is that language users 'hear' the vowel sound produced in the transition between, say, [æ] and [x]. They recognize a 'second half' to the vowel space. However, while such an argument has a certain appeal on the grounds of the continuity of muscular movement in speech production, it tends to fall down as an explanation for the other *Breaking* environment, where vowels were diphthongized in the vicinity of [r] and [l] (plus consonant). Given the front nature of these sounds in many modern dialects, appeals to positional transition in tongue movement are clearly unattractive. The earliest scholars were compelled to conclude that [r] and [l] had also in Old English to be *back* in some way – they had some 'dark' quality. That is, they were to be treated as though they were like the back [ɫ] and [ɼ] in some modern British English dialects (cf. the Scottish pronunciation of [mʌɫʔ] 'milk'. For a more extreme proposal, see Lass and Anderson 1975: pp. 83 ff.

The standard hypothesis seems to be, then, that the dissimilatory contiguity of front vowels like [i] and [e] with proposed back consonantal segments like [ɼ]/[ɫ] resulted in the production of an 'epenthetic' vowel element whose function it was to 'facilitate' the transition between two horizontally contrasting elements: the new post-stressed vowel space taking on the colour of the back segment to its right. It is very important to realize that when any vocalic and consonantal segments are contiguous there is usually manisfested in the acoustic signal some transitional characteristic from one to the other. Indeed, the hearer may often use such transitional information as a cue to the nature of the following (or preceding) segment (Pickett 1980: Ch. 11). For instance, in Modern English, even in a word like [il] '*ill*', where the [l] can be a front, dental sound, instrumentation shows a transitional movement between the end of the vowel signal and the beginning of that for the sonorant. That is, transitions are not only to be found where there is some major positional disparity between contiguous segments. Indeed, the language user may not 'hear' such transitional information – certainly he may not accord it separate, say vocalic, status. Nevertheless, our Old English materials suggest that just this may have indeed happened and some transitional element come to be treated as if it were equivalent to the second element of a lexical diphthong. Yet it is not altogether clear what constitute the precise conditions whereby such transitional elements come to be perceived as sufficiently prominent to be regarded as a 'fully vocalic' second half of a diphthong and not just as some piece of acoustic information signalling that the next segment (a) is not a vowel and (b) shows height or backness differences from the stressed vowel itself.

There are a great many questions regarding possible causations for Old English *Breaking* which we must for the moment leave unanswered, although we shall return to similar matters later in this section. Notably, stressed front vowel diphthongization does not always occur just when the segment to its immediate right is back – we shall see in sect 3.4 ff that it can also occur when that segment is unambigiously palatal and front. Likewise, following back segments do not always provoke it: *Breaking* is constrained not to occur when the segment to the right of the stressed front vowel is an *obstruent* like [k] or [g]. What are the particular phonetic characteristics of [r], [l] and [x] which make speakers hear a transitional vocalic element before them? Some of the answers to these difficult questions will be put in a preliminary fashion in 2.3.6 below.

2.3.4 Did this diphthongization ever really happen?

After committing so much space to a discussion of what we have claimed is a major diphthong producing phonological process, it might appear perverse in the extreme seriously to question whether such a phenomenon ever, in fact, took place. However, we shall see that by asking this question we shall not only gain some insights into how historical phonologists arrive at their conclusions but also have an opportunity to see the operation of some important phonological processes which can affect diphthongs in general and which recur with some regularity throughout the history of the English language. In a now famous paper, Daunt (1939) suggested that it was perhaps naive to interpret Old English spellings such as ⟨eo⟩ and ⟨ea⟩ as if they represented a transition from one vowel state to another; a stressed vowel space with contrastive components. While agreeing with many scholars that both the [l] and [r] sonorants had a 'dark' or back quality like [x] (like, for instance the pronunciation of the [ł] segment in [mʌł] '*Mull*' versus that in [mɪl] '*mill*') she nevertheless put forward the view that the ⟨-o⟩ and ⟨-a⟩ elements in the second half of the ⟨eo⟩/⟨ea⟩ digraphs did not represent a vocalic transition (i.e. the second half of a diphthong) but rather were purely diacritic marks to show that *the following consonants were back*. A spelling like ⟨wæl⟩, for instance, she claims represents a phonetic shape like [wæl], while ⟨weal⟩ denotes [wæł] – the stressed vowels in both items being monophthongal. This purely orthographic convention, she claims, Old English scribes inherited from an Old Irish spelling system in which it was commonplace and with which they were very familiar.

Although Daunt's views are not unattractive, they compel us to look for some evidence which will convince us of a diphthongal interpretation for digraphs like ⟨eo⟩ and ⟨ea⟩. Can we put forward any well motivated arguments for such an interpretation? Perhaps the best argument we can propose is that diphthongizations triggered by the kinds of contexts we have described are so common at all historical periods of our language that they can in some way be considered to represent 'natural' phonological innovation. We shall see in the chapters which follow the extent to which such *Breakings* are a feature of the phonologies of Middle, early Modern and Modern English.

Again, are there any phonetic properties or processes peculiar to diphthongs in general which can be shown to effect those elements spelt ⟨eo⟩, ⟨ea⟩ and ⟨io⟩ in Old English *Breaking* contexts which might lead us to support a diphthongal interpretation for them? In an important paper, Samuels (1952) put forward a whole set of counter claims to Daunt's hypothesis, a principal one centring around a phonetic characteristic common to diphthongs in general. In diphthongal sequences, both of the vocalic 'halves' are not equally prominent. One, often the first, is 'highlighted' or stressed and made to bear the syllable beat (cf. sect. 1.3). Thus, in Modern English, a word like ⟨now⟩ will show the vocalic elements in the diphthong relatively highlighted as [naʊ] and not [naʊ]. However, it is quite common to find the juxtaposed elements in diphthongal vowel space undergoing what is often called a 'stress shift' whereby the second element or half in the sequence comes to be the more prominent of the two. Consider the historical development of the second person plural pronoun '*you*'. Spelt in OE ⟨eow⟩, it apparently contained a diphthongal element whose first half was assigned prominence: [eo]. By the early Middle English period, it appears that for some reason a prominence shift was implemented in this item, such that the diphthong came to be realized as [eo], its first element developing the status of the glide [j]: [jo], the ancestor of our modern [ju] form. Consider too the Middle English dialectal versions for the verb '*to choose*'. In Old English this verb showed a diphthongal [eo] element in its infinitive form, being spelt ⟨ceosan⟩: [čeoz-]. In the twelfth and thirteenth centuries we find that some dialects realize this verb as [čez-] while others show [čoz-]. We might surmise that the latter (and they are the forerunners of the modern [čuz-] forms) arise from just such a relative prominence displacement whereby [čeoz-] → [čeoz] → [čjoz-] → [čooz] → (via the *English vowel shift* – see sect. 4.2.) [čuuz].

Samuels points out that in Middle Kentish texts we find 'broken' diphthongs in words corresponding to Old English ⟨eald⟩ and ⟨heald⟩ spelt as ⟨yealde⟩ and ⟨hyealde⟩. These spellings, he suggests, might be interpreted as reflecting some kind of [æa] → [æa] → [ja] prominence displacement, where the reduced (less prominent) [j] element is recorded graphically as ⟨y⟩. He points also (following Sievers and Brunner 1941: sects 125a and 212.2) to late Old Kentish texts where, for ⟨ea⟩ spellings in pre-[r] *Breaking* contexts, we find representations like ⟨ʒearfoðe⟩ for ⟨earfoðe⟩ where once more the ⟨ʒ⟩ graph may represent a diphthong initial [j] arising from stress shift. For a further discussion, see sections 3.5 and 4.5.1 below.

2.3.5 Exceptions to the *Breaking* process

We have already noted, without offering anything by way of explanation, that the Old English diphthongization process in the vicinity of [r], [l] and [x] segments is far from being a uniform one. Long vowels (and then only [ii] and [æː]) are constrained to diphthongize only in [x] contexts, while [e] → [eo] before [l] only in those instances where the sonorant is followed in turn by [x]. Likewise, we witnessed several important dialectal restrictions upon the change. However, there is one particular set of exceptions which raise some important issues not only about the *Breaking* operation, but also about the nature of phonological behaviour in general. Consider the data in Table 2.28. The items under Type A show diphthongization of the *Breaking* type with which we are by now familiar. The *Postulated pre-Breaking* stage items witness the fronting of the low back vowel [a] in the Germanic examples to the [æ] typical of the English and Frisian Germanic language group (see our discussion of the *Anglo-Frisian Brightening* process in sect. 2.5.2) a change which produces the front vowel input essential for Old English *Breaking*.

The Old English items in pre-[ll] environments of Type B in Table 2.28 however, show *monophthongs* in places where we would typically expect diphthongs produced through *Breaking*. How are we to deal with exceptional behaviour like this? Two possibilities suggest themselves. Firstly, we might argue that while *Breaking* can be expected to occur in the majority of cases where stressed front vowels appear in the vicinity of [r], [l] and [x], there exist in the language random lists of words which, although they contain the contextual trigger for the change, are for some reason entered separately in the dictionary as *Breaking* exceptions. An interesting instance of a phenomenon like this has recently been brought to light by Kerswill (1983) in his study of the pronunciation of adolescents in County Durham, England. He noted that these young speakers showed several variants for the pronunciation of the voiceless dental stop /t/ in word initial position, many involving various degrees of aspiration or fricativization – [tˢ] or [tʰ] – thus [tʰəi] 'tea' and [tˢoə] 'so'. Glottalization of [t] to [ʔ] would never occur in this word initial position *except in the case of the lexical item* '*time*', for which Kerswill found glottalized realizations like [tʔɜɪm]

TABLE 2.28

Non-English		Old English		
	Postulated pre-Breaking shape	West Saxon	Non-West Saxon	
Type A				
Gothic				
⟨alls⟩	*[æll]	⟨eall⟩		*'all'*
⟨kalds⟩	*[kæld]	⟨ceald⟩		*'cold'*
OHG				
⟨barn⟩	*[bærn]	⟨bearn⟩		*'child'*
⟨hart⟩	*[hærd]	⟨heard⟩		*'hard'*
Type B				
Gothic				
⟨nasjan⟩	*[nærian]	⟨nerian⟩		*'to save'*
⟨warjan⟩	*[wærian]	⟨werian⟩		*'to wear'*
⟨taljan⟩	*[tællian]	⟨tellan⟩		*'to tell'*
⟨saljan⟩	*[sællian]	⟨sellan⟩		*'to sell'*
⟨halja⟩	*[hælli]	⟨hell⟩		*'hell'*
Type C				
OHG				
⟨smeruit⟩	*[smiri]		⟨smirian⟩	*'to smear'*
		⟨cyrin⟩	⟨cirn⟩	*'churn'*
Type D				
OS				
⟨irri⟩	*[irri]	⟨eorre⟩	⟨iorre⟩	*'anger'*
1	2	3	4	

'*time*' and [ɔvətʔaɪm] '*overtime*'. Only this particular item behaves irregularly in this respect in his data, and speakers seem to enter it separately in their lexicons as not subject to the 'aspiration' process normally typical of word initial [t]. We shall have cause to see many instances of such a sensitivity of phonological change to *lexical item* types (a phenomenon often referred to as *lexical diffusion*) rather than as a response solely to phonetic considerations, in many places in subsequent sections.

But are the Type B, C data we have presented in Table 2.28 'unmotivated' exceptions like this? Or could we argue that there was something different and deterministic in the phonetic context of Types B and C from those in Type A? That this is indeed the case would seem to be true when we consider the *non-English* and *pre-Breaking* columns where, unlike those under Type A, the second syllable in the items cited contains a high, front vocalic (or vowel like) segment – [i] or [j]. This segment appears to have had two effects: (1) it can provoke the doubling or lengthening (gemination) of an [l] (but not an [r]) sonorant preceding it (in which case it is subsequently deleted) – [taljan] → [tellan] and (2) it can provoke the raising of [æ] to [e] in West Saxon (and other) Old English dialects (see our discussion below of the palatal vowel harmony phenomenon of *i-umlaut*, cf. sect. 2.5.2). Where this syllable 2 initiating [l]/[j] is preserved, *Breaking* will not, it seems, occur; thus while *[bærn] → [bæarn], *[wæri] does not appear diphthongized to *[wæari-]: instead the undiphthongized [æ] has been directly raised to [e]. Likewise, when the [i]/[j] has effected a lengthening of the [l] sonorant, the operation of *Breaking* is also 'blocked', thus we do not find some form like *[tæallian], but again witness a direct raising of [æ] to [e].

But how are speakers of Old English supposed to know when a long [ll] in [tellan] is, as we have without explanation claimed, the product of a following [i] vowel and when it is lexical, as in the case of ⟨eall⟩ – the former blocking *Breaking*, the latter triggering it? We could argue that they in fact have no means of recovering such information and mark items like ⟨tellan⟩, ⟨sellan⟩ and ⟨hell⟩ in their lexicon as being randomly 'blocked for *Breaking*'. But could we claim that it was, in fact, possible for native speakers actually to predict that the [ll] in ⟨tellan⟩ was somehow phonetically distinct from that in ⟨eall⟩ and as such was not an appropriate trigger for the operation of the diphthongization process? It has been argued (notably by Hogg 1971) that we can indeed think in terms of a synchronic phonetic trigger for the [æall]/[tellan] alternation. Recall that we surmised that *Breaking* might only occur if the post-stressed vowel consonant is back. If we consider examples such as *[tællian] and *[nerian] we could argue that the presence of the front [i] contiguous with the [r]/[l] sonorants kept the latter fronted. Even after the loss of the following [i], the sonorants remained as front [r] and [ll]. Speakers of West Saxon would therefore have in their phonetic inventory two types of non-nasal sonorant, the one front, the other back. In the case of words like ⟨tellan⟩, a lexical entry such as /tellan/ would be appropriate, whereas ⟨eall⟩ would be entered as /æɫɫ/. In the same way, the failure of *Breaking* to occur in the Anglian examples set out under Type C in Table 2.28 might be ascribed to the fronting influence of the [i] in the syllable immediately following the [r] segment.

Many modern theoretical phonologists would, however, take an extreme view and suggest that in some way native speakers are able to 'know about' the historical phonology of their language (King 1969: Ch. 3). These scholars would suggest that – even though such forms never appear in the language's pronunciation – native West Saxon speakers would 'know' that forms like [hell] and [tellan] were lexically /hælli/ and /tællian/, unlike [æall] which would be 'known' lexically as /æɫɫ/ and hence trigger the phonological rule of *Breaking*. There is a very important and topical theoretical issue at stake here which we can only note in a book of this kind, referring the reader to the detailed, technical literature (Hooper 1972; Kaisse and Shaw 1985; Kiparsky 1973). We must nevertheless be prepared to keep an open mind and recall that recent research into ongoing phonological change seems to suggest that on many occasions phonological processes are not always as regular or as non-random as we might be led to believe from some of the historical data which has come down to us. Language users appear to be quite capable of randomly applying or not applying even well motivated phonological processes and of generating large numbers of exceptional items to established rule systems (Labov 1966; Pellowe, Nixon, Strang and McNeary 1972). Our example in Type D seems to point to behaviour of this type since, even in a context showing an [i] in the next syllable, the [r] segment is treated as back and provokes *Breaking*. Certainly, by the late West Saxon period we can find non-application of *Breaking* in 'borrowed' foreign words like ⟨pæll⟩ '*pallium*', ⟨balca⟩ '*beam*', ⟨dalc⟩ '*brooch*' and '*fold*' (Sievers and Brunner 1941: sect. 80, note 3.4).

2.3.6 *Breaking* in other fricative contexts

The type of change to the stressed vowel space with which we have been concerned in this section has been one where a 'simple' vowel has come to be realized as a diphthong, i.e. one where there is some complex, side-by-side juxtaposition of two disparate vocalic elements – some kind of positional trajectory in the stressed vowel space area has come into being. The only explanation we have offered so far for this type of innovation has been one dependent upon purely mechanical considerations; whenever palatal (front) vowels come to be juxtaposed with back (labial) segments such as [x], [ʀ] or [ɫ] with which they show a horizontal positional disparity, then some kind of transitional vocalic element is inserted to the 'right' of the stressed vowel area to facilitate the muscular movement of the articulatory organs between it and the following consonantal segments. When we stated that [ɫ], [ʀ] and [x] were the affecting context for this innovatory diphthongal production, it was their horizontal positional characteristic and the opposition between it and that of the stressed vowel which we suggested could be the trigger or driver for the innovation. But, as we have already hinted, such a theoretical stance is less than satisfactory and will require severe modification if we are to provide any kind of coherent account of the motivation for *Breaking* type innovations; by way of an introduction to some alternative explanatory models, let us examine here what appears to be yet another instance of Old English *Breaking* in a fricative consonantal environment.

In addition to the voiceless velar [x] fricative, the phonology of Old English appears to have utilized two other fricative consonantal types – the voiced palatal and velar fricatives [j̊] and [ɣ] respectively. Both could be represented orthographically in Old English by ⟨g⟩, although the former is often editorially marked as ⟨g̊⟩ (Campbell 1959: sect. 50, p. 20). There appears to be some evidence that a *Breaking* type, diphthongization process occurred in late Old English in the vicinity of [j̊] – the voiced palatal (front) fricative (a relatively rare sound in the inventories of the phonologies of modern languages – Maddieson (1984: p. 232)). Consider in Table 2.29 by way of illustration, the spellings of a selection of lexical items from the tenth-century Northumbrian gloss to the *Lindisfarne Gospels* (Ross and Stanley 1956: Bk. 2).

TABLE 2.29 Late Old English pre-[j̊] *Breaking*

West Saxon Old English		10th-cent. Northumbrian Old English	
		[æ]/[æi]	
⟨strægd⟩	'he strewed'	⟨strægd⟩	⟨straigden⟩
⟨frægn⟩	'he asked'	⟨frægn⟩	⟨fraign⟩
⟨mægden⟩	'young girl'	⟨mægden⟩	⟨maiden⟩
		[ɛ]/[ɛi]	
⟨hæg⟩	'meadow'	⟨heg⟩	⟨heig⟩
⟨ðegn⟩	'lord'	⟨ðegn⟩	⟨ðeign⟩
⟨weg⟩	'way'	⟨weg⟩	⟨wég⟩, ⟨we⟩
		[ü]/[üi]	
⟨drȳge⟩	'arid'	⟨dryge⟩	⟨druige⟩, ⟨drui⟩
1		2	3

We are not, of course, suggesting that such a diphthongal innovation
was restricted to Northumbrian Old English, since there is some
evidence for it from other dialectal areas in the ninth and tenth
centuries as well, although the process everywhere appears to have
been a relatively minor one in Old English (Campbell 1959: sects
266–99, pp. 113–15; Wright 1925: sect. 321, p. 168). But what is
interesting about the data in column 3 in Table 2.29 is the fact
that they appear to show several instances where a palatal (front)
stressed vowel has become diphthongized in the environment of a
segment to its 'right' *which is not itself back*, but is palatal. Appeals
to muscular transition type arguments like those we have suggested
for the *Breaking* innovation in Old English proper are clearly
completely inappropriate in cases like this. There is little horizontal
space contrast between the affected stressed front vowels [æ], [ɛ]
and [ü] and the 'affecting' palatal [j̆] segment.

The data we have set out in Table 2.29 point to at least three
kinds of effects which can result from the juxtaposition of palatal
(front) stressed vowels such as [æ], [ɛ] and [ü] with a palatal fricative
like [j̆]. Firstly, as alternants such as ⟨heg⟩/⟨heig⟩, ⟨frægn⟩/
⟨fræign⟩ and ⟨dryge⟩/⟨druige⟩ suggest, a diphthongization such
that [æ] → [æi], [ɛ] → [ɛi] and [ü] → [üi] could be manifested.
Secondly, the ⟨maiden⟩ and ⟨drui⟩ spellings also indicate that alongside the diphthongization, there could also (perhaps simultaneously) occur an effacement, deletion of the palatal fricative [j̆]
segment itself. Thirdly, an alternation such as ⟨weg⟩/⟨wég⟩
(where the *Lindisfarne Gospels*' glossator's ⟨ ′ ⟩ diacritic mark points
to increased stressed vowel duration – see above, sect. 2.2.6 and
Clemoes 1952; Hulme 1896; Ker 1957: pp. xxxiiiff.) would indicate
some kind of [ɛj̆] → [ɛɛj̆] vowel lengthening innovation. What kinds
of explanations can we offer for these types of changes and can
they be described as part of any single, unitary process? Further,
how do they relate to the other *Breaking* phenomena we have
already discussed? At this point we shall only mention a few
possibilities in a rather informal way since we shall have more
opportunity to study a similar, but more extensive enactment in
our discussion of Middle English diphthongization below (cf. sects
3.4–3.4.3). However, three points are worth raising here. Recall
from our discussion in Chapter 1 of what was, we claimed, the
scalar relationship between vocalic and consonantal phonological
segments (cf. sect. 1.3), how both voiced sonorants and voiced
fricatives could be placed with relatively high ranking at the vocalic
'end' of the *sonority hierarchy* (see Table 2.30). Their highly
ranked placement on such a scale arose, we suggested, from the
relatively heavy prominence in their internal, complex structure of

TABLE 2.30 The sonority hierarchy

vls vd obstruents [t,k][d,g]	vls vd fricatives [ç,x][ʝ,ɣ]	sonorants [r,l,m,n]	glides [j,w]	vowels [i,u,a]
			increasing vowel-ness———▶	

vocalic as against consonantal components. That they were in this sense highly vowel-like might mean that speakers could, on occasion, hear them as or perceive of them as being solely vocalic, i.e. as vowels. In this way, it is possible that the palatal fricative [ʝ] was perceived as a pure palatal [i] vowel, and a sequence like, say, [æʝ] was reinterpreted as [æi], where the palatal fricative has come to be reassigned a status appropriate to the non-syllable half of a diphthongal complex. Diphthongization, in this type of instance, will result from the suppression of the (relatively weak) consonantal component in the internal structural 'mix' which makes up [ʝ], leaving its vocalic (palatal) characteristic isolated. Alternatively, with the suppression of the fricative's internal consonantal component there could also simultaneously occur the effacement of the [ʝ] segment's *positional* (i.e. horizontal, vertical) characteristics: if this occurred, the [ʝ] would come to be perceived as a 'vowel-only' segment, and take its positional characteristics (height, frontness) from the in-place stressed vowel to its left, such that [æʝ] → [ææ], [ɛʝ] → [ɛɛ] and [iʝ] → [ii]. Both of the above innovations affecting [ʝ] are often referred to as *vocalizations* (Donegan 1978: p. 109).

On the other hand, alternants such as ⟨frægn⟩/⟨fræign⟩ and ⟨ðegn⟩/⟨ðeign⟩ may suggest that while language users may perceive the fricative as essentially vowel-like, that vowel-ness is still relatively weak compared with that of a 'full' vowel such as, say, [æ]. Consequently, although the voiced fricative segment is not effaced, its vowel component 'spreads' laterally into the stressed vowel space, causing that area to be perceived as a side-by-side complex of two vowel 'halves', the right-hand-side element, 'derived' via the voiced fricative, sharing its positional characteristics. This perception of the voiced fricative as a relatively 'weak' vocalic element produces, we might tentatively suggest, just the kind of *Breaking* diphthongization with which we are now very familiar.

But it is important to note that the presence of the voiced palatal fricative serves, in one way or another, to make the preceding stressed vowel space *complex*. Such complexity can be superficially manifested by a number of different stratagems such as by an

innovatory diphthongal stressed vowel space comprising two halves
contrastive for relative palatality ([æi], [ɛi], [üi]) or through a
durationally increased long vowel which itself is composed of a
dichotomous vowel space whose two halves, although they share
the same positional identity, are distinguished by their relative
prominence; the left-hand, syllable-bearing component being
perceptually more highlighted than its right-hand partner. However,
we shall endeavour to articulate these notions more fully below in
pp. 142–58.

2.4 Monophthongization processes: late Old English developments to *Breaking*-produced diphthongs

At several places in this book we shall come to recognize that one
of the most common and one of the most puzzling features of the
historical phonology of the English language lies in its tendency
to 'undo', neutralize or unscramble those phonological processes
which speakers of an earlier (and often quite recent) period had
produced as innovations. For instance, it is possible for phonetic
contexts which produce vowel raising or lengthening for one set of
speakers to provide the trigger for an opposite set of events like
lowering or shortening for the language users of only a few
generations later. In this section we shall look at just such a
phenomenon; one where a diphthongal stressed vowel space
originally triggered by Old English *Breaking* or the vowel harmony
of *Back Umlaut*, comes to revert to a monophthongal, single vowel
status in contexts which look decidedly similar to those which
triggered the split up in the stressed vowel space in the first
instance. Such monophthongizations are often rather poetically
referred to as *Smoothing* (Campbell 1959: sects 223–7, 312;
Wardale 1955: sect. 36; Moore and Marckwardt 1951: sect. 9.a–c)
and are usually fraught with data which are difficult to interpret in
the extreme. Certainly our own conclusions should be treated in a
very tentative fashion.

Consider, in the first instance, the data in Table 2.31 which seem
to show a contrast between West Saxon forms with a diphthongal
vowel space and their 'equivalents' with monophthongal outputs
in Anglian dialects of the same historical period. Notice that both
those diphthongs derived via the *Breaking* of long vowels
(⟨hēah⟩/⟨sēoh⟩) and short vowels (⟨meaht⟩/⟨feoh⟩) undergo a
monophthongization process, whereby it would appear from the
spelling that [æa]→[æ] and [eo]→[ɛ]/[e]. Our doubts concerning the
value of the latter will be further developed below. The *Smoothing*
thus seems to involve the suppression of the second, non-syllabic

TABLE 2.31

West Saxon		Anglian Dialects
8th century		*8th century*
[æa]		[æ]
⟨meaht⟩	*'might'*	⟨mæht⟩
⟨mearc⟩	*'limit'*	⟨mærc⟩
⟨sēah⟩	*'he saw'*	⟨sæh⟩
⟨hēah⟩	*'high'*	⟨hæh⟩
[eo]		[e]/[ɛ]
⟨feoh⟩	*'cattle'*	⟨feh⟩
⟨Peoht⟩	*'Pict'*	⟨Peht-⟩
⟨eolh⟩	*'elk'*	⟨elh⟩
⟨sēoh⟩	*'see!'*	⟨seh⟩

half of the diphthongal vowel space, bringing with it a diminution of its labiality/backness characteristic and, by definition a heightening of its palatal/frontness feature. Notice in passing that examples of the monophthongization of [io] segments are rare in the surviving data since [io]/[eo] 'collapse' tended to erase them from the language's output (see pp. 36–7 above) although ⟨betwioh⟩/⟨betwih⟩ *'between'*, ⟨tiohhian⟩/⟨tihhian⟩ *'to intend'* alternants are to be found (Moore and Marckwardt 1951: p. 29). But such a 'simple', second element of diphthong deletion process is not typical of much of what is traditionally referred to as *Smoothing*; some of the data from eighth-century Anglian dialects and later (tenth-century) West Saxon suggest that monophthongization and *raising* (in this case, palatalization) were somehow closely related. Consider the items in Table 2.32. The column 2 and 3 forms appear to testify to some kind of change whereby the diphthongal elements in column 1 have not only become monophthongized, but have also been raised, either directly or through some intervening [æ] 'stage'. It is interesting that the raising appears to be considerably constrained. Although those diphthongal vowel spaces deriving (on occasion via *Breaking*) from *short* vowel inputs (cf. ⟨cearf⟩) may or may not undergo the raising in Anglian and late West Saxon, those diphthongal forms derived from *long* vowel spaces everywhere do so. This fact is interesting to us for a number of reasons. Firstly, we recall that during our discussion of long vowel inputs to the Old English *Breaking*

TABLE 2.32

West Saxon		Anglian	Late West Saxon
8th century		8th century	10th century
[æa]		[e]/[ɛ]	[e]/[ɛ]
⟨ēac⟩	'also'	⟨ec⟩	
⟨fleax⟩	'flax'	⟨flex⟩	
⟨cearf⟩	'he cut'	⟨cerf⟩	
⟨nēah⟩	'near'		⟨neh⟩
⟨ēage⟩	'eye'		⟨ege⟩
⟨neaht⟩	'night'		⟨neht⟩
⟨eahta⟩	'eight'		⟨eht⟩
1		2	3

process, we commented upon the fact that, while they appear to have shared the same phonetic, surface realization, namely [æa] (Lass and Anderson 1975: p. 82), speakers still apparently 'knew' that some kind of distinction existed between them since they showed differential responses to subsequent phonological operations: their variable reaction to *Smoothing* seems to illustrate just that. Secondly, we shall see in our section on *Middle English Breaking* (3.4 ff) that while some short vowel inputs to this diphthongization process resist subsequent raising: cf. [dɔuɣtər] '*daughter*' (OE ⟨dŏhtor⟩), long vowel inputs very often show it: [bouɣ] (OE ⟨bōga⟩) '*bow*' → [buu]. There appears to be, in other words, some connection between vowel length and vowel height, one we shall see illustrated at length in our treatment of the *English vowel shift* and Middle English *open syllable lengthening* below. It might even be the case that the *Smoothing* in Anglian and late West Saxon of the 'long' and 'short' diphthongs produced two different kinds of mid vowel monophthong: [æa] → [ɛ], [ææa] → [e]. Consider too the forms in Table 2.33: it would appear from these examples that in late West Saxon and late Kentish dialects speakers reinterpreted 'long' diphthongal vowel spaces as being long high front [ii] vowels in contexts contiguous with the kind of fricative – be it [x] or [ç] we shall discuss below – represented by the graph ⟨h⟩.

Clearly *Smoothing* is not a phenomenon which is easily explainable or even describable in a straightforward fashion. Why should speakers 'undo' a phonological process like Old English *Breaking* in this way? Why should a reversion to monophthongal

TABLE 2.33

West Saxon		Late West Saxon/Kentish
8th century		Early 10th century
[eo]/[æa]		[ii]
⟨lēoht⟩	'light'	⟨liht⟩
⟨nēahst⟩	'nearest'	⟨nihst⟩
⟨nēaht⟩	'night'	⟨niht⟩

status of the 'long' *Breaking* diphthongs bring with it a vowel raising as well? Can this monophthongization/raising be seen as a single phonological process or as two separate and unconnected ones? Without at this stage deciding in favour of one or the other, we shall propose two explanations for the apparently unrelated manifestations of the *Smoothing* innovation. One will see the absence of stressed vowel diphthongization in what superficially appears to be a classical *Breaking* triggering context as a consequence of alterations to that context: the post-vocalic sonorants and fricatives have somehow changed so as no longer to provoke diphthongization in front of them. The other will claim that the raising so clearly associated with long vowel space can be considered as a phonological event which can occur independently of any reference to the nature of these syllable final consonantal shapes.

2.4.1 The instability of contextually derived alternations

In the course of this book we shall see many examples of vowel changes which cause the contemporary language user to have a different conception of his language's vowel space from that held by speakers of that same language before such innovations took place. Vowel changes may cause *mergers* between segments which were previously regarded as distinct and separate in the vowel space. Consider such a merger which has occurred in modern Mid Western US dialects where the [ɐ] sound in words such as ⟨caught⟩ and ⟨dawn⟩ has merged with the [ɑ] sound of items such as ⟨cot⟩ and ⟨Don⟩. The former, as the spelling still suggests, were derived from an earlier [au] diphthong, the latter from a monophthongal [ɔ] vowel. In this dialect until recently speakers would therefore have two separate sets of words, those with [ɐ] and others with [ɑ] stressed vowels: the change of [ɐ] → [ɑ] has neutralized this contrast. Speakers now no longer 'know' that ⟨caught⟩ and ⟨cot⟩ vowels are to be kept distinct in the vocalic inventory, since an [ɐ] segment has been removed from the vowel space and conflated under [ɑ]. As we shall see, in the process of such mergers interesting sociolinguistic phenomena can arise.

The ⟨caught⟩/⟨cot⟩ merger is clearly context free; there are no 'obvious' local phonetic factors triggering the [ɐ] → [ɑ] change. Old English *Breaking*, on the other hand, is obviously context-sensitive, the [æa]/[æ] and [eo]/[e] alternations triggered by a set of contiguous consonantal elements. Now we have seen that in late West Saxon and Anglian Old English these *Breaking* alternations could be neutralized, the diphthongal form being merged with monophthongs. What effect did such a merger have on contemporary speakers' concept of the vowel inventory? Consider again another Modern English merger; the consonantal group [nd] is often conflated with [n] in words like ⟨ban⟩ and ⟨band⟩, both being realized as [bæn]. However, this merger is – like the *Breakings* above – strictly context sensitive. It occurs only in the environment of [z], the plural possessive marker. [nd] and [n] are otherwise kept distinct, as in ⟨banded⟩/⟨banned⟩ and ⟨banding⟩/⟨banning⟩. [nd] clusters have clearly not been 'lost' to the phonology as a result of the merger – the merger is, in this case, purely superficial (Donegan 1978: p. 128). We might then argue that contextually provoked vowel/diphthong alternations produced by rules such as Old English *Breaking* do not involve the speaker in any major realignment in his perception of the vocalic contrasts available in his phonology. We could therefore conclude that such peripheral or superficial modifications are 'unstable' and are liable to 'revert' to their pre-innovation stage. Resulting mergers with, in this instance, monophthongal elements had no major consequence for speakers' perceptions of the vowel inventory and could therefore be more or less freely indulged.

2.4.2 Monophthongization and raising as a unified process
We are still left with the difficult question of the *raisings* which apparently go hand in hand with *Smoothing* both in Old and, as we shall see below, Middle English. Is there any way in which we can relate the monophthongization and the raising? We have inferred above that these two processes could apparently occur independently of any change in the phonetic character of the surrounding context. A change like [mæaxt] → [mæxt] would seem to be implied by the spellings ⟨meaht⟩/⟨mæht⟩, leaving us to deduce that while for one generation of speakers contiguity of short front vowels with a velar fricative [x] had produced a split in the vowel space, for those of another the same environment

appears to have produced the 'opposite' effect. But the spelling evidence should perhaps not be interpreted too literally. We could argue that before the monophthongization a change had occurred whereby the [x], [ɫ] and [ʀ] *Breaking*-producing segments were fronted to [ç], [l] and [r]. If a change such as this did indeed occur – and the orthography would be unlikely to reveal that it did – then as a corollary to Old English *Breaking*, we should expect the vowel space adjacent to these new fronted segments to reflect that frontness/palatality and show a movement away from the the labial (back) end of the spectrum to the palatal (high, front) end. We might therefore argue that in becoming monophthongs by losing their back, labial second half, the diphthongs derived from Old English *Breaking* do just that in Anglian and late West Saxon dialects. A stressed vowel space occupied solely by [e] is clearly more palatal than one split up into [eu] or [eo]. The loss of the labial half of the vowel space results in palatality (frontness) being now spread across the whole of the stressed vowel space.

But how are we to treat what look to be the [æːa]/[eeo] → [ii] and [æːa] → [e] changes also evidenced in the late West Saxon and Anglian materials above in Tables 2.32 and 2.33? Recall the characterization of the vowel space which we presented in Chapter 1 with its three-pointed, triangular configuration, see Figure 2.1.

FIG. 2.1

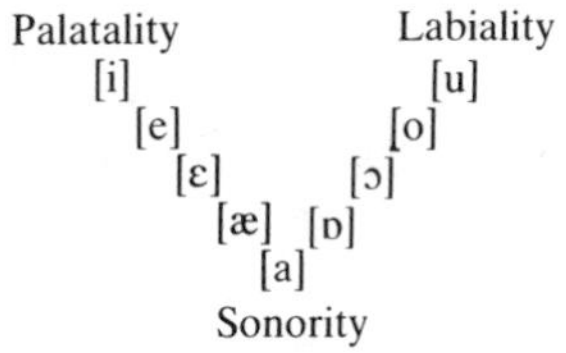

```
        Palatality        Labiality
          [i]               [u]
           [e]           [o]
            [ɛ]        [ɔ]
             [æ]  [ɒ]
              [a]
            Sonority
```

The kinds of [æː] → [ee]/[ii] changes affecting the first half of the 'long' *Breaking*-produced diphthongs clearly point to some kind of palatalization increase (sonority level suppression) in that area of the stressed vowel space. This, taken together with the effacement of the non-syllabic [a]/[o] component of the diphthong, effectively results in a vowel space whose palatality prominence level is considerably enhanced. If such a prominence can somehow be set down to the effect of some contiguous palatal segment, then both the monophthongization and the raising can be seen as the end product of some 'mirror-image' *Breaking* operation. Palatal post-vocalic [r], [l] and [ç] segments cause speakers to perceive a reduction in the non-palatal elements in the contiguous vowel space.

Yet a conclusion like this rests on an assumption for which we have, in fact, little supporting evidence. We have nothing by way of orthographic or other indication which unambiguously points to a 'new' palatal value for the [r], [ł] and [x] segments which, for many interpretations of Old English *Breaking*, are crucially to be interpreted as *labial* (Campbell 1959: p. 174; Wyld 1927: sect. 127). More importantly, even if we were to accept the post-vocalic segment palatalization hypothesis, it would still fail to explain why it is that it is only those segments which are durationally long which regularly undergo palatality increase. Although its import will only become clearer in the next two chapters, we might tentatively suggest that diphthongization and long vowel raising are not to be seen, in fact, as completely unrelated phenomena. Both might be viewed as independent and alternative stratagems whereby language users highlight, foreground or make more 'prominent' the stressed vowel space in pre-sonorant and fricative contexts.

2.4.3 Middle English monophthongization processes

With the purpose of reinforcing some of the observations in the last section, let us briefly consider the case of those regional dialects whose phonologies fail to record the later Old English diphthong to monophthong innovation of *Smoothing*. Consider the data in Table 2.34 where we see the kinds of changes affecting the Old English [æa] stressed vowel space in the period between the twelfth and thirteenth centuries. The contrast between the forms in column 1 and those in 2 and 4 is where the nature of such changes is perhaps best highlighted. Those dialects which had not been involved in the earlier Old English monophthongization (especially those in the South and South Eastern parts of England) again show, by the early twelfth century a loss of the non-syllabic vocalic half of the diphthong, leaving behind the relatively palatal (front) monophthong [æ] we see in the column 2 forms like ⟨æll⟩ and ⟨hælf⟩. However, even by the beginning of this same century most of the dialectal regions with this 'smoothed' [æ] stressed vowel form are beginning to alter it to the pure sonorant [a] vowel shape, thus the forms in column 4 like ⟨all⟩ and ⟨half⟩. Thus, by at least the middle of the twelfth century there are a very large number of regional dialects showing an [a] (low, back) stressed vowel shape in contexts where classical West Saxon had manifested the [æa] diphthong (both derived and lexical) (Wyld 1927: sect. 165). The items in column 3 – in particular those entered under (b) – represent dialectal developments associated with vowels showing increased length. As we saw in sections 2.2.4–2.2.6 dealing with late Old

TABLE 2.34

WS	ME 1100	ME 12th–13th centuries	ME 12th century
[æa]	[æ]	[ɛ]/[ɛɛ]	[a]/[aa]
(a)			
⟨eall⟩	'all'	⟨æll⟩	⟨all⟩
⟨healf⟩	'half'	⟨hælf⟩	⟨half⟩
⟨hearm⟩	'harm'	⟨hærm⟩ ⟨herm⟩	⟨harm⟩
⟨eart⟩	'are'	⟨ært⟩ ⟨ert⟩	⟨art⟩
⟨earm⟩	'arm'	⟨ærm⟩ ⟨erm⟩	⟨arm⟩
		(b)	
		⟨helden⟩ 'hold'	
		⟨cheld⟩ 'cold'	
		⟨beld⟩ 'bold'	
		⟨eld⟩ 'old'	
		⟨berd⟩ 'beard'	
		⟨yerd⟩ 'yard'	
1	2	3	4

English *homorganic lengthening*, certain Old English dialects from the middle of the tenth century showed a process whereby stressed vowels could undergo a durational increase in their timing when they were contiguous with particular kinds of sonorant initial consonantal clusters such as [ld], [rd] and so on. Our column 3 items suggest that the 'historical' [æa] diphthong in such a length-associated environment was perceived by later speakers to be a monophthong whose overall palatality level was greater than that of the diphthong. Thus, in those West and Central Southern dialects of the twelfth and thirteenth centuries where this development is to be found, we apparently witness a 're-enactment' of the late Old English ⟨nēah⟩/⟨neh⟩, ⟨ēage⟩/⟨ege⟩ *Smoothing* type recorded in Table 2.32 above.

But again we should not be surprised by this apparent interdependence between diphthongization and increased palatality level of long vowels in such post-vocalic contexts as [ld] and [rd]. Both these syllable terminations historically trigger vowel lengthening as well as diphthongization; both cause speakers to perceive a highlighted, complex vowel space in their vicinity, and we might suggest that increased palatalization is yet another, alternative stratagem whereby such complex vowel space might be foregrounded, made more perceptually prominent and contrastive (Jordan 1974: sects 59–61; Wyld 1927: sect. 164 ff; Moore and Marckwardt 1951: sect. 30; Roseborough 1970: pp. 36–42; Mossé 1952: sect. 30; Wardale 1955: pp. 49 ff).

2.4.4 The Middle English development of the Old English [eo] diphthong

Given the kind of monophthongization operation we have been discussing so far, it might seem unnecessary to devote a whole section to the effect it has upon [eo] in the period between say 1100 and 1300. We might reasonably expect that there would be a suppression of the second (non-syllabic) half of the diphthongal vowel area, leaving a relatively palatal [e] or [ɛ] element spread across the whole vowel space. As we can see from the data in Table 2.35, this is indeed what happens in certain instances. However, there do appear to be occasions where there are phonetic consequences attendant upon the monophthongization of a kind which are unlike anything we have seen so far. Column 2 shapes show the kind of monophthongization result we might by this time expect, although we shall comment below on the possible [e]/[ɛ] output variation. However, it is the items in the third column which appear decidedly unusual. From as early as the twelfth century and continuing in some dialects for the next three hundred years or so, the [eo] diphthong – either in its lexical form or derived through Old English *Breaking* – is realized as [ø] ([ö]), a retracted (backed), high mid front vowel. However, this particular process was

TABLE 2.35

Old English 8th century		Middle English 12th–13th centuries	Middle English 12th–14th centuries
[eo]		[ɛ]/[e]	[ø]/[øø]
⟨eorþe⟩	'earth'	⟨erthe⟩	⟨orthe⟩, ⟨urthe⟩
⟨heorte⟩	'heart'	⟨herte⟩	⟨horte⟩
⟨steor⟩	'star'	⟨sterre⟩	⟨storre⟩
⟨deorc⟩	'dark'	⟨derc⟩	⟨duerc⟩, ⟨durk⟩
⟨feorrða⟩	'fourth'		⟨furþe⟩
⟨seolf⟩	'self'		⟨sulfe⟩
⟨þeof⟩	'thief'		⟨þuef⟩, ⟨þuf⟩
1		2	3

confined to South Western, Western and Central Midland counties of England as well as to some South Eastern ones (notably Essex), even including some London dialects. Kent, as we shall see below, showed a development for this diphthong all of its own. In manuscripts from the first group of areas scribes were generally careful to keep distinct the two spellings ⟨eo⟩ and ⟨e⟩, the former often used to denote the French pronunciation [ø] in such 'borrowed' words as ⟨people⟩, ⟨preouen⟩ and ⟨meouen⟩. The ⟨e⟩ spelling, on the other hand, was often retained solely as a means of representing lexical monophthongs like [e] and [ɛ] in native English words such as ⟨clene⟩ and ⟨stench⟩. That the ⟨eo⟩ spelling (used mainly, recall, to represent the French [ø] sound) is also to be found in native words which in other dialects would have both lexical and derived [eo] diphthongs suggests that in these dialects the stressed vowel space has undergone some kind of change whereby [eo] → [ø] or [øø] depending upon whether the diphthong was of the 'long' or 'short' variety. What kind of phonetic process is this?

We pointed out in section 1.3 how vowels could contrast along a palatal/labial, front/back parameter: thus [i], [e] and [æ] were opposed to [u] and [o]. However, it is relatively common in many languages for there to be vocalic segments which are 'mixtures' of palatality and labiality: that is, they simultaneously express characteristics of frontness and backness. A good example of this is to be found in some Modern Scottish English pronunciations of the vowels in words like ⟨house⟩ and ⟨mouse⟩ – [hüs], [müs] – where [ü] represents a fronted (palatalized) version of the labial (back) [u]. In the same way, we find that palatal sounds like [e] can be produced with a slightly retracted tongue position to realize a sound which contains a degree of backness, labiality as well: [ø]. A change such as [eo] → [ø] would suggest that the labial/back characteristic of the second half of the diphthongal vowel space is being attracted to the first, syllabic half such that it acquires the roundness characteristic associated with back vowels and is realized as [ø]. Alternatively, we could argue that from being a side-by-side mixture of relatively palatal and labial elements, the entire vowel space comes to be perceived as an *internal* complex of these same elements: [e]⟩[o] → [e/o], i.e. [ø]. Such a 'simultaneous' expression of what had been sequentially discrete (diphthongal) components is, as we shall see below (cf. sect. 4.4.2), one of the most common developmental pathways taken by diphthongal stressed vowel space. Scribal practise seems to have been to spell this [ø] segment in a variety of ways: ⟨u⟩/⟨ue⟩/⟨o⟩/⟨ui⟩ among others, as reflected in the column 3 forms cited above.

There is evidence to suggest that such rounded versions of the

historical [eo] diphthong remained a feature of the South West
Midland dialects of England until as late as the fifteenth century.
However, there appears to be some indication that, even from as
early as the beginning of the thirteenth century in those dialects,
this 'new' monophthong underwent *raising* to [yy] especially when
it derived from long diphthongal sources. For instance we find
rhymes like ⟨neode⟩ '*need*': ⟨hude⟩ '*to hide*' in the thirteenth
century *Laȝamon's Brut*, where ⟨hude⟩ shows a lexical [yy] in turn
suggesting a development of the ⟨neode⟩ item such that [neeod-]
→ [nøød-]→ [nyyd-] (Wyld 1927: sect. 168; Jordan 1974: sects 65–8,
84–6; Wardale 1955: sect. 55; Luick 1964: sect. 357; Mossé 1952:
sect. 30).

However, the [eo]→ [ø]/[øø] change was often limited in its effect
even in those dialectal areas where we have pointed to its
widespread use. By as early as the thirteenth century many South
Western materials show that the 'new' [ø] vowels had become
unrounded to either [ɛ] or [e]. The particular surface shape of the
unrounded segment was a function of vowel length: short [ø]
unrounded to [ɛ], [øø] to [ee], illustrating yet again the co-relation
between a vowel's length and highness values. That such a height
discrepancy in the unrounded variants of the [ø] vowels did in fact
exist can be seen from the subsequent developments of the forms
in question. Those like ⟨herte⟩ and ⟨sterre⟩ (earlier ⟨heorte⟩,
⟨steorre⟩) undergo a stressed vowel lowering process before [r],
appearing as [hærtə], [stærə] in fourteenth-century materials. On
the other hand, items like ⟨der⟩ '*animal*', deriving from a long
vowel source, show no lowering but can instead act as input to
the later *English vowel shift* and be there raised, palatalized to
[diir] '*deer*'.

2.4.5 Special Kentish developments: syllabicity shifting
We have so far examined no less than three ways in which speakers
have come to interpret stressed diphthongal vowel space.
Non-syllabic elements have been effaced, leaving the value of the
stressed half to 'spread' across the entire vowel area; diphthongs
associated with duration-producing contexts have been interpreted
as though they were higher, more palatal long monophthongs,
while what had been side-by-side vowel opposition has come to be
seen as though it were a single but composite vowel internal
mixture. However, there is yet another scenario which, while its
operation is severely regionally constrained in early English, enjoys
(as we shall see) a very wide currency in the later language. Let
us trace the development of the Old English [æa] and [eo] diphthongs
(both lexical and derived) as they surface in the Kent region during

the thirteenth and fourteenth centuries. The data at this period from this area are extremely complex and not easy to interpret and have provoked considerable discussion in the scholarly literature: Dobson 1968: pp. 996 ff; Luick 1964: sect. 359; Wyld 1927: sect. 166; Jordan 1974: sects 61, 85; Wallenberg 1923: p. 85, footnote 3. Consider in Table 2.36 some manifestations of the West Saxon

TABLE 2.36

Middle Kentish 14th century			
West Saxon	⟨heald⟩	West Saxon	⟨eald⟩
⟨heald⟩	(10)	⟨ealde⟩	(6)
⟨hald⟩	(6)	⟨ald⟩	(6)
⟨hyeald⟩	(16)	⟨yeald⟩	(15)
⟨hyald⟩	(10)	⟨yalde⟩	(10)
⟨hieald⟩	(1)		
⟨hyeld⟩	(1)		

Old English items ⟨heald⟩ 'hold', ⟨eald⟩ 'old' (with Breaking produced [æa] diphthongs) as they appear in the fourteenth-century Kentish manuscript – the Ayenbite of Inwyt (Wallenberg 1923: pp. 115–16) – where frequency of occurrence is entered in parenthesis. The majority view seems to be that these spellings indicate two separate developments for the West Saxon [æa] diphthong in this South Eastern dialect. On the one hand, items like ⟨hald⟩ and ⟨heald⟩ are taken (despite the spelling of the latter) to represent a monophthongization to either [æ] or [a] of a type with which we have by now become familiar. On the other, those items showing a stressed vowel space graphically represented by ⟨yea⟩, ⟨ya⟩, ⟨iea⟩ and ⟨ye⟩ are interpreted as representing phonetic shapes like [jææ] or [jɛɛ] (cf. Wyld 1927: sect. 166; Jordan 1974: sect. 61 Remark). What kind of phonetic process are we witnessing in a change like [æa] → [jæ]? Perhaps the most obvious of its characteristics lies in the fact that the first half of the diphtongal vowel space has become less vocalic. Recall from our discussion regarding Table 2.30 how 'glides' or 'semi-vowels' like [j] and [w], while being very high up on the sonorance hierarchy and therefore very vowel-like, were, nevertheless, not so vocalic as vowels themselves showing, as they do, some of the reduced energy associated with the production of consonantal segments. Although we shall have cause to enter into the matter in much greater detail in our discussion of Middle English *open syllable lengthening* and elsewhere (sects 1.3 and 3.5) we should mention here that syllables are constructed in such a way that their central, peak element is usually a vowel. All other components of syllables are less and less vowel-like the further away they are from the vocalic centre of the syllable. Consider a syllable like [kwɪŋk] '*quink*'. Here, the syllable centre or *peak* is the stressed vowel [ɪ]; the segments immediately to the left and right of the peak are, being a glide and a sonorant, still high on the sonority scale, but are not as vowel-like as the vowel itself. Moving further out from these again to the left and right, we meet voiceless obstruents [k], segments which are lowest on the sonority scale as we presented it. The structure of syllables can therefore be characterized as optimally containing a vocalic centre or peak surrounded on both sides by ever decreasingly vocalic consonantal elements (Kiparsky 1979).

But what about those cases where the peak appears to contain more than one vowel? That is, when the stressed vowel space is diphthongal. Do words like [kweɪnt] '*quaint*' show two peaks? Most phoneticians would deny such a claim and say that in this case it is the first vowel in the sequence which represents the peak, the second being 'non-syllabic', more consonantal-like; a fact represented in some transcriptions where the non-syllabic half of the diphthongal space in words like ⟨my⟩ and ⟨house⟩ is frequently represented by the symbols [j] and [w]. If we are willing to accept this oversimplified account of the internal structure of syllables, it would seem that our [æa] → [jæ] change would suggest that language users came to hear the second rather than the first half of the diphthongal space as representing the syllable peak, the original syllable peak bearing segment being reduced in vocalic value and produced as a glide [j]. Such a phenomenon is rather common both in first language acquisition and language change and is usually referred to as *syllabicity shifting* (cf. sect. 2.3.4 above). But why should it occur at all in the case of a diphthong like [æa]? This is a very difficult question to answer, but there does appear to be some evidence to suggest that speakers tend to assign the syllable peak to those vowels which have the greatest *sonority*; that is, those vowels which are the most [a]-like. Thus, a vowel space comprising [æa] may tend to be interpreted as having its peak on the second, more sonorous half of the combination (Donegan 1978: sect. 4.3.2; Andersen 1974).

A good example of just such a syllable shift can be found in the Old Icelandic (ninth-tenth centuries) development (see Table 2.37) where [ea] and [eo] diphthongs undergo a process whereby a syllable bearing first element becomes desyllabified. In consequence, it loses some of its vowel-like qualities and comes to be realized as the 'semi-vowel' [j]. The originally non-syllabic (but highly sonorous) half in [a] now comes to take the syllable beat, so

TABLE 2.37

Old Icelandic syllabicity shifting

[sea]	*'sea'*	→ [sja]
*[dearfr]	*'bold'*	→ [djorfr]
*[eofur]	*'prince'*	→ [jofur]

that a [ja] or [jo] combination results (Gordon 1927: sect. 46, p. 254). A more recent example of this type of phenomenon can be seen in the phonology of some present day Yorkshire English speakers where we occasionally see a development in diphthongs like [uɪ] (with a non-syllabic second half) coming to be realized as [uɪ], accompanied by a reduction in the vocalic value of the new 'unaccented' [u] to [w]. Hence we find a change like the following taking place: [kuɪšən] → [kwɪšən] *'cushion'* (Donegan 1978, p. 116 ff).

To return to our Middle Kentish examples after a long digression; it would seem that spellings such as ⟨hyald⟩, ⟨hyeald⟩ and ⟨hieald⟩ outlined in Table 2.36 above, represent evidence for just such a syllable shift in the stressed vowel space; the prominent peak being now perceived on the second (and more sonorant) half of the diphthongal vowel space, the first half being reduced in vocalic stature to the glide [j], realizing pronunciations for the items in question like [hjæld] (Wyld 1927: sect. 166; Samuels 1952). If this kind of process can happen with low vowel diphthongs such as [æa] in this dialect, surely it should also be the case that the West Saxon [eo] diphthong should follow a similar syllabicity shifting pathway there too? On first examination a contrast between Middle Kentish spellings and those showing [eo] diphthongs in West Saxon would support the view that it can. Consider the examples in Table 2.38. There the ⟨ye⟩, ⟨ie⟩ digraphs

TABLE 2.38

West Saxon		Middle Kentish 12th–14th centuries
⟨eorþe⟩	*'earth'*	⟨yerþe⟩, ⟨ierþe⟩, ⟨ӡerþ⟩
⟨heorte⟩	*'heart'*	⟨hierte⟩
⟨seolf⟩	*'self'*	⟨sielf⟩
⟨leornian⟩	*'to learn'*	⟨lyerni⟩
⟨þeof⟩	*'thief'*	⟨þyef⟩
⟨eode⟩	*'he went'*	⟨yede⟩

would at first glance strongly appear to suggest that, on the analogy of those with ⟨ya⟩ and ⟨iea⟩ we have just examined above, some kind of syllabicity realignment had taken place in the [eo] diphthongs as well. However, there are real problems with this assumption. If we are indeed witnessing a syllabicity shift whereby [eo] → [eo] → [jo] then why do we find spellings with ⟨ye⟩ and not ⟨yo⟩/⟨io⟩? It seems that in some dialects this is indeed what we do find: compare the spellings for the items like 'earth' and 'he went' above with those from the late-fifteenth-century *Guy of Warwick* text in the University Library, Cambridge: there we find orthographic representations like ⟨ʒorthe⟩ and ⟨ʒode⟩, suggesting that some kind of [eo] → [jo] change had indeed taken place. But even here there are difficulties, since in this manuscript we also find spellings like ⟨ʒerthele⟩'*earthly*' (Old English ⟨eorðlice⟩) with a ⟨ʒe⟩ for an expected ⟨ʒo⟩, and we are even confronted with ⟨ʒ⟩ spellings in words where there was originally no diphthongal vowel space forms in the first place – cf. ⟨ʒerbes⟩ '*herbs*' (Old French ⟨erbes⟩). (See Zupitza 1891: p. 246, note 60.) Wyld (1927: sect. 169, p. 123) doubts that the digraph spellings actually represent diphthongs at all, claiming that ⟨ie⟩ 'is a recognized symbol for tense [e] (Laud Homilies write *hieren = heren*) and is consistently used for this in the Essex *Vices and Virtues*'. However, he goes on to say that 'in *yerþe*, by the side of *yerþe*, the *y* may represent a tendency to develop an initial front consonant before *e-*'. (See Moore and Marckwardt 1951: sect. 109.7; Wallenberg 1923: p. 85, footnote 3).

Although it still leaves unresolved cases like ⟨lyerni⟩, ⟨þyef⟩ and ⟨hierte⟩, this last statement has perhaps some value with respect to the ⟨y⟩/⟨i⟩ *word initial* spellings. While the idea is too complex to develop in detail here, we have already suggested that syllables have some kind of overall shape, consisting of a vocalic peak surrounded to its left and right by ever more consonantal-like segments. From the evidence of phonological processes throughout the history of the English language, it would appear to be the case that language users 'prefer' syllables to have a standard configuration. Especially, they tend to 'like' them to have a consonantal segment + vowel peak (CV) starting shape. As a result of such a 'preference' speakers will tend to insert an initiating consonantal segment (an *onset*) in syllables which are introduced by a vowel alone. Consider spellings in the Middle English period like ⟨ʒen⟩ '*eyes/een*', ⟨yeelid⟩ '*eyelid*' and ⟨wocke⟩ '*oak*' where the highly vocalic glide elements [j] and [w] appear before the appropriate palatal and labial vowels. Likewise, we find fifteenth-century pronunciations like [wun] '*one*' for the earlier

Middle English [oon] (cf. Modern Scottish English [jɪn] for this same item). In the Modern period too we find pronunciations like Somerset [jeək] '*ache*' and Yorkshire [wuək] '*oak*'. (See Wyld 1936: pp 306–7; Dobson 1968: sects 428–9; Luick 1964: sect. 435 Anm; Kihlbom 1926.) However, such notions are highly complex and must await a further treatment in sections 3.5 and 4.5.1.

2.5 Vowel harmony processes in Old English

Up till now we have been looking at modifications to and alternations in the stressed vowel space which have been brought about by the effect of *contiguous*, usually following, rightmost segments within the same syllable boundary. For instance, we have seen how part of the stressed vowel space can take on a labial or back 'colour' when it is contiguous with sonorant consonants which themselves show such a backness characteristic – recall the [æɫ] → [æuɫ] diphthongization typical of Old English *Breaking*. Again, we saw too how the vowel space could be 'extended' or 'filled out' through the loss of one of the elements in the syllable to its right. In these instances the temporal extension of the stressed vowel space was seen as a means of 'compensating' for the loss from the syllable of some terminal consonantal element. Thus we witnessed two effects on the stressed vowel space. Firstly, its second half could be 'coloured', made dissimilar to that of the first in the direction of the labial/backness feature of a following, contiguous sonorant (vowel-like) segment, so producing a complex, contrastive vowel space. Secondly, the timing of the stressed vowel space could be extended.

There is, however, a third type of mutation to the stressed vowel area which we have so far left unexplored: namely, where neither diphthongization nor timing changes are involved, but where there occurs a change in say backness/frontness value *across its whole domain*. A good example of an alternation of this type occurs in the Anglian (Mercian and Northumbrian) dialects of Old English involving the short front vowels [æ], [e] and [i] when they are contiguous with following labial sonorants like [ɫ] and [ʀ]. This is, recall, the context which we now recognize as having produced *Breaking* in contemporary West Saxon dialects, but outside that region it appears that rather than only the right half of the stressed vowel space taking on the backness feature of the following sonorant, labiality was spread across its whole area, producing alternations such as [æ] → [a], [e] → [o] and [i] → [u]. Consider the data in Table 2.39. Column 2 forms show the by now familiar

TABLE 2.39 Old English pre-[ł]/[r] sonorant vowel space

Postulated Pre-OE shape	West Saxon Old English	Anglian Old English	
(1)			
[æ]	[æa]	[a]	
*[æłd]	⟨eald⟩	⟨ald⟩	'old'
*[hæłd]	⟨heald⟩	⟨hald⟩	'he held'
*[wærð]	⟨wearþ⟩	⟨warþ⟩	'he became'
(2)			
[e]	[eo]	[o]	
*[werð-]	⟨weorþan⟩	⟨worþa⟩	'to become'
*[werp-]	⟨weorpan⟩	⟨worpa⟩	'to throw'
*[swerd]	⟨sweord⟩	⟨sword⟩	'sword'
(3)			
[i]	[iu]/[eo]	[u]	
*[hwirf-]	⟨sinhweorfende⟩	⟨sinhwurfende⟩	'spinning'
I	2	3	

assimilation between the second half of the stressed vowel space and the backness/labiality characteristics which we claimed were a feature of the sonorants [r] and [ł] in this language. Those in column 3, on the other hand, appear to attest to a spread of this labiality/backness across the entire vowel space such that a new vowel is manifested there: i.e. [i] → [u], [e] → [o] and [æ] → [a]. This Anglian alternation is particularly well attested for the low [æ]/[a] variety while that for the non-low vowel space is rarer and some of these (especially the [e] → [o] change) may well be the result of other (but not unrelated) processes such as the effect of a left contiguous labial [w] element. The innovation outlined above in column 3 forms is traditionally labelled *Retraction* and further details of its operation can be found in Campbell 1959: sects 139–54, pp. 54–9; Nielsen 1981: sect. 55, pp. 129–30; Brunner 1952: sect. 80; Lass and Anderson 1975: pp. 68–9.

  We raise the issue of *Retraction* at this point not just to suggest to the reader that it might be thought of as some kind of 'more-pervasive' *Breaking*, but also because we are about to examine in this section stressed vowel changes which involve complete feature change as well as right-hand half colouring and which, like *Breaking* and *Retraction*, occur in what look to be identical triggering contexts. However, there will be a very important difference between the triggering environments for the processes we are about to describe in this section and those for *Retraction* and *Breaking*. These last, we recall, typically occur within the domain of a single syllable. The affected and triggering segments are both to be found within the scope of a single syllable beat. The set of vowel alternations which we are about to describe in this section occurs in the phonology of Old English characteristically in *disyllabic* contexts. That is, the affecting and affected segments are to be found in separate, distinct syllable environments. Most typically that part of the environment which provokes the change in the stressed vowel peak is to be found at the centre of the syllable which is appended to its right. In Old English many syntactic and semantic relationships (like number, case and tense) can be expressed by appending suffixes to noun and verbal 'stems' or 'roots'. The phonological shape of especially the vowel space of such appendages, accretions or inflexions could often be the cause of alternation in that of the noun or verb stem itself.

In the pages which follow we shall examine what appear to be vowel upon vowel assimilations where the vocalic elements in question *will not be contiguous but be separated by some intervening consonantal element or elements.* The vocalic elements involved will be the peaks of separate syllables. Before we enter into the complex details of this type of process, consider the set of alternations in Table 2.40 involving the low front [æ] and the low back [a] stressed vowels in the noun paradigm for the Old English item ⟨fæt⟩ '*vessel*' (Campbell 1959: sect. 574, pp. 224–5; Luick 1964: sect. 116, p. 127; Wright 1925: sect. 54.3). A simplified display like this

TABLE 2.40 Backness/labial harmony one

	Number	
	Singular	*Plural*
Case	[æ]	[*a*]
subject	⟨fæt⟩	⟨fat⟩ + ⟨u⟩
object	⟨fæt⟩	⟨fat⟩ + ⟨u⟩
possessive	⟨fæt⟩ + ⟨es⟩	⟨fat⟩ + ⟨a⟩
locative	⟨fæt⟩ + ⟨e⟩	⟨fat⟩ + ⟨um⟩

suggests that speakers could alternate between a stressed vowel
space in the 'stem' of this word characterized by [æ] in singular
contexts, and [a] in plural ones. Indeed, no reference might need
to be made to phonological influence whatsoever as far as this
stressed vowel alternation is concerned, since the vowel difference
could be labelled with reference to purely syntactico-semantic
criteria. However, it is interesting to note that those suffixes
which are used by the language to denote the (however very
informally expressed here) *case* relationships such as subject,
object, possessive and locative are distinct syllables in their own
right, showing peak vowels spelt by Old English scribes as ⟨e⟩,
⟨u⟩ or ⟨a⟩, whose phonetic values are traditionally held to be mid
front, high and low back respectively (King 1965; Minkova 1982).
In those versions of the ⟨fæt⟩ item bearing suffixed forms, the
frontness/backness value of the stem vowel space is a direct
function of these phonetic values in the suffixal vocalic element:
[æ] stem vowels are found where there are suffixal ⟨e⟩ spellings
and [a] where the vowel of the inflexion is spelt ⟨a⟩/⟨u⟩. We
might therefore be tempted to conclude that the stressed vowel
syllable one space 'copies' the frontness/backness characteristic
of that of the unstressed peak of the suffix. That this process was
a productive one in the phonology of West Saxon, especially for
low vowels, can be seen from such derivational alternations as
⟨fær⟩ '*journey*'/⟨faran⟩ '*to go*'; ⟨bæcere⟩ '*baker*'/ ⟨bacan⟩ '*to
bake*'; ⟨græf⟩ '*trench*'/ ⟨grafan⟩ '*to dig*' as well as singular/plural
contrasts like ⟨æsc⟩/⟨ascas⟩ '*ash tree*'; ⟨dæg⟩/⟨dagas⟩ '*day*';
⟨flæsc⟩/⟨flascan⟩ '*flask*' (Nielsen 1981: sect. 55, pp. 128–9, sect.
25, p. 237).

This mechanism of vowel peak 'tracing' is described by various
scholars as *Vowel Harmony, Umlaut* or *Metaphony* (Lass 1984:
pp. 171–3; Zimmer 1967: pp. 128–30; Aoki 1968; Clements 1976;
Vago 1980; Andersen 1974). Although not all scholars treat these
processes as representing the same kind of phonological event
(see especially Vago 1980: pp. 155–82) all of them appear to
represent some kind of transfer of all or some of the phonetic value
of the vowel space of one syllable to that of another. This
innovation seems to be able to operate from either right to left (as
in the example we have just cited in Table 2.40 above) or from
left to right. A good example of the latter is cited by Topping
(1973) from the Polynesian language called Chamorro, where items
will show either a front or back stressed vowel space according
to the presence or absence of a preceding definite article-marking
suffix expressed by the high, front vowel [i], as in Table 2.41,
where [u] → [i], [o] → [e] and [a] → [æ] following an [i] in the

TABLE 2.41 Chamorro vowel harmony

[hulat]	*'tongue'*	[i hilat]	*'the tongue'*
[fogon]	*'stove'*	[i fegon]	*'the stove'*
[lahi]	*'man'*	[i læhi]	*'the man'*

preceding syllable: a mirror image process to that we described for Anglian Old English *Retraction* and one we should bear in mind as relevant to our forthcoming discussion of Old English *i-umlaut* later in this section.

A right-to-left, suffix to root vowel harmony can also be seen in Modern Hungarian (as cited by Vago 1980 and Lyons 1967) where the vowel space characteristic of those suffixes which denote locational source *from* and goal *to* in nouns are mapped onto the vocalic element of the noun stem itself. Consider the influence upon the stem stressed vowel (italicized) of the back/front suffix vowels [a]/[e] and [o]/[ö] in the data in Table 2.42 where the

TABLE 2.42 Hungarian vowel harmony

ház + nak	*'to the house'*
ház + tol	*'from the house'*
föld + nek	*'to the earth'*
föld + töl	*'from the earth'*

suffixes in question are + [nak]/ + [nek] 'goal to'; + [tol]/ + [töl] 'source from'. Clearly, a back vowel [a]/[o] in the suffix triggers a back vowel [a] in the stressed vowel space in the 'stem', while suffixal fronted [e]/[ö] peaks make for a fronted [ö] vowel space at the centre of the preceding syllable. Such *vowel harmonization* can extend across many syllables at a time in the phonological systems of some languages. Note, for example, the shared roundness value of syllables two, three and four [u] vowels with the syllable one [o] in an item like [somunumu] in Modern Turkish (Andersen 1980: pp. 21–2). There seems to be little evidence for the existence of such multiple vowel harmonies in the historical phonology of the English language where, in general, assimilation between two vowel peaks appears to be the maximum domain of the process.

We shall proceed to examine three of the most important vowel harmony phenomena which appear to have been operative in the phonology of Old English, returning to a possible Middle English instance in Chapter 3 (see sect. 3.2.5 below). But, as we do so, we

shall look at a set of more traditional proposals which suggest
that what we shall characterize as vowel harmony between
non-contiguous vocalic peaks in disyllabic words might be
regarded, were we to take a different theoretical stance, as being
more akin to the West Saxon *Breaking* and Anglian *Retraction* of
front vowels which are contiguous with [l] and [r] in monosyllables
where direct contiguity with an affecting segment is entailed.

2.5.1 Backness/labial harmony two: Old English *Back Mutation* or *Back Umlaut*

We have already seen the vowel harmony effect achieved in Old
English upon (especially) low front stressed vowels in the first
syllable of disyllabic words when they are followed by another
syllable containing a vowel peak which is back/labial: thus
⟨fæt⟩/⟨fatu⟩ '*vessel(s)*' and spellings like ⟨fadur⟩ (*Cædmon's
Hymn*) corresponding to the ⟨fæder⟩ of 'classical' West Saxon.
By the end of the seventh century, a process not unlike this had
occurred in the phonology of Old English in almost all dialects
except West Saxon where it only ever achieved a rarity status.
What were affected were the short stressed front vowels [i], [e]
and [æ] in the first syllable of di-syllabic words whose second syllable shows a back/labial vowel peak space in what appears to
have been either [a], [o] or [u]. Consider in Table 2.43 the contrasting
forms found in West Saxon with non-West Saxon dialectal materials
(Anglian and Kentish) where the process we are considering was
extremely common. Although these data reflect an oversimplified
picture of the operation of what we claim is an Old English vowel
harmony operation, it would nevertheless be reasonably accurate
to suggest that front vowels like [i], [e] and [æ] show in Anglian and
especially Kentish dialects their second halves to be 'contaminated'
by the sonority/labial characteristic of the vowel in the following
syllable, resulting in a diphthongal stressed vowel space in [io], [eo]
and [æa]. Now clearly such a process is not at all unlike that we
outlined above for *Backness Harmony One* (Table 2.40) save that
it shows the non-palatal colour of the unstressed syllable only
partly reflected in the stressed vowel space: diphthongization
rather than whole vowel backing occurs. The difference between
the two harmonies lies in the extent to which the sonority/labial
colour 'spreads' across the stressed vowel space. For a very
convincing demonstration of the acoustic basis of vowel harmony
in general and for the way it can affect the right half – the transitional element – of the stressed vowel space, see Öhman 1965:
pp. 151–68. The process illustrated in Table 2.43 is variously
referred to in the handbooks as *Back Mutation, Back Umlaut, a-*

TABLE 2.43 Old English backness harmony 2

	West Saxon Old English	Anglian/Kentish Old English	
(1)	[i]	[io]	
	⟨sicol⟩	⟨siocol⟩	'sickle'
	⟨stigol⟩	⟨stiogol⟩	'stile'
	⟨niman⟩	⟨nioman⟩	'to take'
	⟨sidu⟩	⟨siodu⟩	'custom'
(2)	[e]	[eo]	
	⟨efor⟩	⟨eofor⟩	'boar'
	⟨esol⟩	⟨eosol⟩	'donkey'
	⟨fela⟩	⟨feola⟩	'many'
	⟨sprecan⟩	⟨spreocan⟩	'to speak'
	⟨beran⟩	⟨beoran⟩	'to bear'
	⟨medu⟩	⟨meodu⟩	'mead'
	⟨etan⟩	⟨eotan⟩	'to eat'
(3)	[æ]	[æa]	
	⟨hafoc⟩	⟨heafuc⟩	'hawk'
	⟨stapol⟩	⟨steapol⟩	'pillar'
	⟨staþol⟩	⟨steaþol⟩	'foundation'
	⟨faran⟩	⟨fearan⟩	'to go'

/o-Umlaut, and *Gutteral Umlaut* (Wyld 1927: sect. 48, pp. 34 ff; Campbell 1959: sects 205–20, pp. 85–93; Luick 1964: sects 224–34; Lass and Anderson 1975: pp. 102–12).

It should be immediately obvious to the reader that the type of phonological change arising from this vowel harmony is precisely that which we observed to be the result of Old English *Breaking*, namely [e] → [eo], [æ] → [æa], while its [i] → [io] manifestation is not unlike the [i] → [iu] change (recall the ⟨uuiurthit⟩ 'he became' instance in Table 2.16 above) we postulated for Old English *Breaking*, although in that process there was much [iu]/[io]/[eo] 'collapse'. However, despite the similarity between the two phonological events, the *Back Mutation* vowel harmony shows no orthographic evidence for an [iu], [eu] or [æu] diphthongal 'stage', modified by the operation of vowel height adjustment. The inter- and intra-dialectal manifestations of this backness vowel harmony in Old English are complex in the extreme and we cannot

describe them in detail in a general survey like this. Not all the
unstressed back/non-palatal vowels equally readily provoke a
harmony in those of the preceding syllable and, although our
data in Table 2.43 infer that the change was unknown in West
Saxon dialects, this was in fact not the case. For instance we do
find diphthongal vowel space in West Saxon items such as
⟨heofon⟩ 'heaven', ⟨eofor⟩ 'boar', ⟨beofor⟩ 'beaver', ⟨heorot⟩
'hart' and some others, but as Campbell (1959: sect. 210, p. 88)
observes 'analogical removal' is frequent and we can find
evidence suggesting monophthongal vowel space in the items
⟨hefon⟩, ⟨efor⟩ and so on. Given the rarity of this vowel
harmony process in the West Saxon dialect we must expect
evidence of lexical diffusion – the phonological change cannot be
expected to affect equally readily all possible lexical items where
the triggering context is present.

However, to many scholars the failure of the process in West
Saxon is not the result of some diffusion phenomenon, but
predictable from phonological contexts. Many claim that the
operation is constrained by the nature of the consonantal segment
intervening between what we see as the harmonizing vowels.
Campbell (1959), for instance, asserts that 'In Anglian, both *u*- and
a-umlaut of *e* are general before all consonants except *c* and *g*.'
Again, he claims that 'In West Saxon these changes take place only
when the consonant intervening between the vowel affected and
the back vowel which causes the change, is a *labial* or *liquid*
(f,p,w,m,l,r)' (sects 205–6). Intervocalic '*c* and *g*' will constrain the
Back Umlaut from occurring. The importance of such remarks lies
in the way in which they reflect a particular theoretical stance taken
by many traditional philologists. Some of these scholars see
segment assimilation to be a possible phonological event *only when
the affected/affecting elements are contiguous*. The 'jump-over'
assimilation type implied by vowel harmony is viewed with
scepticism by many of these writers. They would hold to the view
that Old English *Back Mutation* is a process whereby the backness
of the vowel in the second syllable is first transferred to the
intervening (and, of course, contiguous) consonantal element and
that this, in its turn, leads to a backness assimilation between itself
and the preceding front stressed vowel. Campbell's 'encouraging'
consonants are mainly labial in their articulatory place and would
appear to have therefore 'reinforced' the liability of a round [u] or
[o] vowel in the following syllable, although it is not clear what kind
of 'labializing' effect might be produced by an [a] vowel in that
position. Perhaps this kind of standpoint is best summarized by
Wyld (1927: sect. 110, pp. 67–8):

> What happened was that the *u* first 'lip modified' the preceding consonant, which in its turn produced a lip- or rounded glide between itself and the preceding front vowel: **witum* became **wit^wum* and then **wi^wt^wum*, thence *wiutum*, and later *wiutun*, later still *weotun*

see also Bülbring (1902: sect. 229). We shall return to this difficult problem in the next section.

2.5.2 Palatal/frontness vowel harmony: Old English *i-umlaut*

Every beginning student of the grammar of Old English quickly realizes that the language has a complex system of noun and verb morphology whereby semantic relationships relating to, for example, number, case and tense contrasts can be indicated by appendages, inflexions to nominal and verbal 'stems'. However, there also occur difficult occasions where, in the apparently random absence of any signalling inflexion or suffix, it is the shape of the stressed vowel of the nominal stem which seems to act as the indicator of case relationship and number value. Perhaps the best way of illustrating these two distinct apparatuses for highlighting nominal case and number differences lies in a comparison between the inflexional morphology of the West Saxon nouns ⟨bōc⟩ '*book*' and ⟨dæg⟩ '*day*' (see Table 2.44). A consideration of the

TABLE 2.44

	Number			
	singular		*plural*	
Case				
subject	⟨bōc⟩	⟨dæg⟩	⟨bēc⟩	⟨dagas⟩
object	⟨bōc⟩	⟨dæg⟩	⟨bēc⟩	⟨dagas⟩
possessive	⟨bēc⟩	⟨dæges⟩	⟨bōca⟩	⟨daga⟩
locative	⟨bēc⟩	⟨dæge⟩	⟨bōcum⟩	⟨dagum⟩

⟨dæg⟩ forms shows us that speakers could 'signal' such semantic concepts as location in time/space or more-than-one-ness by means of accretions to the noun 'root' or 'stem', such that + ⟨um⟩ indicates something like '*to/from the days*'. Upon the shape of the vocalic element in these accretions, we argued above, depended the frontness value of the stressed vowel of the root; a suffix containing a back vowel peak (like ⟨um⟩) would provoke a vowel harmony such that the [æ] stem vowel space was perceived also as being back

– [a]. The ⟨bōc⟩ nominal type is, however, apparently rather different. Like ⟨dæg⟩, it too shows a stem stressed vowel alternation – [ee]/[oo] – but the items showing [ee] vowel space are 'inflexion-less'; there appears to be no vowel harmony trigger for the stressed vowel alternation. It would seem that the language user had to 'know' some kind of rule such that *'when more-than-one-ness is being referred to and a noun like ⟨boc⟩ is involved in a case relationship context where subject of or object of is indicated, then alter the stressed vowel space from [oo] to [ee]; i.e. front it'*. In other words, for such a speaker the stressed vowel alternation would appear to be semantically 'motivated' rather than derived through some known phonological rule process.

On the evidence provided by other Germanic languages related to Old English, scholars have proposed that the Continental ancestor to the latter could have shown a paradigmatic display like that in Table 2.45 for an item like what came to be the Old English ⟨bōc⟩, where we have isolated the inflexional morphology by inserting a + sign (Wright 1925: sect. 410, p. 197; Prokosch 1938: sect. 87, pp. 256–7). What should be immediately clear from a display like this is that those instances where the insular Old English shows 'inflexionless' (suffix-empty) ⟨bēc⟩ forms are the equivalent of those where the Primitive Germanic items witness a suffix containing a vocalic element which is a high, front [i]. (The object plural is clearly an exception to this statement and it would seem that by the time of insular Old English the subject form had been generalized into that case form.) It would now appear that we can propose an account of the [oo]/[ee] alternation in terms of a *vowel harmony*. Were the [oo] vowel space of the root to harmonize with the [i] of the accretion, then we should expect it to become either partially or completely more palatal. That is, we should expect under the first scenario a partial assimilation to realize a diphthong like [oi] or a total assimilation whereby [oo]

TABLE 2.45

	Number	
	singular	*plural*
Case		
subject	*[book + s]	*[book + iz]
object	*[book + un]	*[book + unz]
possessive	*[book + iz]	*[book + oon]
locative	*[book + i]	*[book + umiz]

fronts, retaining its roundness value to [œœ] or, by losing its roundness value, to [ee]. The data we shall present shortly below will
show that precisely these kinds of events may have occurred.
Nevertheless, the data in Table 2.45 show that the vowel
harmony triggering [i] had been deleted from the noun paradigm
of items like ⟨bōc⟩ before the period of our earliest written records,
only its 'result' remaining in the altered stressed vowel of the stem.
It would seem, therefore, that for a child learning what we know
as classical West Saxon, there would be no phonetic motive for the
[oo]/[ee] alternation in such an item; it would have to be 'learned'.

Although it would appear that a palatal/front vowel harmony
like that outlined above must have been a common feature of the
phonology of the earliest Old English, it ceases to be productive
by the sixth or seventh century, that is before most of our earliest
surviving documentation. Our interest in the process will therefore
be mainly (but we shall see not entirely) in its residual effects upon
the Old English lexicon. However, these effects are nevertheless
considerable and are responsible for the marking of many
important semantic/syntactic distinctions in the language. The
palatal vowel harmony itself appears to have initially affected all
long and short back/non-palatal stressed vowel space principally
where it was contiguous with a syllable whose peak was a palatal
vocalic [i] or quasi-vocalic [j] segment.

Let us begin our study of this vowel harmony process firstly by
recalling its right-to-left analogue in Chamorro where [u] → [i], [o] →
[e] and [a] → [æ] when an [i] vowel formed the peak of the *preceding*
syllable. Secondly let us observe some items in early Germanic
languages containing the non-low vowels [i] and [o] in a stressed
vowel space immediately preceding a syllable with a palatal peak
and see how they come to appear in Old English materials from
various dates and sources. Table 2.46 shows a complex display of
forms but a careful study of it will reveal some interesting facts. If
we compare the stressed vowels in the Germanic forms in column
1 ([u] and [o]) with their Old English 'successors' in columns 3(a)
and 2(b), we can see that the harmonizing effect of the second
syllable [i]/[j] has been to front them to [y] and [œ] respectively (the
latter shown by the mainly early Old English ⟨oe⟩ spellings; see
Campbell 1959: sect. 196, pp. 76–7). There has been a change
from a back round to a front round configuration. In other words,
only a partial vowel harmony has occurred – only the frontness
feature of the next syllable [i]/[j] has been 'copied', the fact that it
is non-round has been ignored at this stage. However, if we now
turn to the samples in columns 4(a) and 3(b), we see that changes
like [y] → [i] and [œ] → [e] appear to have taken place; the rounded

TABLE 2.46

Non-English Germanic	Early WS & Dialectal	West Saxon Old English	Late West Saxon Old English
(a) [u]/[uu]		[y]/[yy]	[i]
Gothic ⟨hungrjan⟩		⟨hyngrian⟩	⟨hingrian⟩ 'to hunger'
⟨bugjan⟩		⟨bycgan⟩	⟨bicgan⟩ 'to buy'
⟨kunþjan⟩		⟨cȳþan⟩	'to reveal'
OS ⟨fūsian⟩		⟨fȳsan⟩	'to send'
		⟨dust⟩/⟨dystig⟩	'dust(y)'
		⟨burg⟩/⟨byrig⟩	'city'
(b) [o]/[oo]	[œ]/[œœ]	[e]/[ee]	
OS ⟨olig⟩	⟨oele⟩	⟨ele⟩	'oil'
⟨drobian⟩	⟨gedroefian⟩	⟨drēfan⟩	'to disturb'
⟨ōðil⟩ Prim Gmc	⟨oeþel⟩	⟨ēðel⟩	'home'
*[dɔxtri]	⟨doehter⟩	⟨dehter⟩	'daughter'
1	2	3	4

front vowels have become unrounded or 'spread'. Two points should be made about this unrounding. Firstly, it seems to have occurred after the vowel harmony process ceased to be productive – in other words, it does not represent a change whereby total harmonization between, say, [o] and [i] was achieved. For a detailed discussion of the phonological motivation for such a development, see Lass and Anderson (1975: pp. 286 ff). Secondly, there is a disparity in the rate at which this subsequent unrounding of [y] and [œ] took place. The latter, as we see from the items in column 2(b) occur in West Saxon proper, while the former are later and certainly rarer. Derounding appears to be a function of vowel height, the less palatal the segment the more likely it is to be 'derounded', see Donegan (1978: sect. 3.18.d, p. 85) and Stampe (1979: pp. 39–41). However, the overall direction of this *palatal vowel harmony* for non-low vowels is clear enough: non-palatal vowels in stressed syllables take on the palatal 'colour' of palatal vowels in syllables to their right.

We have deliberately kept separate a discussion of this *palatal harmony* as it affects low back stressed vowel segments because the operation of the process in this area is rather complex and distorted by earlier historical phonological developments. On the analogy of the behaviour of non-low vowels in this harmony environment, we might expect low back vowels like [a] to be fronted to [æ]. The fact is that there is a paucity of short low back vowel segments in the phonological inventory of West Saxon. Such vowels had, in the 'ancestral' Continental stage of the language, become independently fronted to [æ] at a period before the implementation of the *palatal vowel harmony*. This independent [a] → [æ] fronting was a characteristic not only of the precursor of Old English, but also of Old Frisian and is often because of that given the rather poetic title of *Anglo-Frisian Brightening* (Lass and Anderson 1975: pp. 60 ff; Campbell 1959: sects 126–8, pp. 50–1; Luick 1964: sects 116–17, pp. 127–9). The data in Table 2.47 illustrate the non-Frisian/non-English 'retention' of [a] stressed vowel shapes versus their fronted [æ] manifestations in West Saxon Old English. The consequence of this *Brightening* was that at the time of the implementation of the *palatal vowel harmony* there were few [a] vowels in the phonological inventory of the precursor of Old English for the process to affect and, being already fronted, [æ] shapes from the *Brightening* should not be influenced by *palatal harmony* anyway. However, there were some [a] stressed vowel shapes which the *Brightening* had not affected. Firstly, for reasons

TABLE 2.47

Non-English/Non-Frisian Germanic		West Saxon Old English	
Gothic	⟨smals⟩	⟨smæl⟩	'small'
OHG	⟨glat⟩	⟨glæd⟩	'happy'
Gothic	⟨dags⟩	⟨dæg⟩	'day'
OHG	⟨bad⟩	⟨bæð⟩	'bath'
OSax	⟨fast⟩	⟨fæst⟩	'fast'
OHG	⟨wafsa⟩	⟨wæfs⟩	'wasp'

TABLE 2.48

Non-English Germanic	West Saxon Old English	
[aa]	[ææ]	
Gothic		
⟨dailjan⟩	⟨dǣlan⟩	'to divide'
⟨hailjan⟩	⟨hǣlan⟩	'to heal'
⟨haiþi⟩	⟨hǣþ⟩	'heath'

which need not concern us here, *long* [aa] stressed vowels were not inputted to *Anglo-Frisian Brightening* and could therefore be found in *palatal harmony* environments. Compare in Table 2.48 the Old English manifestation of a selection of Gothic forms, where the Gothic ⟨ai⟩ spelling represents a vowel which 'corresponds' to Old English [aa]. Here we see what we expect, the [aa] segment has become palatalized/fronted under the harmonizing influence of the palatal vowel in the next syllable. When we turn to a second context where *Anglo-Frisian Brightening* is 'blocked', namely before nasal sonorants, we confront the classical problem associated with the palatal harmonization of low back stressed vowel segments. Consider the data in Table 2.49. Notice two important characteristics of such data: (1) column 2 forms with examples principally from the early Old English *Epinal Gloss* (Campbell 1959: sect. 193.d, p. 74; Luick 1964: sect. 186, p. 170) show the

TABLE 2.49

Non-English Germanic		Early Old English	West Saxon Old English	
PGmc	*[kampi]	⟨cæmpa⟩	⟨cempa⟩	'warrior'
OHG	⟨anit⟩	⟨ænid⟩	⟨ened⟩	'duck'
OS	⟨mengian⟩	⟨mængan⟩	⟨mengan⟩	'to mix'
		⟨laempihalt⟩	⟨lemphealt⟩	'lame'
		⟨laendino⟩	⟨lendenu⟩	'loins'
PGmc	*[manniz]		⟨mann⟩/⟨menn⟩	'man'/'men'
Go	⟨andeis⟩		⟨ende⟩	'end'
Go	⟨fani⟩		⟨fenn⟩	'moor'
Go	⟨banja⟩		⟨benn⟩	'wound'
Go	⟨kannjan⟩		⟨cennan⟩	'to create'
	1	2	3	

'expected' [a] → [æ] palatal harmony, but (2) the forms in column 3 show that *raising* of [æ] to [e] has also occurred in the same environment. We might, of course, argue that the [æ] → [e] change is not a part of the vowel harmony at all, but represents the raising effect of the preceding nasal sonorant. That nasal sonorants can indeed produce such a raising effect is well recorded (Wyld 1936: p. 222). However, there is also evidence to suggest that the [a] → [æ] → [e] is all part and parcel of the same *palatal vowel harmony* process. Note, for instance, how in a Turkic language like modern Uighur a stressed vowel like [a] fronts and raises when the following syllable contains an [i]. Thus [al+in+maq] → [elinmaq] *'to be taken'* (Andersen 1980: pp. 1–48). Again, we noted above that *Anglo Frisian Brightening* had already produced palatal [æ] vowels from low back [a] shapes, vowels which because of their palatality characteristic we should not expect to be susceptible to a *palatal vowel harmony*. But they are. Stressed [æ] vowels undergo Old English *i-umlaut* to produce a stressed vowel space in [e]. Consider the data in Table 2.50, where we must assume a pre-*palatal vowel harmony* shape for the items in column 2 like *[bæd-], *[tæl-], etc. from the operation of *Anglo-Frisian Brightening*. For further detailed exemplification, see Luick 1964: sect. 189 (a), pp. 175–6; Wright 1925: sect 47, pp. 32–4; Campbell 1959: sect. 194, p. 76. For some reason [æ] is not 'palatal enough' in the vowel harmony context and is perceived by language users as manifesting not only the frontness characteristic of the following syllable [i] peak, *but also an element of its height characteristic*.

TABLE 2.50

Non-English Germanic	West Saxon Old English	
[a]	[e]	
Gothic		
⟨badi⟩	⟨bedd⟩	'bed'
⟨batiza⟩	⟨betera⟩	'better'
⟨hafjan⟩	⟨hebban⟩	'to raise'
⟨taljan⟩	⟨tellan⟩	'to tell'
⟨us-wakjan⟩	⟨weccan⟩	'to waken'

2.5.3 The nature of *palatal vowel harmony* in Old English

Are we able to arrive at any overall formulation for the operation of the *palatal vowel harmony* process which we have claimed to be a feature if not of classical West Saxon itself, then certainly of the language in its late Continental stage of development? We have been arguing for a 'jump over' type of operation through which the palatal nature of the right contiguous syllable's vocalic peak is reflected in that of the preceding stressed syllable itself. For non-low stressed vowels we say that the harmony involved a relative increase in the palatality/frontness characteristic of the stressed vowel such as in Figure 2.2, where the X—Y axis represents

FIG. 2.2 Old English palatal vowel harmony I

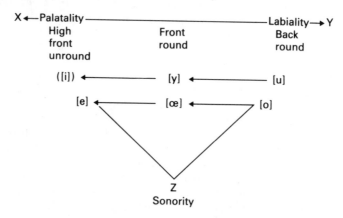

a scale of relative palatality/labiality and the Y—Z axis one of relative labiality/sonority (see sect. 1.2). The effect of *palatal vowel harmony* is therefore to shift 'pure' labial segments like [u] a relatively 'short distance' along the palatality/labiality scale towards the palatality terminus ([y] → [i] unrounding, we suggested, being rare (Campbell 1959: sects 315–16, pp. 132–3)). However, a segment like [o] which is relatively more sonorant than [u], shows a greater degree of 'contamination' and moves completely in the phonology of West Saxon Old English to a relatively pure palatal [e]. On the other hand, the behaviour of the low, back short vowel [a] appeared rather idiosyncratic. Consider Figure 2.3. The 'pure'

FIG. 2.3   Old English palatal vowel harmony 2.

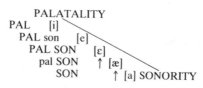

sonorant [a] appears (at least when it is long) to enjoy a 'mild' palatalization to [æ], but [æ] segments themselves are still perceived as too sonorant to stand in a *palatal vowel harmony* environment, and are moved further in the direction of the palatality terminus on the palatality/sonority scale or hierarchy. The *i-umlaut* process therefore appears to be one where speakers perceive stressed vowels to be more palatal and less labial and less sonorant, although the greater the sonority component in the input vowel, the greater will be the number of 'steps' it takes along the pathway to palatality (for a mirror image shift, see our discussion of the modern Swedish vowel shift, pp. 234–5). However, it is very difficult to provide any unified explanation for the rather complex set of data involved in the *i-umlaut* process in the confines of the very simple phonological model within which we are operating in an introductory book of this kind. Nevertheless, historical phonologists have made attempts to do so and the reader is referred to Lass and Anderson (1975: pp. 128–9); Lass (1980) and Anderson and Jones (1974).

The 'results' or 'residue' of the fully productive *palatal vowel harmony* are to be seen constantly and commonly in the derivational syntax of Old English. We have already mentioned singular and plural number contrasts: ⟨tōþ⟩/⟨tēþ⟩ '*tooth/teeth*'; ⟨fōt⟩/ ⟨fēt⟩ '*foot/feet*'; ⟨ac⟩/⟨æc⟩ '*oak(s)*'. Again we noted the directional/locative case relationship signalled by a root vowel alternation originally the product of our vowel harmony: ⟨moder⟩/⟨meder⟩ '*to/from the mother*'; ⟨burg⟩/⟨byrig⟩ '*to/from the city*'. Likewise comparative and superlative adjectival forms show a stem vowel variation historically the result of *i-umlaut*: ⟨lang⟩ '*long*'/ ⟨lengra⟩, ⟨lengest⟩ '*longer, longest*'; ⟨strang⟩ '*strong*'/ ⟨strengra⟩, ⟨strengest⟩ '*stronger, strongest*'. In the same vein we can cite the derivational relationships between certain nominal, verbal and adjectival forms as in ⟨gold⟩ '*gold*'/⟨gylden⟩ '*golden*'; ⟨stan⟩ '*stone*'/ ⟨stænig⟩ '*stony*'; ⟨mann⟩ '*man*'/ ⟨mennisc⟩ '*human*'; ⟨cuman⟩ '*to come*'/ ⟨cyme⟩ '*arrival*'; ⟨hat⟩ '*hot*'/ ⟨hete⟩ '*heat*' and many others (Luick 1964: pp. 166–77).

We noted earlier in this section the fact that both vowel harmonies and assimilations to contiguous sonorants could provoke either a modification to the right hand half of the affected vowel space or show a complete contamination spread across that space by the affecting element. To this point our treatment of *palatal vowel harmony* has suggested that it was of the latter type; all of the affected vowel space was palatality-contaminated, so that a new stressed vowel rather than a diphthong resulted from the process. However, there is some interesting evidence which suggests that *i-umlaut* was in its earliest manifestations a diphthong producing process. That is, some of the earliest spellings we find for Old English point to this *palatal vowel harmony* as operating rather in the same way as Old English *Back Umlaut/labial harmony two*. The palatal assimilation thus appears at first to have been partial, affecting the right hand side of the vowel space only. Campbell (1959: sect. 44) points to rather interesting data which indicate that the earliest recorded English palatal harmonies manifested stressed vowel space spelt as ⟨ui⟩ and ⟨oi⟩ for the *i-umlaut* of [u] and [o] respectively. He cites evidence from several early Old English sources (among them Bede) where, for instance, we find spellings like ⟨oidil⟩ corresponding to the later West Saxon ⟨eðel⟩ (cf. OS ⟨oðil⟩) *'native country'* and ⟨buiris⟩ for the later West Saxon ⟨byris⟩ (OHG ⟨bursa⟩) *'a file'*. He points as well to ⟨ui⟩ spellings for palatal harmonized [u] (normally spelt ⟨y⟩) in the tenth century *Lindisfarne Gospels*, i.e. ⟨druige⟩ (West Saxon ⟨dryge⟩) *'dry'*; ⟨fuilgendo⟩ (West Saxon ⟨fylgende⟩) *'following'* but these he treats as 'archaisms' in such a late text. It is however interesting to note that in the *Lindisfarne Gospels* we also find spellings like ⟨sʷyndria⟩ (alongside ⟨syndrigo⟩, ⟨suindrigo⟩ and ⟨sundrigo⟩) suggesting perhaps that ⟨ui⟩ spellings do not merely represent fossilized orthographic forms, but rather a genuine [ui] diphthong which, through syllabicity shifting (see sect. 2.4.5) could 'demote' the originally peak [u] element to the quasi-vowel [w], to realize a shape like [wi] or [wy]. The early spelling evidence tends to support an interpretation of *palatal vowel harmony* rather like that we proposed for Old English *labial vowel harmony two* (*u-umlaut*) as one where only a partial assimilation of the stressed vowel space to the affecting element was involved. Only at a later date did the 'new' palatal colour of the second half of the stressed vowel space spread across its entire area, such that [ui] → [y] and [oi] → [œ] or alternatively, what was seen as a side-by-side contrast between palatal and labial vowel elements [u\i], came to be perceived as though it were a segment *internal* contrast [u/i], that is [ü] (see sects 1.3, 2.4.4, 4.4).

Yet it is precisely orthographic evidence of the above type which persuades many scholars that *i-umlaut* was not a vowel harmony process at all, but one not unlike Old English *Breaking*. Wyld's (1927) remarks are worth quoting:

> The process of fronting the vowel was due to the front modification of the intervening consonant by the following -i or j. This front modified sound then influenced, and fronted the preceding vowel. When the consonant was back, c or g, it became a pure front ċ ġ, or

if g was followed by j, ċġ; thus *lægiþ became in the first instance *læġiþ 'lays': *sōkja 'I seek' becomes *sōci; *bruggjō 'bridge' becomes *bruċġ, the phonetic values being [j, ṫ, d] (sects 104–19, pp. 65–7).

Campbell too favours the view that 'umlaut palatalizes the intervening consonant, and . . . the umlaut is the assimilation of the preceding vowel to this consonant' (1959: sect. 192, p. 72). This theoretical stance holds therefore that modification to the stressed vowel is brought about by the nature of the right contiguous consonant which has come to contrast with it in frontness assignment. Thus, changes such as [u]→[ui] and [o]→[oi] are seen by these writers as a kind of *Breaking*, the [i] vowel being inserted to 'protect' the back stressed vowel from the newly fronted following intervocalic consonant. The role of the vowel in the unstressed syllable in this model is merely to provide the frontness value characteristic of the intervocalic consonant. It has no direct influence by 'jump over' on the stressed vowel itself. There is certainly no doubt that consonantal segments may be palatalized/labialized when they are contiguous with vocalic elements demonstrating such features. For instance, the phonology of Old Irish seems to show an assimilation whereby consonantal segments take on either a palatal or labial value in agreement with that of the following vowel space. Compare (following Thurneysen 1946: pp. 96 ff) the palatal/labial 'colour' of the consonants [f] and [r] (marked here with a superscripted ^{i} and ^{u} respectively) for the item ⟨fir⟩ 'man' in Table 2.51. The Old Irish examples show a palatalized [f^i] and a palatal/labial [r^i]/[r^u]. The former is clearly predictable from the palatal shape of the following, contiguous front/palatal vowel. For the Old Irish speaker, the palatal/labial value of the [r] sonorant may merely have been a matter for lexical representation, but we can see that its historical development arose through its earlier assimilation to a palatal [i] or [e] vowel or to a labial [u] evident in the pre-Latin

TABLE 2.51 Old Irish consonantal colour

	Old Irish	Pre-Latin	Classical Latin
Case			
possessive	[f^{i}ir^i]	*[wir+i]	⟨viri⟩
locative	[f^{i}ir^u]	*[wir+u]	⟨viro⟩
vocative	[f^{i}ir^i]	*[wir+e]	⟨vire⟩

instances. Many scholars would argue that just this happened in the case of both Old English *Back Umlaut* and *i-umlaut* but that the labial/palatal value of the affected consonant then spread to the preceding vowel space. We have already noted above the claim that Old English *Back Umlaut* in West Saxon dialects operated only when the intervocalic consonantal element was itself labial (i.e. [f], [p], [m]) which suggests that it is the shape of that consonant which is important for the further labialization of the stressed vowel space preceding it. Yet the data supporting West Saxon *Back Umlaut* was so slight as to make generalizations dangerous. Even Campbell who strongly advocates the view that Old English *i-umlaut* arises from the effect of a palatalized intervocalic segment has to conclude that since any kind of consonantal element can occur between the two vowel peaks (and not especially palatalized ones) then 'i-umlaut may be a mere vowel harmony'.

We have shown that vowel to vowel 'jump over' assimilations are quite well attested in the world's languages and appear to operate without any necessary effect on segments intervening between the vowel spaces. At the same time, common vowel to consonant assimilations like the Old Irish cases above, do not imply any further spread of the assimilation to surrounding segments. Finally, it appears to be the case that vowel harmonies can operate across syllable boundaries composed of more than one consonantal segment. Consider (in Table 2.52) the paradigm for the present tense, three person forms of 'strong' verbs like ⟨help + an⟩ '*to help*' in Old English alongside its postulated ancestral shape in Primitive Germanic (see Campbell 1959: sect. 731, p. 297, sect. 331.3, p. 138; Wright 1925: sect. 476, pp. 256–7; Prokosch 1939: sect. 54, pp. 148 ff). It is obvious in the case of the second and third persons that the palatal [i] suffix vowel has caused a *palatal vowel harmony* in the vowel of the stem at some stage prior to our earliest written records, such that [e] → [i]. There is, of course, no corresponding labial harmony when [u] appears in

TABLE 2.52

	West Saxon Old English	Primitive Germanic
	singular	
Pers 1	⟨ic helpe⟩	*[help+u]
Pers 2	⟨þu hilpst⟩	*[help+izi]
Pers 3	⟨he/heo hilpð⟩	*[help+iþi]

syllable two. It would be ponderous to suggest that the suffixal [u] lip-rounded first [p], then [l] thus preventing the stem vowel space from raising to [i]. Scholars who deny direct vowel to vowel effects across intervening segments tend to do do because of their attachment to a theoretical position which sees all assimilation as being contiguity conditioned, a view in turn which arises from an over-dependence on models which see all phonological arrangements as linear. For a different position, see Anderson and Jones (1974) and Durand (1984).

Chapter 3

The Middle English period: the thirteenth to the fifteenth centuries

3.1 The nature of the data

Where the sources of data from the Old English period confound, through their paucity and relatively homogeneous nature, any certainty of our fully understanding the nature of that language's phonology, the period embracing the thirteenth to the fifteenth centuries can paradoxically bewilder the historical phonologist even more as a result of the sheer immensity of the quantity of its extant written materials. Manuscript materials in prose and verse, covering every conceivable topic and written in a variety of styles survive from these centuries (Wells 1916; Hartung 1973). Two characteristics of these data are of particular interest to us. In the first place, we have, for the first time, examples of rhyming verse, which (although, as we shall see, its evidence is not always unambiguous) can provide much interesting testimony to contemporary phonology (Robinson 1971). Secondly, and of even greater importance, the texts which survive from this period are characterized by the very extensive variation they show in their orthographic practice. Especially during the first part of the period, no widely accepted standard of spelling representation is to be found, several regional (and perhaps even personal) spelling norms being in evidence; although spelling methodology can perhaps be identified with individual regional scriptoria, the three hundred years covering our period are marked by an unrivalled variety of almost individual 'solutions' to the problem of the symbolic representation of speech sounds (McIntosh, Samuels, Benskin et al. 1986: pp. 3 ff; Samuels 1972). Evidence of this kind is, of course, clearly of especial interest for the historical dialectologist (Moore, Meech and Whitehall 1935; Samuels 1983) but it can also provide a wealth of as yet largely unexplored detailed information for possible sets of contemporary phonological processes and their temporal as well as regional variation.

The problems associated with the interpretation of the phonological significance of such diverse and non-standard orthographic detail are obviously very complex and we shall only be able to highlight a few of the main difficulties here. A principal problem will lie in determining the extent to which we can treat the spelling as direct evidence for phonetic or phonological correspondence; we shall have to be continually on our guard against interpreting as phonetically significant those spelling alternations which are purely notationally variant or which might be considered to be relics or fossils of phonic realizations which have been long lost from the contemporary phonology.

Perhaps the best method of illustrating some of the difficulties associated with as well as the revalations provided by this enormous spelling variation is to consider some, but by no means all of the alternants associated, throughout our period, with a single item like ⟨length⟩ 'length'; our data are taken from the entries in the *Middle English Dictionary* (Kurath and Kuhn 1984) and from the *Linguistic Atlas of Late Mediæval English* (McIntosh, Samuels, Benskin et al. 1986). Consider the spelling shapes for this item as set out in Table 3.1. The (a) items in column 1

TABLE 3.1 Middle English *'length'* spellings

Orthographic variants	Vowel alternants	Consonantal alternants	Syllabic alternants
(a)	(a)	(a)	
⟨lengþe⟩	⟨lengthe⟩	⟨lenkthe⟩	⟨leneþe⟩
⟨lengthe⟩	⟨langthe⟩	⟨leynkthe⟩	⟨lengeth⟩
⟨lenȝthe⟩	⟨longthe⟩		⟨lenghyth⟩
	⟨linth⟩	(b)	⟨lenkith⟩
⟨lencþe⟩	⟨lynth⟩	⟨lengh⟩	⟨lenketh⟩
⟨lenkthe⟩		⟨lenkt⟩	⟨lenkyth⟩
	(b)		
(b)	⟨leenkþe⟩	(c)	
⟨lengye⟩		⟨lenght⟩	
⟨lenkye⟩	(c)	⟨lenkt⟩	
	⟨leyngthe⟩		
	⟨leeynȝþe⟩	(d)	
		⟨linth⟩	
		⟨lynthe⟩	
1	2	3	4

appear to be straightforward enough; ⟨þ⟩/⟨th⟩ and ⟨k⟩/⟨c⟩
symbols seem to be equivalent and interchangeable markers of
what are perhaps respectively [θ] and [k]. Likewise, we might
interpret the ⟨g⟩ and ⟨ʒ⟩ symbols as representing interchangeable alternants for the voiced [g] shape. In all, these varied
spellings might suggest pronunciations like [lɛnkθ] and [lengθ],
although we have nothing in the spelling to suggest whether a
[lɛŋgθ] variant – with a velar nasal – was a possible output. The
at-first-glance rather odd ⟨y⟩ symbol in the (b) instances can be
interpreted as an equivalent graphic representation for ⟨þ⟩ and
not as an indicator of some otherwise inexplicable [j]-type sound
(Benskin 1982). Full details of the nature, origin and general
function of the Middle English orthographic system can be found
in specialized discussions like Luick 1964: sects 52–62; Jordan
1974: sects 16–19; Moore and Marckwardt 1951: sect. 29, sect.
51; Berndt 1960: pp. 12–16; Jones 1972: pp. 45–51.

Forms in columns 2, 3, and 4 all appear to provide information
concerning genuine pronunciation alternatives. The shapes in
column 2 unequivocally seem to suggest that, for whatever sets of
reasons, the stressed vowel space in the item could vary between
[e]/[ɛ],[o]/[ɔ],[ɪ] and whatever is intended by the graph ⟨y⟩.
Likewise it would appear that the vowel space could also show
diphthongal and lengthened characteristics as attested by the
orthographic shapes in column 2 of ⟨leenkþe⟩ and ⟨leyngthe⟩.
While our earlier discussions of late Old English *homorganic
lengthening* might allow for the former set (sect. 2.2.4), there was
nothing in the kind of 'breaking' processes we found in Old
English which would allow for anything like the latter.

Column 3 items show what seem to be a number of different
innovations affecting the syllable final cluster ⟨ngth⟩, possibly
[ŋgθ]; ⟨nk⟩ shapes perhaps suggest some kind of [ŋg] → [ŋk] devoicing process: ⟨nth⟩ suggests [g] obstruent deletion: while ⟨lenkt⟩
points to the possibility of some kind of [θ]/[t] (continuancy)
alternation. A representation like ⟨lengh⟩ is especially difficult to
interpret, given the problem of ascertaining just what kind of
phonetic segment was intended by scribes when they used the ⟨gh⟩
digraph. That there is evidence, as we shall see below, that it might
indicate a voiced or voiceless velar fricative – [ɣ]/[x] – merely opens
up the difficult question as to the nature of a phonological change
involving [θ] → [ɣ]/[x]. Perhaps it is the spellings in column 4 which
are in many ways the most odd. They appear to show that there
has been some kind of phonological change whereby a
monosyllabic item like [lɛŋgθ] has come to be perceived as though it
were a disyllabic [lɛŋgəθ] or some such. What kinds of factors, one

might wonder, could promote the 'splitting up', 'busting' of the [ŋgθ] cluster by the insertion of a new, epenthetic vowel segment? Such questions of interpretation and explanation will, naturally, figure prominently in the sections which follow, but we should stress at this point that the range of spelling variation we have presented and shall eventually consider as a basis for our phonological discussions, represents only a small percentage of the possible available material. Much research remains to be done if we are ever to elicit the full implications of the vast array of extant Middle English orthographic variation.

Our period shows a general lack of formal grammar books which might have been expected to provide some details of contemporary phonological matters (Edwards 1984). Such as exist normally confine their interest to matters syntactical and morphological (usually after a model of the type set out in the *Ars Minor* by the fourth-century AD scholar, Donatus). What phonological comment there is is usually of a perfunctory nature, as we can typically see from the remarks of the fifteenth-century grammarian John Drury in his treatment of the formation of comparative adjectives and adverbs (Meech 1934: p. 82):

> How formist þu an aduerbe of þe positif degre? . . . Qwan of þe nominatif case? Quanne þe positif dgre end[t] in *ns* or in *rs*. As how? As nominatif, hic hec hoc sapidus: turne þis *s* in to a *ter* and þanne it sapienter. Nominatio, hic hec hoc solers; turne þis *s* in to a *ter*, and þan it is solerter.

Certainly and unfortunately there seems to be nothing relating to the description of medieval English phonology to rival that for the Icelandic language provided by the scribe known as the 'First Grammarian', the author of the *First Grammatical Treatise* – composed in Iceland in the middle of the twelfth century. His statements concerning contemporary phonology are often quite phonetically detailed and he utilizes a rich system of diacritic marks and specialized symbols. At the same time, he often provides sets of lexical items to illustrate the nature of contrasting vowel and consonantal alternants (Haugen 1972: pp. 13–14):

> to the five vowels that already were in the Latin alphabet – a, e, i, o, u – I have added the four that are here written: ǫ, ę, ø, y. Ǫ gets its loop from *a* and its circle from *o*, since it is a blending of these two sounds, spoken with the mouth less open than for *a*, but more than for *o*. Ę is written with the loop of *a*, but with the full shape of *e*, since it is a blending of the two, spoken with the mouth less open than for *a* but more than for *e* . . .

A man inflicted a *wound* (sár) on me; I inflicted many *wounds* (sǫr) on him . . . The priest alone *swore* (sór) the *oaths* (søren). *Sour* (súr) and the *sow's* (sýr) eyes, but better so than if they popped.

However, we shall see in the next chapter, that despite their obvious attractiveness as a means of reconstructing historical phonologies, statements even of this fairly detailed nature can pose as many problems as they apparently solve.

3.2 Vowel lengthening processes in Middle English: *open syllable lengthening*

In our section dealing with vowel lengthening processes in Old English (2.2), we saw how the duration (relative timing) of a stressed vocalic element could be adjusted as the result of various contextual factors. In fact, we came to two rather different sets of conclusions in that discussion. In the first place we saw that speakers had a predeliction for extending the time taken to produce the peak vocalic element in stressed syllables when certain consonantal segments immediately followed it. For instance, our study of *homorganic lengthening* revealed the tendency (and it was, we concluded, probably only that) for there to be an increase in the time taken to produce vowel sounds before sonorant consonants like [l], [r], [m] and [n], especially when these were the first elements in consonantal groups terminated by articulation place-shared voiced obstruents like [d] and [b]. Thus [čild] → [čiild], [lamb] → [laamb] and [feld] → [feeld]. However, apart from noting that such changes were confined to words of a single syllable ([čildrən] '*children*' showing no stressed vowel durational increase), we offered only a very tentative phonetic explanation for such a vowel lengthening process (see sect. 2.2.6).

This was not the case, however, with the second set of vowel lengthening events we described in that section. These, we argued, were accountable for in terms of a tendency for speakers to stretch or elongate the vowel space to 'compensate' for the loss of some post peak segment. Lengthening in these instances was viewed as a balancing, syllable shape stabalizing phenomenon, which in turn suggested – we argued – that speakers had intuitions concerning the 'ideal' composition and nature of those segments which go to make up syllables. Recall for instance the pre-English change whereby the stressed vowel space 'moves into' the area previously occupied by a nasal segment: [uns] '*us*' → [uus], [fimβ] '*five*' → [fiif], as well as those cases where the loss of a syllable final [x] segment seems to trigger an elongation of the precedent stressed vowel space to its left, thus filling out the depleted syllable content: *[slæxan] → [slææan] (2.2.1 above).

Changes to the timing allocated to stressed vowel peaks was also a feature of the phonology of Middle English although at first sight the later set of alternations look rather unlike those we saw in Old English. Certainly they are extremely complex and a great literature exists which attempts both to set out their idiosyncratic manifestations and to provide a unified explanation for what looks like a very disparate set of phenomena. We shall spend most of our efforts in this section examining in some detail one of the best known vowel lengthening processes in Middle English – *open syllable lengthening*. We shall only too quickly see that the process is fraught with difficulties: the theoretical apparatus required adequately to describe the trigger for the change is complex and not always intuitively obvious. The durational alternations associated with the operation are subject to a whole set of apparently unmotivated 'exceptions' and, perhaps above all, this vowel-lengthening rule appears to involve a simultaneous (or resultant or preconditional, depending upon one's theoretical stance) lowering of the affected vowels.

We must state at the outset that we shall arrive at no completely convincing explanation for the causes of the vowel lengthening process we are about to discuss and many of our suggestions must be treated as being very tentative. Let us begin our discussion, however, by looking at some of the more apparently straightforward manifestations of the *open syllable lengthening* rule. Without, for the moment, worrying too much about regional dialectal variations (although as we shall soon see, they are extremely important) let us look (in Table 3.2) at some contrasts in stressed vowel length between items as they appear in West Saxon and, say, thirteenth-century Southumbrian Middle English. There, the forms under (b) represent lexical items adopted into English from Anglo-Norman French forms with short stressed vowels (Bliss 1952–3). Some Middle English spellings for the Table 3.2 items are actually shown as having double vowel graphs – ⟨faare⟩, ⟨naame⟩, etc. – arguing that a lengthening of the stressed vowel has indeed taken place. However, our main information in this respect comes from our knowledge of the subsequent historical behaviour of the stressed vowels in question. Many of the lengthened forms cited above appear from the eighteenth and nineteenth centuries with *diphthongal* outputs – cf. the present day pronunciations [eɪkə], [teɪbəl], [neɪm] and [deɪl]. We shall see in several places in later chapters (notably sects 4.2 and 5.2)

TABLE 3.2 Open syllable lengthening I

West Saxon		Middle English		
(a)				
⟨faren⟩	[farən]	⟨fare⟩	[faarə]	*'to go'*
⟨æcer⟩	[ækər]	⟨aker⟩	[aakər]	*'field'*
⟨fæder⟩	[fædər]	⟨father⟩	[faaðər]	*'father'*
⟨nama⟩	[næmə]	⟨name⟩	[naamə]	*'name'*
⟨dalu⟩	[dalə]	⟨dale⟩	[daalə]	*'valley'*
(b)				
		⟨fame⟩	[faamə]	*'fame'*
		⟨able⟩	[aablə]	*'able'*
		⟨table⟩	[taablə]	*'table'*
		⟨fable⟩	[faablə]	*'fable'*
		⟨grave⟩	[graavə]	*'grave'*

how diphthongal vocalic shapes are often closely associated with
vowel length. Long vowels tend to become diphthongized
(Donegan 1978: sect. 4.4.3). Confronted by a durationally long
vowel space perceived as containing two halves (a peak and a
non-peak – i.e. relatively prominent and obscure portions)
speakers will tend to accentuate or enhance, we shall argue, the
differences between the halves by (among other things) altering
the height characteristics of one of them. Thus, we very often
find changes such that [ii] → [ei] or [əi] or [iə]. That is, words
which have stressed diphthongs in Modern English have very
often developed them form earlier long vowels and modern
diphthongal vowel shapes are often a good retrodictive 'test' for
earlier vowel-length characteristics.

But what is the triggering context for a lengthening change
like [namə] → [naamə]? The Old English *homorganic lengthening*
process we examined in our last chapter operated *within the
domain of a single syllable*. That is, a change such as [gans] → [gaas]
witnesses vowel length adjustment to 'make up for' the
replacement of the nasal consonantal element in the right-
hand-side part of the syllable. On the other hand, we shall see
that the most characteristic feature of our Middle English
vowel lengthening rule lies in the fact that its domain extends over
and across a syllable boundary and that its effect is constrained to
the stressed vowel of items comprising *two syllables*. It is at first
sight difficult to see how a change of the type [dalə] → [daalə] can
relate to notions such as vowel timing adjustment or stretching to

compensate for lost or replaced segments. To understand just how such a notion might be appropriate to open-syllable lengthening, let us digress a little to examine what we might mean by a *syllable*.

This is a highly technical area of phonological theory and there is an enormous literature available for study (Lehiste 1970; Lass 1984: pp. 248–70). Most scholars agree that language users have intuitions concerning the organization of the sounds of their language which take into account units which are larger than single segment size. That is, for Modern English speakers a word like [dɔg] '*dog*' is considered not to be just a sequence of individual phonetic segments [d]⟩[ɔ]⟩[g] but to be some kind of higher level construct whereby it has a *peak* or *centre* (the vocalic element), an *onset* (the [d] segment) and a *coda* or *terminator* (the [g] segment). Such *onset* + *peak* + *coda* configurations are called syllables. Not all syllables require onsets and codas, but *all require a peak*. Some possible combinations of the syllable constituting elements might therefore be those in Table 3.3. Bearing in mind the fact that

TABLE 3.3 Syllable shapes

Onset	Peak	Coda	
–	æ	–	'*a*'
–	æ	t	'*at*'
p	æ	–	'*pa*'
p	æ	t	'*pat*'

we are presenting an over-simplified, overgeneralized picture, we might nevertheless propose that speakers tend to view all the words in their language as being constructed of syllables whose structural 'template' might comprise a structure like

ONSET + PEAK + CODA

Syllables comprising the structure of individual words will tend to be mapped on to this 'template' in some way; there will be, as we shall explore below, an intuition for the existence of some kind of 'ideal' or characteristic syllable shape. Critical to our present argument is the notion that there exists in different languages an interaction between the durational length of individual segments and syllable shape on the one hand and accent/stress placement on the other. In the case of the latter, there seems to be some evidence to suggest that the timing interval is constant between accented items within words and in utterances. For example in the nursery rhyme

> Thrée blínd míce
> Sée hów they rún

the duration of elapsed time between *how* and *run* (despite the intervening unstressed *they*) is the same as that between *blind* and *mice*. Languages like this are called *iso-accentual* and include English and Thai. On the other hand, there are languages (especially French, Polish and possibly Spanish) which show timing equalization between syllable types: all syllables, be they CV, CVC, CVCC or VC, are equally long in temporal duration. Such languages are *iso-syllabic* (Pike 1943; Abercrombie 1967; Lehiste 1970) although not all scholars accept the validity of these claims (denOs 1983; Cutler 1980; Lehiste 1970). Note the following observations by Donegan (1978: p. 5 and sect. 4.4.1):

> Temporal compensation is a matter of mapping different sorts of segmental representations onto the timing patterns set up by the language. In a language with syllables of equal length, for example, the vowel of a closed syllable (CVC) will be shorter than that of an open (CV) syllable, other things being equal . . . . And in language groups with accent groups of equal length (ideally), the accented vowel of a monosyllabic word (CVC) will, other things being equal, be longer than that of a disyllabic (CVCVC) or trisyllabic (CVCVCVC) word. In many languages, particularly stress-timed languages, these principles may interact

> Iso-syllabism also plays a role in stress-timed languages like the Germanic ones, in that accented syllables show some tendency to all be equally long, and unaccented ones, to be equally short. Thus, accented vowels in open syllables may lengthen, and those in closed syllables, especially heavily closed syllables . . . may shorten.

The main importance of these observations for us is that if all syllables are viewed as having an *onset + peak + coda* configuration and if this structure is given some 'fixed' timing or duration value, then those syllables which have part of this syllable structure 'missing' will tend to 'stretch' other of their elements to make the syllable adjust to the allotted time span. For instance, in a syllable which is *coda*-free, e.g. {dæ}, the vocalic element will tend to be elongated to equalize overall duration with one like {dæd} with a *coda* slot filled. In this way we might argue that syllables like the former – 'open' syllables – will tend to have longer vocalic elements than *coda* terminated syllables ('closed' syllables) in iso-syllabic languages. Conversely, those syllables with heavy or complex *codas*, e.g. {dʒɪŋks} *'jinks'* will tend to show vowel length durational *reduction* to accommodate the time taken to produce the post peak set of consonantal segments (where the { } symbols are used to denote syllable termini).

How do observations like these relate to the thirteenth-century Middle English changes we have outlined above, whereby [farən] → [faarən] and [ablə] → [aablə]? We are, in each case, dealing with words of two syllables, i.e. having two vocalic peaks. How do such words fit the syllable template of *onset + peak + coda* which we have discussed above? One way in which we might map them on to such a template is shown in Table 3.4. Such a representation

TABLE 3.4 Disyllabic syllable shapes

	Syllable one			Syllable two		
	Onset	Peak	Coda	Onset	Peak	Coda
1	f	a	–	r	ə	n
2	–	a	–	bl	ə	–

is highly controversial as we shall see in our later discussions, but let us notice a few of its more interesting characteristics at this stage. Note, firstly, that we have shown the coda to syllable one in each case to be *empty*. We have chosen to represent the intervocalic consonantal elements – [r] and [bl] – as though they were the onset to syllable two. Why, we might ask, do we not propose representations like those in Table 3.5. Proposal (3) looks the least

TABLE 3.5

	Syllable one			Syllable two		
	Onset	Peak	Coda	Onset	Peak	Coda
1	f	a	r	–	a	n
2	–	a	b	l	ə	–
3	–	a	bl	–	ə	–

likely of all since we do not find in the English language monosyllables terminating in a [-bl] cluster. Words such as ⟨able⟩ in the modern language show a disyllabic structure like {eɪbəl}. Proposal (2) is rather unlikely as well since although we do find syllables terminating in [-b] and initiated by [l] (as in [kæb] *'cab'* and [lɛt] 'let') it does not capture our intuition that as a cluster [bl] can act as an onset, thus [blou] 'blow'. Proposal (1) is the one which might be the most difficult for us to reject since [r] can be monosyllable final in many dialects, thus [fær] 'far'. We shall have cause to return to such matters, which we only raise as problems here, in later sections notably 3.5–3.5.2 and 4.5–4.5.2. Meanwhile we shall at this point, without formal justification, prefer an interpretation like that in Table 3.4, on the grounds of the widely held proposal that all syllables are, where possible, *onset non-empty* (Kiparsky 1979; Giegerich 1985: p. 46). That is, they have a minimal structure of {CV}.

Mapping the items affected by the Middle English *open syllable lengthening* rule listed above in Table 3.2 on to the syllabic template proposed in Table 3.4, we immediately see that syllable one is left 'open' – {₁fa{₂ran. Syllable one under this interpretation has a *zero coda* and, given the tendency for syllables to receive equivalent durational articulation, the stressed vowel space is 'stretched' to compensate. *Open syllable lengthening* can, therefore be viewed in the terms of our model as a type of compensatory lengthening. We can perhaps illustrate this timing adjustment process by considering the behaviour of stressed vowels in the early Middle English period before a range of syllable final consonantal clusters in words of two syllables:

(1) Stressed vowels in syllables terminated by clusters such as [lt], [nk], [mp] and [rs] do not act as input to *open syllable lengthening* because their first syllable is not 'open'; [lt] etc clusters cannot act as syllable initiating onset clusters – *{₁bo{₂lten. However, both [l] and [t] can be syllable terminating and initiating elements, so that the syllable composition of ⟨bolten⟩ might be displayed as {₁bol₁}{₂ton₂}. As such, its syllable one has a coda and is by definition 'closed'. Stressed vowel lengthening is therefore inappropriate since it would realize a syllable shape like {₁bool{₂, one which would 'offend' the template structure we proposed in Table 3.3 above. Thus, items such as ⟨bolten⟩ 'to fetter', ⟨linken⟩ 'to chain', ⟨limpen⟩ 'to happen' and ⟨acursen⟩ 'to curse' all have *short, unlowered* stressed vowels throughout this period.

(2) On the other hand items with intervocalic ⟨st⟩ clusters showing short vowels in West Saxon, undergo *open syllable lengthening* in the thirteenth and fourteenth centuries. Words such as ⟨restes⟩, ⟨gestes⟩, ⟨brestes⟩ (the possessive case shapes of ⟨rest⟩ etc) appear with new lengthened stressed vowels later in the period: [rɛɛstəs], [gɛɛstəs] and so on. Again, Anglo-Norman French words with short stressed vowels before ⟨st⟩ clusters

show them as *lengthened* once they are 'borrowed' into Middle English: thus there are long first syllable vowels in ⟨coste⟩ '*coast*', ⟨giste⟩ '*joist*', ⟨host⟩ '*host*', ⟨tasten⟩ '*taste*', ⟨wasten⟩ '*waste*', ⟨feste⟩ '*feast*', ⟨paste⟩ '*paste*', ⟨tosten⟩ '*toast*' as well as the ⟨able⟩, ⟨table⟩ etc. instances presented in Table 3.2. *Open syllable lengthening* is operative in these cases just because [st] and [bl] can, as clusters, initiate syllables; the fact that they do so leaves the preceding syllable in an 'open' state – {₁to {₂sten.

(3) In West Saxon Old English, items such as ⟨wisdom⟩, ⟨hlæfdige⟩ and ⟨wifmon⟩ showed stressed vowels which were lexically *long*: [wiisdəm], [hlææfdijə] and [wiifmən]. However, by the thirteenth century in many dialects the stressed vowels appear to have been shortened, so that we find [wisdəm]. Clearly neither [sd], [fd] nor [fm] can act as syllable initiating clusters; however, each of the elements of the cluster on its own is capable of being a coda and an onset, thus {₁wiis₁} {₂dəm₂}. Under this interpretation, their syllable one, having a coda, is 'closed' and, with a *long* stressed vocalic element, contravenes the template configuration given in Table 3.3. The effect of the vowel shortening has been to realize just that template shape.

We should make a further point about the ⟨st⟩ cluster types in (2) above. The forms we cited were those with inflexional morphology – i.e. the possessive case forms ⟨gestes⟩, ⟨brestes⟩ contructed from the subject case form shapes ⟨gest⟩, ⟨brest⟩. The latter represent 'closed' syllable contexts where stressed vowel lengthening is inappropriate. The addition of the vocalically initiated inflexional forms like the possessive ⟨es⟩ and dative ⟨e⟩ in the singular dictates that on becoming disyllables the elements show a transfer of an element which was previously a coda to an onset position, thus {₁gest{₂ → {₁ge{₂st-. It is interesting to notice too that the lengthened vowel of the disyllabic, inflected shape has become generalized throughout the noun paradigm to inflexionless subject forms where, according to our syllable timing compensation theory, it would be inappropriate. There appear to be some cases, however, where this analogical generalization of the long stressed vowel throughout the paradigm did not occur, since we find inflexionless ⟨staff⟩ [stæf] with short peak vowel in the thirteenth century against its inflected plural shape ⟨staves⟩ [staavəz], reflected in the Modern English ⟨staff⟩/⟨stave⟩ alternation. Indeed, it seems that such inflexion/morphology provoked lengthenings led to the existence throughout the thirteenth and fourteenth centuries of long and short syllable one vowel variants in many lexical items. Words like ⟨blake⟩/⟨blak⟩ 'black' (cf. the personal name *Blake*) and ⟨smale⟩/⟨smal⟩ can apparently rhyme with items showing either short or long (through *open syllable lengthening*) stressed vowels. Consider these rhymes from Chaucer's poetry:

(1)   For feere of blake beres, or boles *blake*
      Or elles blake develes wole hem *take*
                        Nun's Priest's Tale, 11, 2935–6

(2)   How Sir Thopas, with sydes *smale*
      Prikyng over hill and *dale*
                        Sir Thopas, 11, 836–7

where ⟨blake⟩ and ⟨smale⟩ are seen to rhyme with the long [aa] vowels of ⟨take⟩ and ⟨dale⟩ produced by *open syllable lengthening*. On the other hand, we find in the next quotations from Chaucer ⟨blak⟩ and ⟨smal⟩ in contexts where the words with which they rhyme are lexically short and are not in *open syllable lengthening* affecting environments.

(1)   And why that ye been clothed thus in *blak*
      The eldeste lady of hem alle *spak*
                        Knight's Tale, 11, 911–12

(2)   Fair was this yonge wyf, and there *withal*
      As any wezele hir body gent and *smal*
                        Miller's Tale, 11, 3233–4

For further examples, see Terajima (1985: pp. 100–3).

3.2(1) Lengthening and lowering of mid vowels
The remarks we have so far made about this thirteenth-century *open syllable lengthening* change are generalized in the extreme. Not only have we put forward an extremely simplistic presentation of the nature of syllable structure, we have deliberately utilized a set of data which has allowed us to avoid facing some rather complex issues in relation to the overall *open syllable lengthening* process. For example, one such problem stems from the fact that the effect on stressed vowels in *open syllable lengthening* contexts in our period is not just one of lengthening but, in many instances, a shift in vowel height is involved as well. Without at the moment providing the evidence supporting the stressed vowel shapes we shall cite, consider the data in Table 3.6 (typical of those to be found in most standard Middle English handbooks) illustrative of the effect of our innovation upon the short high mid vowels [e] and [o]. The behaviour of the stressed vowels in the *open syllable*

TABLE 3.6 *Open syllable lengthening 2*

West Saxon		Middle English (13th century)		
⟨beren⟩	[berən]	[bɛɛrə]	⟨bere⟩	'to bear'
⟨mete⟩	[metə]	[mɛɛtə]	⟨mete⟩	'meat'
⟨ofer⟩	[ovər]	[ɔɔvər]	⟨ouer⟩	'over'
⟨nosu⟩	[nozə]	[nɔɔzə]	⟨nose⟩	'nose'
⟨þrotu⟩	[θrotə]	[θrɔɔtə]	⟨throte⟩	'throat'

lengthening environment manifests, in the above cases, *a decrease in vowel height*, from [high, mid] configurations like [e] and [o] to [low, mid] like [ɛ] and [ɔ]. Since the spelling forms clearly provide no motivation for this conclusion, we might justifiably ask upon what grounds is this kind of judgement made. One way we could assess the height of vocalic elements is by reference to specially devised spelling systems like those we have already met with in the *Ormulum*. However, Middle English scribes do not appear to have developed sepcific ways of graphically realizing the difference between high and low mid vowels. Alternatively, we might make reference to the evidence provided by rhymes. Poetic rhymes are notoriously difficult to interpret and are often the product of considerable licence (Skeat 1892; Langhans 1921; Kökeritz 1954). However, let us look in a fairly general way at some of the evidence which comes from rhyming poetry in the thirteenth and fourteenth centuries to see what clues it can provide for the height values of the newly lengthened mid vowels from *open syllable lengthening*.

Before we attempt this, however, let us provide a very general survey of the kinds of long mid vowels already present in the vowel space of many thirteenth-century English dialects. The dialectal variation is, of course, extremely complex but for the general Midland and parts of the London region in this period there appear to have been two distinct kinds of front and back long mid vowel as in Table 3.7. All of these can derive via phonological changes

TABLE 3.7 Middle English long mid vowels

	Front	Back
+high +mid	[ee]	[oo]
+low +mid	[ɛɛ]	[ɔɔ]

which occurred in many dialects at the beginning of the Middle English period:

(a) [ee] vowels came into being through the monophthongization of the 'long' [eo] diphthongs in Old English words like ⟨hēoldan⟩, ⟨stēor⟩ and ⟨dēor⟩ (see 2.4.3 and 2.4.4 above, and Jordan 1974: sect. 84). They also arose from the continuation of the lexically long Old English [ee] segments in words like ⟨hēr⟩ and ⟨slēp⟩ (Jordan 1974: sect. 51.2).

(b) Long [oo] vowels often appear as the continuation of such segments from the Old English period, as in items like ⟨tooth⟩, OE ⟨tōþ⟩ 'tooth'; ⟨bok⟩, OE ⟨bōc⟩ 'book' and ⟨doom⟩, OE ⟨dōm⟩ 'judgement' (Luick 1964: sect. 174; Jordan 1974: sect. 53; Wyld 1927: sect. 163).

Both the back and front long low mid vowels [ɔɔ][ɛɛ] are derived in our period through phonological processes like the following:

(c) Long low and back [aa] vowel sounds became rounded and raised to [ɔɔ] at the beginning of our period in items like [hɔɔm] ⟨hoom⟩ (OE ⟨hām⟩ 'home'); [mɔɔrə] ⟨more⟩ (OE ⟨māra⟩ 'more') and [lɔɔrə] ⟨loore⟩ (OE ⟨lār⟩ 'lore'), etc. – cf. Jordan 1974: sect. 44 and Luick 1964: sect. 369.

(d) Although there are great complexities in detail, Old English [ææ] low front segments appear by the thirteenth century to be raised in some dialects to [ɛɛ] (Jordan 1974: sects 48–51; Luick 1964: sect. 369). Thus, for OE ⟨nǣdl⟩ 'needle', ⟨ǣl⟩ 'eel' and ⟨þǣre⟩ 'there', we find in many Middle English dialects spellings like ⟨nedl⟩, ⟨el⟩ and ⟨ther⟩. The general assumption in the handbooks is that these last represent long, low mid vowel [ɛɛ] stressed vowel shapes. See sections 3.3 – 3.3.2 below.

The question to which we must now address ourselves is – on to to which of these mid vowel shapes were the outputs to the *open syllable lengthening* of [e] and [o] mapped? The rhyming evidence is, unfortunately, far from consistent and presents rather a complex picture. Nevertheless many handbooks suggest that by and large they rhymed only with [ɛɛ] and [ɔɔ] and that assonance with high mid segments like [ee] and [oo] was extremely rare. Let us consider a stanza from the famous fourteenth-century poem *Pearl* (British Museum manuscript Cotton Nero A.x) written in a predominantly North-Western dialect (Gordon 1963):

> More meruayle con my dom adaunt:
> I seȝ byȝonde þat myry *mere*
> A crystal clyffe ful relusaunt;

> Mony ryal ray con fro hit *rere*.
> At þe fote þerof þer sete a faunt,
> A mayden of menske, ful *debonere*;
> Blysnande whyt watȝ hyr bleaunt.
> I knew hyr wel, I hade sen hyr *ere*.
> As glysnande golde þat man can *schere*,
> So schon þat schene an-vnder shore.
> On lenghe I loked to hyr *þere*;
> þe lenger, I knew hyr more and more.
>
> 11, 157–69

The rhymes ⟨mere⟩/⟨rere⟩/⟨debonere⟩/⟨ere⟩/⟨schere⟩ and ⟨þere⟩ show stressed mid vowels from a variety of 'sources'. ⟨ere⟩, ⟨þere⟩ and ⟨rere⟩ (OE ⟨ǣr⟩ '*before*', ⟨þǣre⟩ '*there*' and ⟨rǣran⟩ '*to rise up*') show [εε] outputs as raisings from Old English [ææ] segments. On the other hand, ⟨mere⟩ and ⟨schere⟩ (OE ⟨mere⟩ '*a pool of water*' and OE ⟨sceran⟩ '*to cut*') derive, via *open syllable lengthening*, from a short [e], high mid segment in Old English. Evidence like this would therefore tend to suggest that in their open syllable contexts the stressed vowels in these last two items have, in the thirteenth century in this dialect, been realized as [εε].

Again the ⟨shore⟩/⟨more⟩ rhyme in lines 167 and 169 is illustrative of the output of the *open syllable lengthening* of the back vowel [o]. ⟨more⟩ derives via the rounding and raising of [aa] in OE ⟨māra⟩ '*more*', a vowel shape which must also, presumably, characterize the vowel in ⟨shore⟩ – [šɔɔrə]. Nevertheless, the picture is not always as clear as this as we can see from another rhyme from *Pearl*:

> I þoȝt þat noþyng myȝt me *dere*
> To fech me bur and take me halte,
> And to start in þe strem schulde non me *stere*
> 11, 1157–9

Here the vowel in ⟨stere⟩ derives from the lexically *long* Old English diphthongal ⟨stēoran⟩ '*to steer*', usually resulting in a Middle English high mid [ee] sequence. On the other hand, ⟨dere⟩ represents an *open syllable lengthening* output from Old English ⟨derian⟩ [derjən] '*to dare*', suggesting that the result of the lengthening rule is one where no lowering is involved. But the subject is too complex to be dealt with in depth in a book like this and the reader is referred to more specialist works: Luick 1964: sects 393–394; Wyld 1927: sect. 173; Stockwell 1961; Heck 1906; Grundt 1974 and Lieber 1979.

3.2(2) Lengthening and lowering of high vowels
We will treat the *open syllable lengthening* development of high
vowels separately because they are subject to a rather special set
of conditions and constraints – constraints which, within the terms
of explanation we shall offer, are crucially important for any
attempt to provide an overall motivation for the whole
open syllable lengthening process. Let us begin by looking at Old
English words of two syllables whose stressed vowel peak is either
[i] or [u] and compare the shapes these vowels take on after the
operation of our lengthening operation as well as in the *trisyllabic*
forms such items show when subject to morphological accretion.
The examples in Table 3.8 feature prominently in most treatments
of high vowel *open syllable lengthening*. The spellings for the

TABLE 3.8 *Open syllable lengthening* of high vowels

Old English	14th century Middle English	14th century inflected/morphologized forms	
(a) High Front			
⟨wicu⟩	⟨wik⟩	⟨wekes⟩	*'week'*
⟨giefan⟩	⟨gif⟩	⟨geves⟩	*'give'*
	⟨spir⟩	⟨speres⟩	*'spear'*
⟨widua⟩		⟨wedwys⟩	*'widow'*
⟨wifel⟩	⟨wevel⟩		*'weevil'*
⟨bitul⟩	⟨betel⟩		*'beetle'*
⟨clipian⟩	⟨clepen⟩		*'to call'*
⟨ifel⟩	⟨evel⟩		*'evil'*
⟨bysig⟩	⟨besi⟩	⟨bisily⟩	*'busy-'*
⟨myrig⟩	⟨meri⟩	⟨mirily⟩	*'merry-'*
(b) High Back			
⟨wudu⟩	⟨wud⟩	⟨wodes⟩	*'wood'*
⟨sunu⟩	⟨sun⟩	⟨sones⟩	*'son'*
⟨guma⟩	⟨gum⟩	⟨gomes⟩	*'man'*
⟨duru⟩	⟨dur⟩	⟨dores⟩	*'door'*
⟨sumor⟩	⟨somor⟩	⟨sumeres⟩	*'summer'*
⟨ðunor⟩	⟨thoner⟩	⟨thuneres⟩	*'thunder'*
I	2	3	

disyllabic shapes in columns 3(a) and (b) clearly suggest that in addition to any durational increase, the stressed vowels have undergone a lowering of some kind. But again we have to ask after the phonetic value of the segments graphically represented by ⟨e⟩ and ⟨o⟩. Once more the rhyming evidence for these values manifests a complex picture with little in the way of consistent effect. If anything, it suggests that while the *open syllable lengthening* of [i] and [u] did indeed involve a lowering to a mid vowel position, that position is almost as equally likely to be [εε] or [ɔɔ] as the [ee] and [oo] favoured by so many standard accounts (Jordan 1974: sects 25–6). Consider the following passage from *Pearl*:

> Anende ryȝtwys men ȝet saytȝ a *gome*
> David in Sauter, if euer ȝe syȝ hit:
> 'Lorde, þy seruant draȝ neuer to *dome*,
>   11, 697–99

where ⟨dome⟩, with lexical [oo] (OE ⟨dōm⟩ '*judgement*') is seen to rhyme with ⟨gome⟩ (OE ⟨guma⟩ '*man*') suggesting that the latter had undergone *open syllable lengthening* such that [u] → [oo].

However, we are on far less firm ground when we try to establish the phonetic value for the *open syllable lengthening* of the high, front [i] vowel. That some kind of mid vowel is involved is evident enough from the spellings in columns 2 and 3 in Table 3.8 above, but the rhyming evidence seems to suggest that the value of the mid vowel is as likely to be [εε] as [ee]. Consider firstly the following passage from Chaucer's *Troilus and Crisede*, Book III, 11, 1640–3:

> My deere frend, that I shal so me *beere*
> That in my gylt there shal no thynge be lorn,
> N'y nyl nought rakle as for to greven *heere*
> It nedeth naught this matere ofte *stere*

Two of the italicized items ⟨bere⟩ and ⟨stere⟩ are available for *open syllable lengthening* since they derive from short vowel forms in disyllables in Old English; ⟨beran⟩ [berən] '*to bear*' and ⟨styrian⟩ [stürjən] '*to stir*' respectively. The latter has undergone a Middle English change whereby, in this dialect [ü] has been fronted to [i] or [I]. According to our observations immediately above, the *open syllable lengthening* output of [berən] should be [bεεrən], suggesting that the [i] vowel in Middle English ⟨stiren⟩ has likewise been lengthened and lowered such that [stεεrən] results. However, ⟨heere⟩ derives from the Old English

form ⟨hēr⟩ which shows a lexical long [ee] vowel. What is the
rhyming value of the stressed vowels in these cases then, [εε] or
[ee]? Consider again another instance from *Pearl*:

> And, as lombe þat clypper in hande *nem*,
> So closed he hys mouth fro vch query,
> Quen Jueȝ hym iugged in *Jerusalem*
> 11, 802–4

The phonetic value of the final syllable of ⟨Jerusalem⟩ is suggested by its rhyme at 1. 816 with ⟨bem⟩ 'cross', derived from
OE ⟨bēam⟩ [bæǣam] with a diphthongal element which often
ends up in Middle English as [εε]. The *open syllable lengthening*
of ⟨nimen⟩ '*to take*' would therefore appear to result in a 'two
height' drop to a low mid position in this instance, 'leapfrogging'
over the [ee] high, mid position. However, a different picture seems
to be painted in an example like the following from the
early-fifteenth-century mainly Northern text *Roland and Otuel*
(Herrtage 1880) where we find a rhyme like:

> So thikke þaire dynttis to-gedir *pelyde*,
> thaire armours hewenn laye in þe *felde*
> Als floures þat strewede were
> 11, 502–4

Here, the ⟨felde⟩ form should show a lengthened [ee] shape, the
result of late Old English *homorganic lengthening* (sect. 2.2.4) a
process which, while affecting stressed vowel duration, leaves
vowel height unaltered. ⟨pelyde⟩, the singular past tense form of
the verb ⟨pilian⟩ '*to strike*' would therefore appear to manifest an
open syllable lengthening change such that [i] → [ee].

Perhaps the best we can say is that Middle English *open syllable
lengthening* is a rule which lowers and lengthens stressed vowels in
disyllabic words with certain syllable boundary configurations. The
precise nature of the degree of lowering is difficult to determine
and clearly best the subject of the scholarly monograph: Heuser
(1900); Bliss (1952–3); Eckhardt (1936); Keller (1920); Orton
(1952); Dobson (1962). Yet even the limited data we have
presented here suggest the lowering was not necessarily of a 'single
step at a time' nature and that 'two-step' height loss (leapfrogging)
appears also to have been possible. The importance of this
observation concerning the general nature of 'vowel shifts' will
become clear in Chapters 4 and 5 – see pp. 210–11 and 288–90
below.

3.2.1 *Open syllable lengthening* in other languages

It is interesting to note in passing that an *open syllable lengthening*-type rule is also to be found operative in the historical phonology of both Dutch and German. Probably in the fourteenth century, Middle High German shows what looks like a compensatory vowel lengthening process in stressed 'open' syllables in disyllabic words such that: [vibəl] → [viibəl] ⟨wibel⟩ '*weevil*'; [kugəl] → [kuugəl] ⟨kugel⟩ '*a bullet*'; [lebən] → [leebən] ⟨leben⟩ '*to live*'; [honəg] → [hoonəg] ⟨honig⟩ '*honey*' and [vagən] →[vaagən] ⟨wagen⟩ '*a carriage*' (Russ 1982: pp. 125 ff; Wright 1917: sect. 105; Reis 1974). Notice, however, the absence of any lowering in this Middle High German process, although this too is to be witnessed in certain dialects of the period, notably Thüringian where [i] and [ü] are lengthened and lowered to [ee] and [öö] respectively. Some centuries earlier (probably during the eleventh) Middle Dutch shows an *open syllable lengthening* lowering and lengthening phenomenon as well, compare for example the OHG ⟨sunu⟩ '*son*', Middle Dutch [zoonə] ⟨sone⟩; OHG ⟨situ⟩, Modern Dutch [zeedən] ⟨zeden⟩ 'morals' and OHG ⟨gibit⟩, Middle Dutch ⟨gevet⟩, Modern Dutch ⟨geeft⟩ '*he gives*' (van Bree 1977, Pelt 1960).

3.2.2 Lengthening and lowering as a unified process

Section 3.2 clearly showed that, although it is not always easy to categorically state the precise phonetic value of the resultant stressed vowel, Middle English *open syllable lengthening* was not merely an innovation to the phonology which increased vowel duration but one which initiated vowel lowering as well. This fact has led to considerable controversy in the scholarly literature not least because (a) the lowering is sporadic – it does not affect all of the vowels in the vowel space equally readily, (b) it appears constrained to *disyllabic* contexts; the presence of a third syllable attached to a classical *open syllable lengthening* context blocks the stressed vowel lengthening/lowering process. This is clear from the trisyllabic examples in column 3(b) in Table 3.8 above: cf. the [sumər]/[sɔɔmər]/[sumərəz] alternation. At the same time, there appear to be a whole set of lexical items which, although they otherwise appear to satisfy the conditions for triggering *open syllable lengthening*, still consistently show short stressed vowels throughout the Middle English period. We cannot pretend to be able to offer a unified or totally inclusive set of explanations for these characteristics of the change nor, indeed, can we hope to even summarize the many suggestions contained in the established literature. Rather we shall have to be content both to note some of the major observations which other writers have made and to put forward some tentative suggestions of our own.

We have given the impression in our discussion so far that *open syllable lengthening* was an 'across the board' type of phenomenon. Any stressed vowel in the appropriate disyllabic context might be subject to it. However, one of the earliest observed features of the rule was its disparate behaviour with respect to high as against non-high vowel segments. The high vowels [i] and [u] only regularly undergo the innovation in the thirteenth century in regional dialects North of the Humber. Southumbrian dialects of that date regularly show unlengthened/lowered high vowel sounds, *even when mid and low vowels are regularly affected by the process*. Thus, in Southern and Midland dialects in the thirteenth century we find lengthened/lowered outputs like [bɛɛrə] ⟨bere⟩ '*to carry*', but [drivən] ⟨driuen⟩ and [ritən] ⟨writen⟩ with no *open syllable lengthening* effect (Jordan 1974: sects 36–8, pp. 62–5). It is only in the latter part of the fourteenth century that we find the change affecting high vowels in these dialects and then only sporadically.

Is this fact merely a dialectal curiosity or can it tell us anything about the reasons why vowel lowering should be attendant upon what we have claimed to be a compensatory vowel durational increase? It seems to be fairly well established that vowel duration and height are closely interconnected phenomena. For example, some languages will show a phonological inventory whereby non-high vowels exist in short and long 'pairs', thus [a]/[aa], [e]/[ee], [o]/[oo] but where there are no long 'partners' for the high vowels [i] and [u] (cf. Samoan and Classical Latin (Donegan 1978: sect. 2.3.5.1)). Indeed, it seems to be the case that there is some *intrinsic* (causal) relationship between height and the duration of vocalic segments. Klatt (1973 and 1976) has convincingly shown that the higher a sound is in pitch, the shorter will its duration appear to become (all other things being equal). Low back vowels are intrinsically longer than high front and high back segments. Under laboratory conditions listeners will persist in treating the vowel in a word like [baθ] '*bath*' as longer than that in [bif] '*beef*', even when the timing duration of the former has been deliberately reduced (Jakobsen, Fant and Halle 1961; Perkell 1969; Petersen and Lehiste 1960: pp. 701–2; Elert 1964; Klatt 1976; Hongmo 1985 and O'Shaughnessy 1981).

This correlation of [i] and [u] with durational brevity might therefore account for the dialectal and temporal discrepancy in the *open syllable lengthening* rule. Southern dialects while 'willing' to see the lengthening/lowering of [a] and even [e]/[o], resisted it in intrinsically short contexts like [i] and [u]. (Why this resistance was apparently less in Northern dialects is, of course, a fair cause for speculation). Indeed, the very existence of a length/height parameter might provide a motivation for the introduction of a rule like *open syllable lengthening* into the phonology in the first place. There has always been considerable speculation as to whether there was any kind of sequential order in the operation of the rule: some scholars have seen the process as one containing two discrete parts – lowering and lengthening are separate manifestations. Indeed, some have argued that the lengthening only took place after an earlier stressed vowel lowering rule had been operative. Dobson (1962) argues in this vein, pointing to the fact that only in those dialects where lowering had already occurred did a subsequent lengthening take place. (For other accounts, see Luick 1964: pp. 209 ff; Bliss 1952–3: pp. 40–7; Stockwell 1961.) We should like to suggest here, on the other hand, that we are, in fact, not dealing with two separate phonological processes at all. Rather, the compensatory stretching of the vowel durational timing in the open syllable context produced (especially for non-high vowels) a *concomitant* lowering of vowel pitch quality. In this framework, lowering and lengthening are a simultaneous phenomenon; lengthening is a causal factor in the perception of lower pitch.

3.2.3 Some further thoughts on *open syllable lengthening*
The reader will have realized by now that we are in the presence of a very complex change, one which taxes our accepted views of phonological modelling. However, a recurrent concern in our discussion has had to do with the notion of 'compensation'. The implications lying behind this kind of notion are twofold: (a) there appear to be units of phonological structure (like syllables) of more than single segment size (b) in a language where all accented syllables are treated as having the same timing duration, there will be a tendency to extend the duration of the vowel space of those which are 'coda-less' or 'open'. A stressed syllable like {kæ-} will tend to be perceived as shorter than one like {kæt}; an increase in the vowel duration of the former to [kææ] establishing the syllable length equilibrium (Lass 1984: pp. 256–8).

Many writers have suggested that the domain of *open syllable lengthening*-type processes is not confined to the shape of the first stressed syllable; rather the process results from intuitions speakers have for some 'preferred' syllabic configuration appropriate to disyllabic words as a whole. Recall that our change

is uniquely a disyllabic word affecting phenomenon. Words of
three or more syllables, whose first is 'open' and for which
compensatory lengthening would be appropriate, do not show
evidence of being affected by the change: recall alternations
like [bɛɛsə] ⟨besi⟩/[bɪsɪlɪ] ⟨bisili⟩ and [θɔɔnər] ⟨thoner⟩/
[θunərəz] ⟨thuneres⟩ in Table 3.8 above (Luick 1964: sect.
392; Koeppel 1900). Jordan infers that words of two syllables are
to be viewed as having some kind of 'accent' balance. He suggests
that in early Middle English unstressed syllables are becoming
weaker, losing their accentual prominence, with the result that
this prominence is transferred to the strong, accented first
syllable to maintain some kind of balance of accent/stress across
the disyllable as a whole (1974: sect. 20, p. 41). Grundt (1974)
introduces the notion of a 'vowel duration ratio' as a feature of
disyllabic items – a ratio that can be disturbed by the 'weakening'
of unstressed syllables and which has to be restored or compensated
for by an equivalent increase somewhere else in the disyllablic
construction.

An interesting case of what might constitute just such a balancing
act between syllabic 'weight', as manifested by vowel duration, can
perhaps be seen in the phonology of some dialects in the early
twelfth century whereby lexical long vowels become shortened in
trisyllabic contexts. Consider the data in Table 3.9 (Luick 1964:
sect. 353, pp. 328–9). In many of the Table 3.9 cases the lexicon
of the modern language still shows a diphthongal/monophthongal
alternation in such pairs as [ould]/[ɔldəmən], [sauθ]/[sʌðərən] and so
on. Many 'explanations' for such long/diphthongal versus short
vowel contrasts have been offered (notably Kiparsky 1979:
pp. 179–81). In an attempt to maintain the 'closed-syllable-
short/open-syllable-long' hypothesis Stampe (1979: pp. 47–53)
argues for resyllabification of elements in the medial syllable in
trisyllabic words. Stampe claims that while in the disyllabic
(*open syllable lengthening*) cases, the coda to syllable one is
'empty', thus {₁blii{₂ðe ⟨blīþe⟩, in trisyllabic contexts what was

TABLE 3.9

West Saxon		Early Middle English		Late Middle English
⟨hāliʒ⟩	'holy'	⟨haliʒdæʒ⟩	'holiday'	⟨halidai⟩
		⟨haliʒdōm⟩	'holy place'	⟨halidom⟩
⟨blīþe⟩	'happy'	⟨blithelice⟩	'happily'	
⟨sūþ⟩	'south'	⟨suþerne⟩	'southern'	
⟨āld⟩	'old'	⟨alderman⟩	'an elder'	

the onset to syllable two becomes reinterpreted as the coda to syllable one, thus {₁bliið{₂ə{₃lič ⟨blithelic⟩. The effect of this is to 'close' syllable one, simultaneously reducing its stressed vowel duration to make it fit the canonical syllable shape template. But Stampe provides no independent motivation for such a resyllabification.

A different kind of solution is suggested by Lehiste's (1970: p. 40) proposal relating to the relative timing of vowel segments in polysyllabic words:

> Another factor which influences the duration of a sound is its position within a higher level phonological unit . . . . It appears that in some languages the word as a whole has a certain duration that tends to remain relatively constant, and if the word contains a greater number of segmental sounds, the duration of the segmental sounds decreases as their number in the word increases.

See also in this respect Klatt (1976) who observes that syllabic length decreases by up to a factor of 15 per cent in words of more than two syllables (Hongmo 1985). The implications of observations like these for our Middle English data might be, we tentatively suggest, that not only do syllables have some kind of preferred length characteristic, but so do *combinations* of syllables. A disyllabic configuration like [metə] is 'too short' in this respect and shows stressed vowel stretching to achieve some 'canonical' [mɛɛtə] shape: on the other hand, shapes like [suuðərnə] are 'too long' and show stressed vowel durational reduction to achieve a 'canonical' [suðərnə] configuration. But such are highly metaphorical observations and require testing for some correlation with either phonological or perceptual structure correlates (Ohala and Kawasaki 1984).

3.2.4 'Exceptions' to *open syllable lengthening*

In this and the following section we shall briefly examine two sets of apparent exceptions to the *open syllable lengthening* process. That is, we shall look at lexical items of two syllable composition whose first syllable is open and which should therefore show compensatory lengthening of the stressed vowel, but which persistently maintain a short vowel there. We shall observe, however, that it will be difficult to offer explanations for both sets of exceptions without recourse to phonological notions which are of a highly abstract and controversial nature. The first group of words which fails to undergo *open syllable lengthening* when superficially the environment for its application is met is comprised mainly, but not entirely, of 'borrowings' or 'loans' from

Anglo-Norman French into Middle English. We need not list all
the items in question here (see Bliss 1952–3 for a full account)
but we can mention:

⟨alum⟩; ⟨felon⟩; ⟨talon⟩; ⟨valor⟩; ⟨baron⟩; ⟨baril⟩; ⟨coral⟩;
⟨moral⟩; ⟨peril⟩; ⟨comon⟩; ⟨revel⟩; ⟨panel⟩ and ⟨chanel⟩.

Here too we might include items like ⟨gospel⟩ and ⟨hostel⟩ which,
with their syllable two initiating {st clusters, would normally
expect to have their stressed vowel lengthened as is the case in
[gest]/[gɛɛstəz] (see above, sect. 3.2, pp. 105–6).

As a first reaction we might conclude that Middle English
speakers excepted many of the above forms from *open syllable
lengthening* just because they were non-native items. But there
is ample evidence to show that at this period many adopted foreign
words underwent English phonological processes readily enough –
cf., for example, the stressed vowel lengthening in such words of
Anglo-Norman French origin as ⟨able⟩, ⟨chaste⟩, ⟨blamen⟩ and
⟨dame⟩ (Jordan 1974: sects 214 and 225 ff). That we are in fact
dealing with a situation which is phonologically motivated is
suggested by the fact that in most of the above examples the second
(unstressed) syllable has a particular type of segmental make-up:
[ləm]; [lən]; [lər]; [rən] etc. That is, usually both onset and the coda
to the peak are *sonorants*. At least the post-peak position is
always so – ⟨hostel⟩; ⟨record⟩; ⟨copor⟩ and ⟨botom⟩. It is
interesting to notice too that in this particular unstressed syllable
environment, the parallel Middle High German *open syllable
lengthening* process is often blocked as well. For instance, Middle
High German forms like ⟨himel⟩, ⟨komen⟩ and ⟨hamer⟩ all show
short stressed vowel reflexes in the modern language (Russ 1982:
pp. 129–30; von Kienle 1960: sect. 35; Wright 1917: sect. 105 ff).

Scholars have proposed at least two types of explanation for
exceptional *open syllable lengthening* behaviour like the above.
One group contends that segment durational increase does indeed
take place, but that the lengthened segment is the intervocalic
sonorant. In this way, [barən] → [barrən]. This sonorant lengthening, it is suggested, has the effect of 'closing' syllable one
($\{_1bar_1\}\{_2rən_2\}$) thus making it unsusceptible to lengthening
(Malsch and Fulcher 1975: pp. 303–14). Such a proposal fails, of
course, to account for the ⟨gospel⟩, ⟨hostel⟩ instances. Others
(notably Dobson 1962), suggest that there has a been a 'substitution for the normal combination of unstressed vowel and liquid or
nasal [boren ⟩ born] thus again closing syllable one'. (See also Russ
1969: p. 129; Paul 1888 II: sect. 35). We might very tentatively

add to these suggestions (following Jones 1984: pp. 257–68) that failure of *open syllable lengthening* in such contexts has again to do with the ways in which speakers structure 'higher level' items like syllables and words. We have made reference in the last section to such notions as the 'accent distribution' and 'durational loading' appropriate for disyllablic and trisyllabic words. We might add to these criteria for syllable composition that of *vowel/vocalic prominence weighting*. By this we mean the overall level within a syllable of vowel-ness (sonority) taken as a sum of its component segmental parts. For instance, a syllable such as {kɪt} is intrinsically *low* in vowel-ness since both voiceless obstruents and high front vowels are low in vocalicness for their phonological class. Recall our comments on the sonority hierarchy in section 1.3 and regarding Table 2.30. On the other hand, a syllable like [lal] is *high* in sonority; sonorants like [l] are, as we have seen in several places, highly vowel-like, while [a] is the most sonorous of all the vowels (Stevens and House 1956; Fant 1956).

If speakers do indeed have (perceptual) intuitions about some kind of preferred weighting of the overall distribution of vocalicness across syllables and words, then *open syllable lengthening* can be viewed as a mechanism whereby such a weighting is regulated. Items like ⟨carel⟩, for instance, would – in this view – 'resist' the change just because the high concentration of vocalicness in the second syllable would make any further accretion of sonority through stressed vowel lengthening 'non-canonical': a shape like *[kaarəl] is over heavy in the amount of sonority deemed appropriate for disyllabic words. Indeed, failure to apply *open syllable lengthening* to items like ⟨copor⟩, ⟨botom⟩, ⟨hostel⟩ and ⟨gospel⟩ suggests that the vowel weighting factor in syllable two, which is crucial to the assessment of the disyllable's overall sonority contour, is confined to the peak and post-peak (rhyme) area. Nevertheless, such notions obviously need further investigation and development before they can be in any way convincing. For an attempt along such lines, see Anderson and Jones (1974) and Jones (1976; 1984).

3.2.5 Middle English *open syllable lengthening* as a vowel harmony process

We have stressed, throughout our treatment of this thirteenth-century innovation, that it was somehow rather unlike any of the other phonological processes we had considered up to that point. Especially it appears to show none of the assimilatory characteristics typical of changes like Old English *Breaking* or *Retraction*, while unlike the *homorganic lengthening* innovation it shows vowel 'shifting' to increased levels of sonority (lowering) accompanying durational increase. But perhaps the most prominent characteristic of *open syllable lengthening* – the bisyllabic nature of its provoking context – might alert us to the possibility that, after all, it can be seen as a 're-enactment' of some of the changes we described in Chapter 2. This impression becomes even stronger when we realize that in some languages (notably Faroese), open syllables in disyllabic words show not a vowel space lengthening, but a diphthongization innovation; cf. the ⟨maður⟩ [mɛavur] *'man'* instanced cited by Lockwood (1955: pp. 9–12). Diphthongal innovations in the stressed vowel area of disyllabic items were, we recall, the outstanding characteristic of *vowel harmony two* (*back umlaut*) where, for instance, [sɪkul]/[sɪokul] *'sickle'* and [gætu]/[gæatu] *'gate'* alternants were attested (Table 2.43 above). In those cases we argued that partial 'contamination' of the right hand half of the vowel space in the first syllable was instigated through a *vowel harmony* with some back, labial vowel segment at the peak of syllable two. The Faroese *'open syllable lengthening'* instance looks not at all unlike the Old English labial harmony in its effect.

If Middle English *open syllable lengthening* can be interpreted as a type of vowel harmony operation, then we should need to argue that the syllable two vowel peak was relatively heavily sonorant in its internal composition – perhaps an [ə] or [ʌ] low central element (King 1965; Minkova 1982). As such, its effect on the precedent vowel space would be to intensify any sonority component in its internal structure or to add sonority to that structure where none existed before. Sonority addition would, of course, entail lowering (depalatalization, delabialization – see Fig. 2.2) and such sonority increase could, we have argued, simultaneously bring about an increase in perceived vowel temporal duration.

3.2.6 Middle English *open syllable lengthening* and homorganic clusters

There is yet another set of items which seems to show idiosyncratic developments in what would normally be Middle English *open syllable lengthening* producing contexts. Although items showing unstressed syllable peaks initiated and terminated by sonorant continuants – ⟨baril⟩, ⟨felon⟩ – tend not to show, we have argued, durational increase or vowel lowering to their stressed vowel space despite conforming in other respects to the environment favoured by our thirteenth-century process, there are occasions on which such items are associated with quite distinct and at first glance unconnected innovations. Consider in Table 3.10 instances involving two syllable items whose vowel peaks 'enclose' a segment which is a bilabial nasal and whose second syllables are terminated by a sonorant continuant consonant. The sets of alternants there show an unstressed syllable configuration with [məl] → [mbəl] (Jordan 1974: sect. 212, p. 191; Luick 1964: sects

TABLE 3.10

	13th–15th-century Middle English	
⟨bremel⟩ ⟨bramel⟩	⟨brembel⟩ ⟨brimbel⟩ ⟨bremble⟩	*'bramble'*
⟨hamer⟩ ⟨hamour⟩ ⟨hamur⟩	⟨hamber⟩ ⟨hambir⟩ ⟨hambyr⟩ ⟨Hambermakyr⟩	*'hammer'*
⟨humer⟩ ⟨Humerdalgate⟩	⟨Homber⟩ ⟨humbre⟩ ⟨houmber⟩	*'river Humber'*
⟨chimer⟩	⟨chimber⟩	*'sleeveless robe'*
⟨momele⟩ ⟨mumlen⟩ ⟨mummelen⟩	⟨momble⟩ ⟨mombil⟩ ⟨mumble⟩	*'to mumble'*
⟨scamel⟩ ⟨shamille⟩ ⟨shamele⟩	⟨schambil⟩ ⟨schambyll⟩	*'slaughter house'*
⟨semeli⟩	⟨sembli⟩	*'visually pleasing'*
⟨hymlice⟩ ⟨hemelic⟩	⟨humbloke⟩	*'hemlock'*
⟨plumer⟩ ⟨plomer⟩	⟨plumber⟩ ⟨plomber⟩	*'lead worker'*
⟨semele⟩ ⟨semeli⟩	⟨semeble⟩ ⟨semble⟩ ⟨sembele⟩	*'assembly'*

I   2

204.1, 675, 764). We have already tentatively suggested (and we shall do so again – see pp. 230 ff.) that the stressed vowel space in such items remains unlengthened (and hence 'unforgrounded'), since the item is already inherently highly vowel prominent, given the continuant nature of its syllable two onset and coda segments. But why should there appear such an 'additional' voiced obstruent [b] segment at the first syllable's termination, and why should such an epenthetic stop be mainly constrained to appear just when the intervocalic sonorant is the (bilabial) [m] nasal. While we can occasionally find alternations like ⟨spinel⟩/⟨spindel⟩ 'spindle', ⟨alor⟩/⟨alder⟩ 'alder tree', and ⟨ðuner⟩/⟨thunder⟩ 'thunder', ⟨win⟩/⟨wind⟩ 'wine', ⟨soul⟩/⟨sould⟩ 'soul' and ⟨mil⟩/ ⟨mild⟩ 'mile' (Luick 1964: sects 719, 765, 782), they are rare and we find no outputs like *⟨aldum⟩ for ⟨alum⟩, *⟨mordel⟩ for ⟨morel⟩ or *⟨chandel⟩ for ⟨chanel⟩. Both questions are inter-related but extremely difficult to answer especially within the limited theoretical compass of an introductory book such as this. However, let us explore two highly tentative suggestions which might enable us to see the [b] consonantal epenthesis characteristic of the column 2 types in Table 3.10 as at least connectable with some of the general observations we have already made concerning Middle English *open syllable lengthening* and other vowel-lengthening processes. We have made much of the notion of vowel-length increase as a reaction to the loss of a right-positioned segment within the scope of the domain of the same syllable. Such 'compensatory lengthenings' were appealed to as at least partial explanations for pre-Old English and West Saxon alternations such as [fimβ]/[fiif] 'five', [gans]/[gaas] 'goose' and [hansa]/[hoos] 'army' and so on – see Table 2.10 above. There our argument went that syllables had some kind of 'canonical' shape (perhaps defined in terms of the maximum and minimum number of segments in their composition); one such 'preferred' syllabic configuration was for there to be at least two elements to the right of the stressed vowel peak itself, as in the [fimβ] instance. Any loss of one of these elements (particularly that contiguous with the stressed vowel) led to a 'filling out' of the vowel space to compensate for the syllable component contraction (deChene 1979). We might therefore argue that something analagous is happening in the ⟨hambor⟩/⟨hamer⟩ type alternations set out in Table 3.10. Long-stressed vowel shapes such as *[haamǝr] were prohibited on the basis of the 'over-vowelly' constraint suggested above, but one like [hambǝr] could surface since, while it filled out the syllable one rhyme shape (the 'new' [b] allowing the nasal to be reinterpreted as a member of syllable one) the 'filling out' does not involve the addition of any extra vowel quality (Haggard 1973).

But what is the significance of the general constraint upon the distribution of the 'epenthetic' consonantal shape in those items with highly vocalic syllable two configurations? Why should co-articulating [b] insertion be apparently more readily tolerated in an item like ⟨hamber⟩, than [d] insertion in, say, *⟨aldum⟩? Once more a complete answer to this kind of question would involve us in much complex theoretical discussion and we shall only be able to present informal proposals here. While we have been arguing for a scale of relative prominence whereby vocalicness (however defined) is decreasingly present in segments such as vowels, glides, sonorant continuants, fricatives and obstruents, it is possible to show that such a hierarchy can operate within a much finer level of phonetic detail. For instance, it can be demonstrated that not all of the sonorant continuants are equally 'vowelly': [r] would seem to be the most marked for this feature, next [l] and least of all the nasals [n] and [m]. O'Dochartaigh (1978) has shown, for instance, that in modern Scottish Gaelic we can find both vowel lengthening and diphthongization in all continuant sonorant contexts; shapes such as [baar], [daul], [keun] and [kaum] forms surface in many regions where the language is still spoken. In some parts of Scotland, however, this stressed vowel foregrounding process is regularly blocked in nasal contexts; thus, while we frequently find shapes such as [baar] and [daul] in these regions, there are many occasions where only undiphthongized and unlengthened [kem] and [kam] forms will appear. On the basis of this kind of data we might therefore propose the setting up of a vocalicness hierarchy for the continuant sonorants which might at least provisionally look like:

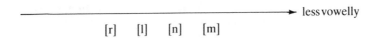

While the high relative vocalicness of [r] and [l] accords well with our observation that items such as ⟨valor⟩ and ⟨baril⟩ are significantly prominent in this respect to prohibit the addition of more of that same quality, those like ⟨hamor⟩ and ⟨bremel⟩ with their intervocalic bilabial nasals will show, on the above hypothesis, a relatively overall *reduced* level of vowel prominence. If such is indeed the case, is there then any sense in which we can argue that a form such as [bræmbəl] is (however marginally) overall more highly vocalic than, say, [bræməl]? Can, that is, shapes such as [bræmbəl] be seen as some kind of alternative lengthening stratagem to that 'normally' found operative in Middle English *open syllable lengthening*? Such a stratagem, we might suggest, while producing an increase in overall vocalic prominence, does not 'overstate' such a level of prominence as would a 'non-canonical' shape such as *[bræææməl].

We outlined in Chapter 1 (1.3) how nasal (and other) sonorants could be viewed as *complexes* of both vocalic and consonantal components simultaneously expressed. Segments such as [m], we hinted, had some kind of internal structure which we might see as comprised of a labial vowel element [u] and a voiced obstruent occlusion like [b]; the simultaneous expression of [u] and [b], we could suggest, produces [m] (for a more detailed treatment of this notion, see Anderson and Ewen (1987: pp. 162–4)). We might tentatively suggest that in the ⟨hambor⟩ type instances in Table 3.10, such an internalized [b] element has come to be linearly realized to the right of the nasal of which it is a component part (indeed, there is evidence to suggest that the [m] in [mb] clusters is rather different, especially as regards its overall duration, from the 'stand alone' [m] (Haggard 1973)). Such a right linear addition of the voiced obstruent can be seen as a stratagem for the addition of extra vocalic prominence to the syllabic environment of which [m] is a part: recall too the vowel length 'cueing' function of voiced co-articulating obstruents in nasal initial clusters in section 2.2.6. Yet while the obstruent's voiced status is indeed responsible for the appearance of additional vowel highlighting in the affected syllable, the fact that it is an obstruent suggests that such an addition is a 'weak' one, all that is appropriate, as we have been suggesting, in already highly vowel prominent (potentially *open syllable lengthening*) contexts like [hæmər] and [bræməl].

It is worth bringing back into focus at this point our suggestion that the late Old English *homorganic lengthening* process was only operative before consonantal clusters which were *voiced* obstruent terminated – [mb], [nd], [rd], etc – the presence of the voiced characteristic of their terminating obstruent we saw (following Raphael 1975) being responsible for the much greater vocalic resonance of the precedent nasal in an item like ⟨bend⟩ compared with one like ⟨bent⟩ – section 2.2.6 above. Yet the impression that we had in our discussion of that late Old English process that somehow [mb] is a 'short' cluster, one which does not strongly or consistently provoke a perception of vowel length in its immediate vicinity is reinforced by a number of other factors. We have shown above that on most occasions stressed vowel lengthening contiguous with sonorant initial homorganic clusters is at best a patchy affair. Indeed, although the matter requires further researching, the textbooks tell us that by the late fourteenth century such lengthening processes were often 'undone' and most especially so in [mb] and [nd] enviromnents. Only pure labials and palatals remained durationally lengthened before [mb] (Jordan 1974: sect. 22, pp. 43–4), all other vowel segments having, as a result of their sonority characteristic, a greater inherent durational content (cf. sect. 3.2.2 above) were perceived as durationally short in such a context (Mossé 1952: sect. 18).

We can perhaps strengthen such impressions by observing the rather different ways in which syllables terminated by sonorant initial homorganic clusters like [mb], [ld] and the like behave, in word final position, vis-à-vis the availability for deletion of the cluster finalizing voiced obstruent, such that [klimb] → [klim] 'climb' – see the examples in Table 3.11. There column 1 forms show orthographic variants some of which – those in ⟨ow⟩, ⟨ou⟩ and ⟨oo⟩ – appear to show explicitly that stressed vowel length is perceived in the pre-sonorant initial cluster context. Items in column 2, however, seem to suggest that syllable final 'cluster simplification' could occur whereby the articulatory place sharing obstruent comes to be effaced leaving the continuant sonorant in syllable coda position. This phenomenon appears to be one achieving statistical significance only from the fifteenth century and then perhaps most commonly in texts of a Northerly dialectal provenance, although there is some slight evidence for it even in Old English; cf. alternations such as ⟨dum⟩/⟨dumb⟩ and ⟨wom⟩/⟨womb⟩ in the tenth-century Northhumbrian gloss to the *Lindisfarne Gospels* (Ross and Stanley 1956; Campbell 1959: pp. 190–1; Luick 1964: sect. 764.1). Nevertheless, although more investigation into the phenomenon is required, it would appear that this obstruent effacement is principally constrained to occur in bilabial nasal initiated clusters, those instances of [nd] → [n] and [ld] → [d] being apparently extremely rare (at least on the general evidence provided by the entries in the *Middle English Dictionary*). Although it is possible to come across instances like ⟨For eauereuch chil þe cleopeþ ful⟩ (*Owl and Nightingale*, 1315 (Atkins 1922)); ⟨He ne moucte no more liue/For gol ne siluer ne fer no gyue⟩ (*Havelock* 358–59, (Skeat (1868)); ⟨Elde, or olde/ ole, forweryde⟩ (*Promptorium Parvulorum* (Mayhew (1908)); ⟨þet weren twa hun manna⟩ (*Lambeth Homilies* 1225 (Morris 1868–73)); ⟨But huusen hym as an hound/houne⟩ (*Piers Plowman* A.1, 48, (Skeat 1873)); ⟨& nim al i þire hond nime castles & mi lon⟩ (*Laȝamon's Brut*, 13355, (Madden 1847)), where 'cluster simplification' has apparently affected items like ⟨child⟩, ⟨gold⟩,

TABLE 3.11

12th–15th-century Middle English			
[mb]			
⟨dumb⟩ ⟨domb⟩ ⟨doomb⟩ ⟨dowmb⟩	⟨dum⟩ ⟨doom⟩ ⟨domme⟩	⟨domp⟩ ⟨dompe⟩	*'dumb'*
⟨comb⟩ ⟨camb⟩ ⟨Cambesmyth⟩	⟨cam⟩ ⟨came⟩ ⟨camsmyth⟩ ⟨comemaker⟩		*'comb'*
⟨lamb⟩ ⟨loomb⟩ ⟨lomb⟩	⟨lam⟩ ⟨loom⟩ ⟨lamme⟩	⟨lamp⟩ ⟨loomp⟩ ⟨lowmpe⟩	*'lamb'*
⟨jaumbe⟩ ⟨jambe⟩ ⟨yaumbe⟩ ⟨chaumbe⟩	⟨jamme⟩ ⟨jame⟩		*'door post'*
[nd]			
⟨lond⟩ ⟨londe⟩ ⟨lend⟩ ⟨leinde⟩	⟨lon⟩	⟨lont⟩	*'land'*
⟨graund⟩ ⟨grund⟩ ⟨grond⟩	⟨groun⟩ ⟨groune⟩ ⟨grun⟩ ⟨gron⟩	⟨grunt⟩	*'ground'*
[ld]			
⟨gold⟩ ⟨goold⟩ ⟨gowlde⟩ ⟨guld⟩	⟨gol⟩		*'gold'*
⟨cild⟩ ⟨child⟩	⟨cil⟩		*'child'*
1	2	3	

⟨old⟩, ⟨hund⟩ '*dog*', ⟨hund⟩ '*hundred*' and ⟨land⟩, they appear to be exceptional and the effacement regular only in post labial contexts. Yet it is interesting to note too that paradoxically and perhaps for reasons of *lexical diffusion* (see pp. 273–4 below) the *Middle English Dictionary* notes no examples between the twelfth and fifteenth centuries of the now universally effaced [b] in the ⟨tomb⟩ item. It is worth emphasizing also that second element deletion is even rarer in [rd] clusters.

Once again it would appear as if we are dealing with a general constraint involving bilabial nasal initial clusters and it is this fact which may indeed provide us with a rationale for its occurence. We argued above that it was the relatively low vowel content status of [m] nasals which 'permitted' the insertion of additional vocalic weight in the form of the linearly placed voiced [b] obstruent in such otherwise length-prohibiting contexts as ⟨hamor⟩. It is this same fact too which, we might claim, predicts that this very obstruent will delete (not be perceived) in monosyllabic terminations: *vowel + [mb]* clusters are relatively less vocalic in overall syllable weight than those in *vowel + [rd]/[ld]*. As such they tend not to attract vowel space foregrounding in the shape of stressed vowel durational increase to the same extent as the latter; alternatively they are simply perceived as altogether less vowel prominent – it is the deletion of the [b] which, we wish to argue, constitutes one stratagem whereby this overall low level of vowelly-ness can be manifested. Indeed, in such items the stressed vowel space itself may remain relatively long – as in the ⟨doom⟩ case, for instance, in Table 3.11 – with sonority reduction alternatively recorded through the effacement of the syllable terminal [b]. In the terms of this kind of argument, [b] insertion or deletion can be considered as one stratagem whereby the (minimum) amount of vowel prominence can be added to or substracted from syllable configurations. Clearly, too, one might interpret the syllable final [b] → [p] (much rarer [d] → [t]) obstruent devoicing in the column 3 items of Table 3.11 as yet another manifestation of this syllable vowel level reduction stratagem. Yet we shall show below that there may be other more general, but not unrelated, factors at work in cases like this.

3.3 Vowel length and vowel raising : the Middle English vowel shift

We saw in the last sections how stressed vowel height (i.e. relative palatality/labiality versus relative sonority) could apparently be affected by or at least connected with the durational characteristic of the vowel space. Although the historical phonology of English suggests that raisings and lowerings of vowels are not phenomena solely confined to the domain of extended vocalic length, we shall nevertheless see that such height variation is particularly common there; indeed, it will seem at first sight that in such long vowel contexts the raising and lowering alternations in the vowel space can appear to be 'unmotivated' and require no affecting phonetic context – they seem to be 'context free'. But such a correlation between vowel length and vowel height is not the only conclusion to be drawn from our discussion of *open syllable lengthening*. It is important to consider the possibility that such relationships can be seen as *metaconditions* upon the global phonological vowel space. In other words the domain of operation of such a dependent lowering process is not any individual long vowel, but *all* the long vowels in the phonological inventory. The very general and unitary effect of such processes on that inventory is often referred to as 'vowel shifting' and we shall see in what follows and in several sections thereafter just how important is an appreciation of the nature and operation of such 'vowel shifts' for our general understanding of historical phonological processes as a whole.

In the following pages we shall examine the set of innovations affecting the inventory of *non-high* long vowels (both lexical and derived) in the approximate period between the twelfth and the end of the fifteenth centuries. The evidence for such alternations will once more be provided by our interpretation of the orthographic data in contemporary manuscripts as well as by the evidence from the rhymes in poetic texts and in consequence be of rather limited intrinsic value. Yet we shall be able to see even from such sources that there are well defined changes occurring in the stressed long vowel inventory, changes which can perhaps be seen as the forerunners of those which, as we shall show below in section 4.2, occurred between the fifteenth and seventeenth centuries and which are verifiable during that later period on the basis of a more diverse set of criteria than merely orthography and rhyme. Let us begin by looking at a small selection of possible spelling representations for those (non-high) long vowel segments (both derived and lexical) which are to be found in many dialects in the late Old English and early Middle English period (say from the tenth to the twelfth centuries) contrasting them with their equivalent spelling versions some two hundred or so years later. The long vowels in question are [aa], [ææ], [ee], [ɛɛ], [oo] and [ɔɔ]. The spelling contrasts set out in Table 3.12 are, of course, extremely general and we shall fill in some of the detail con-

TABLE 3.12

Late OE/earlyME			13th/15th century Middle English	
Long vowel value	Spelling form	Example	Spelling form	Example
[aa]	⟨a⟩, ⟨aa⟩	⟨mara⟩ ⟨bat⟩ ⟨ban⟩ ⟨stan⟩	⟨o⟩, ⟨oo⟩	⟨more⟩ ⟨bot⟩⟨boot⟩ ⟨bon⟩⟨boon⟩ ⟨ston⟩⟨stoon⟩
[ææ]	⟨a⟩, ⟨æ⟩	⟨æfre⟩ ⟨clæne⟩ ⟨sæ⟩ ⟨stræt⟩	⟨a⟩, ⟨æ⟩, ⟨e⟩	⟨evre⟩ ⟨clene⟩ ⟨se⟩⟨see⟩ ⟨stret⟩
[ee] [ɛɛ]	⟨e⟩, ⟨eo⟩	⟨deor⟩ ⟨ʒear⟩ ⟨sen⟩/ ⟨seon⟩ ⟨le(o)rne⟩ ⟨e(o)rðe⟩ ⟨bred⟩	⟨e⟩, ⟨i⟩	⟨dere⟩ ⟨yer⟩ ⟨sen⟩/ ⟨sien⟩ ⟨lerne⟩/ ⟨liern⟩ ⟨erthe⟩ ⟨bred⟩⟨brid⟩
[oo] [ɔɔ]	⟨o⟩	⟨rode⟩ ⟨blod⟩ ⟨don⟩ ⟨boc⟩ ⟨toþ⟩	⟨o⟩, ⟨ui⟩ ⟨ou⟩, ⟨u⟩	⟨rode⟩⟨roude⟩ ⟨blod⟩⟨blood⟩ ⟨bluid⟩⟨blud⟩ ⟨don⟩⟨doun⟩ ⟨bok⟩⟨buik⟩ ⟨buk⟩ ⟨toth⟩⟨tooth⟩ ⟨tuth⟩

cerning their phonetic and dialectal manifestations as we proceed (Samuels 1985; McIntosh, Samuels, Benskin *et al.* 1986). Table 3.12 is quite deliberately selective both in the illustrative lexical items themselves and in the spelling shapes chosen to represent their stressed vowel space, since at this stage we wish only to point in a very general way to any innovative phonological processes such spellings might indicate. In general it is clear that the spelling representations characteristic of the period between the thirteenth and fifteenth centuries appear to suggest that while in some instances the late Old English and early Middle English long stressed vowels *may* have retained their phonetic value into that later era, there appears to have been an overall tendency – if we interpret the orthography at its face value – for there to have been a global *raising* of these vowels. Thus, we see temporal spelling contrasts like ⟨mare⟩/⟨more⟩ '*more*', ⟨stræt⟩/⟨stret⟩ '*street*', ⟨boc⟩/⟨buk⟩ '*book*' and perhaps even ⟨bred⟩/⟨brid⟩ '*bread*'. Clearly there are places where the spelling evidence is of only the most general interest and provides little in the way of phonetic detail – the ⟨e⟩ and ⟨o⟩ graphs, for instance, are of no value as indicators of the high or low mid status of the vowels in question, i.e. whether they are [ee] or [ɛɛ], or [oo] or [ɔɔ]. Yet digraphs like ⟨ou⟩, ⟨ui⟩ and ⟨ie⟩ may represent, as we shall see, specialized efforts to show just such phonetic detail. Obviously if we are to make any meaningful observations about possible Middle English long stressed vowel alternation, we shall have to support such spelling evidence like that above with data from rhymes and from the retrodictions possible from our knowledge of subsequent developments to the system.

Let us proceed to examine each of the long vowel segments in turn to see what kinds of changes they may have undergone between the temporal *termini* we have chosen.

3.3(1) [aa] segments, lexical and derived

The Middle English ⟨o⟩, ⟨oo⟩ and ⟨oa⟩ spellings for the vowel space of those items which in Old English and early Middle English showed [aa] vowels would suggest that some kind of 'raising' – labial 'contamination' in this instance – had occurred; cf. ⟨lamb⟩/⟨lomb⟩ '*lamb*', ⟨ald⟩/⟨old⟩ '*old*', ⟨rad⟩/⟨rod⟩ '*road*', ⟨hlaf⟩/⟨lof⟩ '*loaf*' (Jordan 1974: sects 74–5; Wyld 1936: pp. 105–6; Berndt 1960: pp. 41–3; Luick 1964: sect. 369 ff). Most observers suggest that a phonological change came about such that in these items, [aa] → [ɔɔ]. The affected [aa], in addition to its lexically entered form, is also the consequence of the Middle English *open syllable lengthening* of [a]. But as we have just observed, such an ⟨o⟩/⟨oo⟩ spelling format is non-specific as to the highness value of the back mid vowel; are we dealing with a change such that [aa] → [ɔɔ] or one where [aa] → [oo]? One argument for an [ɔɔ] interpretation might be if we could demonstrate that items with this newly labialized vowel rhymed with those showing an [ɔɔ] derived via the *open syllable length-ening* of [o] (see pp. 106–8). That there is some evidence for just such a 'merger' of the two back mid vowels from these sources we have already shown in section 3.2.1, where we pointed to the existence in *Pearl* of rhymes involving the items ⟨shore⟩ and ⟨more⟩, the former [šɔɔrə] through the operation of the *open syllable lengthening* of [o], the latter apparently therefore illustrating an [aa] → [ɔɔ] labialization. Chaucer too rhymes the [ɔɔ] from *open syllable lengthening* in ⟨bifoore⟩ with items showing historic long pure sonorant [aa]: ⟨moore⟩ *'more'* (OE ⟨māra⟩) (*Pardoner's Tale*, 393–4), ⟨goore⟩ *'garment'* (OE ⟨gāra⟩) (*Merchant's Tale* 3237–8) and ⟨soore⟩ *'pain'* (OE ⟨sār⟩) (*Wife of Bath's Prologue* 631–2). Yet the majority of commentators suggest that 'good' poets of the thirteenth, fourteenth and later centuries avoided rhyming just such sounds (Wright and Wright 1973: p. 25; Jordan 1974: p. 73), claiming instead that the labialization of [aa] was not so far 'advanced' as the low, mid [ɔɔ] of *open syllable lengthened* [o]; the former, they argue, was some kind of 'wide' [ɑɑ] sound (Liberman 1966). The circuitousness of such arguments will be obvious to the reader since, if indeed there is a proven reluctance to rhyme the two kinds of mid back vowel sounds, then it might as readily be because the result of *open syllable lengthening* was not [ɔɔ], but some slightly more labial, higher [ǫǫ], the labialization of [aa] achieving the former value.

The case is even further complicated by the fact that there is some evidence to suggest that the labialization of the Old English [aa] stressed vowel actually went as far as the high, mid [oo] position. Chaucer, for example, will rhyme (albeit occasionally) items such as ⟨hoom⟩ *'home'* (Old English ⟨hām⟩) with ⟨dom⟩/⟨doom⟩ (*Monk's Tale*, 3127) the latter showing a lexical [oo] vowel from the Old English period; other Chaucerian rhymes suggesting a similar vowel homophony are ⟨he goth⟩ *'he goes'* (Old English ⟨gāþ⟩) with ⟨sothe⟩ (Old English ⟨sōþ⟩ [sooθ] *'truth'*) and ⟨forsothe⟩ with ⟨bothe⟩ (Old English ⟨bāþe⟩ [baaθ] *'both'*). But the evidence is extremely complex and the reader is referred for more detailed information to Berndt 1960: p. 43; Jordan 1974: sect. 45, p. 75; Smithers 1948–9; Dobson 1968: p. 674, note 2; and Luick 1964: sect. 391, Anm. 4, p. 401.

Yet whatever detailed interpretation we are to accord it, it does seem clear that evidence of the kind we have outlined above points to some kind of labialization throughout the Middle English period of the pure sonorant [aa] segment; we appear to be witnessing varying degrees of 'contamination' of this sonority component by some labial colour, resulting in the production of long vowels 'mixed' for components of labiality and sonority, a process traditionally described as a 'raising', and which we might display as in Figure 3.1, where, following our discussion in section 1.3 (cf. Fig. 1.4), we treat segments like [ɔ] and [o] ('mid' vowels) as being complex, and showing various 'weightings' of the two primary *labial* [u] and *sonorant* [a] components. It is interesting to observe at this

FIG. 3.1

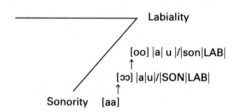

point that in Northern (especially Scottish) dialect areas in this
historical period, the 'contamination' of the long pure sonorant [aa]
took a different *pathway* – contamination by *palatality* occurred. The
[aa] segment appears to have been progressively palatalized such
that [aa] → [æǣ] → [εε] → [ee] and even, apparently, achieving a
palatal value resembling [ii]. Certainly from the early fourteenth
century there is clear evidence to suggest that in these Northern
dialects, the original [aa] had come to be seen as the long
'equivalent' of the short, relatively palatal [æ]. Such a palatalization
development is to be seen reflected in such modern Scottish English
pronunciations as [beeθ]/[beθ] '*both*' (Old English ⟨bā⟩);
[heem]/[hjem] '*home*' (Old English ⟨hām⟩) and [tee] '*toe*' (Old
English ⟨tā⟩) among many others (Wilson 1926: p. 33; Murray
1873: pp. 110–11).

3.3(2) [oo] segments, lexical and derived

As some of the spellings we have presented in Table 3.12 suggest,
many items which historically showed [oo] (high, mid) back vowels
are coming to be represented by ⟨ui⟩ and ⟨u⟩ spellings in the
Middle English period as well as retaining their 'original' ⟨o⟩
forms. Those long high mid [oo] stressed vowels derived through
the operation in Northern dialects of Middle English *open syllable
lengthening* of [u] (see pp. 110–12) are increasingly from the
thirteenth century being spelt there with such ⟨u⟩ and ⟨ui⟩ graphs.
These spellings would lead us to suspect that this [oo] vowel, 'mixed'
for sonority and labiality (although weighted in favour of the
latter – see Fig. 1.4) was losing its sonority component and having
its labiality element highlighted to realize some kind of 'pure' labial
[uu] segment; cf. such spellings as ⟨abuif⟩ (Old English ⟨abufen⟩)
'*above*'; ⟨duir⟩ (Old English ⟨duru⟩) '*door*'; ⟨luif⟩ (Old English
⟨lufu⟩) '*love*', for what would be Northern *open syllable lengthened*
shapes in [əboovə], [doorə], and [loovə] respectively. In other words,
the labiality 'loss' occasioned by the application of *open syllable
lengthening* has been 'restored'. Likewise, those [oo] segments
which are non-derived and typical of the stressed vowel space in
both Old and early Middle English in items like ⟨blōd⟩ '*blood*',

⟨bōc⟩ '*book*', ⟨he dōeþ⟩ '*he does*', ⟨fōt⟩ '*foot*' and ⟨gōd⟩ '*good*' can be found spelt in Northern, later Middle English dialects as ⟨bloud⟩/⟨bluid⟩, ⟨buik⟩, ⟨he dus⟩, ⟨fuit⟩, ⟨guid⟩/⟨goud⟩, the ⟨ui⟩, ⟨u⟩ and ⟨ou⟩ graphs strongly suggestive of pure labiality (Wyld 1936: p. 234; Berndt 1960: pp. 42–3; Dobson 1968: sect. 156). Yet it is extremely difficult to support such spelling evidence from that of rhymes. Likely instances such as ⟨stunde⟩/⟨londe⟩ (*King Horn*, ll. 167–8) and ⟨grunde⟩/⟨honde⟩ (*Floris and Blanchfleur*, ll. 303–4) although they look promising in appearing to show an [oo] (through the operation of late Old English *homorganic lengthening* – cf. pp. 24–9) in ⟨honde⟩ and ⟨londe⟩ rhyming with items with lexical [uu], such correspondences are very rare in the period and may in the above instances be the result of special South West dialect characteristics.

These last data showing the homogenizing of the mixed labial/(weak) sonorant segment [oo] to the pure labial [uu], when they are taken together with those we have presented for the development of the Old English and early Middle English pure sonorant [aa], suggest that something inclusive was happening to the long vowel inventory during our period. We seem not to be dealing with a set of alternations affecting individual long vowel segments, but the alternations all appear to have a single 'effect' – diluting the sonority component in all those long vowels characterized by showing it; pure sonorants become contaminated, made mixed, by the addition of varying levels of *labiality* (or, in Northern dialects, *palatality*), while those which are already mixed or complex show a progressive suppression of their sonority component to the extent that those which are weakly marked for it 'revert' to pure labials (cf. Fig. 1.4). According to such a schema, we have sets of *vowel shift* type changes such that [aa] → [ɔɔ] → [oo] and [oo] → [uu]. Although we shall develop the idea in considerably more detail in the corresponding section in the following chapter (see pages 202–4), we might characterize this unified movement towards the *labiality* point in the vowel space triangle as in Figure 3.2.

FIG. 3.2

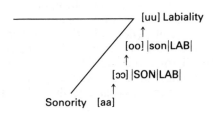

3.3(3) The palatalization of long mixed palatal/sonorant segments
Is it possible for us to show that there was in Middle English a set
of changes to long stressed vowels showing some *palatality* element
in their composition 'parallel' to the *sonority* → *labiality* vowel shift
effect we have attempted to demonstrate for back long vowels?
Can we demonstrate a concomitant sonorance reduction along the
pathway of increasing *palatalization* for long vowels mixed for
sonority/palatality in our period? We have already seen, of course,
that such a pathway was taken in the alternations affecting the pure
sonorant [aa] in Northern and Scottish Middle English dialects, such
that instead of the 'expected' desonorization vowel shift in the
direction of increased labiality found in Southern dialects (where
[haam]→ [hɔɔm] and even→ [hoom] *'home'*) we witnessed the sonority component increasingly contaminated by *labiality* such that [aa]
→ [æææ] → [ɛɛ] and even → [ee], cf. Modern Scottish English
[heem] *'home'*. While we shall show in the following pages that just
such a matching palatality orientated vowel shift did indeed exist
in many dialects in the Middle English period, the details of its
operation are extremely complex and raise, as we shall see in the
next chapter, a number of important theoretical issues. In what
immediately follows, we shall try to address two separate problems:
(1) what is the evidence for the vowel shift as it affects the least
palatal of the long vowel segments in the Middle English
inventory – [æææ]? Was its palatalization range limited to [ɛɛ] or did
it extend as far as [ee], and are there any conditions constraining
that extension? (2) we have already shown that by the thirteenth
century many Middle English dialects have an innovatory [ɛɛ]
(low, mid) segment in their long vowel inventory, triggered by
the operation of *open syllable lengthening* on [e]. To what extent
does this segment lose its sonorancy component and palatalize
to [ee]?

3.3(4) Increased palatalization of [æææ]
Even in the Old English period itself there is considerable evidence
to suggest that a palatalization of [æææ] had occurred. Such a process
seems to have been inoperative in the 'classical' West Saxon
dialectal region, but observable almost everywhere else. That such
a raising of the mixed *palatal/sonorant* [æææ] occurred in non-West
Saxon dialects can be seen if we compare spellings from texts
written in such dialects like ⟨ded⟩ *'deed'*, ⟨her⟩ *'hair'* and ⟨beron⟩
'they bore' with their West Saxon 'equivalents' ⟨dǣd⟩, ⟨hǣr⟩ and
⟨bǣron⟩ (Campbell 1959: sect. 128, pp. 50–1). The incidence of
such ⟨e⟩/⟨ee⟩ spellings for a long vowel space characterized in
West Saxon by ⟨æ⟩, increases dramatically in the Middle English

period and examples can be seen in Table 3.12 above. But clearly such ⟨e/ee⟩ spellings have limited value in themselves as indicators of the extent to which the sonorancy component of the original [ææ] has become 'diluted'. Do the Middle English (indeed the Old English) ⟨e⟩ graphs represent [εε] or [ee] or both? The handbooks and specialized literature contain a mass of complex and often conflicting evidence on this question, but there would certainly appear to be a strong case for arguing that the palatalization of [ææ] increased to both [εε] and [ee] values. For instance it is possible throughout the thirteenth and fourteenth centuries to find rhymes between items whose stressed long vowel space is [εε] derived via *open syllable lengthening* on the one hand and those showing a derivative of the 'original' Old English [ææ]. In Chaucer's *Canterbury Tales*, for instance, we find rhymes between items like ⟨unhele⟩ and ⟨wele⟩. The latter we would expect to be realized as [wεεlə] through the operation of *open syllable lengthening* on a shape like [welə], Old English ⟨wela⟩ 'prosperity'. On the other hand, the Old English West Saxon spelling for the former – ⟨unhælu⟩ *'illness'* – represents an [ææ] vowel space one which, if the rhyme is to be trusted, has undergone a palatalization as far as [εε] – [unhεεlə].

Yet there is also ample rhyming evidence to suggest an [ææ] → [ee] palatalization in some Middle English dialects. Chaucer again frequently rhymes the item ⟨se⟩ *'sea'* (Old English ⟨sæ⟩) with items whose stressed vowel space is unambiguously lexically *high*, mid [ee]: for instance, we find ⟨se⟩ in rhyming combinations with ⟨me⟩ *'me'* (*Troilus and Cresyde*, 5.886–7); ⟨he⟩ *'he'* (*Troilus and Cresyde*, 2.443–6); ⟨she⟩ (*Canterbury Tales* II, 1107–9): and again with [ee] segments derived from the monophthongization of the Old English [eo] diphthong (see sect. 2.4 above) – ⟨see⟩ *'to see'* (*Canterbury Tales* I, 3031–2); ⟨tree⟩ *'tree'* (*Troilus and Cresyde* 3, 8–10) (references to Chaucer's works are to the Robinson (1977) edition). The works of the Kentishman Gower provide us with much evidence for such [ee] level palatalizations, often it seems graphically represented by ⟨ie⟩ – cf. ⟨diel⟩ *'part'* (Old English ⟨dæl⟩) (Samuels and Smith 1981; Samuels 1985).

3.3(5) Increased palatalization of [εε]

The by now very familiar Middle English [εε] derived through the operation of *open syllable lengthening* also appears to have been affected by this generalized tendency to increase the palatality component of mixed palatal/sonorant long vowel segments. Note, for example, such Chaucerian rhymes as between the items ⟨stele⟩ *'steel'* and ⟨stele⟩ *'to steal'*; the former represents the Middle

English retention, continuation of the Old English high, mid [ee] in this item (Old English ⟨stēle⟩), while the latter shows the operation of *open syllable lengthening* upon the durationally short [e] of Old and early Middle English ⟨stelan⟩ – [stelən], producing [stɛɛlə(n)]. For many other instances of such lengthened [ɛɛ] with lexical [ee] rhymes, see Ogura 1980: pp. 44 ff; Berndt 1960: pp. 36–47 and Wyld 1936: pp. 29–31.

Although we have presented only an extremely small set of the possible data relating to the manifestations in the thirteenth and fourteenth centuries of the spelling and pronunciation possibilities for the long [æ: æ], [ɛɛ] and [ee] segments from all historical sources, it would still appear that we are able to argue from them for the existence of the presence in the phonology of some general 'instruction' or overall condition such that 'long vowels mixed for palatality and sonority show a palatality increase, a sonority suppression'. As we saw above, such metaconditions on the phonological inventory can be productive of 'vowel shifts', in this case such as in Figure 3.3. It is perhaps worth mentioning in passing

FIG. 3.3

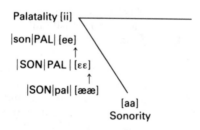

here that even in texts of the fourteenth century we can also see evidence for the palatalization of the high, mid [ee], even though this process is usually held to be operative much later in that century or even considered as a fifteenth-century innovation. Compare such mid-thirteenth-century spellings as ⟨brid⟩, ⟨bryd⟩, ⟨bryed⟩ for what was historically the Old English ⟨bread⟩, whose [æa] diphthong we saw monophthongized to [æ æ] or [ɛɛ] in Middle English (see sect. 2.4.2 above). Such an [ɛɛ] manifestation we might expect to palatalize to [ee] by the fourteenth century in many southern dialects, but our spellings above would suggest that in this period a complete suppression of sonority and the realization of a 'pure' palatal [ii] was at least a possibility for the stressed long vowels of some items.

3.3.1 The first English vowel shift

Our characterization above of changes such as [aa] → [ɔɔ] and [ææ] → [ɛɛ] as non-unique but rather part of a wholesale set of changes, metaconditions, 'conspiracies' or whatever we like to call them affecting the entire long vowel inventory of Middle English is not without controversy. We need to observe that, contrary to many of the phonological changes we have so far described in this book, we have provided no affecting phonetic context, no phonetic 'trigger', 'driver' or motivator for any of the long vowel raisings in the period. Instead, we have seen them as self-induced, independent in some way. Needless to say, not all scholars view these phonetic events in such a light, seeing what they consider to be clear affecting phonetic contexts in the items where the long vowel raising occurs (although, as far as one can see, no such motivation is ever provided for the changes affecting the pure sonorant [aa] segment in early Middle English). The most popular view, espoused by Berndt (1960) and Wyld (1936), is that the long vowel raisings are the result of their contiguity with a *dental* consonantal segment in their syllable coda – cf. items such as ⟨dæd⟩, ⟨mæd⟩, ⟨sæd⟩, ⟨hæþ⟩, ⟨stræt⟩ and so on – this dental element, being 'high', imparting its palatal value to the preceding long vowel and so instigating an alternation like, say [ææ] → [ɛɛ]. A whole range of 'dental' consonants (including [d, t, č, n and l]) is seen as constituting such an affecting environment, while the list of common items manifesting the long vowel raising causes these scholars to extend this group to include coda consonantal elements like [v, m, k, p and r] (cf. affected lexical items like ⟨læfan⟩, ⟨clæne⟩, ⟨wæcan⟩, ⟨slæpan⟩ and ⟨þær⟩) (Terajima 1985: pp. 49–54)). Yet it is hard to see how such a segment grouping readily fits with any obvious natural phonetic class and, while several of its members do demonstrate palatality characteristics, the list is so large it could be made to justify more than one phonetic motivation. But we have also seen above that, for example, [ææ] palatalizations can occur when the syllable is coda-empty – ⟨se⟩, ⟨sle⟩, ⟨fle⟩ etc. Are we to list word/syllable boundary among those consonantal segments described above? Whatever, if any, phonetic, properties syllable boundaries might be said to have – palatality heightening would hardly seem to be one of them (Lass 1971; Lass and Anderson 1975: pp. 177–9). Some writers, most recently Terajima (1985: p. 123) even view the labialization of the back vowels as the direct result of the consonantal type following the long stressed vowel and, on the basis of the lexical items affected, cite a list much like that given above as motivation for the front vowel raisings. It is even less easy to see how segments like [n, m, t, s, z] and so on could possibly have any labializing influence in any phonetic framework, while once more changes like [aa] → [ɔɔ] quite regularly appear in non-coda terminated syllables – ⟨wo⟩, ⟨tho⟩, ⟨fro⟩ etc.

We have to bear in mind once more that much of traditional historical phonological scholarship rests on the assumption that phonological change most often resulted from the effect of the phonetic make-up of *contiguous* segments. We have, of course, seen much evidence of that assumption in our discussion of Old English *Breaking* (see sects 2.3.1–2.3.6). Lexical items are seen as composed of linearly (temporarily) arranged segments, and change in one segment is very often, if not always (it has been traditionally argued), the consequence of its proximity to another segment which will either reinforce the phonetic properties of the first if it shares them, or 'mutate' them in its own direction if it does not. Linear phonological models of this type usually cite as examples of segment contiguity induced changes those like [ɛdɪnbʌrʌ] → [ɛdimbʌrʌ] (place of articulation reinforcement) and [æɫ] → [æaɫ] (where the frontness/backness 'discrepancy' of the [æ] and [ɫ] temporarily contiguous segments results in the 'mutation' of the vowel space in the direction of the 'affecting' syllable terminating [ɫ]). And while traditional historical phonological scholarship does admit of isolative or independent change (often by default), the model's pressure to produce combinatorial changes and to elicit affecting phonetic contexts is so strong that triggering environments can sometimes be produced regardless of their appropriateness. Yet we must bear in mind that it is only because we look through the viewpoint of the linear model that we are forced to see vowel changes like [sæaæ] → [sɛɛ] with their lack of consonantal coda, as isolative or context free. Non-linear models of phonology are able to see in the concept of vowel length itself some kind of phonetic environment which might be responsible for alternation. Recall that we have been treating long vowel and diphthongal vowel spaces as composed of two halves. Only *one* of these halves constitutes the syllable peak – the other half is less prominent and could be seen as in some way 'dependent' upon the syllable bearing portion. That central/dependent relationship can be, we informally suggest here, a type of phonetically affecting context in a broad sense, capable of producing regular and predictable alternations to the stressed vowel space. We shall return to the motivation for such context-free vowel changes in the section parallel to this in the following chapter, while the reader is referred to Anderson and Jones (1974) and Durand (1984) for more detail on the tenets of non-linear phonologies. We shall see too that there may also be a set of (related) *perceptual* factors behind the tendency speakers appear to have both to vary the height co-efficient of long vowel segments and to cause them to diphthongize or, indeed, to effect both types of alternation simultaneously.

3.3.2 The Middle English vowel shift

Even though the set of alternations involving long stressed vowels which has been the subject of this section occurs across an extended time span and with fairly diverse regional dialectal manifestations, we have been proposing that there might be a sense in which that set of changes could be viewed as some kind of uni-directional event, a type of unitary metacondition affecting the entire long vowel inventory – such an event we tentatively labelled a *vowel shift*. We have been suggesting that rather than be characterized as an unrelated set of phonological events occuring at random in the grammar through time, the mainly Middle English labializations and palatalizations to the original and subsequently derived (non-high) long vowel inventory could be seen as some kind of overall or global *process*; a process in general involving the desonorization of vowels showing extended durational characteristics. The evidence we provided suggested that this generalized occurrence began in Old English itself and with those long vowels which showed a minimal palatality in their sonority/palatality 'mix'–[ææ]. But especially from around the beginning of the twelfth century there seemed to be operative some kind of constraint on the level of sonority 'allowed' in the production and perception of long vowels. Those pure sonorants – like [aa] – showed, according to dialect, either palatal or labial intrusion, whereby they became mixed, or complex (non-pure). On the other hand, all other long vowels mixed for palatality or labiality with sonority saw an increase in the predominance of the former at the expense of the last. This essentially negative (constrain sonority) 'schema' resulted, we claimed, in a general *vowel shift* (vowel raising) effect in the phonological vowel space. The overall result of these desonorizing changes (in acoustic terms, a spectral diffusing effect) we might schematically illustrate in a highly idealized fashion represented diagramatically in Figure 3.4. We shall see below that this Middle English vowel shift was the precursor of that other 'great' vowel shift – also producing, among other things, a similar raising of long vowels – which is so well documented in the handbooks as occurring between the fifteenth and seventeenth centuries and which has ongoing effects in and ramifications for the phonology of many of the dialects of the modern language.

FIG. 3.4

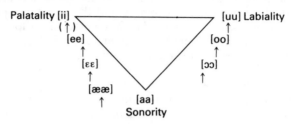

3.3.3 The irregular application of palatalization/labialization

We must mention here a problem which will feature more and more in our discussions as we proceed; the schema as we present it above in Figure 3.4 for the long vowel-shifting phenomenon in Middle English, although it serves to capture the general direction of vowel movement occasioned by the shift, is obviously highly idealized. It clearly does nothing to show that the desonorizing of the long vowel segments in the phonology was an extremely complex matter, not affecting all long vowel segments equally or in the same way. More particularly it fails to show that there are occasions when the shift can have a 'double application' or 'leapfrogging' effect; i.e. the desonorization of [ææ] to [εε] is on some occasions apparently followed up by a further desonorization of the [εε] to [ee]. We need to know what are the constraints on such re-applications of the raising process; why do they appear to occur with the long vowel segments of some lexical items and not with others? Equally our schema in Figure 3.4 does nothing to highlight one of the consequences of this apparent irregularity in the application of our phonological process. It would seem that both re-application of the vowel shift as well as its failure can lead to the same lexical item appearing in the grammar with two pronunciations. It is not uncommon, for example, to find in some Southern Middle English dialects in the fourteenth century, items like ⟨se⟩ 'sea' ⟨slee⟩ 'slay', ⟨clene⟩ 'clean', ⟨dede⟩ 'deed', etc. (derived etymologically from an Old English [ææ] stressed vowel element) having 'alternate' pronunciations like, for example, [slεε] and [slee] (Wyld 1936: pp. 29–30; Berndt 1960: pp. 41–2; Ogura 1980: p. 44). Such discrepancies in the extent of desonorization (or raising) have occasioned much controversy in the standard literature (especially Dobson 1968: sects 117–21; Mackenzie 1927) where by way of explanation there has been proposed a model for historical phonological changes which sees them as the direct result of their having *different inputs* or *sources*. That is, an [ee] level of palatalization will imply that the [ææ] from which it derives is in some way different (probably itself more palatal) than that which produced a palatalization level which only reached [ɛɛ].

Perhaps it is Wyld (1936: p. 29) who espouses this kind of position most enthusiastically in holding for a 'different origin/different fate' model as an explanation for what he considers to be divergent Middle English [ɛɛ]/[ee] outputs from the palatalization of Old English [ææ]. This Old English [ææ] has two different historical 'sources'. One of these is the lexical [ææ] descended from the [aa] of West Germanic, the other is that [ææ] derived through the operation of the Old English vowel harmony of *palatal umlaut* which palatalized the lexical Old English [aa] to [ææ] (Campbell 1959: sects 132, 193, 2.23 ff). Among others, Wyld (1936: pp. 194–96, and Wright and Wright (1973: sect. 52) argue that the [ææ] vowels from these two different sources undergo the Old and Middle English 'independent' palatalization process differentially. The derived [ææ] via *palatal umlaut* tends in Middle English to appear more commonly palatalized to the extent of [ee] than does that [ææ] from the West Germanic [aa] which is claimed normally only to reach an [ɛɛ] 'level'. But such an hypothesis has many limitations, not least is its assumption that speakers in say the fourteenth century were somehow able to 'recover' the historical sources of the [ee]/[ɛɛ] vowels in their inventory. But even if it could be demonstrated that speakers possess such historical knowledge of the origins of items in their phonology, the question would still remain as to what constituted the *phonetic* difference between the two source differing [ææ] long vowels. It is extremely difficult to produce any convincing evidence that one of these [ææ] shapes in Old English was, say, more palatal than the other.

In sections 4.2.1. and 5.2.1 below we shall outline some recent proposals which suggest that differential phonological rule application is, if anything, the norm in natural language change. Speakers will apply, not apply, reapply phonological processes on the bases of a number of different criteria – many of them of a non-phonetic kind; the nature of the lexical item itself might, for example, promote or block such an application as might considerations of a general sociolinguistic nature.

3.4 Diphthongization processes in Middle English: Middle English *Breaking*

We spent some considerable time in Chapter 2 discussing the various types of diphthongizations affecting stressed vowels in Old

English as well as the various contexts giving rise to those diphthongizations. Essentially, we saw that before what are reputed to be back consonantal segments like [ɫ], [ʀ] and [x] the stressed vowel space was split into two sections or halves, the first an inputted front vowel [æ], [i] or [e], the other a vocalic element reflecting the backness or labial 'colour' of the affecting consonantal trigger. The vowel space before this back or labial environment was regularly realized as [æa], [eo] and [io]. What we shall try to show in the sections which follow is that from as early as the twelfth century, although a precise *terminus a quo* is difficult to justify, a whole set of new diphthongs was produced in the phonology of Middle English in environments very reminiscent of those which produced the earlier Old English *Breaking*. It will be interesting to see to what extent this Middle English diphthongization process can be described as a repetition of the Old English version; indeed, a comparison between the two events will perhaps enable us to formulate more clearly what is meant by claims that phonological processes can be diachronically recurrent and that historical phonological change can perhaps be seen in terms of the re-enactment of a limited set of processes triggered by a finite set of phonetic conditioning factors. Certainly such a comparison between the two temporarily discrete events might assist us in our search for an explanation for their appearance in the speech of language users in the first instance.

Let us begin by examining the behaviour of stressed vowels between the approximate dates of 1200 and 1500 in the immediate vicinity of what the spelling suggests might be some kind of fricative consonantal element. Consider the range of spellings at Table 3.13 for the numeral '*eight*' found in Middle English manuscripts in certain dialect areas between the twelfth and fifteenth centuries. In cases like this and in as many others as

TABLE 3.13

12th & 13th centuries	14th & early 15th centuries	15th century
[ɛ]	[ɛɪ]	[ɛɪ]
⟨ehte⟩	⟨ey3t⟩	⟨eyte⟩
⟨ehhte⟩	⟨eighte⟩	
⟨eht⟩	⟨ey3the⟩	
	⟨ei3te⟩	
1	2	3

practical subsequently, we continue our policy of providing a variety of the spelling variants available at a particular period for an individual item, not merely to give the reader a 'feel' for what the orthographic representation of the language looks like, but also to try to demonstrate some of the principles by which the historical phonologist arrives at conclusions concerning spoken forms through their written representations. Recall that those diphthongs produced via the *Breaking* of front vowels before [x] in Old English had undergone monophthongization (*Smoothing*) in late Old English (see sect. 2.4). The items in column 1 above show just such monophthongal outputs – probably [ɛ] shapes resulting from the Southumbrian *Smoothing* of [æa] before [x]. Do the ⟨h⟩/⟨gh⟩/⟨3⟩ spellings therefore represent some kind of voiced or voiceless velar fricative [ɣ]/[x]?

The items in column 2 show a stressed vowel space which, from the spelling, would appear to be diphthongal: ⟨ey⟩, ⟨ei⟩. The phonetic value of this we might assume to be something like [ɛɪ]. If this is indeed the case, then it would appear that by the fourteenth century in some dialects the stressed vowel space has been 'split up' – made internally contrastive – to produce a diphthong before whatever kind of fricative ⟨h⟩/⟨3⟩/⟨gh⟩ represents. We remember that in Old English *Breaking* stressed front vowels like [e] showed a labial ([u]-like) transition in the context of back, velar fricatives like [x]. We might therefore deduce that the appearance of a front transitional vowel like [ɪ] in our ⟨eighte⟩ examples above suggests that the following fricative is also front, perhaps the *palatal* fricative [ç] and not the velar fricative [x]. Indeed, as we shall see below, the ⟨3⟩/⟨gh⟩ spellings might also represent a palatal, front fricative which is voiced: [j]. At any rate, the [ɛ] → [ɛɪ] diphthongization before the fricative [ç] is not altogether unlike that we described under Old English *Breaking* and is indeed referred to in some manuals as *Middle English Breaking*. The particular process illustrated in Table 3.13 is by and large confined to dialects south of the Humber although even there it is relatively sporadic and only appears in any numbers after the close of the thirteenth century (Jordan 1974: sect. 97). The form ⟨eyte⟩ in column 3 seems to infer that after the diphthongization has taken place, the affecting [ç] fricative context has been deleted from the syllable. However, we should bear in mind here the comments we have already made in Chapter 2 in our discussion of Old English vowel lengthening processes whereby certain segments (notably those high up on the sonorance hierarchy) could be 'substituted for', vocalized, by vowel-like elements sharing their height and backness characteristics (see sect. 2.3.6). Consequently the ⟨eyte⟩ spelling

may indicate that a process like [ɛçt] → [ɛit] has taken place,
where the [ç] has been directly vocalized to [i] and does not
represent a diphthongal output of [ɛ] triggered by a contiguous
fricative which has subsequently been deleted. At least we might
bear in mind the possibility that processes like fricative vocalization
and *Breaking* might not be unrelated. For a further discussion, see
sections 3.4.2 and 5.3.2 below. In the meanwhile, let us take a more
detailed look at the various manifestations of Middle English
Breaking.

3.4.1 Middle English *Breaking* in voiceless velar fricative environments: diphthongization of back mid vowels

Perhaps the single characteristic of Middle English *Breaking* setting
it apart from what its name infers is its Old English 'counterpart'
is the fact that its operation is not confined to affect only front
stressed vowel inputs. Rather, both front and back short and long
vowels may act as input to the process especially when they are
non-high. However, the effect on back vowels is probably later and
occurs in a more limited dialectal area than does, say, the
diphthongization of [ɛ] in palatal fricative contexts which we briefly
outlined in the last section. Let us illustrate the diphthongizing
effect on back vowels (both long and short) of a contiguous
unvoiced velar fricative consonantal element [x] across a fairly wide
temporal span of Middle English materials and, for reasons which
will become clear immediately below, in Northern dialects which
appear to evidence rather peculiar diphthongal shapes – see Table
3.14. Column 2 forms are very revealing. They are mainly taken
from fourteenth-century materials and show ⟨ou⟩, ⟨ow⟩ spellings
where only ⟨o⟩ is to be found at the stressed vowel position in
column 1. This kind of evidence suggests at its face value that the
stressed vowel space has been split into two halves, diphthongized,
the second of which shows a transition to a high, back configuration
[u]. The affecting context – the immediately following consonantal
segment – is variously spelt as ⟨ȝ⟩, ⟨h⟩, ⟨gh⟩ and would appear
to represent some kind of velar, back fricative either the voiceless
[x] or (for reasons we shall explore below) perhaps also the voiced
[ɣ]. The effect it produces upon the stressed vowel space is just
that we described for Old English *Breaking* in a similar context –
the second half of the vowel space becomes [u]-like (or labial).
However, it is important to recall our discussion in section 2.3.3
where we showed that many scholars had explained the
appearance of a new [u] element in Old English *Breaking* as the
result of the muscular movement involved in the transition from a
front vowel segment like [e], to a back fricative configuration like

TABLE 3.14

13–16th century	13th–15th century	15th century	Northern dialects
[o]/[oo]	[ou]	[uu]	
OE ⟨genōh⟩ 'enough'			
⟨inoh⟩	⟨inouh⟩	⟨enughe⟩	⟨enewe⟩
⟨anog⟩	⟨anou3⟩	⟨enugh⟩	
⟨enogh⟩	⟨inowghe⟩		
	⟨inou⟩		
	⟨ynow⟩		
OE ⟨plōg⟩ 'plough'			
⟨ploh⟩	⟨plou3⟩	⟨plughe⟩	⟨pleugh⟩
⟨plogh⟩	⟨plow3⟩	⟨plugh⟩	⟨plewes⟩
	⟨plough⟩		⟨plewger⟩
	⟨plowhe⟩		
	⟨plow⟩		
	⟨plo⟩		
OE ⟨dohter⟩ 'daughter'			
⟨dohhter⟩	⟨dou3ter⟩		⟨deu3tren⟩
⟨dohter⟩	⟨douhtur⟩		
	⟨dowhter⟩		
	⟨dowter⟩		
	⟨doutres⟩		
1	2	3	4

[x]. Some kind of [u] 'off-glide' was said to have been produced by that tongue positional shift between extreme horizontal articulatory positions. But clearly no such argument can be appealed to for those cases in Table 3.14 since the stressed vowel space in items like ⟨dohter⟩ is already back, and no front-back tongue placement transition is required. So we may have to remain sceptical about the kind of 'explanation' we have offered for Old English *Breaking*. Instead, we shall explore the possibility a little later below that the second half of the vowel space becomes [u]

coloured just because segments like [x] can be themselves rather
[u]-like in their physical (especially) acoustic characteristics.

Notice too that Middle English *Breaking* does not appear to
show any kind of diphthong height harmony operation like that
we found for its earlier 'manifestation' in Old English (sect.
2.3.1). We do not, for example, find the second – [u] – half of
the diphthongal vowel space taking on the height characteristics
of the first half, such that [ou] → [oo]. Rather, as the instances
like ⟨plughe⟩ in column 3 suggest, the whole vowel space can
become entirely [u] coloured; the height/backness features of the
non-syllabic half become generalized. However it is worth noting
that our ⟨dohtor⟩ example, with its short stressed vowel space,
shows no raised [uu] forms in column 3, a fact which might
perhaps lead us to speculate that the *Breaking* diphthong produced
by short stressed vowels was [ɔu] – with a low mid initial element
– rather than the [ou] characteristically produced from long vowel
inputs to the process. We have already commented in sect. 2.3.2
on how 'long' Old English *Breaking* produced diphthongs are
associated in their subsequent development with 'raising'; and the
reader should recall similar behaviour affecting such 'long' diphthongs when they underwent monophthongization or *Smoothing*
in late Old English and early Middle English (see sects 2.4 and
2.4.2). However, we must stress that the overall effect of the
Middle English *Breaking* of back vowels like [o] is rather patchy
and even in the fourteenth and fifteenth centuries, especially in
some Northern regions of the country, monophthongal [o]/[oo]
vowel shapes remain contiguous with [x]/[ɣ] and we regularly
find spellings like ⟨dohter⟩, ⟨enogh⟩, ⟨bogh⟩.

The special Northern developments illustrated in column 4
above, are worth examining at this point. Around the end of the
thirteenth century there is evidence to suggest that in such dialects
[oo] sounds were being independently raised and fronted to [üü] –
notice some Modern Scottish English pronunciations of words like
⟨foot⟩ and ⟨book⟩ which derive from forms with long stressed
[oo] vowels (cf. OE ⟨fōt⟩ and ⟨bōc⟩) as [füt] and [bük]
showing a recent shortening). A change like this also appears to
have occurred with those [oo] vowels in the vicinity [x]/[ɣ], such that,
for example, [oox] → [üüx]. However, by the end of the fifteenth
century, the first element of the long vowel had become fronted
or unrounded, through a process of dissimilation, leaving a
diphthongal combination like [iu], a combination frequently spelt
⟨ew⟩ or ⟨eu⟩. In consequence, we find the Scottish or Northern
English forms (with fricative 'loss') – ⟨bewes⟩ *'boughs'* and

⟨slewen⟩ '*they slew*' (Southumbrian [slouən]). For a fuller discussion of dissimilatory processes affecting long vowels and diphthongs, see our treatment of the *English vowel shift* below (sect. 4.2.2) and Donegan (1978: pp. 113 ff).

The back mid vowel which was subject to Middle English *Breaking* in the examples cited in Table 3.14 above was the high [o]/[oo] version. Recall from our discussion in sect. 3.3.1 that in early Middle English there was produced another set of long mid back vowels from the raising of Old English [aa] vowels: cf. changes like OE [haam] ⟨ham⟩ → early ME [hɔɔm] '*home*'. In a pre-[x]/[ɣ] context this [ɔɔ] vowel was also affected by Middle English *Breaking*, producing a [ɔu] output which was not subject to the fifteenth-century raising to [uu] (despite its association with long vowel contexts) as were the [ou] inputs characteristic of the items in column 2 in Table 3.14 above. Consider the data in Table 3.15.

TABLE 3.15 Old English ⟨dāh⟩ '*bread*'

12th–15th centuries	14th–15th centuries	Northern dialects
[ɔɔ]	[ɔu]	[a]/[au]
⟨doh⟩	⟨dowhg⟩	⟨daugh⟩
⟨dogh⟩	⟨dough⟩	⟨daghe⟩
	⟨douw⟩	
	⟨dowe⟩	
1	2	3

The column 3 forms show a peculiarly Northern development resulting from the fact that there the [aa] → [ɔɔ] raising did not generally occur in early Middle English. Nevertheless, a form like ⟨daugh⟩ would suggest that even a low, back vowel space like [aa] could have its second element 'coloured' by the contiguity of an [x]/[ɣ] to produce some kind of [au] diphthong.

In both Tables 3.14 and 3.15, we have subdivided the second column, where the lower division forms appear to show stressed vowel space diphthongization but 'loss' of the affecting [x]/[ɣ] context, thus ⟨inou⟩, ⟨plow⟩, ⟨dowter⟩ and ⟨douw⟩. This kind of phenomenon we noted too in our discussion of Old English *Breaking* in [j] contexts (see sect. 2.3.6 above) and there appear to be at least two possible explanations for the development, and these we shall discuss in section 3.4.2 immediately below.

3.4.1(1) Diphthongization of low vowels

Those low vowels (both short and long) which developed in Middle English as the result of the monophthongization (*Smoothing*) of West Saxon [ææ] diphthongs as well as from the shortening of lexically long [ææ] vowels, can act as input to the process of Middle English *Breaking* before [x]. Consider in Table 3.16 the sets of spellings to be found throughout the Middle English period for the items corresponding to Old English ⟨hleahtor⟩ '*laughter*' and ⟨ræhte⟩ '*he reached*'. Once again a comparison between the monophthongal stressed vowel space in the forms of column 1 and the digraphic representations of ⟨au⟩ and ⟨aw⟩ in column 3 suggest that a change like [a] → [au] has occurred in that vowel space when contiguous with the voiceless velar [x] fricative represented by spellings such as ⟨gh⟩, ⟨h⟩ and ⟨ʒ⟩. The monophthongal low, back forms in column 2 are especially typical of Northern dialects where we can also find alternations such as ⟨saʒ⟩/⟨saugh⟩ '*he saw*'; ⟨aʒte⟩/⟨aughte⟩ '*he fought*'; ⟨faʒt⟩/⟨faught⟩ '*he faught*' and so on. However, even in the dialects where this *Breaking* to [au] is common, the effect is nevertheless patchy and [a] is still frequently to be found there contiguous with [x] even in late Middle English texts.

The instances in column 4 are interesting since they seem to show the possibility of a monophthongization of the Old English [æa] diphthong to an [ɛ] as well as an [æ] vowel space in late Old English and early Middle English (sect. 2.4.2 above) and such that, say, [hlæaxtər] WS ⟨hleahtor⟩ → [hlɛçtər] where, notice,

TABLE 3.16

12th century	13th–14th centuries	14th–15th centuries	13th–15th centuries
[æ]/[a]	[a]	[au]	[ɛɪ]/[ɛ]
⟨læhtræs⟩ ⟨lahtræs⟩	⟨laghter⟩ ⟨lahtre⟩ ⟨laʒter⟩	⟨laughter⟩ ⟨lauʒtre⟩ ⟨lauhter⟩	⟨lɛɪʒter⟩ ⟨leihter⟩ ⟨hleihtres⟩
	⟨rahte⟩ ⟨raght⟩ ⟨raʒt⟩	⟨rauhte⟩ ⟨rawght⟩ ⟨raughte⟩ ⟨rawghte⟩	⟨reght⟩ ⟨reygte⟩
1	2	3	4

the new front stressed vowel appears to have provoked a fronting of the velar fricative [x] to [ç]. In the Middle English instances in column 4, this [ɛç] combination has resulted in a splitting of the vowel space to realize the [ɛi] diphthong characteristic of the Middle English *Breaking* we have already discussed in section 3.4.

3.4.2 Middle English *Breaking* in voiced fricative contexts: Middle English [ǰ] *Breaking*

The majority of scholarly accounts of the *Breaking* process in both Old and Middle English tend to constrain the occurrence of this stressed vowel diphthongization event to pre-fricative contexts which are *voiceless*. Old English *Breaking* was triggered when stressed front vowels had to their right a continuant consonantal element like [x], while the Middle English 'equivalent' of the process, affecting vowels of either backness value, was induced by a contiguous [ç] or [x]. But we have already suggested above that the stressed vowel space in some Old English dialects could be modified when contiguous with a *voiced* version of the palatal fricative–[ǰ]. We observed, for instance in section 2.3.6, how stressed vowel diphthongization could be induced in such a phonetic environment in late Old English – recall such alternants as [fræǰn]/[fræiǰn] '*he asked*'; [heǰ]/[heiǰ] '*hay*' – while earlier in section 2.2.2 we noted the lengthening effect on short vowels of a contiguous voiced palatal [ǰ] or velar [ɣ], as in such examples as [reǰn]/[reen] '*rain*' and [wæɣn]/[wææn] '*wagon*'. We shall attempt to show in this section that in many Middle English dialects as well the stressed vowel space contiguous with voiced fricative segments like [ǰ] and [ɣ] became linearly complex (i.e. comprised of two (often contrasting) halves). But the process is, as we shall see, far from being a simple one and speakers appear to have utilized several stratagems to express the acoustic information they perceived when stressed vowel space appeared alongside such voiced fricative segments. Consider the data in Table 3.17 (Jordan 1974: pp. 120–3). Such data are very similar to those we presented in Table 2.29 for late Old English pre-[ǰ] *Breaking* (Campbell 1959: sect. 269). As the column 1 ⟨daȝ⟩ form suggests, undiphthongized stressed vowel space could still occur as late as the twelfth century, especially in texts from Northern dialectal areas. Column 2 shapes seem unambiguously to show that some kind of [ɛ] → [ɛi] diphthongization occurred in the stressed vowel space in the vicinity of the voiced [ǰ] fricative, a process identical to that we saw in such alternants as ⟨eht⟩/⟨eyȝt⟩/⟨eighte⟩ '*eight*' in voiceless [ç] neighbourhoods in Table 3.13 above. Column 3 shapes appear

TABLE 3.17 Middle English [ǰ] *Breaking*

West Saxon Old English			12th–15th-century Middle English		
[æ]			**[æ[i]/[ɛi]**		
⟨dæʒ⟩	[dæǰ]	'*day*'	⟨daʒ⟩		⟨dei⟩ ⟨dai⟩ ⟨day⟩
⟨clæg⟩	[klæǰ]	'*clay*'	⟨cleiʒ⟩ ⟨cleigh⟩		⟨clay⟩ ⟨clei⟩ ⟨clai⟩
[e]			**[ei]/[æi]**		
⟨hēg⟩ ⟨hīg⟩	[heeǰ] [hiiǰ]	'*hay*'	⟨heigh⟩ ⟨heiʒe⟩ ⟨heyʒ⟩		⟨hai⟩ ⟨hei⟩ ⟨ai⟩
			1	2	3

to suggest that there has been some effacement of the affecting [ǰ] context after the diphthongal innovation – cf. too the ⟨eyte⟩ spelling in Table 3.13. But before we offer any explanation for this diphthongization and possible [ǰ] effacement, let us look (in Table 3.18) at what appears to be evidence for a 'parallel' Middle English *Breaking* of back stressed vowels when they are contiguous with a following voiced velar fricative, [ɣ]. The twelfth-through-fourteenth-century spellings there for the Old English ⟨ploga⟩, ⟨agan⟩, ⟨boga⟩ and ⟨dragan⟩ items show a complicated enough picture of the *Breaking* process (Luick 1964: sects 372–3). As the column 1 shapes suggest, undiphthongized vowel space could be found throughout the period in this pre-[ɣ] environment, although such forms are probably most typical of Kentish and West Midland dialects and are rare even there after 1400 (Berndt 1960: pp. 51–55). The column 2 forms seem to show that the voiced velar [ɣ] segment has induced a splitting up of the precedent stressed vowel space into two halves or components the second of which shows a labial, [u] colour; a process clearly parallel to the Middle English *Breaking* in [x] environments which we have outlined above in section 3.4.1. However, on closer examination our data in Table 3.18 present us with a rather more complex situation. For instance, the spelling representations in column 1 for what is historically the

TABLE 3.18 Middle English [ɣ] *Breaking*

OE ⟨ploga⟩ 'plough' [ploɣə]		
⟨plo3⟩, ⟨plog⟩ ⟨ploh⟩, ⟨ploch⟩	⟨plough⟩, ⟨plouh⟩ ⟨plowhe⟩, ⟨plou3⟩	⟨plou⟩ ⟨plouw⟩ ⟨plowis⟩ ⟨plowes⟩
OE ⟨agan⟩ *'to own'* [aɣən]		
⟨aghe⟩, ⟨a3en⟩ ⟨a3hen⟩, ⟨ogen⟩	⟨ough⟩, ⟨ouh⟩ ⟨augh⟩	⟨oun⟩, ⟨ou⟩ ⟨owen⟩
OE ⟨boga⟩ *'bow'* [boɣə]		
⟨bo3e⟩, ⟨bogh⟩ ⟨boch⟩, ⟨bohe⟩	⟨bough⟩ ⟨bouwhes⟩	⟨bow⟩, ⟨bouwe⟩ ⟨bawe⟩, ⟨boues⟩ ⟨bowe⟩
OE ⟨dragan⟩ *'to draw'*		
⟨dra3hen⟩ ⟨dra3en⟩ ⟨drahen⟩ ⟨dragen⟩	⟨drauhen⟩ ⟨drau3en⟩ ⟨he drough⟩	⟨drau⟩ ⟨drawen⟩ ⟨he drowe⟩
•I	2	3

voiced velar [ɣ] fricative are clearly open to a number of interpretations: ⟨gh⟩, ⟨g⟩, ⟨h⟩, ⟨ch⟩, ⟨3⟩ and ⟨3h⟩ orthographic shapes are to be found for this segment. While the ⟨g⟩ and ⟨3⟩ combinations appear regularly in both Old and Middle English orthographic inventories as representations for [ɣ] (Campbell 1959: sect. 50; Wyld 1927: sects 86 and 153; Wright and Wright 1973: sects 290–9), those in ⟨ch⟩ and ⟨h⟩ are equally regularly used to denote the voiceless [x]. Indeed there is evidence to suggest that syllable and especially word final devoicing of both voiced obstruents and voiced fricatives is a common process in the historical phonology of English (Jordan 1974: sect. 197; Wright and Wright 1973: sects 238–9; Campbell 1959: sect. 446; and sect. 3.5 below) – cf. such alternants as ⟨bind⟩/⟨bint⟩, ⟨strengþ⟩/⟨strenkþ⟩. If such a [ɣ] → [x] devoicing has occurred in all syllable final positions, then the set of instances in column 2 in Table 3.18 could be entered under the Middle English *Breaking* in pre-[x] contexts outlined in sect.

3.4.1 above. Yet the ⟨plouʒ⟩, ⟨ough⟩, ⟨bough⟩ and ⟨drauʒen⟩ shapes would still appear to lend support to a [ɣ] diphthong-producing context.

Column 3 forms are of especial interest and may shed some light upon the question of the voice value of the velar fricative. In that column we see a selection of items with a stressed vowel space composed of two contrasting halves, but where any etymological [ɣ] ([x]) trigger is absent. Similar types of example to this we have already mentioned in our discussion of [ĵ] *Breaking* (Table 3.17) where we witnessed what appeared to be [ĵ] deletion subsequent to diphthong inducement – cf. the ⟨cleiʒ⟩/⟨clei⟩ and ⟨heigh⟩/⟨hai⟩ alternants. In this context also recall our discussion in section 2.2.2 dealing with the so-called 'compensatory' lengthening of stressed vowels in pre- and subsequently 'deleted' [ĵ] fricative contexts: [reĵn]/[reen] '*rain*'. Innovations of these types leave us with the problem as to whether we are dealing with some kind of trigger effacement after that trigger has produced its effect; thus [heĵ] → [heiĵ] → [hei], or some other process whereby the language user interprets, processes segments like [ĵ] and [ɣ] as though they were the pure vowel second-half elements of a diphthongal vowel space.

There is little doubt that the voiced [ĵ] and [ɣ] fricatives bear a considerable resemblance in their acoustic 'fingerprint' to the palatal and labial pure vowels [i] and [u] respectively (Maddieson 1984: ch. 6; Fant 1956). In the simplest of terms, the constriction formed in the speech tract for for both [ĵ] and [i] tends to produce a signal with a relatively high acoustic pitch, whereas the effect of the [ɣ] and [u] type of tract narrowing is to lower that relative pitch. Very generally, palatal signals generate a relatively high-pitch tone, labials a low. If therefore the acoustic effect of the palatal/velar fricatives and palatal/labial vowels is so similar, then speakers might interpret such signals as 'interchangeable' given the appropriate phonological circumstances (Durand 1954; Ohala and Lorentz 1977). We have already drawn attention to the fact that speakers have some kind of knowledge as to the componential structure of suprasegmental events such as the syllable (see sect. 3.2 above). Syllable structure, we argued, comprised three components – a central, peak item, around which were grouped onset and a coda elements. In addition, it is often claimed that the peak + coda element (often referred to as the *rhyme*) can itself have some kind of 'ideal' or canonical configuration, such as in Table 3.19. Thus, well formed rhymes (with full coda) for English could include shapes such as [it], [iit] and [eit], where the peak is viewed as potentially at least composed of a two element or twin half vowel space (Giegerich 1985: pp. 121–2). What we

TABLE 3.19 Rhyme template

Rhyme		
Peak		Coda
vowel	vowel	consonant

wish to tentatively suggest here is that when speakers are exposed to an item with a voiced fricative final ([ǰ]/[ɣ]) rhyme coda, there is a tendency for such a configuration, say in an item like [boɣ-]

TABLE 3.20

Rhyme		
Peak		Coda
vowel	vowel	
[o]	Empty	[ɣ]

in Table 3.20 to be interpreted as if it were in Table 3.21. The original fricative coda, according to this interpretation, has not been deleted following some diphthongizing effect on the stressed

TABLE 3.21

Rhyme		
Peak		Coda
[o]	[u]	Empty

vowel space; rather, given the highly vowel-like nature of such voiced fricative segments, they are reinterpreted by speakers as if they were the second, non-syllabic half of the peak vowel space: the process often referred to as *vocalization*. As we shall again see immediately below in our discussion of Middle English *Breaking* in sonorant [l]/[r] environments, a stressed vowel space before such [ǰ]/[ɣ] fricatives allows for at least two perceptual stratagems. While both involve the vowel space becoming linearly complex (i.e. where the peak is no longer viewed as second-half empty), the one achieves this by the complete suppression of the relatively weak consonantal component in the [j]/[ɣ] internal structure (see Table 1.2) to leave behind a 'pure' palatal or labial [i]/[u] vowel; the other 'spreads' the vocalicness associated with the voiced fricatives into the vacant non-syllabic slot in the peak area but leaves the coda still filled by the [j]/[ɣ] segment. Although we have not provided sufficient evidence to prove the assertion, even though *voiceless* fricative vocalizations appear to be found (cf. the ⟨dowter⟩, ⟨ynow⟩ instances in Table 3.14), replacement of fricatives by pure vocalic elements appears to occur more readily when the former are *voiced*.

Let us return to Table 3.18 where the items in column 3 would unequivocally appear to suggest the implementation of the first of the two perceptual stratagems tentatively outlined in the last paragraph. Yet there still remain some problems: what, for example, are we to make of examples such as ⟨plowis⟩, ⟨owen⟩ and ⟨drawen⟩? What does the ⟨w⟩ symbol represent in such cases? We have assumed in many of the column 2 shapes, e.g. ⟨bowhes⟩ and ⟨plowhe⟩, that the ⟨w⟩ is an orthographic representation for the labial vowel which is the second half of a diphthongal vowel space. If we apply this interpretation to an instance like ⟨plowis⟩ *'ploughs'*, we would appear to be suggesting that the item has a two syllable structure like $\{_1plou_1\}\{_2əs_2\}$, where the syllable one coda is *empty*. However, if we interpret the ⟨w⟩ symbol as the phonetic [w] segment and therefore as some kind of a sonorant consonant (Lass and Anderson 1975: sect. 3.2), the syllable structure of the item might now appear as $\{_1plo\{_2w_1\}əs_2\}$, where [w] simultaneously terminates syllable one and onsets syllable two (see below, sects 3.5 and 3.5.1). But before we could accept this second interpretation we should require to examine in more detail what are the phonetic characteristics of [w] and how such a segment could come to be derived from [ɣ].

In order to suggest answers to some of these questions, let us consider an important set of innovations affecting the voiced velar fricative [ɣ] throughout the Middle English period although, as we shall see, there is some evidence for it as a minor phenomenon in Old English as well. Consider the data in Table 3.22 with Old and Middle English items realizing [ɣ] and [rɣ] clusters in intervocalic positions. Column 2 forms seem to suggest that in an immediately post sonorant [l]/[r] environment, the voiced velar fricative [ɣ] has come to be perceived as a [w]-type segment, and not as a non-syllabic [u] labial vowel (Berndt 1960: pp. 129–31, 160–1; Jordan 1974: sect. 186; Brunner 1952: sect. 38; Wright and Wright 1973: sect.

TABLE 3.22

West Saxon Old English		Middle English 13th–15th centuries		
⟨galga⟩ [galɣə]	'gallows'	⟨galghes⟩ ⟨galhes⟩	⟨galwes⟩	⟨galowes⟩ ⟨galewis⟩
⟨halga⟩ [halɣə]	'saint'	⟨halghe⟩ ⟨halȝe⟩ ⟨halhen⟩	⟨halwes⟩ ⟨halwen⟩	⟨halowes⟩ ⟨halewes⟩ ⟨halowen⟩
				⟨haligh⟩ ⟨halogh⟩
⟨fealga⟩ [fæalɣə]	'fallow'	⟨falghe⟩	⟨falwe⟩ ⟨falwes⟩	⟨falow⟩
				⟨falugh⟩
⟨morgen⟩ [mɔrɣən]	'morning'	⟨morghen⟩ ⟨morgan⟩	⟨morwen⟩ ⟨morwoun⟩	⟨morewan⟩ ⟨morowen⟩
				⟨maregan⟩ ⟨mareȝen⟩
		1	2	3

298). The Old English alternants ⟨earh⟩/⟨earwe⟩/⟨arewe⟩ 'arrow' suggest that this type of process had an ever earlier pedigree (Campbell 1959: sect. 360). But what kinds of factors could motivate such an [l/rɣ] → [l/rw] change and why, if it is going to mutate at all, should [ɣ] alternate with [w]? Let us address this second question first since it will also have some considerable bearing on the column 3 data presented in Table 3.18. The segment [w] is traditionally described as *labio-velar* in its articulatory characteristics; that is, such a sound simultaneously exhibits features which can independently occur in velar segments like [u] and labial segments such as [f] or [β]. The mechanism whereby [w] segments are realized is one where there are *two* simultaneous constrictions in the oral tract – one at the velar, the other at the labial position. The acoustic effect of a constriction at either of these points in the tract is to lower the overall relative pitch of the segment; a double constriction characteristic of the labio-velar [w] emphasizes this lowering effect. Additionally, the acoustic effect of either constriction in isolation is very similar to the extent that the production of one, say a velic constriction, may lead to the perception of the other (Ohala and Lorentz 1977; Lehiste 1967; Maddieson 1984: ch. 6). Likewise the doubly articulated labio-velar [w] can be interpreted as, alternate with or mutate to, segments which are either labial or velar. For instance the Indo-European labio-velar regularly becomes realized in many of its 'daughter' languages as a labial – cf. the [kw]/[p] contrast between Latin ⟨equus⟩ [ɛkwus] and Greek ⟨hippo⟩ [hɪpo], while in those languages where the labio-velar [w] may determine the articulatory place of a contiguous nasal, it is the *velar* [ŋ] nasal which surfaces: cf. the [wee]/[ŋwee] '*white clay*' alternants cited by Welmers (1962) for the African language of Kpelle. Such an acoustic similarity between velar constrictions such as [ɣ] and the labio-velar [w] might not only provide us with a physical motivation for the fricative/glide alternation in the [halɣə]/[halwə] instances in Table 3.22 but also make us the more prepared to accept the ⟨plowis⟩ type instances in Table 3.18 as representative of a $\{_1plo\{_2w_1\}es_2\}$ syllabic construction rather than one like $\{_1plou_1\}\{_2əs_2\}$. Yet the phonetic/phonological conditions under which a segment like [ɣ] is realized as a pure [u] labial vowel rather than as a glide [w] are too elaborate to investigate in a general survey of this type.

It is interesting to recall that the [lɣ]/[rɣ] trigger for the change under discussion here is very like one of the most powerful contexts for the inducement of Old English *Breaking*. Sonorant initial clusters such as [lx] and [rx] were strong triggers for that process which made the stressed vowel space linearly complex – cf. such shapes as ⟨hearh⟩ [hæarx] '*temple*' and ⟨eolh⟩ [eolx] '*elk*' (see sect. 2.3.1(4)). In such cases, the post-sonorant fricative was, of course, voiceless. But given the fact that Middle English *Breaking* is unconstrained as to the backness value of the stressed vowel it affects, it is surprising not to find some sort of diphthongization in what looks so likely a *Breaking* trigger as [l/rɣ]. But we argued that the additional linear complexity to the stressed vowel space was not the only change brought about by both Old and Middle English *Breaking*; the syllable containing the sonorant initial cluster was also perceived to be 'more vowelly' – both vowel slots in the peak position had come to be filled. We might tentatively suggest that just such a *Breaking* indeed occurs in these pre [lɣ] contexts, but in a guise which has led many other writers to view it as a totally unrelated phenomenon. We shall suggest below (in sect. 3.4.6) that there are in fact alternative phonological stratagems for manifesting the effects we associate with *Breaking*. We might merely point to the possibility at this point that the column 3 ⟨morowen⟩ types, with their extra syllabicity component, might represent the form of such stratagems.

3.4.3 Diphthongization by [w] vocalization

It should by now come as no surprise that, given the acoustic similarity of effect of constrictions in the labial and velar tract areas, labial [w] segments, especially when they appear in syllable coda position, should be 'heard' as an integral part of the vowel peak area, in much the same fashion as we claimed for the vocalic mutations to [ɣ] and [j] fricatives above. Consider the data in Table 3.23. The column 1 and 2 forms are again interesting in that they appear to provide evidence for the perceptually 'ambiguous' nature

TABLE 3.23

West Saxon Old English		13th–15th-century Middle English	
⟨eowu⟩ [eowu]	'female sheep'	⟨ewe⟩ ⟨awe⟩	⟨eu⟩ ⟨yeue⟩ ⟨yowe⟩ ⟨yoo⟩ ⟨ouwe⟩ ⟨owherde⟩
⟨dēaw⟩ [dæaw]	'dew'	⟨dewe⟩ ⟨dæw⟩ ⟨deawe⟩ ⟨deuʒ⟩ ⟨deuh⟩ ⟨dieuʒ⟩	⟨deu⟩ ⟨dywe⟩
⟨fēawe⟩	'few'	⟨feawe⟩ ⟨veawe⟩ ⟨fæwe⟩ ⟨fewe⟩ ⟨feyʒ⟩	⟨fæu⟩ ⟨feue⟩
⟨clawu⟩ [klawu]	'claw'	⟨clawe⟩ ⟨clauwes⟩ ⟨clawes⟩ ⟨clowes⟩	⟨clou⟩ ⟨claues⟩ ⟨clauen⟩ ⟨cleys⟩ ⟨cleu⟩ ⟨clei⟩
		1	2

of the [w] glide segment. Its high vocalic status on the sonority hierarchy enables it to be interpreted as the (labial) right hand half of the stressed vowel space; what had been for one set of speakers a sequence of:

ONSET	PEAK		CODA
	vowel$_1$	vowel$_2$	
[d]	[e]	EMPTY	[w]

has become interpreted by another set as having the complex vowel peak, empty coda structure of:

ONSET	PEAK		CODA
	vowel$_1$	vowel$_2$	
[d]	[e]	[u]	EMPTY

The ⟨yeue⟩, ⟨yowe⟩, ⟨yoo⟩ spellings are especially interesting in this regard in that they appear to suggest a development (mainly in Northern dialectal areas from the late thirteenth century) whereby the innovatory [eu] diphthong underwent a 'syllabicity shift' (see sect. 2.4.5 above) such that from a linearly complex combination where syllable one [e] was the more prominent, there occurred an innovation with the effect that syllable two [u] came to be perceived as the central peak component, the [e] being viewed as on the periphery of the stressed vowel space. This peripheral, marginal status brought with it a reduction in vocalic content or prominence, such that [e] was perceived as its 'equivalent' palatal 'glide' [j], thus the ⟨yeue⟩, ?[ju] and ⟨dywe⟩, ?[dju] shapes (for a fuller discussion of this phenomenon, see the data in Table 3.34 below). It is worth observing as well that in some of the column 1 items, where the [w] coda is generally retained, we see what appears to be some kind of [w] → [ɣ]/[x] fricativization process – ⟨deuh⟩, ⟨deuȝ⟩ and ⟨feyȝ⟩. Given what we have said above about the 'interchangability' of the velar fricative and labio-velar segments (cf. the [galɣa]/[galwe] alternation types), such a development should cause little surprise, and it is a common feature of many modern Scottish English speakers who often realize (voiceless) palatal glides as fricatives: cf. [šü] realizations for [hj̊ü] 'Hugh'.

3.4.4 Middle English *Breaking* in the sonorant consonant [r] and [l] environment

We have already seen in Chapter 2 how stressed vowels in the vicinity of sonorants like [r] and [l] – especially, we argued, when the latter were labial – provoked a splitting up of the front stressed vowel space to manifest a labial, [u]-like, second half. Thus, *[æld] → *[æuld] → [æald] 'old'. Is there a parallel development in Middle English? The answer is in the positive, but only to a very limited extent. The pre-[r]/[l] vowel space in Middle English times is an environment subject to a great many apparently different kinds of influences, notably durational increase and even raising and lowering. Diphthongization, however, is not particularly common in such contexts although it does occur, especially in pre-[l] environments. Yet even in this context the process is severely dialectally constrained in a fashion which is as yet not completely clear – Berndt (1960: pp. 66 ff) – and it appears in almost all its manifestations to be relatively late (mainly fifteenth-century). Consider the data in Table 3.24. Columns 2 and 3 seem to show that in this pre-[l] environment the stressed vowel space was subject to the same two kinds of perceptual 'constraints' as were operative,

TABLE 3.24 Middle English *Breaking* in pre-[l] sonorant contexts

12th–13th centuries	*14th–15th centuries*	
'gold'		
⟨gold⟩	⟨gould⟩	⟨goud⟩
⟨goold⟩	⟨gowlde⟩	
	⟨gouldes⟩	
'hall'		
⟨hale⟩	⟨haul⟩	⟨Haustede⟩
⟨halle⟩	⟨haule⟩	⟨Houstede⟩
⟨alle⟩	⟨haull⟩	
	⟨hawlle⟩	
'bold'		
⟨bold⟩	⟨bauld⟩	⟨bowde⟩
⟨boold⟩		⟨bowdly⟩
'false'; Old French ⟨fals⟩/⟨faus⟩		
⟨fals⟩	⟨fauls⟩	⟨faus⟩
⟨vals⟩	⟨faulssemblant⟩	⟨faussemblant⟩
1	2	3

as we have just observed, in the pre-voiced-fricative [ǰ] and [ɣ] contexts. Column 2 types show the vocalicness associated with the relatively vowel-like [l] 'spreading' into the precedent vowel space, thus filling out the potentially two slot peak area there. Column 3 shapes suggest an [l] vocalization; the vowelly [l] being perceived as the second (labial) half of the stressed vowel area; as a result some affected items are reinterpreted as being coda empty. It must be stressed, however, that column 2 types appear to be extremely rare (at least from the data available in the *Middle English Dictionary*). Those in column 3 are perhaps marginally more common, especially in Northern texts, although the ⟨Hau-⟩ for ⟨hall⟩ types are only apparently to be found in place names from Devon and Lancashire (EPN, 24, Ekwall 1922). It might be argued too that the ⟨faus-⟩ shapes in column 3 represent a direct 'borrowing' from French where a very similar [l] vocalization process had been operative (Pope 1966: sects. 135, 389) but given the phonetic 'naturalness' of such an [al]/[au] alternation, we can assume that both [fauls] and [faus] shapes are just as likely to be a genuine production of the phonology of late Middle English itself.

3.4.5 Middle English *Breaking* in other sonorant and fricative environments

A central point which we have been trying to stress in our discussions of both Old and Middle English *Breaking* is that the 'contamination' of the right hand side of the stressed vowel space was not simply a response to the dictates of some mechanical lingual muscular transition between contiguous segments contrasting in their horizontal place of articulation – i.e. between a front vowel segment like, say, [e] and some back fricative [x] or sonorant [ʀ] or [ɫ]. The kind of diphthongal innovations associated with our *Breaking* phenomena were essentially constrained to occur in post-stressed vowel contexts which were themselves highly 'vowelly'. Recall our discussion in at section 1.3 where we expressed the view held by many modern theoretical phonologists that the segment inventories of natural languages should be viewed as existing along a *scale* of either relative vocalic or consonantal prominence. Speech sounds were to be seen as part of a sonority hierarchy (Lass 1984: pp. 285 ff; Anderson and Jones 1977: ch. 3; Anderson and Ewen 1987: pp. 97–100). According to this model all phonetic segments are valued along a parameter which expresses their relative vocalic content; all segments are seen as part of a *scale* or *hierarchy* reflecting the degree of relative vocalic- or consonantal-ness in their make up or composition; such a make up could be defined according to a number of criteria both acoustic and articulatory and might include, for instance, relative degree of stricture in the oral tract associated with a segment's production. At one terminus of such a scale would be vowel segments themselves (although not all would be classified as equally vocalic), voiceless obstruents would occupy the other while segments like the sonorants [r], [l]. [m], [n] and so on, while they demonstrate some consonantal characteristics, would nevertheless have an internal structure placing them relatively high up near the 'pure' vocalic terminus of the scale:

Sonority scale

obstruents fricatives sonorants glides vowels

An essential element in the *Breaking* triggering context, we argued, was the presence of some relatively highly vocalically prominent segment to the right of the stressed vowel; post-stressed vowel voiceless obstruents therefore tended not to produce any effect on the preceding vowel space of a diphthongizing (or lengthening) kind.

In the light of these observations we might wish to ask the question as to whether stressed vowel diphthongization could occur in a wider range of sonorant and fricative type environments, a range that might, for instance, include the nasal sonorants as well as [r] and [l] and fricative types like [š], [ž], [č] and [ğ] as well as [x] and [ç]. That there is a stressed vowel diphthongiz-ation in the immediate context of an [š] fricative in most Middle English dialects in the thirteenth and fourteenth centuries can be seen from the selection of orthographic representations in Table 3.25 for the items ⟨fresch⟩ '*fresh* ' and ⟨asce⟩ '*ash*

TABLE 3.25

1	2	3
⟨fresh⟩	⟨freish⟩	⟨firsh⟩
⟨frech⟩		⟨firesc⟩
⟨fresse⟩		⟨verisse⟩
⟨freesh⟩		
⟨asshe⟩	⟨aisshe⟩	⟨esshe⟩
⟨ash⟩	⟨aish⟩	⟨esk⟩
⟨asse⟩	⟨hais⟩	⟨esche⟩
⟨has⟩	⟨aisse⟩	⟨ex⟩
	⟨Aychs⟩	⟨hees⟩
	⟨Ays⟩	

tree'. The ⟨ei⟩, ⟨ai⟩, ⟨ay⟩ spellings in column 2 would point to some kind of [e]/[eɪ] alternation in the stressed vowel space in this pre-[š] context, while some of the ⟨i⟩ and ⟨e⟩ spellings in column 3 point to the possibility of raising as well – both innovations showing an overall increase in vowel ⟨palatality⟩ in the [š] fricative environment (Jordan 1974: sect. 102; Luick 1964: sect. 404).

TABLE 3.26

1	2	3
⟨frensch⟩	⟨freinsch⟩	⟨vrinsh⟩
⟨frenss⟩	⟨freinch⟩	
⟨frence⟩	⟨vreinch⟩	
⟨french⟩	⟨freins⟩	
	⟨friensh⟩	
⟨henge⟩	⟨heinge⟩	⟨hyngys⟩
⟨heengis⟩	⟨heyngges⟩	⟨hinge⟩
⟨heenge⟩		

Consider again (in Table 3.26) a set of orthographic variants for stressed mid vowels in nasal sonorant contexts illustrated from the items ⟨frensh⟩ *'french'* and ⟨henge⟩ *'hinge'*. Our data comes from fourteenth- and fifteenth-century materials of mainly Southumbrian dialectal provenance. Note too such spelling alternants as ⟨strengþe⟩/⟨streinþe⟩ *'strength'* and ⟨lengþe⟩/⟨leinþe⟩ *'length'*. Once more, the ⟨ei⟩, ⟨ey⟩ spellings in the column 2 examples point to some kind of [e] → [eɪ] diphthongization in this pre-*nasal* sonorant environment. The possibility of such a partial palatalization of the stressed vowel space in this context could also spread across its whole area can be seen from the 'pure' palatal [i]/[ɪ] segments in the column 3 ⟨hinge⟩ type examples, increased palatalization (raising) being, as we have already observed (sect. 2.2.4), a feature of pre-nasal contexts in general. Yet that this diphthongization process is more complex than we have so far been suggesting can perhaps best be seen from a consideration of examples like those in Table 3.27 which represent the tenseless infinitive and past tense singular verb forms of the items ⟨blencen⟩ *'to deceive'*, ⟨mengen⟩ *'to mix'*, ⟨sengen⟩ *'to singe'* and ⟨drencen⟩ *'to drench'*, *'soak'* as they appear in Southumbrian dialects of the fourteenth century (although some dialects manifest the process much earlier) (Jordan 1974: sect. 103; Luick 1964:

TABLE 3.27

Infinitive	Past singular	Infinitive	Past singular
⟨blenchen⟩	⟨blenchede⟩	⟨mengen⟩	⟨mengede⟩
⟨blenken⟩	⟨blenchte⟩	⟨meingen⟩	⟨menget⟩
⟨blinchen⟩	⟨blenkede⟩	⟨mingen⟩	⟨minget⟩
⟨blinken⟩	⟨blinchede⟩		⟨meingde⟩
	⟨blinkete⟩		⟨meinte⟩
	⟨bleinte⟩		⟨mæingde⟩
	⟨blente⟩		⟨maingde⟩
⟨drenchen⟩	⟨drengde⟩	⟨sengen⟩	⟨senged⟩
⟨dreinchen⟩	⟨drainte⟩	⟨singe⟩	⟨sengt⟩
⟨drengen⟩	⟨dreinte⟩		⟨seinde⟩
⟨drinken⟩			⟨seinkt⟩
			⟨saind⟩
			⟨saynd⟩

sect. 404). These data are of especial interest for at least two reasons. In the first place, it would appear that the diphthongization process 'prefers' to occur pre-nasally only when that nasal is itself part of a complex consonantal cluster whose second element (a) shares the horizontal and vertical articulatory position of the nasal and (b) is a continuant consonant with a fricative quality; in other words, the diphthong triggering environment consists of sonorant initial co-articulating (homorganic) clusters such as [nǧ], [nč], and [nš], thus ⟨heinge⟩, ⟨dreinch⟩, ⟨freinsch⟩. What is interesting is that while both 'stand-alone' non-nasal sonorants and fricatives such as [x], [ç] (and even, as we shall see below, stand-alone affricatives like [ǧ]) can provoke the diphthongizing effect on the stressed vowel space (cf. such alternants as ⟨hall⟩/⟨haull⟩, ⟨boh⟩/⟨bough⟩ and ⟨age⟩/⟨ayge⟩), solitary nasals regularly have no such effect, but appear to need 'reinforcement' from the co-articulating fricative consonant. In this context it is interesting to recall our earlier observations on the late Old English *homorganic lengthening* process (sect. 2.2.3) where we saw that stressed vowels historically first became lengthened before nasal sonorant clusters and that the second (co-articulating) element in these clusters was a *continuant fricative*; the Old English lengthening process was triggered by clusters such as [ms], [mβ] and [nθ], thus *[fimβ] → *[fiimβ] *'five'*. Consequent upon the lengthening, one element of the triggering cluster (the nasal sonorant) was effaced, such that *[fiimβ] → [fiif].

It is just such a segment deletion condition upon nasal initial homorganic clusters which brings us to our second interesting point about the data in Tables 3.26 and 3.27. It would appear that in several cases there the diphthongization process is affected by or at least related to the effacement of the second, affricative element in the nasal initial cluster. In the verb forms in question, the past tense singular is signalled morphologically by the presence of a suffix or postposed accretion to the verb 'root', thus [mɛnǧ + əd], [sɛnǧ + əd], and as many of our spellings testify, this suffix could be 'desyllabified' (vowel effaced), such that shapes like [mɛnǧd] could surface. It seems that in the thirteenth and fourteenth centuries, a diphthongal stressed vowel space was only 'permitted' in such contracted suffixal environments on condition that the second element of the nasal initial cluster was itself effaced. Thus [mɛɪng(ə)d] → [mɛɪnd], [sɛɪnǧ(ə)d] → [sɛɪnd]. We tentatively argued above that the reason for the [fiimβ] → [fiif] contraction had to do with the permitted or 'canonical' amount of vowel-ness appropriate to syllables; a syllable peak + termination combination like [iimβ] was too vocalic in some way, an 'acceptable level' being achieved by the suppression of the relatively vowel-like [m] segment. Likewise, we might equally tentatively propose here, stressed vowel plus coda configurations like [ɛɪnǧd] were 'too vowelly' in much the same way; vocalic reduction being achieved in this instance by the effacement of the fricative content of the delayed release [ǧ] or [dʒ] segment, leaving behind the dental voiced obstruent. Such 'compensatory' adjustments we can only treat metaphorically and speculatively at this point, especially given the limitations of the kind of descriptive phonological framework we are employing, but we shall return to them again, especially in our sections dealing with syllable shapes and their phonetic consequences (cf. sects 3.5 and 4.5).

The diphthongizations and raisings described above in pre-nasal cluster environments represented, we argued, an increase in the overall level of palatalness in the stressed vowel space, such that [ɛ] → [ɛɪ] or [i]/[ɪ]. In the examples we provided it was mainly the 'mixed' (palatality/sonority) mid [ɛ] vowel which was affected in the Middle English period. However, although it may be a very minor phenomenon, there also appear to be some instances where a low, palatal [æ] or [ɑ] shows a contamination of a palatality element in its 'right hand side', such that processes like [æ] → [æɪ] or [ɑ] → [ɑɪ] are to be found. We raise these statistically relatively rare items at this point not so much for their importance for the phonology of Middle English but as the forerunners of an apparently identical set of changes (affecting by and large, it seems, the same lexical items) which play an important role in the development of English phonology in the sixteenth and seventeenth centuries. The instances we have in mind involve a stressed vowel space, probably generally durationally long, which derived from an [au] diphthong in the Middle English period itself. This [au] diphthong, which we shall discuss in some detail below (see sect. 4.4.1), appears to be a feature of the phonology of that version of French spoken in England from at least the eleventh century, known generally as Anglo-Norman. Particularly, Anglo-Norman showed a development whereby low back [a] vowels diphthongized to [au] in nasal environments. Note such Anglo-Norman, Central (Parisian) French alternants in our period as ⟨auncient⟩/⟨ancient⟩ 'ancient'; ⟨braunch⟩/⟨branch⟩ 'branch', ⟨daunger⟩/⟨danger⟩ 'danger', ⟨chaumber⟩/⟨chamber⟩ 'chamber'. In this pre-nasal + co-articulating obstruent/continuant context (i.e. in front of [mb], [nt], [nč], [nǧ]), the Anglo-French [au] becomes monophthongized to what was a relatively palatal [ææ] or to [ɑɑ]. There would appear to be some evidence to suggest that his new long vowel itself became subject to a diphthongized process in some Southern dialects of Middle English in the fourteenth century. Thus, for the Anglo-French ⟨raunge⟩ 'row' we find in this period such spellings as ⟨raunge⟩, ⟨raunche⟩, ⟨range⟩, ⟨rainge⟩ and ⟨raynges⟩: for Anglo-French ⟨chaungen⟩ 'to change' we have ⟨changen⟩, ⟨chaingen⟩, ⟨chaynge⟩, while for the personal name *Grainger*, we can find such alternant versions as ⟨Willelm le Graunger⟩, ⟨Robert the Grainger⟩, ⟨Walter le Granger⟩ and even ⟨Henri le Greunger⟩ (*Middle English Occupational Terms*, Thuresson 1950: pp. 102–3; Luick 1964: sect. 436; Jordan 1974: sect. 224). This development of the Anglo-French [au] diphthong through [ææ] to [æɪ] was not confined to pre-nasal environments, but could apparently also be triggered by 'free standing' voiced delayed release affricatives like [ǧ], such that both in the thirteenth and fourteenth centuries we can find alternants like ⟨auge⟩, ⟨age⟩, ⟨ayge⟩ 'age', ⟨gauge⟩, ⟨gage⟩, ⟨gayge⟩ 'gauge', ⟨rauge⟩, ⟨rage⟩, ⟨rayge⟩ 'rage' (Luick 1964: sect. 436). But both the dialectal provenance and overall frequency of this [au]/[ææ]/[æɪ] alternation are matters of some uncertainty and its range and statistical level of occurrence in this period require much further investigation.

As we shall see in the chapters which follow, the *Breaking* processes we have observed to be so typical of many regional dialects in both Old and Middle English have counterparts and reflexes in the language of a much later date and are, indeed, still characteristic of many modern English speech communities. The diphthongization process itself we have tried to characterize in terms of a 'destabalization' or contamination of the main 'colour' characteristic (palatality, labiality, sonority or their 'mixes') of the stressed vocalic space in lexical items. The contextual trigger for such a contamination we showed was the contiguity to the right of the stressed vowel of some non-obstruent phonetic segment; some segment which showed features of continuancy, a relatively unobstructed vocal tract, and which in some order of 'preference' was a non-nasal sonorant, a voiceless fricative, a nasal sonorant or a delayed release continuant affricative. In nearly all instances some kind of 'support' for such segments was required to effect the diphthongizing process, support in the form of a place of articulation sharing obstruent or continuant consonant. However, expressed in such terms, the affecting context would seem to provide little in the way of explanation as to why diphthongization should be triggered before it at all. Even at this point, however, it is worth recalling that we have tried to suggest over and over again from our data selections that such environments were not just diphthong producing, but also could cause innovations to the stressed vowel space which involved length change and even raising. The type of context we have described which is responsible for such an apparently disparate set of effects is characterized essentially as one *where a stressed vowel is contiguous with segments which are themselves highly vocalic in their internal composition*. In such cases the syllable peak and its terminator comprise a sequence which represents a highly vowel-like extended space. In several places below, but especially in our discussion of vowel shifts (cf. sect. 4.2.2), we shall show that such extensive 'vowel stretches' are for some reason accorded by speakers an exaggerated or heightened level of perceptual prominence – stratagems are found to make them observationally more 'obvious'; their signal is enhanced and enriched. Such an enhancement, enrichment might be achieved by a number of different routes or stratagems – increased vowel or sonorant consonant duration, 'splitting up' of the stressed vowel space (diphthongization), driving the stressed vowel closer to one of the 'pure' vowel parameters resulting in vowel shifts like raisings and lowerings. Just why such highlighting or emphasis should be seen as appropriate in these vowelly segment 'stretches' is one to which we shall return much later below.

3.4.6 Other *Breaking* stratagems: bi-continuant cluster busting

The enhancement, enrichment or foregrounding of the stressed vowel space provoked by its proximity to consonantal sonorant and fricative segments has other manifestations across the whole temporal span of the English language. We have shown several times now that this foregrounding can take the form of side-by-side linear contrast (diphthongizations), durational increase and even height adjustment to the stressed vowel space. One consequence of the first two of these effects, we argued, is the production of two vowel 'halves', halves which bear a relative prominence characteristic to each other; one is the more 'stressed' or bears the syllable pulse, while the other usually (but not always – see the *syllabicity shift* instances at sect. 2.4.5 above) the one linearly to its right is non-syllabic and unstressed; thus by a process like Old English *Breaking* we have [æld] → [æɑld]. Such an intervocalic prominence differential can be achieved by another stratagem, one which again involves vowel insertion or epenthesis. Rather than see additional vowel-ness realized to the immediate right of the stressed vowel and within the confines of the same syllable structure as in the [æɑld] instance, that extra sonority can be added to the right of the affecting sonorant consonant itself, in the process 'splitting up' the triggering consonantal cluster and creating an additional syllable beat in the item's structure (Luick 1964: sect. 316; Jordan 1974: sects 145–9; Campbell 1959: sect. 360). Consider the data in Table 3.28. The examples in columns 2 and 4 clearly show this 'splitting up' of the [rx] and [xt] clusters, additional

TABLE 3.28

Old English		13th–15th-century	Middle English	
[xt]				
⟨dohtor⟩		⟨daughter⟩ ⟨doughter⟩	⟨dohuturis⟩ ⟨dogheter⟩	'*daughter*'
⟨dohtig⟩		⟨doughti⟩	⟨dougheti⟩ ⟨duȝhuti⟩ ⟨duhhitȝ⟩	'*valiant*'
⟨hleahtor⟩		⟨laghter⟩	⟨lahuter⟩	'*laughter*'
⟨niht⟩		⟨night⟩	⟨nyhyt⟩	'*night*'
⟨meahtig⟩		⟨mighti⟩ ⟨miȝti⟩	⟨miȝety⟩ ⟨mihety⟩	'*strong*'
⟨fyrhto⟩	⟨fyrihto⟩	⟨firht⟩		'*fear*'
⟨worht⟩	⟨wyriht⟩	⟨wruhte⟩		'*work*'
I	2	3	4	

vocalicness being added to the right of the continuants which are, as we have seen in our discussion of both Old and Middle English *Breaking*, such powerful diphthong and vowel length producing forces for the vowel space preceding them. The overall result is, in fact, not at all unlike Middle English *Breaking* as it affects some of these items: a shape like [douxtər], for instance, shows the production of a syllable one configuration where there exist two side-by-side vocalic elements 'in place' of the original simple [o] vowel space. At the same time, the extra vowelness of the diphthong produces a prominence differential such that [o] is the more contrastive, syllable pulse-bearing member of the pair. The column 4 shape like [dɔxətər], ⟨dohuter⟩ also manifests just such an overall increase in vocalic level within the item, on this occasion realized through the production of a new vowel peak internal to the [xt] cluster. Once again there occurs a prominence differential between the stress bearing syllable one vowel peak and the innovatory segment in syllable two: from being a syllable terminating cluster, the [x] and [t] segments are now realized as syllable initiator and terminator respectively. We shall return to another possible motivation for such a change below, see sect. 3.5.2.

   This type of phenomenon is widespread throughout the phonology of Middle English, but it appears to be especially common in the more Northerly dialectal areas of the country and in texts of a post-1350 date, although as can be seen from the column 2 examples in Table 3.28, some instances would appear to be a feature (albeit a limited one) of the phonology of late Old English as well (Campbell 1959: sect. 360). It is interesting to see the contrast between the impetus for this process whereby new, relatively non-prominent syllable peak vowels are formed and that for late Old English *homorganic lengthening* (sect. 2.2.4). Recall that the context which produced stressed vowel length in English of the tenth century was one where a nasal or non-nasal sonorant was the first member of a two segment consonantal cluster the second of which was normally a *co-articulating voiced stop*: [nd], [mb], [ŋg], [ld], [rd]. Lengthening in [rl]/[rn] contexts was, we suggested in section 2.2.4, relatively rare. Yet it is just such environments that our present syllable peak innovation appears to prefer to operate: the impetus for the change being the contiguity with a stressed vowel of a consonantal cluster *both of whose members are continuants* – [rn], [rm], [rl], [rθ] and [rx]. We might tentatively suggest that it is the combined effect of these highly vocalic double continuant clusters which provokes the manifestation of a 'new' vowel between them. At any rate, it would seem to be the case that segment configurations such as say [bord] and [erl] provoke a perception of increased overall vowel prominence in the listener. The place in the item's segmental structure where that perceived additional vowel-ness is located appears to be a function of the nature of the termination of its syllable final cluster. Clusters ending in obstruents lead to the perception of vocalicness internal to the syllable to which they were the coda (hence the [bord/boord] alternation); those with a continuant occlusion can realize additional vowel-ness in the shape of a new syllabic peak at the 'right hand end' of the item's structure, thus [erl]/[erəl].

In this respect it is worth reminding ourselves as well of one of the constraints upon the operation of that other lengthening change which we have discussed above – *open syllable lengthening*. There, we will remember (sect. 3.2.6), stressed vowel lengthening was blocked or resisted in items like ⟨baril⟩, ⟨cannon⟩, ⟨common⟩; that is, in items whose second syllable was composed of a peak whose *onset and coda were both continuant sonorants*. Just such a configuration is what our unstressed vowel epenthesis, illustrated in Table 3.29, in fact, 'achieves', and such a distribution of vowel-ness across the bi-syllabic items listed in columns 3 and 4 there makes them too inelligible for the acceptance of a complex (long) vowel space through the operation of *open syllable lengthening*.

TABLE 3.29

Old English	13th–15th- Middle English century		
[rn] ⟨lærness⟩	⟨lernesse⟩ ⟨lerenesse⟩		'emptiness'
⟨fern⟩ ⟨fearn⟩	⟨fern⟩ ⟨farn⟩	⟨feren⟩ ⟨feron⟩ ⟨farron⟩	'fern'
⟨bearn⟩	⟨barn⟩ ⟨bern⟩	⟨baren⟩ ⟨barin⟩	'offspring'
[rm] ⟨hearmian⟩	⟨harmen⟩ ⟨haremi⟩		'to injure'
⟨feorm⟩	⟨ferm⟩	⟨fereme⟩	'farm'
⟨earm⟩	⟨arm⟩	⟨arum⟩ ⟨arome⟩	'arm'

TABLE 3.29 (contd)

Old English		13th–15th- Middle English century		
[rl]				
⟨eorl⟩	⟨erl⟩ ⟨eerl⟩	⟨eryl⟩ ⟨erel⟩		'earl'
⟨ceorl⟩	⟨cherl⟩ ⟨churl⟩	⟨cherel⟩ ⟨cherol⟩		'commoner'
⟨carl⟩	⟨carl⟩	⟨carile⟩		'man'
⟨deorling⟩	⟨darling⟩	⟨dereling⟩		'dear one'
	⟨harlot⟩	⟨harelot⟩		'prostitute'
[rθ]				
⟨eorþe⟩		⟨erthe⟩	⟨erethe⟩	'earth'
⟨eorþlic⟩		⟨erthli⟩	⟨erethli⟩	'earthly'
[rx]				
[ðerh⟩	⟨ðerih⟩	⟨þurh⟩	⟨þuruh⟩ ⟨þoruʒ⟩	'through'
⟨burh⟩	⟨burug⟩	⟨borgh⟩ ⟨burh⟩	⟨borough⟩ ⟨boreges⟩	'town'
⟨earh⟩		⟨argh⟩	⟨areh⟩ ⟨areʒ⟩	'timid'
[ns]				
⟨Frencisca⟩		⟨Frensh⟩ ⟨French⟩	⟨Frenish⟩ ⟨Frenysch⟩	'French'
[ln]				
⟨myln⟩	⟨mylen⟩	⟨milne⟩	⟨milen⟩	'mill'
[lf]				
⟨wylf⟩	⟨wylif⟩			'wolf'
1	2	3	4	

Items showing syllable terminations of the kind most typically associated with late Old English *homorganic lengthening* in general fail to undergo the cluster 'splitting' process of the type described above, and while we do on occasion find alternants such as those in Table 3.30, on the whole obstruent terminated clusters remain 'intact' throughout the Middle English period for items like ⟨bald⟩, ⟨cald⟩, ⟨cild⟩, ⟨fold⟩, ⟨gold⟩, ⟨word⟩, ⟨sword⟩, with shapes such as *⟨worod⟩, *⟨folod⟩, *⟨ciled⟩, etc. failing to surface.

TABLE 3.30

	Old English		*13th–15th-* Middle English century		
[mb]			⟨chamber⟩	⟨chameber⟩	*'room'*
[rd]	⟨wyrd⟩		⟨wurde⟩ ⟨werde⟩	⟨werid⟩ ⟨wirid⟩	*'fate'*
[ŋg]	⟨engel⟩	⟨enegel⟩	⟨angel⟩		*'angel'*

3.5 Syllable shapes and their phonetic consequences

We have spent much time suggesting (in a very informal fashion) that in some way speakers recognize not only that phonological entities such as syllables exist and have a certain structural content, but that that very structure can itself have a 'preferred', 'ideal' or 'canonical' form. While it is difficult to find any great degree of unanimity in the scholarly literature as to what might constitute a universally acceptable definition for syllable structure itself, there are, nevertheless, some areas of general agreement (Lehiste 1970). We have already discussed the proposal that syllables can essentially be thought of as identifiable higher order units comprised of combinations of segments and not just as representative of some arbitrary number of linear sequences of sounds. While, in the case of an instance such as [kæt], we may think of the syllable as a phenomenon comprising three segmental units, an *onset*, a *peak* and a *coda* occurring in a simple precedential relationship, we have also already seen (in, for instance, sect. 3.2.6) how some phonetic/phonological processes are constrained in their occurrence with reference to some 'higher order' structure within the syllable – the *rhyme* – of which the *peak* and *coda* are componential units. Indeed, much of our discussion in this present chapter and Chapter 2 of the various *Breaking* and vowel lengthening phenomena was concerned with the ways in which the structure of the stressed syllable *rhyme* component was perceived. It could be 'too short', 'over long' or show too much or too little 'vowelly-ness'; various 'compensatory' adjustments could be made, we argued, to achieve some kind of perceived ideal configuration for this sub-structure within the syllable (Giegerich 1985: pp. 97–8).

In this section we shall pursue notions like this still further and try to show how a whole set of apparently unconnected (certainly in the standard literature) phonetic alternations can be viewed as in fact sharing a single characteristic – i.e. they can be interpreted as a response to the dictates of speakers' perceptions as to what constitutes some ideal syllable structure. But before we look at any of these individual alternations, let us briefly and informally discuss one important aspect of syllable structure which we have so far only briefly hinted at (cf. sects 1.3 and 3.4.3). We are by now very familiar with the notion of the *sonority hierarchy*; however, it is essential to re-emphasize that this concept has an important part to play in any description of what might constitute syllable structure (especially that of the English language). Kiparsky (1979) and others have convincingly demonstrated that a syllable can be viewed as though it were some kind of sonority/vocalicness 'pulse'; a pulse which, commencing from a position of minimum sonority or vowel-quality value, progresses through a peak or maximum for such a property, returning to a minimal expression of the same. We might represent such a pulse in terms of a graph like that expressed at Fig. 3.5 for a monosyllabic structure like [plæŋk] '*plank*'. Such a mapping of a relative sonority/vocalicness 'envelope' against the temporal sequence of the individual seg-

FIG. 3.5

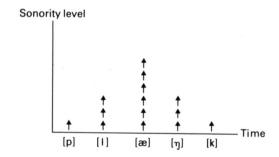

ments which go to make up the [plæŋk] item clearly shows how that sequential order is, in fact, a direct function of the inherent sonority characteristics of each segment. Our graph shows that the syllable can be viewed as some kind of pulse whose centre or peak (in this case [æ]) is maximally marked for sonority and, as we move away from that centre to right and to left, there is a 'fading' of vocalic quality in the segments, markedly so as we reach the syllable's 'edges' or periphery. For English at any rate, the temporal, linear sequence of elements which go to make up syllables bears a direct relationship to the intrinsic vowel content of those very segments: those, like voiceless obstruents – with relatively low vocalic prominence – will tend to occur 'first' and 'last' in syllables (i.e. be at the syllabic periphery). Others, such as the relatively highly sonorant [l] and [r] types, will tend to cluster around the syllabic centre, which itself will be characterized by the most highly sonorant of all segments – the vowels. Thus, for English, syllable initial [lp-] and syllable final [-kn] clusters would be impossible on the basis of this hypothesis, since sequences such as these do not conform to the prediction of our model that segments closest to the syllable peak should be more 'vowelly' than those at the syllable 'edge'. Our model for the syllable sees it therefore as a highly vocalic peak which demonstrates 'vocalic fading' as one moves either to the right or left syllable margin (Lass 1984: pp. 208 ff; Fudge 1969; Anderson and Jones 1974). Consider the data in Table 3.31. There the column 1 Old English shapes like ⟨æpl⟩, ⟨nedl⟩ and ⟨botm⟩ would orthographically appear to represent items showing a single syllable pulse clearly counterexemplifying the very interdependence between segment sequence and inherent relative sonority we have outlined above, as they show syllable final consonantal clusters like [-pl], [-dl] and [-tm]; in such cases the syllable edge segment is clearly more vowelly than that nearer the syllabic centre. If anything, the distribution of the syllable final ⟨dl⟩, ⟨tn⟩ type spellings is concentrated in the very earliest Old English texts (Campbell 1959: sect. 363), while the clearly bi-syllabic types in column 2 regularly surface in later Old English materials. In fact, the spellings in the first two columns in all likelihood are to be treated merely as straightforward *orthographic* variants; those in column 1 almost certainly represent outputs like [æpəl], [nedəl], [bɔtəm] and so on. Note too such fourteenth- and fifteenth-century spelling alternants like ⟨bedegar⟩, ⟨bdegar⟩ *'rose plant'*, where ⟨bd⟩ would seem to be simply an orthographic device for [bəd-].

However, the column 3 Middle English forms are interesting in that a typical shape like ⟨apple⟩ found there can be interpreted as a *bi-syllabic* configuration like {₁a{₂plə₂}, the second syllable

TABLE 3.31

Old English		12th–15th- century	Middle English		
[-pl]					
⟨æpl⟩	⟨æppel⟩	⟨apple⟩	⟨appel⟩		*'apple'*
⟨eapl⟩ ⟨appel⟩		⟨applene⟩	⟨eppel⟩		
		⟨apple⟩			
[-tm]					
⟨botm⟩ ⟨bodam⟩		⟨botme⟩	⟨bottem⟩		*'bottom'*
⟨bytme⟩		⟨bodne⟩	⟨bottim⟩		
		⟨bothme⟩			
[-ðm]					
⟨fæðm⟩		⟨fadme⟩	⟨fadom⟩		*'fathom'*
		⟨vedme⟩	⟨feþem⟩		
		⟨fathme⟩	⟨fethem⟩		
[-dl]					
⟨nedl⟩ ⟨nedel⟩		⟨nedle⟩	⟨nedel⟩	⟨neld⟩	*'needle'*
		⟨nædle⟩	⟨nidel⟩		
		⟨kindlen⟩	⟨kindelen⟩	⟨kinlin⟩	*'kindle'*
		⟨kindlin⟩	⟨kindel⟩	⟨kenle⟩	
			⟨kindelle⟩		
[-kn]					
⟨tacn⟩ ⟨tacen⟩		⟨tæcne⟩	⟨taken⟩	⟨tanc⟩	*'token'*
		⟨takne⟩			
[-gr]					
	⟨hungor⟩	⟨hungre⟩	⟨hunger⟩		*'hunger'*
		⟨hongre⟩	⟨honguer⟩		
			⟨hungær⟩		
			⟨Hungurhill⟩		
1	2	3	4	5	

vowel (represented orthographically as ⟨e⟩) showing a canonical onset cluster in [pl-] (although we shall discuss the more precise details of syllable membership assignment later in this section). Likewise, forms such as ⟨fadme⟩ and ⟨botme⟩ might be argued to show a possible syllable division like $\{_1fad_1\}\{_2me_2\}$ and $\{_1bot_1\}\{_2me_2\}$, given our model's claim that [dm]/[tm] clusters cannot syllable terminate, thus blocking a division like $\{_1fadm_1\}$

$\{_2e_2\}$. We might argue too that the column 4 items like ⟨appel⟩, ⟨fadom⟩ and ⟨nedel⟩ actually 'derive' from syllable configurations such as $\{_1a\{_2ple_2\}$ and $\{_1ned_1\}\{_2le_2\}$ in which, for reasons that need not concern us here, the syllable two peak vowel has been effaced resulting in some non-canonical syllable shape like, say, $*\{_1apl_1\}$. We might suggest that an appropriate syllable configuration could be re-established lies in the realization of the inherent vocalic property of the syllable final sonorant [l]/[m] in the shape of a linearly precedent [ə]-like vowel, in this way creating a new vocalic peak: so $\{_1fadm_1\} \rightarrow \{_1fa\{_2dəm_2\}$ or some such. The similarity between this kind of process and the 'cluster busting' we have outlined above in section 3.4.6 is obvious – cf. recall where we found there alternants such as ⟨dohter⟩/⟨dohuter⟩; ⟨erl⟩/⟨eril⟩ and ⟨ðerh⟩/⟨ðerih⟩.

Yet these last instances suggest too that the constraints on syllable final cluster sequences is not simply a matter of their relative vocalic prominence. We saw on pp. 123–4 above how the sonorant consonants were themselves ranked according to their relative inherent vowel-like qualities along some decrease in sonority scale like:

[r]   [l]   [n]   [m]

decreasing vowel-ness

In the light of this kind of observation, syllable final terminations such as [-rl] or [-rn] (and certainly [-rx]) conform to the dictates of this sonority/sequence paradigm; that is, there would seem to be no reason why speakers should 'tamper' with such sequences in any way. Yet it would appear that we require to modify our model to include some kind of notion such that there has to be some prescribed degree of 'sonority separation' between the cluster elements before they can conform to the canons of our syllable pulse shape above. [rl], [rn] and even [rx] – with its sonorant/continuant fricative sonority difference – do not appear to be sufficiently vowel-distinct (as are [nt] and [rd] for example) to be allowed as stable syllable terminating combinations. Their relative vocalic 'closeness' leads to the perception of enhanced vowel foregrounding and the realization of a new syllable peak; thus $[\theta\varepsilon rx] \rightarrow [\theta\varepsilon r\iota x]$.

It is extremely interesting to observe from some of the examples in column 5 of Table 3.31 how speakers seem to have developed another stratagem whereby [-dl] and [-kn] sonority level/sequential position-defying codas were made to 'conform' to the canonical syllable final configuration. Alongside shapes such as

⟨sedle⟩/⟨sedel⟩ *'seat'*, ⟨tæcn⟩/⟨tacen⟩ *'sign'* and ⟨nedle⟩/
⟨nedel⟩ *'needle'* we find others like ⟨tanc⟩, ⟨seld⟩ and ⟨neld⟩
(Luick 1964: sect. 693, 2.b and sect. 714.3) in which the sequential
order of the syllable final clusters has been 're-arranged' to achieve
a sequence showing sonority level 'fading' at the approach to the
syllable boundary. A syllable configuration based motivation like
this for such a *metathesis* effect might colour our views when we
come to discuss reasons for the more widespread [r] metathesis
(⟨curd⟩/⟨croud⟩) types to be discussed at section 3.5.3.

In the meantime, let us turn our attention to a second set of

TABLE 3.32

	12th–15th-century Middle English		
[nd]/[nt]			
	⟨þusend⟩	⟨þusent⟩	*'thousand'*
	⟨feond⟩	⟨feont⟩	*'enemy'*
	⟨frend⟩	⟨freont⟩	*'friend'*
[ld]/[lt]			
	⟨child⟩	⟨chilt⟩	
	⟨hild⟩	⟨hilt⟩	*'sword'*
	⟨scaffold⟩	⟨scaffalt⟩	
[ŋg]/[ŋk]			
	⟨bring⟩	⟨brink⟩	
	⟨þink⟩	⟨þing⟩	*'thing'*
	⟨kyng⟩	⟨kynck⟩	*'king'*
	⟨song⟩	⟨sonk⟩	
	⟨offringe⟩	⟨offrink⟩	*'offering'*
[b]/[p]			
	⟨godsibb⟩	⟨godsip⟩	*'parent'*
	⟨wardrobe⟩	⟨wardrop⟩	*'cupboard'*
	⟨syllabe⟩	⟨syllap⟩	*'syllable'*
		⟨silip⟩	
[v]/[f]			
	⟨giv⟩	⟨gif⟩	*'give'*
	⟨luv⟩	⟨luf⟩	*'love'*
	⟨above⟩	⟨abuf⟩	*'above'*
	⟨haue⟩	⟨haf⟩	*'have'*
[d]/[t]			
	⟨ballad⟩	⟨ballat⟩	*'ballad'*
	⟨abbod⟩	⟨abbot⟩	

alternants which appear to be the result of some understanding on the part of language users as to what constitute the appropriate shapes for the structure of syllables. The data in Table 3.32 are traditionally described as instances of 'word final devoicing' (Jordan 1974: sects 193, 200, 217; Berndt 1960: pp. 182–3; Luick 1964: sect. 713.1). Although they are temporarily and regionally complex in their distribution, data like these seem to suggest that segments at the syllable edge especially, as we shall see below, those associated with the periphery of the rhyme, are perceived as minimally vocalic, given their maximal distance from the highly vocalic syllable centre. Devoicing is, of course, one means whereby overall vocalic reduction can be achieved in the internal composition of segments. But it is not the only one; given the characteristics of the kind of sonority hierarchy we have been suggesting, overall vowel/sonority reduction can also be achieved, for instance, by the substitution of obstruency for continuancy (as in [fɛð-] → [fɛd-]) or even by the replacement of one relatively highly vocalic sonorant continuant like [r] by another, less vocalic type on the 'local' sonority scale, like, say, [l] or a nasal (as in [purpər] → [purpəl]). Although there are other ways of accounting for such phenomena, we might speculate here that the data in Table 3.33 represent precisely the same kind of syllabic margin vowel level reduction as those in the previous list (Berndt 1960: pp. 187 and 195; Luick 1964: sect. 673; Jordan 1974: sect. 206). Indeed intuitive knowledge of syllable structure of this kind may also have a part to play in accounting for certain types of consonantal epentheses in syllable final position in such thirteenth- and fourteenth-century alternants like ⟨fesan⟩/⟨fesant⟩ 'pheasant'; ⟨paten⟩, ⟨patein⟩/⟨patent⟩ 'Eucharist plate'; ⟨plought⟩, ⟨ploght⟩, ⟨ploiʒt⟩/⟨ploh⟩, ⟨plouh⟩ 'plough' and ⟨inoght⟩, ⟨inouʒt⟩, ⟨enoght⟩/⟨inoh⟩, ⟨enough⟩ 'enough' (Wyld 1936: p. 309; Luick 1964: sect. 675, Anm. 2). In such cases we might see something akin to the 'compensatory' vowel filling-out processes we met with in our discussions on vowel lengthening phenomena above (see sect. 2.3.1); an item like ⟨ploh⟩, for example, shows a 'complete' leftwards vocalic quality 'fade' from the peak – an identical deterioration pathway becoming possible on the other 'side' of the stressed vowel through the realization of a syllable final voiceless (minimally vocalic) obstruent.

Yet there appears to be an even more striking but not unrelated consequence of what we claim to be speakers' intuitions concerning the general well-formedness of the combinations of segments which go to make up the vowel crescendo/descrescendo syllable pulse effect. While we shall see that the phenomenon in question is a

TABLE 3.33

	12th–15th-century Middle English		
[ð]/[d]			
	⟨fithele⟩	⟨fidel⟩	*'violin'*
	⟨fethele⟩	⟨fidle⟩	
	⟨morther⟩	⟨morder⟩	*'murder'*
	⟨morthre⟩	⟨mordre⟩	
	⟨morth⟩	⟨morde⟩	*'murder'*
	⟨merthe⟩		
	⟨fether⟩	⟨feder⟩	*'feather'*
	⟨fither⟩	⟨fedres⟩	
	⟨birthen⟩	⟨birden⟩	*'weight'*
	⟨burthen⟩	⟨bourden⟩	
[n]/[m]			
	⟨confort⟩	⟨comfort⟩	
	⟨confit⟩	⟨comfit⟩	*'confectionary'*
	⟨ranson⟩	⟨ransom⟩	
	⟨randon⟩	⟨random⟩	
[r]/[l]			
	⟨purpur⟩	⟨purpul⟩	
		⟨purple⟩	

very prominent feature of the later language, there is much evidence throughout the period embracing the twelfth to the fifteenth centuries to show that items characterized by an *onset empty* syllable shape (i.e. those whose first segment was a vowel of some kind) were subject to being perceived as if, in fact, they actually had an onset characteristic, usually manifesting itself as some highly vocalic 'glide' like [w] or [j]. Consider the data set out in Table 3.34. It is important to observe that all of the items cited there under column 1 show a vowel space which is durationally long either lexically, or through the operation of either of the two stressed vowel lengthening processes which we have discussed above – *open syllable lengthening* and the ninth-century *homorganic lengthening*. In fact we only cite a very small number of instances

TABLE 3.34

	12th–15th-century MiddleEnglish		
⟨eende⟩ ⟨eynde⟩ ⟨ente⟩	⟨yende⟩ ⟨yinde⟩ ⟨zind⟩ ⟨ʒend⟩	⟨hende⟩	*'end'*
⟨erthe⟩ ⟨eerthe⟩ ⟨erethe⟩ ⟨ierthe⟩	⟨yerthe⟩ ⟨ʒerthe⟩ ⟨ʒereth⟩ ⟨ʒerþ⟩	⟨herþe⟩	*'earth'*
⟨once⟩ ⟨ones⟩ ⟨ons⟩ ⟨oones⟩	⟨wunus⟩ ⟨wons⟩ ⟨wones⟩ ⟨ʒons⟩		*'once'*
⟨olde⟩ ⟨oulde⟩ ⟨ole⟩	⟨wolde⟩ ⟨yolde⟩ ⟨yolle⟩ ⟨ʒelde⟩	⟨holde⟩ ⟨halde⟩	*'old'*
⟨othe⟩ ⟨outh⟩	⟨woth⟩	⟨hoth⟩ ⟨hoit⟩	*'oath'*
⟨oc⟩ ⟨oek⟩ ⟨auch⟩	⟨wooke⟩	⟨hoc⟩ ⟨hokke⟩ ⟨hock⟩	*'oak'*
⟨other⟩ ⟨othere⟩ ⟨othther⟩	⟨wother⟩ ⟨woder⟩		*'other'*
1	2	3	

of the 'glide epenthesis' phenomenon in Table 3.34 and many others could be quoted, including shapes like ⟨vus⟩ *'us'*, ⟨wonlyche⟩ *'only'*, ⟨wote⟩ *'oats'*, ⟨Wolster⟩ *'Ulster'*, ⟨yeven⟩ *'evening'*, ⟨yeny⟩ *'any'*, ⟨yegg⟩ *'egg'* and ⟨yerbys⟩ *'herbs'*, (Kihlbohm 1926: pp. 79–81, 163–8; Luick 1964: sect 435; Wyld 1936: p. 308; Ekwall 1980: sect. 82). Superficially, at any rate, column 1 and 2 forms show a contrast in their stressed vowel space value which looks to be like [ee]/[je] and [ɔɔ]/[wɔ]. The first (syllable beat bearing) element has for some reason apparently come to be vocalically 'demoted' to the status of a (more consonantal in internal composition) 'glide' element; some kind of *devocalization* process might appear to be operative – a palatal [j] glide substituting for a relatively palatal [e] vowel, a [w] glide for a relatively labial [ɔ], although we have to note such apparent counterexamples to this palatal and labial 'matching' in instances such as ⟨ʒons⟩ *'once'*, ⟨ʒorthe⟩ *'earth'* and ⟨yolde⟩ *'old'*.

Various suggestions have been proposed for such a word initial 'glide epenthesis'. Kihlbohm's (1926) view is that the 'glide' segment is realized, presumably on the basis of some version of the 'ease of articulation' hypothesis, to avoid 'hiatus'; that is, [j]/[w] segments appear just in those contexts where at syllable and/or word boundaries two vowel segments are in direct 'contact'. Thus we find [j] epenthesis in examples such as ⟨Long time after the zynd of the said Michell terme⟩ (1472) (*Rolls of Parliament* 6, 154.a), where ⟨z⟩ orthographically represents the [j] palatal glide inserted between the otherwise contiguous vowel ter-minating/initiating items [ðə] and [ɪnd]. But why should 'hiatus' need to be avoided in this way and why should 'glide' segments ease the transition between contiguous vowels more readily than, say, segments like [r] or [l], or even [d]? Anyway, the [j] epen-thesis is nowhere confined to such hiatus-type environments, cf. ⟨þe chambur at neþer ʒend of the hale⟩ (1474) (*Stunor*, 147). But we shall return to a more detailed discussion of this syllable 'interface' context in the next section.

We might recognize that a change like [ee] → [je] is one which we have already had reason to discuss in our section on *syllabicity shifting* in section 2.4.5, where we described fourteenth-century Kentish alternants like ⟨heald⟩ and ⟨hieald⟩ *'he held'* in what were stressed vowel diphthongally foregrounded *Breaking* environments. Could we not also argue that the examples in column 2 of Table 3.34 showed just such a syllabicity shift, such that [ęe] → [eę] → [je] and [ɔ̨ɔ] → [ɔɔ̨] → [wɔ]? However, we must bear in mind two points. Firstly, spellings such as ⟨wooke⟩ (as well as the Kentish ⟨hjealde⟩) at least support the possibility of 'glide epenthesis' even when vowel length and diphthongization are retained: i.e. where the syllable-bearing peak vowel remains intact and has not, apparently, been desyllabified and then 'replaced'. Secondly, and perhaps more pertinently, a term like 'syllabicity shifting', is merely a label; in itself it does nothing to explain why speakers might come to re-assign prominence to a different 'side' of a durationally extended vowel space in the first instance. Many different types of factors can be involved, of course, be we should like to suggest at least provisionally that speakers can interpret an

TABLE 3.35

Onset	Rhyme		
	Peak		Coda
	syllable centre		
Empty	[e]	[e]	[nd]

onset empty + complex vowel shape like Table 3.35 as one where the onset slot is fillable by available phonetic material, as in Table 3.36. The syllable edge 'vocalicness fade' effect which is so

TABLE 3.36

Onset	Rhyme	
	Peak	Coda
[e]	[e]	[nd]

characteristic of our model of the syllable pulse will dictate that the newly established [e] onset is interpreted as less vocalic, namely as, say, [j] – although as we shall see there are other possibilities – thus establishing a 'new' vocalic [e] syllable-bearing peak. In this way the entire syllable is now perceived as showing the typical vocalic crescendo ⟩ descrescendo effect. In the same fashion, we might argue, speakers will be inclined to hear a sequence like [ɔɔns] as [wɔns], although it would appear that for some the palatal/labial nature of the new onset glide did not need to reflect those characteristics of the 'replaced' vowels – cf. the ⟨ʒons⟩ [jɔns] and ⟨yolde⟩ [joold] cases – it being sufficient that the onset was vocalically less prominent than its contiguous stressed vowel space.

In view of the fact that this kind of phenomenon is almost always constrained to occur with *complex* (long or diphthongal) syllable peaks, we could suggest too that alternations like [ee]/[je] and [ɔɔ]/[wɔ] can be viewed as yet other manifestations of a stratagem whereby such complex vowel space could be further highlighted or foregrounded. Indeed, we might consider such a process to be an alternative stratagem to *Breaking*; a vowel space comprised of two non-phonetically contrastive components coming to be 'heard' as one where there is some kind of phonetic opposition. In the cases we have been discussing immediately above, that contrast is one between relative vowel prominence associated with the segments' internal structure, rather than (as with most of the other *Breaking* types we have so far looked at) one where a vowel height or backness opposition is involved. Yet the matter may be more complex than this, since there are many instances of such 'glide insertion' – especially in the language of a later date – where the affected syllable already manifests an onset consonant: cf. such ⟨bwoy⟩ *'boy'* spellings of the late sixteenth and seventeenth centuries as well as such present-day pronunciations as [kjæind] *'kind'* and [kwɪšən] *'cushion'* (Wyld 1936: p. 310).

Column 3 forms in Table 3.34 show what appears to be some kind of alternative [h] epenthesis to that involving [j]/[w]. This syllable initial, pre-vocalic 'aspiration' is an extremely common feature of the phonology of English in every period and we shall deal with it in some detail (as well as point to the similarities between it and the [j]/[w] and other epentheses) in the parallel section to this in the following chapter (cf. sect. 4.5.1).

3.5.1 Syllable contact points

Our discussion in the previous section mainly centred around the ways in which phonetic segments react when they appear at the 'edges' of syllables in *monosyllabic* contexts. We shall move on now to a brief discussion of what kinds of phonetic consequences befall those segments which are to be found at some point of contiguous contact with those of another syllable. For example, the type of phenomenon we shall be discussing relates to the kinds of intuitions speakers have concerning the phonetic characteristics of a segment like [m] in some modern pronunciations of the item [bræməl] *'bramble'*, a segment which appears to stand at the junction of two adjacent syllables. We have already attempted in section 3.2 to raise the question as to which of the two syllables in a word like [bræməl] the [m] segment should be assigned. At least two possibilities suggested themselves there:

(a) $\{_1\text{bræm}_1\}\{_2\text{əl}_2\}$

(b) $\{_1\text{bræ}_1\}\{_2\text{məl}_2\}$

In our discussion of Middle English *open syllable lengthening* we favoured the second interpretation largely on the basis of two criteria: (1) that syllables should, where possible, be *onset full* and (2) the need to see the 'filling out' of the durationally short [e] → [ɛɛ] in a change like [breməl] → [brɛɛməl] as a 'compensation' for some empty syllable one coda position. However, there is at least one other possible interpretation of a syllable structure for an item like [bræməl], one which sees the [m] segment as *simultaneously the coda to syllable one and the onset to syllable two*. The classic justification for this last kind of interpretation is that of Hooper (1972), the complex details of which we shall only briefly summarize here. Have we, for instance, any principled means for deciding in an item like, say, [pɛtrɔl] *'petrol'* to which of the word's two syllables the 'medial' [t] and [r] segments belong? Are we to interpret the item as showing syllable boundary structure like {pɛ}{trɔl}, {pɛt}{rɔl} or whatever? Hooper pointed to the fact that segments like [t] and [r] have distinctive phonetic characteristics dependent upon whether they are found at syllable onset or coda positions. For instance, a segment like [t] is much more likely to undergo glottalization to [ʔ] when it is syllable final than when it is syllable initial. In this way we are likely to find realizations like [pɛʔ] *'pet'* and not so frequently those like *[ʔu] *'to'*. That pronunciations like [pɛʔrəl] are possible would then favour a syllable bracketing interpretation like {pɛt}{rɔl}. Yet Hooper argues too that while [r] segments are usually always fully voiced in syllable initial position, they can be *devoiced* (at least partially) when they appear as the second element of consonantal clusters initiated by segments like [t]; thus the [r] in [rʌn] is fully voiced, while that in an item like [tri] *'tree'* is relatively unvoiced. In the case of the item [pɛtrəl] the [r] segment is characteristically relatively *unvoiced*, suggesting that it is not seen as syllable initial and arguing in favour of a syllable bracketing interpretation like {pɛ}{trəl}. But how can we reconcile this syllable boundary placement interpretation with that so strongly supported by the glottalized [t]? Hooper sees a solution in the acceptance that the [t] segment can *simultaneously* terminate syllable one and initiate syllable two; thus the item ⟨petrol⟩ will have a syllable bracketing structure like:

$$\{_1 p\varepsilon \{_2 t_1\} r\mathupsilon l_2\}$$

As the coda to syllable one the [t] could readily be glottalized to [ʔ], and as the non-initiator to syllable two, the [r] segment could be relatively unvoiced; in this way, a form like [pɛʔrɔl] readily surfaces. Such an ambisyllabicity potential for those elements occurring at syllable boundaries or interfaces can prove to be, as we shall show in what follows, a vital fact in explaining what can otherwise only be viewed as anomalous phonological innovation. Consider the data in Table 3.37. The column 2 ⟨nempne⟩-type expressions appear to show the 'addition' of

TABLE 3.37

	12th–15th-century Middle English			
(a)				
	⟨hersumnesse⟩ ⟨hersumnisse⟩	⟨hersumpnesse⟩		*'obedience'*
	⟨nemnen⟩ ⟨nemne⟩	⟨nepne⟩ ⟨nempned⟩	⟨nemeni⟩	*'to name'*
	⟨remnant⟩	⟨rempnant⟩ ⟨rembnand⟩	⟨remenaunt⟩	*'remainder'*
	⟨somnen⟩	⟨sompne⟩ ⟨sompnoun⟩	⟨somonen⟩	*'to summon'*
	⟨condemnen⟩ ⟨condemnyd⟩	⟨condempnen⟩ ⟨condempnacioun⟩		*'to condemn'*
	⟨damnen⟩ ⟨demnen⟩ ⟨dammen⟩	⟨dampnen⟩		*'to condemn'*
	⟨chemne⟩	⟨chimpne⟩	⟨chimene⟩	*'chimney'*
(b)				
	⟨emti⟩ ⟨emty⟩	⟨ampti⟩ ⟨empti⟩		*'empty'*
	⟨demstre⟩	⟨dempster⟩	⟨demmepster⟩ ⟨demester⟩	*'a judge'*
	⟨controllour⟩	⟨compterollour⟩		*'a judge'*
	⟨comsen⟩	⟨compsen⟩		*'to commence'*
	I	2	3	

some (epenthetic) voiceless [p] segment immediately to the 'right' of a bilabial (voiced) nasal in what looks like a syllable final position; such examples at first sight look extremely awkward in view of what we have said above concerning the appropriateness in such a context for the appearance of an innovatory *voiced* [b] obstruent; recall the ⟨hamor⟩/⟨hambor⟩ cases in Table 3.10. Are the Table 3.37 instances to be regarded then as mere unmotivated exceptions to this voice sharing homorganic cluster production in 'open' syllable contexts, or can we show that a voiceless co-articulating segment surfaces under conditions which we can rigidly specify? Notice that the ⟨nemnan⟩ type items show a syllable structure where 'medial' segments are unambiguously *non*-ambisyllabic at syllable contact point:

$$\{_1nem_1\}\{_2nan_2\}$$

A cluster like [mn] is unacceptable in English as either a syllable initiating or terminating unit in monosyllabic items – although the fact that it can be 'cluster busted', as we might by now expect, is clear from the column 3 cases, of which more below. It is important to realize that it is apparently *only* in such non-ambisyllabic contexts that a voiceless epenthetic stop can be used to 'fill out' the structure of syllable one (but note the single ⟨rembnand⟩ instance), not surprising in the light of our discussion of the [fɪnd] → [fɪnt] syllable final 'devoicings' which were the topic of the previous section. Alternants such as [bræmbəl]/[bræmblə] permit a *voiced* [b] intrusion just because that [b] can be interpreted as at once the terminator to syllable one and the onset to syllable two, according to the theory which seeks to show that segments at syllable interface can be (indeed, as we shall see, 'prefer' to be) members of both syllables simultaneously, thus

$$\{_1bræm\{_2b_1\}əl_2\}$$

No such possibility exists for the [p] intrusion in ⟨nemnan⟩, since in English syllable initial *{pn- clusters never surface. The same kind of argument holds for the cases under (b) in Table 3.37, where a shape such as *[ĕmbtə] '*empty*' is debarred given the impossibility for *{bt- clusters to act as syllable onsets in English monosyllables. What we are claiming, therefore, is that a segment's voicing characteristic in such an epenthesis process is, among other things, a function of that segment's ability to act in a capacity which is either ambisyllabic or syllable unique. According to such a model, therefore, {bræm{b}əl} and {bræm{b}lə} are acceptable syllable bracketing structures, while one like {nemb}{nən} dictates that the syllable one coda show a devocalization effect (in this case [b] → [p]) since that coda is uniquely within the domain of the first syllable and can show no ambisyllabic affinity with syllable two.

An interesting parallel to these data can be found in the phonology of some modern German dialects (Anderson and Jones 1974: pp. 105–6; Jones 1976; Hooper 1972). Many of these dialects show, as did Middle English, a tendency for syllable final obstruents to become devoiced, cf. alternants such as [veg]/[vek] '*road*'. Such an obstruent devoicing also occurs in an items like [radlə] ⟨radle⟩

'*to cycle*' realizing [ratlə], and is a function of the obstruent's status as uniquely the terminator of its own syllable. The syllable structure of the item can only be represented as {rad}{lə}, the {d} uniquely within the domain of syllable one, there being no possibility in Modern German for syllable initial or terminating {dl-/-dl} clusters. Yet in items such as ⟨segle⟩ '*I sail*' and ⟨lieble⟩ '*I love*' no [g]→[k] or [b] → [p] devoicing (devocalization) occurs in those very dialects where [ratlə] surfaces, because in their case we meet a syllable bracketing structure like:

$$\{_1se\{_2g_1\}lə_2\}$$
$$\{_1li\{_2b_1\}lə_2\}$$

the [g] and [b] voiced obstruents showing ambisyllabicity characteristics, and where {gl- and {bl- can act as phonologically acceptable syllable two onsets. Our argument goes that speakers recognize two different 'kinds' of obstruents dependent upon their place in syllable status; those which are uniquely syllable terminal are available for devoicing; others, which although coda-like, simultaneously illustrate syllable initiating possibilities, are not.

This apparent predisposition on the part of speakers (all the while adhering to the general sonority 'profile' of syllable segment sequence as outlined above) to see syllable onsets as *voiced* (or at any rate, relatively vocalic), as against codas as *voiceless* is supported by several different kinds of historical phonological processes, among them the mainly thirteenth century (and probably South West Midland regional) change whereby syllable initial fricatives become voiced. Compare such alternants as [fæðer]/[væðer] '*father*'; [fɔks]/[vɔks] '*fox*'; [flɛš]/[vlɛš] '*flesh*' and the Kentish [zɛlf] '*self*'; [zwɔrd] '*sword*' (Jordan 1974: sects. 207–8, 215; Berndt 1960: pp. 178–80). Compare too, in this respect, the process whereby syllable final voiceless obstruents are 'vocalized' in those circumstances where the items in question undergo morphological accretion – the addition to the word of a suffix can transform a segment from being uniquely single syllable bound and final, to one where it is ambisyllabic, hence: ⟨wolf⟩/⟨wolues⟩ '*wolf(s)*'; ⟨staf⟩/⟨staues⟩ '*stick(s)*'; ⟨fif⟩/⟨fiues⟩ '*(of) five*'; ⟨twelf⟩/⟨twelues⟩ '*(of) twelve*' and ⟨knif⟩/⟨kniues⟩ '*(of) knife*' (Berndt 1960: p. 151; Luick 1964: sect. 658). It is also in the terms of this tendency for syllable onset segments to be perceived as relatively more vocalic than codas that we might tentatively speculate upon such occasional Middle and later English renderings of the items ⟨chimney⟩ and ⟨named⟩ as ⟨chimbli⟩, ⟨nembled⟩. If the syllable one final [b] segment is perceived as having an ambisyllabic status and therefore seen to be simultaneously the onset to syllable two, then one stratagem for rendering the otherwise non-phonological syllable initiating *{bn cluster 'canonical' is to increase the vocalic status of the [n] element to its articulatory place equivalent but more vowel prominent congener, [l].

3.5.2 Stratagems for achieving ambisyllabicity

We have tried to show in the previous section how particular phonetic effects can crucially depend upon the characteristics of what we might call the *syllable interface*. We have identified two important features of this syllable boundary position or juncture point: on the one hand, in the case of an item like ⟨nemnan⟩, the segments at the point of interface (here [m] and [n]) are uniquely associated with the domain of their respective syllables one and two; on the other hand, in the case of an item like ⟨brembel⟩, we have argued that there is evidence to suggest that the [b] element in the [mb] cluster shows phonetic characteristics of *dual* syllable membership (it is ambisyllabic). That is, this last item is perceived as having a syllable boundary placement configuration like

$$\{_1 br\text{æ}m\{_2 b_1\} \text{ə} l_2\}$$

where [b] is simultaneously the coda to syllable one and the onset to syllable two. At this point we should like to present what look like some interesting data which suggest that at least two other kinds of (otherwise apparently unrelated) innovatory processes – common, as we shall see throughout the history of the English language – result from speakers' 'knowledge' that at syllable interface, phonetic segments may show dual syllable membership – a phenomenon often referred to as syllable *overlap* or *interlocking* (Anderson and Jones 1974: pp. 107–12; Kohler 1966). Consider what look to be a rather heterogeneous set of data in Table 3.38 (Berndt 1960: pp. 186, 204; Luick 1964: sect. 713). Two points are especially worth our attention in these data. The first is that all of the items in columns 1 and 3 show a syllable interface where there is no segment ambisyllabicity option, thus:

$$\{_1 seld_1\}\{_2 ku\theta_2\}$$

$$\{_1 \varepsilon ln_1\}\{_2 bo\gamma \text{ə}_2\}$$

$$\{_1 f\text{æ}st_1\}\{_2 n\text{ə}n_2\}$$

$$\{_1 g\text{ɔ}d_1\}\{_2 s\text{ɪ}b_2\}$$

sequences such as [dk]. [nb], [stn] never acting as syllable onsets or

TABLE 3.38

Old English		12–15th- Middle English century		
⟨milds⟩ ⟨milts⟩		⟨miltsa⟩ ⟨mildse⟩ ⟨mildsce⟩	⟨milse⟩ ⟨milce⟩ ⟨milche⟩	*'mercy'*
⟨seldlic⟩	⟨sellic⟩		⟨selli⟩ ⟨sillice⟩	*'rare'*
⟨elnboga⟩	⟨elboga⟩		⟨elbo⟩	*'elbow'*
⟨seldcuþ⟩		⟨sildecouth⟩	⟨selcouth⟩ ⟨selcude⟩ ⟨selcuht⟩	*'wondrous'*
⟨self-hælu⟩		⟨self-hele⟩	⟨selfele⟩ ⟨selhele⟩	*'plant'*
⟨godspel⟩		⟨godspelle⟩	⟨gosspel⟩ †⟨godespel⟩	*'gospel'*
⟨god-sunu⟩		⟨god-sone⟩	⟨gossone⟩ ⟨cossone⟩	*'godson'*
⟨godsibb⟩		⟨godsibbe⟩ ⟨godsib⟩	⟨gossibbe⟩ ⟨gosseb⟩ ⟨gossip⟩ †⟨goddesibbe⟩	*'godparent'*
⟨myrgþ⟩		⟨mirght⟩ ⟨mirhthe⟩ ⟨merhþe⟩	⟨mirthe⟩ ⟨murʒe⟩	*'joy'*
⟨freondscipe⟩		⟨frendshipe⟩	⟨frenship⟩ ⟨fronship⟩ ⟨frenchip⟩	*'friendship'*
		⟨chapfare⟩ ⟨cheapfare⟩ ⟨chapuare⟩	⟨cheffare⟩ ⟨chaffere⟩ ⟨chaffre⟩	*'commerce'*
⟨fæstnian⟩		⟨fastnen⟩	⟨fasten⟩	*'fasten'*
⟨Norþfolc⟩ ⟨Suþfolc⟩		⟨northfolk⟩ ⟨suthfolk⟩	⟨Norfolk⟩ ⟨suffolk⟩	
I	2	3	4	

codas in English, thus making impossible overlapping syllable divisions such as

$$*\{sɛl\{d\}kuθ\}$$

$$*\{sɛld\{k\}uθ\}$$

At the same time, [ds] terminations are ruled out as they offend the syllable pulse sonority level/sequence relationship ([ds] sequences appearing at word end only when [s] is some kind of morpheme structure marking plurality or 'possession'). Secondly, the items in both columns 2 and 4 clearly show *segment effacement*, and cluster reductions/simplifications, such that, for instance, [ldl] → [ll]; [ds] → [s]; [dsp] → [sp]; [nds] → [ns] and [stn] → [st]. For such an effacement it is difficult to find either any persistent single phonetic feature characterizing the effaced segment or to discover any overwhelming commonality in the phonology of the triggering context as defined in terms of the surrounding phonetic segments. While dental obstruent [d]/[t] loss is common, so too is that of [f], [g], [p] and [θ] in the sample we have quoted. Although the contexts in which such loss occurs can be typified as very generally pre-fricative and post-[l] sonorant (-[st]; -[s]; -[f]; -[sp]; [l]-[s]; [l]-[k] and [l]-[l]) they provide little in the way of immediately obvious phonetic causation for the segment deletion phenomenon. What we should like to suggest is that it is the *effect* of just such a segment effacement to alter a syllable interface situation from one where no overlapping occurs to one where segments with ambisyllabic characteristics are to be found; the segment 'loss' is, we claim, a stratagem whereby ambisyllabicity is achieved, thus:

$$\{_1\varepsilon ln_1\}\{_2boy\partial_2\} \quad \rightarrow \quad \{_1\varepsilon l\{_2b_1\}oy\partial_2\}$$

$$\{_1frɛnd_1\}\{_2skIp_2\} \quad \rightarrow \quad \{_1frɛn\{_2s_1\}Ip_2\}$$

$$\{_1g\mathfrak{d}d_1\}\{_2spɛl_2\} \quad \rightarrow \quad \{_1g\mathfrak{d}\{_2s_1\}p\partial l_2\}$$

$$\{_1n\mathfrak{d}r\theta_1\}\{_2folk_2\} \quad \rightarrow \quad \{_1n\mathfrak{d}r\{_2f_1\}olk_2\}$$

For further details of such a proposal, see Jones (1976).

It seems to be the case, for reasons upon which we can but speculate here, that speakers tend to 'avoid' syllable interfaces whose terminal points or contiguous edges show unique syllable domain reference. Overlapping at such junctures seems to be 'preferred'. As the forms marked † in Table 3.38 above suggest, in addition to and alongside a stratagem like segment loss as a means of achieving ambisyllabicity at interface, there appears to be yet another pathway open to speakers whereby the same kind of result can be brought about. Consider the forms in Table 3.39. The

TABLE 3.39

12th–15th-century Middle English	
⟨godspel⟩	⟨godespell⟩
⟨gosling⟩	⟨goseling⟩
⟨demster⟩	⟨demester⟩
⟨remnant⟩	⟨remenant⟩
⟨selduþ⟩	⟨sildecouth⟩
⟨selfhele⟩	⟨selfehale⟩
⟨gostli⟩	⟨gosteliche⟩
1	2

column 2 shapes show the kind of 'cluster busting' phenomenon we have already witnessed in several places above and indeed look rather similar to some of the forms in column 3 in Table 3.37 (a) – recall there such spellings as ⟨chimene⟩, ⟨nemeni⟩ alternating with ⟨chimne⟩, ⟨nemne⟩. Our Table 3.39 materials show originally two syllable items realized with a 'new' third syllable, manifested as an innovatory peak vocalic element inserted at the non-overlapping syllable one/two interface. The effect of such a vowel epenthesis is immediately obvious: segments earlier uniquely terminal or instigating at syllable interface now take on a new syllable overlapping function at the boundaries of syllables two and three, thus

$$\{{}_1g\text{ɔ}s_1\}\{{}_2li\eta g_2\} \rightarrow \{{}_1g\text{ɔ}\{{}_2s_1\}\text{ə}\{{}_3l_2\}i\eta g_3\}$$

$$\{{}_1g\text{ɔ}st_1\}\{{}_2li_2\} \rightarrow \{{}_1g\text{ɔ}\{{}_2st_1\}\text{ə}\{{}_3l_2\}i_3\}$$

In this way we might argue that the otherwise unrelatable consonantal deletion and vowel epenthesis processes characteristic of the alternants in Tables 3.38 and 3.39 represent different pathways towards the same perceptual goal – *disallow syllable edge segments at syllable interfaces which are unique to their own syllable domain.*

3.5.3 'Shuffling' the linear sequence of segments in syllables: *metathesis*

We mentioned above in passing how speakers in our period could apparently 're-arrange' the sequential (linear) order of segments in syllables on those occasions when such a sequence contravened the dictates of the 'syllable pulse' model we proposed in section 3.5: recall how shapes such as ⟨nedl⟩ *'needle'* and ⟨sedl⟩ *'seat'* – with their coda final [dl] sequence defying the post-peak vowel-level 'fade' effect – came to be perceived as [nɛld] and [sɛld]. In this respect too, compare the Old English 'segment shuffling' manoeuvre whereby an item like ⟨wursm⟩ *'foul matter; puss'* with its sequentially 'misplaced' [s] preceding a relatively more inherently vowel valued [m] sonorant, is realized as ⟨wurms⟩ to show a rhyme segment sequence which tallies with the principle of post-peak vowel level decline. However, throughout the temporal span of the English language (although the phenomenon is possibly more particularly in evidence in some regional dialects between the thirteenth and sixteenth centuries) there occurs a well-documented segment sequence re-ordering crucially involving the highly inherently vocalic sonorant [r]. The data are well known and are set out in detail in most handbooks: Jordan 1974: sects 164–6; Campbell 1959: sects 459–60; Berndt 1960: pp. 196–7; Luick 1964: sects 714, 716. Fully satisfactory explanations for the phenomenon of [r] movement or *metathesis* are, nevertheless, difficult to come by and the motivations we offer in what follows must be regarded as highly tentative only.

Such an [r] sonorant 'movement' takes two forms: (1) those [r] segments which were etymologically in a pre-peak vowel position become moved into what is a post-peak slot: (2) those which are historically post-peak come to be found at syllable onset. Such a movement appears constrained to occur in two principle contexts, the first of which is illustrated by the data in Table 3.40. What is immediately obvious about the materials there is the discrepancy in [r] sequential placement between the column 1/2 items and those in column 3. Equally obviously, the rhymes of the former are extremely 'heavy' in their internal vocalic prominence composition; the peak vowel has to its right at least two segments whose internal vowel level is relatively high, a context which – as we might by now expect – is liable to produce perceptions of even greater vowel prominence or foregrounding. In the case of the ⟨beorht⟩, ⟨beornan⟩ shapes, that post-peak vowel density 'spreads' to the left into the vowel space itself producing there a vowel contrast of the *Breaking* (diphthongization) type. The column 4 instances witness this coda vowelly-ness concentration as it were 'spreading' to its right, and expressed through 'cluster busting'; the [rn] sequence being reinterpreted as a new syllable peak with [r] and [n] at its periphery – cf. the ⟨fern⟩/⟨feren⟩ *'fern'* and ⟨lern⟩/⟨leren⟩ *'learn'* alternations discussed in section 3.4.6. It is worth bearing in mind that our evidence in section 2.3.1 does not point to [rn] as a particularly 'prolific' *Breaking* producing environment; nor was that cluster a very successful producer of new long vowels to its left in the ninth-century *homorganic lengthening* process. Items like

TABLE 3.40

Old English		13th–15th-century Middle English		
(a)				
⟨beorht⟩		⟨bright⟩ ⟨briht⟩ ⟨bryghte⟩		*'bright'*
⟨fyrhto⟩	⟨firht⟩ ⟨furht⟩	⟨fright⟩ ⟨freyhte⟩ ⟨freiht⟩ ⟨freit⟩	⟨fyrihto⟩	*'fear'*
⟨wyrhta⟩		⟨wriht⟩ ⟨wryht⟩	⟨wyrihto⟩	*'wright'*
⟨þurh⟩	⟨thurh⟩	⟨thrugh⟩ ⟨through⟩	⟨thoruh⟩	*'through'*
(b)				
⟨ærnan⟩	⟨arnen⟩ ⟨ærnen⟩ ⟨hearne⟩	⟨rennen⟩ ⟨rinnen⟩		*'run'*
	⟨erninge⟩ ⟨eorninge⟩ ⟨urninge⟩	⟨renning⟩ ⟨rinninge⟩		*'running'*
⟨birnan⟩ ⟨biernan⟩ ⟨beornan⟩	⟨birnen⟩ ⟨bernen⟩ ⟨beornen⟩	⟨brinnen⟩ ⟨brennyng⟩		*'burn(ing)'*
1	2	3	4	

⟨corn⟩, ⟨horn⟩ and ⟨morn⟩ only sporadically showed increased duration as a feature of their stressed vowel space, a fact confirmed by their subsequent failure to undergo the palatalizing, labializing effect of the *English vowel shift* of the fourteenth and subsequent centuries. Such a 'failure' to lengthen might, we suggest, reflect the fact that a vowel + [rn] sequence was already seen as sufficiently vowel prominent to resist any further vocalic addition or heightening.

It is important to stress how clusters like this could *inhibit* the addition of additional vocalicness in front of them; we saw how items such as ⟨canon⟩, ⟨common⟩ and ⟨baril⟩ showed no increase in vowel duration despite otherwise conforming to the syllable shape dictates for the lengthening/lowering thirteenth-century *open syllable lengthening* process. The reason for this, we tentatively suggested, was that outputs such as *[baarəl] were perceived as 'over-vowelly', suggesting that there existed in speakers' phonologies some kind of intuition that items had an overall level of vowel-ness beyond which increase was non-phonological. The corollary of this is, of course, that there existed other configurations like, say, [metə] which fell short of that overall preferred vowel density level and which, as a result, could be inputted to a change like *open syllable lengthening* to produce a shape like [mɛɛtə]. In the light of such remarks, the removal of the highly vocalic [r] from the codas of column 3 items like ⟨firght⟩, ⟨wirght⟩ and ⟨thourh⟩ might be seen as a stratagem for *vocalic level reduction in the rhyme*; post-peak [rx], [rn] sequences are 'too vowel heavy' for mono-syllables, a conclusion supported by the data in Table 3.41 where we see [r] movement out of rhymes showing [s]/[š] fricatives.

TABLE 3.41

Old English		13th–15th-century Middle English			
⟨cærse⟩	⟨cresse⟩	⟨carse⟩ ⟨cerse⟩ ⟨cærse⟩	⟨cresse⟩ ⟨crasse⟩		'cress'
⟨fersch⟩		⟨fersh⟩ ⟨firsh⟩ ⟨versh⟩ ⟨versse⟩	⟨fresh⟩ ⟨frech⟩ ⟨freishe⟩ ⟨freysche⟩	⟨firesse⟩ ⟨verisse⟩	'fresh'
⟨gærs⟩	⟨græs⟩	⟨gars⟩ ⟨gerse⟩	⟨gras⟩ ⟨grace⟩ ⟨gris⟩	⟨gares⟩	'grass'
1	2	3	4	5	

But, as we noted at the outset of this section, [r] movement can be onset-to-coda directed as well. Consider the items in Table 3.42; it is clear from that presentation that the items in column 1 (a) are distinguished by the fact that (unlike their counterparts in Table 3.40) they show rhymes which are vocalically 'lightweight'; their post-peak segments show a pronounced 'fade' effect in being voiced or voiceless obstruents rather than continuant sonorants or

TABLE 3.42

Old English		13th–15th-century	Middle English	
(a)				
⟨brid⟩		⟨bridde⟩ ⟨brude⟩	⟨birde⟩	*'bride'*
⟨greot⟩		⟨gret⟩ ⟨grot⟩ ⟨grit⟩	⟨gert⟩ ⟨girt⟩	*'gravel'*
⟨ðridde⟩		⟨thrid⟩	⟨third⟩	*'third'*
		⟨crudde⟩ ⟨cridde⟩	⟨curd⟩ ⟨curddys⟩	*'cheese'*
(b)				
⟨frost⟩		⟨frost⟩	⟨forst⟩ ⟨vorst⟩ ⟨first⟩	*'frost'*
		⟨cruste⟩ ⟨croste⟩	⟨curst⟩	*'crust'*
		⟨cruskin⟩	⟨curskin⟩	*'tankard'*
⟨cristalla⟩		⟨cristal⟩	⟨cirstalin⟩	*'crystal'*
⟨crisp⟩	⟨cirps⟩	⟨crisp⟩	⟨cirsp⟩ ⟨cirps⟩	*'curly'*
I	2	3	4	

fricatives. Yet the (b) cases seem to contradict this characteristic with their post-vocalic peak fricative [s] coda component. However, all the syllable one terminations in the (b) instances are, in fact, *clusters* of [st], [sp] – the very clusters, we claimed in our discussion of Middle English *open syllable lengthening* (pp. 104–6), which behaved at syllable interface as though they were single obstruent segments. Recall how *open syllable lengthening* operated on an item such as ⟨waste⟩ but not on ⟨linken⟩ since [st], [sp], [sk] clusters were seen as uniquely *ambisyllabic*. All the items cited in Table 3.42 therefore witness a monosyllabic (or syllable one) configuration where the bulk of the syllable's vocalic weight or emphasis is confined to its *onset* area. In such cases, it appears (we might very tentatively suggest) that speakers prefer to reinterpret such configurations by transferring that weight to the coda; the [r] movement in this way activates a more highly vocalic (but still not *too* vocalic) rhyme, the rhyme being, as we have repeatedly shown, the place in the syllable where vowel heightening, foregrounding, more generally takes place. It is certainly worth noting that this onset-to-coda [r] movement is never to be found in items such as ⟨fraught⟩, ⟨fraunchise⟩, ⟨freli⟩, ⟨fremman⟩, ⟨front⟩, ⟨frothe⟩, where to do so would produce 'over heavy' post-peak clusters.

The ⟨crisp⟩/⟨cirsp⟩/⟨cirps⟩ alternants are puzzling, given the sequence reversal of the [sp] cluster which appears to be associated with the [r] movement. A similar phenomenon occurs with Old English alternants such as ⟨frox⟩ [frɔks]/⟨forsc⟩ '*frog*', but this innovation (unlike ⟨cirps⟩) might be provoked by the vowel-fade effect we claimed to be characteristic of coda consonantal sequences. This onset-to-coda [r] movement is another of those 'patchy' processes and is almost certainly lexical item specific in its application; many items exist in the inventory of Middle English where, although the conditions for its application are to be found, no [r] movement occurs: ⟨crib⟩, ⟨Crist⟩, ⟨crike⟩, ⟨crest⟩, ⟨croke⟩, ⟨frek⟩, ⟨fredom⟩, ⟨red⟩, ⟨rod⟩.

Chapter 4

The sixteenth to the eighteenth centuries

4.1 The nature of the data

The period spanning the sixteenth through the eighteenth century offers the historical phonologist what can only be described as a complete transformation in the kinds of evidence available for the reconstruction of contemporary phonetic detail as well as ongoing phonological change. It is especially noticeable that the level of 'direct' evidence increases dramatically during this era and there survive extensive data compiled by scholars some of whom, by any set of standards, show sophisticated and advanced views on the speech habits of real speakers. The sixteenth – eighteenth-century interest in all matters linguistic stems from a number of different factors, among them the general advance in understanding of human physiology and anatomy, leading to detailed description of the human vocal tract, together with an almost obsessive concern for some supposed rectitude in human speech form and substance, a concern only heightened by the manifest discrepancy between the nature of the spoken word and the written system used to represent it. Much of the comment upon current language use is, as we shall see, of a very direct kind and of a type not at all unlike that we are accustomed to find in modern grammars and technical manuals dealing with phonetics. At the same time, the period supplies a very rich source of supplementary evidence for the nature of the spoken word in the form of spelling books, foreign-language grammars, shorthand manuals and the occasional non-standardized spelling variants which are to be found in the various versions set up by printers in the process of manuscript to book production (Simpson 1935).

Plentiful too is the (not always unambiguous) evidence of rhyming equivalence, while it is also possible to find many pointers to phonological relatedness in the punning habits of several writers; thus, in Shakespeare's *Two Gentlemen of Verona* (Leech 1969) we find a word game centring on the homophonous nature of ⟨one⟩ and ⟨on⟩ under [ɔn] in the dialogue between Valentine and Speed in Act 2, Scene 1, ll. 1–2:

Speed: Sir, your glove.
Valentine: Not mine. My gloves are on.
Speed: Why then, this may be yours, for this is but one.

But by far the most important and insightful evidence for the contemporary state of the language's phonology and phonetics is provided by the large number of phoneticians, grammarians, spelling reformers and educationalists in the period (Cercignani 1981: pp. 1–23). In the course of this chapter we shall have many opportunities to examine in some detail the evidence provided by several of such sources and we shall endeavour to assess both the strengths as well as the weaknesses of the types of comment they offer. Even at this point it is worth coming to terms with the fact that, despite the detail and variety of the data left to us (often in the form of elaborate phonetic alphabets and detailed physiological descriptions), we shall remain confused and perplexed over many important matters of fact and interpretation. The existence of greater and more detailed data will on many occasions only serve to make some of the phonological problems appear more complex and resistant to explanation.

   As an introduction to some of the tantalizing evidence which contemporary spelling reformers, phoneticians and the like can offer the student of English between the sixteenth and eighteenth centuries, we shall briefly examine a few of the observations of one of the earliest members of such a group – John Hart (?–1574). Hart's feeling for the ineptitude of his current orthography as a systematic reflection of the spoken language (a frustration still felt by many today (Wijk 1959; Follick 1975)) is given clear expression in his *An Orthographie* (1569) ('conteyning the due order and reason, howe to write or paint thimage of mannes voice, most like to the life or nature') (Danielsson 1955–63; p. 171):

But in the moderne and present maner of writing . . . there is such confusion and disorder, as it may be accounted rather a kind of ciphring, or such a darke kinde of writing, as the best and readiest wit . . . can . . . attaine to the ready and perfite reading thereof, without a long and tedious labour, for that it is vnfit and wrong shapen for the proportion of the voice.

To these 'darke' writings, Hart offers two principle solutions. In the first place, he is anxious to set up a system of spelling where the least possible amount of overlap or mismatch between symbol and phonetic entity is manifested. At the same time, he attempts to provide detailed and specific descriptions of the nature of the articulatory mechanisms involved in the production of individual speech sounds. To the first end he is careful to select sets of symbols whereby as close a correlation as possible can be imposed between an individual graph and a specific sound in his phonological inventory. For example, in his *An Orthographie* (Danielsson 1955–63; p. 195) he sets out his solution for dealing with the ambiguous phonetic significance of the ⟨th⟩ spelling in standard orthography:

> we have a paire of soundes for which we doe vsurpe the th, alone, which I, with Sir *Thomas Smith* doe leaue, and vse for eche one a diuerse figure: and whereas he vseth for them the English Saxon letters called the thorne d, thus, ð or the Gréeke Δ for thone, and the Gréeke θ or Saxon þ for thother, I haue followed the readynesse of the hande, as is sayde for the dʒ, and tʃ, and haue deuised for this couple ð, for thone, d, or dh, and þ for th.

And this concern to provide as direct a mapping between sound and symbol as possible leads Hart to the production of a full-blown, highly developed and even by modern standards, quite sophisticated 'phonetic alphabet'. Consider, as an instance of this invention, the following version of the *Credo* represented in the phonetic script utilized in Hart's *A Methode* (1570) – a 'comfortable beginning for all vnlearned, whereby they may bee taught to read English' (Danielsson 1955–63; p. 247):

> Ei bi-līv in God ðe fāðr aul-mih-ti, mā-kr ov hevn and erþ, and in dʒe-zus Krist hiz uonli sun our lord. Huitʃ uas kon-sēvd bei ðe hol-li gōst, born ov ðe vir-dʒin māri. Suf-ferd undr pons pei-lat, us kriu-si-feid, ded and biu-ri-ed, hi des-sen-ded in-tu hel. Ðe þird dē hē rōz agēn from, ðe ded. Hi as-sen-ded intu hēvn, and sitþ on ðe riht hand ov God ðe fāðr aul-mih-ti. From ðens hi ʃaul kum tu dʒudʒ ðe kuik and ðe ded. Ei bi-lıv in ðe hol-li gōst, ðe hol-li ka-þo-lik tʃurtʃ, ðe kom-mu-ni-on ov sents, ðe for-giv-nes of sinz. Ðe re-zur-rek-si-on ov ðe bod-di. And ðe leif evr-last-ing. So bi it.

Even a preliminary glance at materials like these show that there are substantial points of difference between modern and mid sixteenth century pronunciation. Notably, spellings like ⟨riht⟩,

⟨aulmihti⟩ point to the realization of some post-stressed vowel
fricative segment, with Hart's ⟨h⟩ symbol perhaps indicating a
sound like [c], much as in many Northern English and Scottish
dialects where [nıct], [rıct] realizations of ⟨night⟩ and ⟨bright⟩
are commonly to be found. But it is the symbols used by Hart to
represent the stressed vowel space which most strongly point to
subsequent phonological innovation. Representations like
⟨Krist⟩ and ⟨sēnts⟩, for example, point to what were for Hart
monophthongal pronunciations, where many modern dialects would
produce a diphthongal vowel shape in [kraist]/[kræist] and [seints].
At the same time, representations such as ⟨dʒēzus⟩ and
⟨konsēvd⟩ would suggest that in the mid-sixteenth-century
pronunciations like [dʒeezus] and [kənseevd] were possible for such
items, pronunciations still heard from modern speakers in the
North-West of England and in many parts of Ireland. For large
numbers of other speakers, however, some kind of [ee] → [ii]
innovation has occurred. Likewise, Hart's ⟨māri⟩ shape points to
a stressed vowel pronunciation less palatal and more sonorant than
those like [meirı] and [merı] current in many dialects today.
Finally, Hart's ⟨kum tu dʒudʒ⟩, if we are to treat his transcription
at its face value, suggests that, as is still the case in many parts of
Northern England, the stressed vowel in ⟨come⟩ and ⟨judge⟩ was
close to, if not identical with, that of ⟨to⟩, and that ⟨come⟩/⟨to⟩
did not show the modern [ʌ]/[u] alternation.

Hart's 'phonetic' spelling is clearly carefully thought out and
detailed; not only is there a genuine attempt to map sound on
symbol, but he tries to indicate syllable boundaries and vowel
length. Yet, as every student knows who has tried to learn a foreign
language with the aid of even a modern narrow phonetic
transcription, judgements of a fine phonetic kind are extremely
difficult to achieve and it seems almost impossible to rid such
transcriptions of all levels of ambiguity. The specialized spelling
adaptations of the sixteenth and seventeenth centuries are no
different in these respects and, as we shall continually see
in the main body of this chapter, we are consistently faced
with problems of symbol interpretation and inconsistency of
usage.

Some of these difficulties can, however, be resolved since both
Hart and several of the grammarians, phoneticians and spelling
reformers of the period regularly provide highly detailed
articulatory descriptions and sound segment classifications, both of
which can often be used to clarify points of dispute arising from
uncertainty in interpretation of phonetic scripts. Table 4.1 from

Table 4.1

The Letters placed according to their Nature; 1. In respect of the Organs by which they are framed. 2. Of their sound; Semi-vowels, Aspirated, Sem-imutes, Mutes. 3. The several degrees of Aperture or closure either of the Organs or the found. Whether

Consonants framed by the

	Lips			Tongue							In the Throat			
	upper, lower, or both.			tip, moved or fixed to the						middle, moved to the	the root of the Tongue fixt			
	Extremity of both Lips.	Lower Lips to upper Teeth.	Lips shut.	Lower Teeth.	Breathed more dense.	Upper Teeth.	Gums.	Formost Palate.	Middle Palat.	Middle Palate.	in the inmost Palat, Breathed thro' the		In the Throat only.	
											mouth	Nose.		
Semivowels.	W	V	M	Z	Zh	Dh	N	L	R	Y	Gh	Ng	H	
Aspirated.	Hw	F	Hm	S	Sh	Th	Hn	Hl	Hr	Hy	Ch	Hng	:::	
Semimutes.			B			D					G			
Mutes.			P			T					C			

Vowels, upper, lower, or both:

	Open		Middle found		Close	
Guttural					v	
Labial	o				u	
Lingual	æ	a	e	e	i	

(v) is the Radical among the Vowels

All the Consonants according to their several feats, depend upon the Three Mutes, as the Radicals; from which all the rest are framed, according to the several Definitions of their Formation.

Christopher Cooper's *The English Teacher* (1687), is a good
example of the kind of systematic classification of speech sounds
typical of the scientific attitude to language description emerging
in our period. With its paradigmatic arrangement based largely on
articulatory place reference and its specialized terminology, it can
be clearly seen as a forerunner of the kinds of models for phonetic
and phonological description which were until quite recently widely
current. It is worth citing here too at some length Hart's detailed
observations concerning the nature of vowel production (*An
Orthographie*, Ch. iv; Danielsson 1955–63: p. 190) since it is
important to stress that (despite what subsequent research has
shown to be its limitations) throughout the three-hundred-year
span we shall be considering in this chapter, speculation in matters
phonetic could be quite meticulous:

> I finde that we vse fiue differing simple soundes or voyces,
> procéeding from the brest, without any maner of touching of the
> tongue to the palet or foretéeth, or of the lippes close ioyning
> togither: or eyther of the lippes to their counter teeth. Their due
> and auncient soundes, may in this wise be verye sensibly perceyued:
> the first, with wide opening the mouth, as when a man yauneth: and
> is figured *a*. The seconde, with somewhat more closing the mouth,
> thrusting softlye the inner part of the tongue to the inner and vpper
> great teeth (or gummes for want of teeth) and is marked *e*. The
> thirde, by pressing the tongue in like maner, yet somewhat more
> foreward, and bringing the iawe somewhat more neare, and is
> written *i*. The fourth, by taking awaye of all the tongue, cleane from
> the téeth or gummes, as is sayde fore the *a*, and turning the lippes
> round as a ring, and thrusting forth of a sounding breath . . . thus
> *o*. For the fift and last, by holding in lyke maner the tongue from
> touching the téeth or gummes . . . and bringing the lippes so neare
> togither, as there be left but space that the sounde may passe forth
> with the breath, so softly, that (by their ouer harde and close
> ioyning) they be not forced thorow the nose, and is noted thus *u*.
> And holding the top of your finger betwixt your téeth, you shall the
> more sensiblye feele that they are so made with your sayd
> instrumentes.

Yet even given all these detailed descriptions, formulations and
specialized alphabets, we shall soon see how many uncertainties
remain as to what constitutes even a general statement for the
nature of the phonology of our period. Indeed, in spite of such aids
our knowledge is of so limited a kind that we are still not able to
state with absolute certainty even how Shakespeare pronounced
his own name (Cercignani 1981: pp. 1–3).

4.2 Vowel length and vowel shifting: the *English vowel shift*

Two important and interesting facts emerged from our study of vowels with extended duration in Middle English in sections 3.2–3.3.2 above. The first of these was the apparent causal relationship between the durational value of the stressed vowel space and its highness value. Vowel length appeared to entail or at least be associated with 'shifts' in relative vowel height – either in overall increase in palatality/labiality (raising) or sonority (lowering). We observed, for instance, that the process of Middle English *open syllable lengthening* was rather inappropriately named since that particular phonological innovation involved not just stressed vowel lengthening, but also the *lowering* of all those non-low vowels which could be inputted to it, such as we can see in Figure 4.1. For some reason or set of reasons this stressed vowel

FIG. 4.1 Middle English *open syllable lengthening*

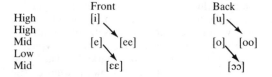

lengthening process in open syllables did not merely produce simple lenghtened versions of the input vowel, such that [i] → [ii] or [u] → [uu] (although we did note that just such was the case with some of the Middle High German dialects which also showed an innovation of this kind – see sect. 3.2.1) but lengthening apparently brought with it a concomitant shift of vowel height down 'one step', so that purely palatal and labially coloured vowels like [i] and [u] came to be perceived in this open syllable environment as lowered (that is, sonority 'contaminated'), as well as being durationally extended. That is, [i] and [u] outputted from the process as [ɛɛ] and [ɔɔ] respectively. We tentatively suggested that one causal factor for this attendant lowering with durational increase was the intrinsic tendency for long vowels to be perceived as lower – that is, there is some inherent connection between vowel height and vowel duration; the longer the vowel, the lower it was 'heard', we argued (following Klatt 1973). However, this is a phenomenon which we shall explore in more detail later in this section and we shall wish to suggest there that the length/'lowering' correlation is an over simple one for the kinds of phenomena associated with

open syllable lengthening processes. For instance, we shall produce evidence to show that this extended duration context is
just as likely to produce stressed vowel *raising* and even
diphthongization in the lengthened stressed vowel space. We
shall try to argue below that the lowering, raising, diphthongization
of contextually lengthened as well as lexically long vowels might
be viewed, in fact, as part of a single perceptual stratagem
associated with the production and recognition of those vowel
spaces which possess extended durational characteristics. However,
one very important feature tends to be hidden in general
discussions of phenomena like *open syllable lengthening*. The fact
that we have a set of vowel alternations triggered by a definable
phonetic context disguises the fact that the *result* of the rule process
is some kind of *vowel shift* affecting most of the derived long
vocalic items in the language's inventory. This Middle English
innovation shows the characteristics of what might be seen as
some kind of metacondition upon one definable and recognizable
area of the phonology – *all derived, innovatory long vowels which
are non-low become lower*.

This particular *vowel shift* is apparently phonetically motivated,
it has a recognizable context for its operational domain. But there
are others – and this was the second important point raised in our
discussion of Middle English long vowels – which do not,
superficially, in terms of a particular view of the causation of
phonological change, appear to be motivated in this way but which
nevertheless involve similar wholesale 'juggling' or redistribution
of large areas of the language's phonological structure. We saw
especially that there were apparently context free changes in the
stressed vowel space in many Middle English dialects where some
kind of unitary loss of sonority characteristic was being manifested.
Pure sonorants like [aa] were coming to be contaminated by labial
characteristics, while those segments mixed for labiality and
sonority saw that former 'colour' heightened. Changes such as [aa]
→ [ɔɔ] → [oo] and even → [uu] were taking place, changes paralleled
in the long front vowel set where palatality highlighting was being
manifested (cf. sects 3.3.1–3.3.2 and sect. 1.3). These sets of
changes we tentatively suggested could be seen not as individual
idiosyncratic events, but as representing some kind of unified
reaction on the part of the whole long vowel inventory of the
language, as expressed in Figure 4.2. We were careful to stress,
however, that a representation like Figure 4.2 was highly idealized
and that the application of the desonorizing tendency in long
vowels was extremely complex and constrained by a number of
different kinds of criteria.

FIG. 4.2

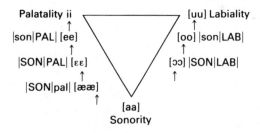

We shall see in what follows that important theoretical issues both for general models of phonological behaviour as well as historical change attach to explanations for vowel shifts in general, as well as for the particular version set out above, most especially for those which are supposed to occur without any *phonetic* motivation and which are supposed to be *context free*. But before we can arrive at such a point, we shall immerse ourselves in a fairly detailed investigation of what is one of the most intensively studied as well as widely documented of these supposedly *context-free* meta-processes in the historical phonology of the English language – the vowel shifting associated with lengthened stressed vowels which had a profound effect on the general appearance of English from at least the late fifteenth to the late seventeenth century, an effect which is still ongoing in many versions of the modern language. The phenomena we are about to describe, which can in many respects be treated as continuations and extensions of those chronologically earlier shifts discussed in section 3.3.2 are generally referred to in most of the standard handbooks as the *great vowel shift* and are of such complexity that our treatment of them here will of necessity be over-simple and effectively be no more than a summary of the main points relating to the interpretation of what is in fact a rather diverse set of phonological events. It will be no accident that we shall try to leave the reader with the impression that the data for this vowel shift event are not 'tidy'; indeed, we shall endeavour to stress the fact that the neatness often ascribed to the overall effect of the *great vowel shift* in many scholarly treatments is hardly justified by the primary evidence. Furthermore, we shall see that this neatness of description might itself be the direct result of a particular theoretical stance relating to the motivation for such context-free vowel shifts themselves.

In order to illustrate at least some of the major processes which will be our concern in the pages which follow, let us consider Verse xii from a most important text known as the *Welsh Hymn* or the

Hymn to the Virgin. Despite its name, this poem is written in English but according to the metrical, prosodic conventions of writers in the Welsh language of its period. In all probability it was composed by a Welshman at the beginning of the sixteenth century or perhaps even a little earlier (Dobson 1954; Forster 1926; Holthausen 1920). Its importance for the student of historical English phonology lies in the fact that it appears to show an attempt by a native Welsh speaker to represent the sounds of his English contemporaries using an orthography which was partly Welsh, partly English based. An approximate and rather literal translation of Verse xii might be: *'O trustworthy queen, who wears a crown, before we die ready prepared to thank you at the cross. Then may all we, thine own, go to the light. Agree to grant, with me, that I may see thee with my sight.'*

   The Welsh Hymn

  O trysti *kreist* tat werst a *kroun*
  er *wi* dei *down*, a redi dicht
   tw thank tw thi
   at te *rwt-tri*
  Dden went awl *wi*
   ddein own, tw licht
  Tw grawnt agri
  amen, wy *mi*,
  ddat *ei* mae *si*,
   ddi tw *mei* sicht!

When we come to compare the spellings of the forms we have highlighted in the selected verse with their equivalents in the language of say a hundred or so years earlier, we can immediately see in Table 4.2 that some rather dramatic phonological changes appear to have occurred. These would seem to be of two principal types. The spellings from the *Hymn to the Virgin* under the (a) instances there show digraph forms like ⟨ei⟩ and ⟨ow⟩ suggestive of a diphthongal stressed vowel space, whereas the corresponding late Middle English items show what we know to be etymologically the long pure palatal and labial vowels [ii] and [uu] respectively. On the other hand, the examples under (b) seem to show that where the late Middle English items have a long high mid [ee] and [oo] vowel space, the equivalent forms in the *Hymn to the Virgin* witness those segments apparently raised (sonority level reduced) to [ii] and [uu] – the Welsh ⟨w⟩ symbol most likely denoting a high back, [u], segment – an operation we have already witnessed at a much earlier date (see sects. 3.3–3.3.2) (Dobson 1968: vol. I,

TABLE 4.2 Fifteenth-century diphthongization and raising of long
stressed vowels

Welsh Hymn	15th-century Middle English	
(a)		
[ei]	[ii]	
⟨kreist⟩	⟨crist⟩	*'Christ'*
⟨dein⟩	⟨ðin⟩	*'thy/thine'*
⟨mei⟩	⟨min⟩	*'my/mine'*
⟨ei⟩	⟨i(c)⟩	*'I'*
[ou]	[uu]	
⟨kroun⟩	⟨krun⟩	*'crown'*
⟨down⟩	⟨dun⟩	*'down'*
(b)		
[ii]	[ee]	
⟨wi⟩	⟨we⟩	*'we'*
⟨mi⟩	⟨me⟩	*'me'*
⟨si⟩	⟨se⟩	*'se'*
[uu]	[oo]	
⟨rwt⟩	⟨rode/roode⟩	*'rood(tree)'*

pp. 2–6). The exact nature of the first half of the vowel space in
the diphthongal instances under the (a) examples is a matter of
some dispute among scholars, but there seems to be general
agreement that by 1500 (or perhaps even much earlier) many
lexical items which had contained a long stressed vowel space in
[ii] or [uu] witness those segments becoming diphthongized to
[ei]/[ou] or perhaps [əi]/[əu]. Evidence for this diphthongization of
late Middle English [ii] and [uu] is especially common in the
Hymn to the Virgin as can be seen from spellings there such as
⟨geiding⟩, ⟨abeiding⟩, ⟨deifyrs⟩, ⟨wythowt⟩, ⟨owr⟩ equivalent
to the late Middle English ⟨giden⟩ *'to guide'*, ⟨abiding⟩
'expectancy', ⟨divers⟩ *'various'*, ⟨wiðut⟩ *'outside'*, ⟨ur⟩ *'our'*. That
this diphthongization process affecting long high vowels was
perhaps in fact considerably earlier than the date of the *Welsh
Hymn* can be seen from the instances cited by Wyld (1936:
pp. 223–6) from the *Life of St. Editha* (1420) – ⟨y-leyche⟩ *'like'*,

⟨ley3t⟩ 'light', ⟨wiy3t⟩ 'wight' – as well as from the *Paston Letters* (1425–30) – ⟨abought⟩ 'about', ⟨faunde⟩ 'found' and ⟨withaught⟩ 'without'. Yet we might be inclined to attribute the *Welsh Hymn* spellings to scribal idiosyncracy with no special significance for phonological changes like raising or diphthongization. That we would be rash to do so is clear from the fact that many, if not most words derived from late Middle English equivalents showing [ii] and [uu] stressed vowels appear in many present day English dialects with diphthongal shapes as, for instance, in items like [main], [kraist], [haus], [daun]. Indeed, some modern Northern British English (especially Northumbrian and Scottish) dialects still show contrasting [uu]/[u]/[au]/[ʌu] pronunciations for items which in late Middle English had a stressed [uu] vowel space as in ⟨house⟩, ⟨mouth⟩, ⟨south⟩ and so on (see sect. 5.3 below).

Is it possible to turn to more direct contemporary comment to find unequivocal evidence of the kinds of vowel changes we have described in Table 4.2, especially for the two diphthongization processes? As we have noted in the previous section, there are extant many statements by writers of foreign language grammar books as well as by those individuals who were attempting reform of their contemporary spelling systems writing in the half century or so later than the author of the *Hymn to the Virgin*. These provide some very clear evidence for the fact that some kind of diphthongization (a dissimilation between the two vowel space halves) of both [ii] and [uu] had taken place or was in the process of actively occurring. Consider, for instance, the following statement by the spelling reformer John Hart from his *The Opening of the Unreasonable Writing of our English Toung* (1551) (Danielsson 1955–63: p. 129). Conscious of some kind of lack of phase or 'lag' effect between the symbols in his orthographic inventory and the sounds of his phonology, Hart complains that the symbol ⟨i⟩ in contemporary usage is being made to represent pronunciations other than, say, [i] or [ɪ], and as such being 'abused':

the *i*, we abuse in two wais: the first is in that we geve it a brode sound (contrary to all people but the skotts): as in this sentence. he borowed a swerd from bi a mans side to save thie life: where we sound the *i* in bi, side, thie and life as we shuld doo the *ei* dipthong . . .

Although using a metaphorical expression like 'broad' to describe the pronunciation of the ⟨i⟩ graph in the words he highlights, there would seem to be little doubt that Hart has heard pronunciations for such words where the stressed vowel space is not homogenous but dissimilatory. The same kind of conclusion can be drawn from the remarks of William Salesbury who, writing a year earlier, tells us in his *A Brief and Plain Introduction* under his discussion of *The sound of I* (Ellis 1869–89: Part I, p. 111) that:

> I in Welsh hath the mere pronunciation of *i* in Latine, as learned men in our time use to soūd it, and not as they yt with their Iotacisme corrupting the pronunciation make a diphthong of it, saying: veidei, teibei for vidi, tibi . . . And *i* is never sounded so broad in Welsh as it is in thys English word I (ego)

Here again we see the diphthongal pronunciation characterized as being 'broad' and it is interesting to note Salesbury's distaste for the innovatory pronunciation since such prejudices will figure large in many of the comments made by phoneticians in the sixteenth and seventeenth centuries whose writings we shall allude to below. Even as late as 1669 we find William Holder writing in his *Elements of Speech* that 'Our vulgar (i.) as in (ſtile) ſeems to be ſuch a Dipthong . . . compoſed of *a.i* or *e.i* and not a ſimple Original Vowel' (Holder 1669: p. 95).

Specific statements as to the diphthongal nature of ⟨ou⟩/⟨ow⟩ spellings for what had been late Middle English [uu] are not so easy to come by from sources similar to those like Hart and Salesbury, although in his *De Pronuntiatione Graecae Linguae* (1555) John Cheke notes (Alston 1969: p. 126):

> De v litera quia ea paucis doceri potest, pauca dicamus. V latinu scriptura simplex, sono coniunctum est. quare diphthongus potiusquam uocalis censeri debet. Id enim sonatur, quasi cum *o* coniungetur.

Whatever sound in represented by the symbol ⟨u⟩ or ⟨v⟩, it would appear from Cheke's remarks that it can on occasion not be a 'simple' vocalic sound, but a complex one, (the first) part of which is realized by that sound represented by the symbol ⟨o⟩. It would not be unreasonable to interpret such a statement as indicating a diphthong like [ou].

In addition to such innovatory diphthongization processes, the data we produced from the *Hymn to the Virgin* showed that long high mid-stressed vowels like [ee] and [oo] were subject to a raising to [ii] and [uu] respectively, a process we have already seen evidence of in our Middle English *vowel shift* materials in section 3.3.2. On this raising process there is much comment by phoneticians and spelling reformers in the following half century and later. Witness, for example, how in his *The Opening of the Unreasonable Writing* John Hart (1551) comments upon the discrepancy between the

graph ⟨e⟩ and its various combinations and any correlation it might
be expected to have with its 'matching' sounds [e]/[ee] and [ɛ]/[ɛɛ];
in Hart's time it is clear that many items spelt with an ⟨e⟩ symbol
at their stressed vowel spot were pronounced by many speakers as
high and front – as the 'pure' palatal [ii] (Danielsson 1955–63:
p. 129):

> We abuse . . . the *ee*, which most communely we use properli: as
> in theis wordes *better* and *ever*: but often we change his sound
> making yt to usurp the power of the *i*, as in *we*, *be*, and *he*.

In a similar fashion Hart's *The Opening of the Unreasonable Writing*
points to the fact that graphs like ⟨o⟩ or ⟨oo⟩, while they may
still in some dialects and certainly could historically represent some
kind of high mid [oo] sound, by the middle of the sixteenth century
had to be interpreted as connoting a vowel space which was high
and back – a 'pure' labial [uu] (Daniellson 1955–63: p. 131):

> Now see you whether we doo well to writ the *o* in theis wordes, do,
> to, & other (signifijing in latine *alius*) when yt ys the proper sound
> of the *u*

Similar sentiments are also reflected by Salesbury in his *Dictionary
in Englysche and Welsche* (1547) (Ellis 1869–89: Part I, p. 93)
where we find the comment:

> *O* takes the sound of (Welsh) *o* in some words, and in others the
> sound of *w*; thus To, *to*, digitus pedes; so, *so* sic; two, tw, duo; To,
> tw, ad; . . . but two oo together are sounded like *w* in Welsh, as
> GOOD gwd, bonus; POORE, pwr, pauper

where the Welsh sound represented by ⟨w⟩ was almost certainly
a high back [u] type segment. But we cannot stress forcibly
enough the fact that the details of such 'direct' evidence by
contemporary writers is extremely complex and difficult to interpret in a coherent fashion; not all writers in the sixteenth and
seventeenth centuries provide us with the same kind of incon-
trovertible evidence for the diphthongal and raising innovations
(Dobson 1968: sects 137, 160). Still, from what we have outlined
above there would seem to be some support for the view that at
least by the year 1500, for some speakers, late Middle English
stressed [ii] and [uu] vowels were showing alternations whereby
their first 'halves' were coming to be lowered (i.e. more
sonorant); what had been pure long vowel spaces were now
linear, sequential 'mixtures' of labiality/palatality and sonority.
At the same time, the late Middle English long high mid 'mixed'

vowels [ee] and [oo] were showing their sonority component diluted and targeting to pure palatal and labial positions in [ii] and [uu] respectively.

Before going on to discuss what kind of unitary phonological process the raising and diphthongization of stressed long vowels might represent, let us examine briefly the manner in which the other stressed long vowels in the language's inventory reacted during our period. Recall, that largely as a result of Middle English *open syllable lengthening* (sects. 3.2–3.3), many late medieval English dialects manifested two kinds of 'mixed' mid vowels: the one high and mid – [ee] and [oo], the other low and mid – [ɛɛ] and [ɔɔ]. Instances of the latter relatively more sonorant vocalic elements are to be found in the stressed vowel positions in late Middle English items such as ⟨beneðe⟩ '*beneath*'; ⟨*even*⟩ '*even*', ⟨grete⟩ '*great*'; ⟨steke⟩ '*steak*'; ⟨breke⟩ '*break*'; ⟨clere⟩ '*clear*'; ⟨before⟩ '*before*'; ⟨hope⟩ '*hope*'. A comparison of the late Middle English [ɛɛ] and [ɔɔ] pronunciations of the stressed vowels in these items and their present day equivalents is rather interesting. In all instances some kind of *raising* has taken place (in some cases accompanied by diphthongization), *but that raising has not occurred to the same 'degree' in all cases*. On the one hand (and this seems to represent the commonest situation with the front vowels) items like ⟨beneðe⟩, ⟨even⟩ and ⟨clere⟩ show stressed vowels which have become pure palatals [ii] (or perhaps palatally introduced transitions like [iə]); in other words, a 'two step' raising has occurred whereby apparently [ɛɛ] → [ee] → [ii]. On the other hand, items such as ⟨grete⟩, ⟨steke⟩ and ⟨breke⟩ would seem from the evidence of their modern 'standard' British pronunciation in [ei] to have undergone a 'single step' only raising transition whereby [ɛɛ] → [ee] (the diphthongization of [ee] to [ei] being, as we shall see below (cf. sect. 5.3), a late-eighteenth-century phenomenon). The items like ⟨before⟩ and ⟨hope⟩ showing low mid [ɔɔ] segments have, on the other hand, only raised by one 'step' to [oo] (and generally not to [uu]). Although we shall have to fill in much greater detail as we proceed, it would seem from a comparison of the Modern pronunciations and those postulated for the late Middle English period, that the long stressed vowels [ɛɛ] and [ɔɔ] reflect, as did [ee] and [oo], some kind of raising process (like that we saw in our earlier, Middle English materials in sect. 3.3.2), a movement away from relative sonority to a shape which tended to maximize palatality and labiality.

The unusual behaviour of the low mid front vowel [ɛɛ] in this innovatory process of 'vowel shifting' is worth examining in some detail, both for the light it sheds on the kinds of evidence available to us from contemporary sources for phonological change, but also because it raises some issues of potential theoretical interest. The examples we have cited in the previous paragraph apparently illustrate vowel height changes whereby [εε] → [ee] and [εε] → [ii]. The latter might suggest that 'two step' jumps in height like [εε] → [ii] were phonologically possible; on the other hand, an [εε] → [ee] movement might lead us to prefer a model which sees all vowel height shifts as constrained to one-step-at-a-time procedures. Under the latter thesis, those items above showing Modern English [ii] type stressed vowel pronunciations (⟨beneðe⟩, ⟨even⟩) must have gone through some [ee] 'stage'. We shall spend a little time on these matters not merely because they relate to one of the most important phonological processes in the diachronic development of English, but also because a detailed study will reveal how their treatment in many of the standard handbooks is too idealized and over-generalized.

4.2(1) Innovations affecting Middle English stressed /εε/

The evidence which survives to us from both sixteenth- and seventeenth-century sources on the exact nature of the vowel sound corresponding to late Middle English [εε] is not at all clear-cut, and there seem to be equally strong claims that it could be heard unchanged as [εε], raised by one 'step' to [ee] and even further to [ii]. Some of the most phonetically reliable evidence from this period is to be found in the *Logonomia Anglica* of Alexander Gil written in 1619 (Dobson 1968: pp. 131 ff). Gil developed what for his time was a sophisticated set of alphabetical symbol and sound equivalences which shows a highly developed 'phonetic script' type of notation with both specialized characters and diacritically marked detail (Jiriczek 1903: pp. 28–9). His evidence for the ways in which Middle English [εε] was pronounced during his own lifetime is worth examining in depth since on the one hand it shows us just how difficult it is to interpret even the fairly detailed phonetic comment of writers of Gil's status, but also on the other how such writers often took up stances which were prescriptive and judgemental concerning the innovations which were occuring in the vowel inventory of their phonology. A brief sample from one of Gil's transcriptions is worth our consideration (Jiriczek 1903: p. 124: Gil (1619)):

Brëk hëvi hart

Mjn eiz, no eiz, but fountainz of mj tërz:
Mj tërz, no tërz, but fludz tu moiſt mj hart:
Mj hart, no hart, but harbour of mj fërz:
Mj fërz, no fërz, but filing of mj smart.
Mj smart, mj fërz, mj hart, mj tërz, mjn eiz
Ar bljnd, drj'd, spent past, wäfted with mj krjz

Firstly, observe how Gil uses the ⟨j⟩ symbol especially to denote the [ei]-type diphthongal pronunciation in those items showing a stressed [ii] vowel in late Middle English – ⟨mjn⟩, ⟨mj⟩, ⟨bljnd⟩ – while we see the ⟨i⟩ symbol in the item ⟨filing⟩ suggesting that in his dialect too, like that of the author of the *Hymn to the Virgin* more than one hundred years earlier, the long high mid [ee] of the late Middle English [feelɪŋg] '*feeling*' had been raised to become the pure palatal [ii]. But there is nothing in his rhymes to point to any precise value for his ⟨ë⟩ vowel spellings. Their use with items such as ⟨tërs⟩ and ⟨fërs⟩ could signify no more than that they represented [ɛɛ], the phonetic value we might expect in late Middle English for the stressed vowels in such words, etymologically descended as they were from [æræ] type segments – cf. the Old English spellings for these items as ⟨tēar⟩ and ⟨fǣr⟩, suggesting a vowel space wholly or partly realized as [ææ], a segment later raised by possibly as early as the thirteenth century to [ɛɛ] as we saw in section 3.3.2 above (Ogura 1980; Jordan 1974: pp. 240–1).

The evidence for the status of late Middle English [ɛɛ] provided by his transcription system is, in fact, rather difficult to interpret. While he does distinguish two *e* symbols ⟨e⟩ and ⟨ë⟩, giving as contrastive examples ⟨best⟩ '*best*' and ⟨bëst⟩ '*beast*' (Middle English [bɛɛst]) suggestive of some kind of qualitative difference in pronunciation, the precise nature of that difference is difficult to evaluate. Gil uses the same diacritic mark to differentiate the stressed vowel space in items like ⟨kin⟩ '*blood relation*' and ⟨kïn⟩ '*sharp,/enthusiastic*'. This last, which if it corresponds to our modern [ɪ]/[ii] contrast obviously involves something more than just vowel height; durational variables (as well as laxness/tenseness) are also present. We shall see several examples in the pages which follow of the tendency shown by many of even the most sophisticated writers in this period to confuse or conflate length differences with those involving vowel quality, notably height. At one point Gil himself infers that the symbolic ⟨e⟩/⟨ë⟩ contrast was merely one showing *duration*: 'E, breuis est hac formâ *e* ut in *net* "rete": et longa sic, ë; ut in nët *neate*' (Jiriczek 1903: p. 24). Yet his notation would at least seem to point to the possibility that the kind of [ɪ]/[ii] relationship holding between ⟨i⟩/⟨ï⟩ was mirrored in that between what is represented by ⟨e⟩/⟨ë⟩; superficially, at any rate, we might deduce that this last infers an [ɛ]/[ee] contrast rather than one of simple length like [ɛ]/ ɛɛ].

But that raising of late Middle English [ɛɛ] vowels had in fact occurred among Gil's contemporaries, *but to [ii] and not to [ee]*, is unambiguously shown from both his transcription method and his

direct comment. Items like late Middle English [lɛɛvə] *'permission'*
and [mɛɛtə] *'meat'* are recorded in the *Logonomia Anglica* as ⟨lïv⟩
and ⟨mït⟩. The low mid-quality of the stressed vowel in the latter
item in late Middle English is by now familiar to us through the
lowering and lengthening process of Middle English *open syllable
lengthening* which has acted upon an inputted late Old English
shape like [metə] to produce a shape like [mɛɛtə]. It is interesting
to observe, however, that for Gil the new [ii] pronunciations in
items like [miit] and [liiv] were clearly stigmatized and characteristic
of the pronunciation of those members of society of whom he very
strongly disapproved. Such pronunciations he ascribes to the
speech habits of those effeminate individuals whom he describes
as 'Mopseys', and his attitude towards them is uncompromisingly
derogatory. Such speakers, he claims, 'chirp' or 'whimper'
(⟨pippiunt⟩) ⟨I pre ya gï yar skalerz lïv ta plë⟩ rather than produce
what he considers to be the more polite ⟨I prai you giv yür skolars
lëv tu plai⟩ where, alongside 'wayward' pronunciations of ⟨ya⟩
for ⟨you⟩ and ⟨skalerz⟩ for ⟨skolars⟩, we see Gil's disapproval of
the [liiv] pronunciation for what he would prefer to hear as ⟨lëv⟩
([lɛɛv]/[leev]). Again, he draws our attention to the fact that these
same Mopseys gluttonously devour (⟨liguriunt⟩) their ⟨biccherz
mït⟩ *'butcher's meat'* rather than more politely consume their
⟨bucherz mët⟩ (Gil 1619 pp. 17–18: Jiriczek 1903: p. 33; Wolfe
1972: pp. 52 ff; Dobson 1968: pp. 150–1, 650 ff).

Yet when we turn to Robert Robinson's famous *The Art of
Pronunciation* of 1617 (Robinson 1617) we appear to be faced with
evidence which quite categorically shows a 'one-step' vowel raising
of [ɛɛ] to [ee], and [ee] to [ii]. This work is an important source for
much of our understanding of early-seventeenth-century
pronunciation, and it is perhaps especially well known for
Robinson's *Scale of Vowelles* (Dobson 1968: p. 23; Wolfe 1972:
pp. 48–9) which we reproduce in Figure 4.3, and upon which we
have superimposed an outline of a cross-section of the human oral
tract: Robinson's AB parameter marks the roof of the mouth, while
his C symbol denotes the position of the root of the tongue.
Robinson's symbols have been the subject of much speculation as
to their contemporary phonetic value, but it can reasonably be
assumed from his own comments that the ten symbols are arranged
in short/long groups of five, those positioned above the dots
marking the lengthened versions of whatever is meant by the
preceding symbol at the interface of the joined lines. Dobson
(1968: pp. 206–7) interprets the symbols and their layout at Table
4.3. It is very clear from Dobson's interpretation and, as we shall
see below, from Robinson's own comments upon the *Scale of*

FIG. 4.3

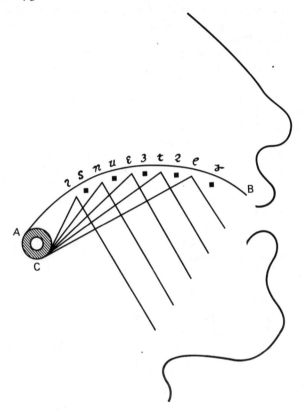

TABLE 4.3 Phonetic values for the *Scale of Vowelles*

	Position 1		Position 2		Position 3		Position 4		Position 5	
	Short	long	Short	long	Short	long	Short	long	Short	long
Robinson's symbols	ƨ	ſ	n	u	ε	ʒ	τ	ʔ	e	ɣ
Dobson's values	[ʊ]	[oo] [ɒ]		[ɒɒ] [æ]		[εε] [ε]		[ee] [ɪ]		[ii]

Vowelles that the five vowel pairs are not merely reflective of vowel-durational contrast; i.e. we do not see represented simple length contrasts like, say, [ɛ]/[ɛɛ] and [o]/[oo] within the various positions. Change of durational status appears to bring with it a change in the quality of the perceived 'long' version. In fact, Robinson's vowel *scale* is just that: it does not merely illustrate those places where qualitatively identical long and short vowels are positionally articulated in the oral cavity, rather it strongly suggests that what are perceived as vowel-length differences are also on some occasions to be associated with different tongue positions and configurations. Again using Dobson's (1947) interpretation of the symbol values, let us consider in Figure 4.4 Robinson's positions

FIG. 4.4

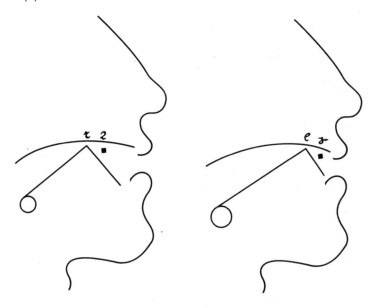

four and five. These representations clearly show that Robinson sees the tongue position for what he calls the 'long e' and the 'long i' as being further forward in the mouth, more palatal, than that of their short 'equivalents'. It might therefore be inferred that in such cases we are not, for instance, dealing merely with some kind of duration only contrast between [ɛ] and [ɛɛ], but some kind of frontness/palatality discrepancy such that the 'long' versions of [ɛ] and [ɪ] are, in fact, [ee] and [ii] respectively. The possibility of such an interpretation is reinforced by Robinson's own statement (1617: f. 35^r) that long vowels are to be seen as being:

> framed in the place of its short, but by the helpe of a longer organe, extended almost to the place of the next short vowell

in other words, the 'long' version of [ɛ] is almost of the same degree of palatality as [ɪ], from which we might deduce that a sound like [ee] rather than [ɛɛ] was intended to be understood. We might therefore argue that Robinson's evidence suggests that the [ɛɛ] which historically had been the long congener of [ɛ] had, by this time, come to be perceived as a more palatal [ee] sound.

4.2(2) Innovations affecting Middle English [aa]

Thus far, we have shown that those long front vowels which were mixed and only partially palatal in their nature – i.e. the non-[i] segments – were having that palatality component increased, such that [ee] → [ii] and [ɛɛ] → [ee] and even [ii]. The reasons for vowel shifts of this kind and the consequences such innovations have for the vocalic phonology of the language as a whole, we shall discuss in detail below. But before we attempt that task, let us turn to another set of sixteenth- and seventeenth-century palatalizations of the vowel space (primarily raisings), this time those which were to affect long vowels which in early Middle English at least had been low and back – [aa]. We have shown above that Middle English *open syllable lengthening* produced a new set of [aa] vowels from original [a] inputs; indeed here we witnessed the only context where that vowel lengthening mechanism did not bring with it a qualitative vowel change in the affected vowel space. Thus it seems that in the thirteenth and much of the fourteenth centuries, speakers in many Southern dialects of England realized a [aa] stressed vowel space in items like ⟨bathe⟩ '*bathe*', ⟨hare⟩ '*hare*', ⟨name⟩ '*name*', ⟨able⟩ '*able*', ⟨table⟩ '*table*', ⟨age⟩ '*age*', ⟨acre⟩ '*acre*' and ⟨ale⟩ '*ale*' (Luick 1964: pp. 397 ff; Dobson 1968; Bliss 1952–3). Many present-day, especially Southern British English regional pronunciations of such items show an [ei] diphthongal vowel space, suggesting that this long vowel too (like [ɛɛ] and [ee]) has undergone some kind of historical process of palatalization through raising and fronting. Indeed, even in some late Middle English dialects from as early as the fourteenth century there is evidence for an initial palatalization of the [aa] vowel to some kind of fronted [ææ] sound (Dobson 1968: sect. 100, p. 595). However, we shall show in what follows that there is much to suggest that the palatal 'contamination' of Middle English [aa] went much further in the course of the sixteenth and seventeenth centuries to reach values of both [ɛɛ] and [ee]. The diphthongization of that highly palatal [ee] vowel space so characteristic of many Modern pronunciations of words such as ⟨able⟩ and ⟨chaste⟩ was a development first observable, as we shall see later, in the late eighteenth century (cf. sect. 5.3).

Once again we shall find the kinds of evidence available to us for the sixteenth- and seventeenth-century pronunciation of those words which had [aa] stressed vowels in Middle English extremely difficult to interpret and often apparently contradictory. Only a fraction of that evidence can be presented here (and perhaps we could be accused of bias in the types of exemplification we ultimately select) but at least our discussion should serve once more to convince the reader that the vowel-shifting processes we are discussing are anything but straightforward or homogenous. The *Scale of Vowelles* from Robinson's *The Art of Pronunciation* of (1617) is once again of considerable use to us. Recall that Robinson used the special symbols ⟨ɛ⟩ and ⟨3⟩ to denote what corresponded (at least in Dobson's (1947) interpretation) to the vowels [a] or [æ] and [ɛɛ] respectively (see Fig. 4.5).

FIG. 4.5

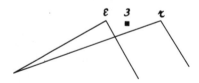

Recall that for Robinson the lengthened vowel values are not merely to be treated as durationally extended 'equivalents' of their short vowel versions. The longer vowels on this scale are to be viewed as being produced nearer to the articulatory position of the next frontmost segment. Thus, if we take ⟨ɛ⟩ to represent [a] or [æ], the ⟨3⟩ must be interpreted as being closer in its realization to the more palatal ⟨ɕ⟩, i.e. [ɛ]. If this is the case, then we might safely interpret ⟨3⟩ (if it is to be viewed as 'extended almost to the place of the next short vowell' – in this case [ɛ]) as [ææ] or [ɛɛ]. But while it would clearly be foolish to attempt to assign any precise value to Robinson's symbols, it is important to bear in mind that those between positions two and five, at any rate, seem to represent a *scale of relative palatality* and on the basis of that we can assert with some confidence that the lengthened version of some [a] type sound has, concomitant with this lengthening, had its palatality co-efficient increased to [ææ] if not even to [εε]. (But see Dobson (1968: p. 208) for a more detailed interpretation.) From Robinson's evidence it would therefore seem that an item like ⟨name⟩ (etymologically derived from one with an [aa] stressed vowel space) would have been heard at beginning of the seventeenth century with a vowel space somewhere 'between' [aa] and [εε], in all probability the item would have sounded [næææm] or even perhaps [nε̞ε̞m].

Evidence for what looks like the relatively more palatal [εε] pronunciation of Middle English [aa] seems to come from the anonymous 'R.R.' 's English translation of William Lyly's *Short Introduction to Grammar* written in Latin in 1540 (R.R. 1641). This translation (called *An English Grammar*) was published in 1641 and is claimed by 'R.R.' to contain 'easie and profitable Rules for parsing and making Latine. Very usefull for all young scholars, and others, that would in a short time learn the Latine tongue'. Under a section dealing with 'OF ORTHOEPY' ('the way of speaking purely and rightly') Lyly states that there are certain pronunciation vices to be avoided when using Latin, among them *Ichnotes*. This particular malpractice relates to those occasions (clearly to be shunned) where there is

a certain slenderness of speaking so often as we do pronounce certain syllables, more slenderly, and smally then is fit: as, say

Nunc, now		Nync
Tunc, then	pronouncing	Tync
Aliquis, somebody		Eliquis
Alius, another		Elius

(R.R. 1641: p. 3). Notice, as with the comments of Gil we have already recorded above, metaphorical terms like 'slenderly' and 'smally' are used to describe the innovatory pronunciations for the [aa] (created by *open syllable lengthening* in the Latin items ⟨Aliquis⟩ and ⟨Alius⟩), and that the new pronunciations are stigmatized – they are observed to be the hallmark of speech which is not considered to be 'polite'. Yet Lyly is not held to be the best of phoneticians (Dobson 1968: p. 599, sect. 101) and we cannot be confident that his ⟨E⟩ spellings in ⟨Eliquis⟩ and ⟨Elius⟩ in fact denote stressed vowel palatalization to the extent of [εε] rather than something more close to [ææ].

There are no such reservations concerning the phonetic

observational capabilities of Christopher Cooper who was born
somewhere near the beginning of the seventeenth century and who
died in 1698 (Dobson 1968: vol. 1, p. 281). Cooper's two great
works are his *Grammatica Linguae Anglicanae* (1685) (Jones 1911)
and *The English Teacher* of 1687 (Sundby 1953). Cooper provides
us with a most detailed account of the vocalic inventory of the
speech of his contemporaries and the conclusions we can draw from
his observations upon the pronunciations of those vowels
etymologically derived from Middle English [aa] are extremely
valuable, although once more they are not always easy to interpret.
He tells us (*The English Teacher* (Cooper 1687: p. 5)) that his
language has what he calls an *e lingual* vowel sound,
corresponding to the stressed vowels in his ⟨ken⟩ and ⟨men⟩ items
– it would seem the vowel [ɛ]. But like Robinson, and many other
phoneticians of the sixteenth and seventeenth centuries, Cooper is
careful to point to the fact that stressed vowel lengthening does
not always simply imply mere durational increase, it also often
simultaneously entails other changes to a vowel's make-up, notably
to its height. Indeed, his comments upon vowel lengthening in
general are worth considering in some detail. Some vowels, he
claims, show no qualitative difference under durational increase:

> The lengthning of the sounds, *a* in *ass*, and *o* in *nor*; as in *last*,
> *north* is distinguished by no signs; for in them there is no difference,
> than the measure of time in pronunciation; when as in others the
> short Vowel hath a distinct sound for its long one.

(Cooper 1687: sect. 11, p. 10). A few pages later, he asserts under
a section entitled *The true lengthning of short Vowels*:

> The true shortning and lengthning of the Vowels, and how every
> one of the short Vowels hath, for its long one, a neighbouring
> sound, distinct from it self, and a degree more subtle; or a
> dipthong; may be easily known from what hath already been said.
> But for a farther confirmation of this matter, I will compare the
> short Vowels with those sounds that are put instead of the long;
> and than set down the same short sounds compared with
> Examples; wherein they are sounded long according to their own
> true power. The *Vowels* according to the common institution are
> compared after this manner.

1	2	3	4	5	6	7
Can	met	will	folly	cut	meet	foot
cane	meet	wile	fole	–	need	food

. . . These short vowels, lengthened in their own true sound,
should be compared as in the following Examples.

1	2	3	4	5	6	7	8
Can	ken	will	folly	full	up	meet	foot
cast	cane	weal	fall	fole	–	need	food

From whence appeares that

(a)	in can		(e)	in ken, cane
(e)	in ken		(i)	in will, weal
(i)	in will	borrows its long	(ui)	in wile a dipthong
(o)	in folly	vowel from	(o)	in full, fole
(u)	in full		(ou)	in fuel a dipthong
(u)	in but			the same dipthong

.What conclusions can we arrive at concerning the seven-teenth-century pronunciation of the Middle English stressed [aa] vowel from observations such as these? Clearly Cooper is unhappy with his contemporary *orthography* which, although it will neatly supply matching pairs of *symbols* for short and long vowel sounds (as in the first set of illustrated pairs), nevertheless obviously fails to represent in any consistent fashion the clear discrepancy in sound between the long and short vowel 'equivalents'. Consider the use of the identical ⟨a⟩ graph for the stressed vowels in the items ⟨Can⟩ and ⟨cane⟩ in his examples. In the second set of examples, the latter, which derives via *open syllable lengthening* from [kanə] ⟨cane⟩ '*a hollow stick*', is paired in its 'own true sound' not with [æ]/[a] vowel items, but with the [ɛ] of ⟨ken⟩. Such evidence strong-ly suggests to us that the [ææ] sound so typical in the previous century for stressed vowels of this Middle English [aa] origin, have come by the mid-seventeenth century ("secundum" *genuinam pronuntiationem; Grammatica Linguae Anglicanae* (Jones 1911: p. 57)) to be further palatalized by raising to at least [ɛɛ]. But recall Cooper's injunction that short and long pairs (with the exception of *a* and *o*) are to be regarded as qualitatively *different* – a sentiment which might lead us to interpret the ⟨ken⟩/⟨cane⟩ alternation as one not reflecting an [ɛ]/[ɛɛ] but rather an [ɛ]/[ee] contrast. In other words we might interpret Cooper's formulations as suggesting palatalization of Middle English [aa] stressed vowel space to a *high* mid configuration. But not all commentators interpret these data in this way and other views may be had in Wolfe 1972: pp. 92 ff; Jones 1911: pp. 17 ff; Ellis 1869–89: pp. 82–3; Ekwall 1980: pp. 16–17; Dobson 1968: pp. 594–606.

However we evaluate Cooper's evidence for the pronunciation of the stressed vowel in ⟨cane⟩ – type words, it is important to observe that he makes no mention of any social or 'politeness' level of acceptability associated with it. The same can not be said for the observations upon stressed vowels derived from Middle English [aa] made some seventy years or so earlier by Alexander Gil in his *Logonomia Anglica* (Gil 1619). In the very same passage where he condemns his effeminate Mopseys for brutishly devouring their ⟨bucherz mït⟩ rather than their ⟨bucherz mët⟩ (see page 213), Gil also comments adversely on their habit of eating the ⟨këpn⟩ [kɛɛpən] '*capon*' rather than the ⟨käpn⟩ [kæ æpən]. Gil's ⟨këpn⟩ rendering of this item, whose stressed vowel in Middle English would probably have shown [aa] through the operation of *open syllable lengthening*, witnesses a vowel space which has been raised as far as the low mid [ɛɛ]. Gil's explicit comment is to the effect that palatalization of this [aa] as far as the fronted [æ æ] is all that is socially acceptable in his time. But he goes on to point to the fact that these dreadful Mopseys not only show a stigmatized ⟨këpn⟩ pronunciation but, he complains, 'just about' pronounce the word as ⟨kïpn⟩ (Gil 1619: p. 18). Their stressed vowel pronunciation is *not quite (fere)* so purely palatal as his ⟨ï⟩ symbol would suggest, but is to be viewed on this occasion at least as being somewhere between the [ɛɛ] of his ⟨ë⟩ and the [ii] of this ⟨ï⟩. Gil has no specific symbol for a long [ee] segment, so we might interpret his ⟨feré kïpn⟩ as [keepən]. In other words, the early-seventeenth-century stigmatized pronunciation is the one most close to the modern 'standard' Southern British shape [ei]. But for Gil it would appear that both [ɛɛ] and [ee] realizations for what was late Middle English stressed [aa] were a sign of the 'vulgar' and the regional – cf. his reference to rustic, dialectal pronunciations like ⟨beað⟩ [bɛəð] for '*both*', where the etymologically long [aa] vowel (vide Old English ⟨bā⟩) could only have been palatalized to the extent of [æ æ] (i.e. fronted) in polite usage known to Gil (Jiriczek 1903: p. 32; Dobson 1968: sect. 101, p. 601). Yet we might just argue that when three quarters of a century later Cooper, in attesting to [ɛɛ]/[ee] pronunciations in words like *able, chaste, name, capon*, accepts them without prescriptive comment, such raised palatal outputs had become the norm in this phonological context, and that perhaps even palatalization to the degree of [ee] was acceptably 'polite' to warrant no especially adverse comment from such an observant phonetician.

4.2.1 Possible motivations for such large scale processes

We have tried in the description of the *Middle English vowel shift* (in sections 3.3–3.3.2) to show that it was an extremely complex set of processes, subject to 'irregular' application and geographic variation. Yet perhaps the over-riding impression one has of the fifteenth – seventeenth-century *English vowel shift* from standard handbooks on the history of the pronunciation of English is the representation of these events (or something very similar) as a very uniform process characterized in the familiar display shown in Figure 4.6 (Jespersen 1961: sect. 11; Zachrisson 1913: pp. 71 ff; Wyld 1936: pp. 223 ff, sect. 112; Wolfe 1972: p. 1; Lass 1984: pp. 126–8; Wells 1982: pp. 184–6).

FIG. 4.6   The 'Great' vowel shift

Such sets of raised and diphthongized alternations, apparently affecting elements in the global vowel space in some unitary fashion and within the space of a relatively short chronological period, have always caused severe difficulties for the historical phonologist since they lack any obvious 'trigger' in the way of influencing phonetic context. One can make no appeal to familiar change instigators as some 'following consonant', 'vowel in the following syllable' or whatever. As a result, such 'context-free' sets of changes have tended to be explained in *phonological* rather than phonetic terms. In the case of the events under discussion here, it is the nature of the phonological space itself which has been seen by the majority of scholars as the framework within which some motivation for the vowel shift is to be found. Lying behind such explanations is the assumption that language users do not simply 'know about' their sound system in terms of inventories or lists of individual vowel and consonantal sounds, rather they can have intuitions about the ways in which these sounds are spatially organized in relationship to one another. More especially, language users are held to have intuitions as to the nature of the corporate vowel space within which the individual vocalic elements operate. The phonological part of the speaker's grammar contains information concerning the *spatial symmetry* of the arrangement of individual vowels in relationship to others in the overall vocalic inventory. This symmetry is part and parcel of speakers' 'knowledge' of their phonology and any individual phonetic change which (co-incidentally) unbalances that symmetrical arrangement can cause some kind of compensatory 'reaction' in the overall system of vowel organization. For instance, a language – like some dialects of late Middle English, for example – which has a long vowel inventory like [ii], [uu], [ee], [oo], [ɛɛ] and [ɔɔ], demonstrates a very 'neat' vowel space symmetry with occupied space at all three (non-low) heights for front and back vowels (see Fig. 4.7). In such

FIG. 4.7   Middle English long vowel segments

Front	Back	
[ii]	[uu]	High
[ee]	[oo]	High/mid
[ɛɛ]	[ɔɔ]	Low/mid

a system all the non-low height/frontness slots are 'filled', and there is a clear spatial organizational symmetry. Many writers have argued that phonological change is constrained by the existence of symmetries of this kind. Any changes which might result in the 'distortion' of the symmetry are to be avoided or 'compensated' for. Such distortion, it is argued, can occur in two main ways. In the case of the symmetry cited immediately above, independent sets of phonetic changes to individual long vowels (say transforming them into diphthongs) could result in the production of a *hole* or *gap* in the symmetrical pattern. Again, the creation of some 'new' long vowel could cause the addition to the symmetry of an element which has no matching 'partner' (King 1969; Prins 1972; Yamada 1984; Martinet 1955). The appearance of such symmetry distorting vowel segments will, it is claimed, cause the symmetry itself to 'react' or 'adjust' in the direction of restoration of some similarly patterned global vowel space configuration. Most importantly, *chain reactions* can be set up as a result of any deformity to the language user's perception as to an established regularity in the way in which individual vowel elements are arranged.

   Let us examine briefly two types of symmetry irregularity and the ways in which global vowel space 'readjustment' can result. Consider a situation where in a language like late Middle English with a (partial) long vowel inventory like that outlined in Figure 4.7 above, there occurred some independent phonetically mo-tivated process whereby high long vowels showed an increase in the sonority component of their first 'halves' – i.e. [ii] and [uu] become diphthongized to, say, [ei] and [ou] respectively. Such a change (illustrated in Fig. 4.8) has consequences for the previously symmetrical global long vowel space, in that it creates 'gaps' in the system. It is often argued that as a result of some kind of *symmetry preservation constraint* speakers will instigate innovations in their phonology whereby the original symmetry is restored, and the

FIG. 4.8

$$[ei] \longleftarrow [empty] \qquad [empty] \longrightarrow [ou]$$
$$[ee] \qquad\qquad [oo]$$
$$[\varepsilon\varepsilon] \qquad\qquad [\mathfrak{I}\mathfrak{I}]$$

'gaps' left by the diphthongization filled. One method whereby this might be achieved, would be for the lower [ee] and [oo] vowels to raise into the positions held by the original high vowels. But that move, in its turn, would leave 'gaps' in the symmetry of the vowel space at the high, mid positions. As a direct consequence, so goes the argument, these gaps too will be filled through the mechanism of the raising of [εε] and [ɔɔ] into the [ee] and [oo] slots. Clearly a kind of *chain reaction* is established in such a scenario, and it is this which gives the driving force to the vowel shift phenomenon. Such gap-filling reactions have been referred to as *pull chains* (Jespersen 1961: sect. 8; Samuels 1972: pp. 25 ff; Dobson 1968: sect. 137 ff; Martinet 1955: pp. 241 ff).

Yet another kind of chain reaction can be instigated inside phonological symmetries in situations where additional elements are this time added to the global vowel space to 'unsettle' the symmetrical order. Consider again a symmetry like that outlined in Figure 4.7 appropriate to some late Middle English dialects,

FIG. 4.9

Front	Back	
[ii]	[uu]	High
[ee]	[oo]	High/mid
[εε]	[ɔɔ]	Low/mid
[ææ]	[empty]	Low

into to which is inserted a new [ææ] segment, the result of an independent process which has palatalized that phonology's [aa] vowel space: here the result of the palatalization has been to cause an asymmetry in the vowel space with an *empty* slot in the low/back position (Figure 4.9). One solution would be, of course, to fill the vacant slot with some new [aa] segment. However, an alternative, symmetry restoring stratagem would be to let the relatively palatal [ææ] vowel 'merge' with the next most palatal segment [εε], thus restoring the vowel balance by taking the offending [ææ] 'out' of the system altogether. Thus, all those lexical items with a stressed [ææ] vowel space would, under this theory, become re-entered in the dictionary alongside those containing the 'original' [εε]. But many writers have argued that such a solution has a high 'cost', namely there would be a dramatic increase in homonyms; the number of minimal pair lexical items distinguished by a vocalic [ɛɛ]/[ææ] contrast would be dramatically reduced, and the original [ɛɛ] vowel would have to take on an additional communicative 'load' (Martinet 1955: p. 241; Samuels 1972: pp. 132 ff). To avoid such a *merger* brought about by the invasion of its phonological space by the further palatized [ææ], the original [ɛɛ] will be forced out of its slot and, in its turn, become identified with the next most palatal segment near it, namely [ee]. Thus a *push chain* type of reaction is set up in the phonological vowel space, necessitated not only by some constraint upon the preservation of symmetry but by one which makes appeal to some kind of *avoidance of merger principle*.

It is important to realize too that the corollary of this model will be that some items will have to be 'pushed out' of the global vowel space. For instance, it is a recurrent theme in the work of those who propose such push chain hypotheses, that the high segments [ii] and [uu] have metaphorically 'nowhere to go' when their space is invaded by the [ee] and [oo] from the level beneath them. It is often rather naively stated that the already high tongue positions of both [ii] and [uu] infer that further raising for them would result in contact of the tongue with the roof of the mouth, thus producing some kind of consonantal element. The only 'route' open to these high segments in the attempt to avoid collapse with [ee] and [oo] segments undergoing raising, is their displacement 'outside' the long vowel symmetry – they become realized as diphthongs. Such a view is clearly rather crude, since dipthongization would clearly not be the only 'avoidance' stratagem available (fronting, for example, might be another possibility for high back [uu] segments), while the assumption that there cannot be several possibilities for height differentiation among 'high' vowels like [ii] and [uu] is based upon a rather unsophisticated view of the phonetic possibilities (Ladefoged 1971: pp. 67–80).

It is essential to note the important characteristics of both chain reaction models we have outlined above. Essentially both treat vowel shifts as unified, unitary phenomena whose motivation is phonologically based. Importantly, the vowel shifts involved are not the product of some affecting phonetic 'context'. While both types involve some kind of instigator or 'driver', the drivers themselves need not be connected in any way to the effects they set off. The symmetry distorting processes (like the diphthongization of [ii] or the palatalization of [aa]) need in themselves bear no relationship to the kinds of processes undergone in the chain reaction. Their occurrence is purely co-incidental to the push or pull chain effect. But the actual chain reaction is a wholly dependent, inter-active occurrence. It is essentially a (phonological) cause and effect syndrome motivated and constrained by global (and often non-phonological) constraints such as *preserve the symmetry of the vowel space organization* and *avoid phonetic output merger*. While we shall go on to see to what extent chain reaction type shifts like those outlined above are an appropriate expression of the alternations affecting long stressed vowels in the sixteenth and seventeenth centuries as we have described them, we shall also wish to propose another – non purely phonological – set of explanations for such vowel shifts. We shall postpone until the corresponding section in the next chapter a discussion of the difficult area of what effect phonetic mergers may have upon ongoing sound changes (see sects 5.2–5.2.2) period.

The bulk of the scholarship which has centred around the fifteenth – seventeenth-century *English vowel shift* – from which we shall desist ascribing the epithet 'great' since it is hard to see on what grounds it is particularly outstanding among other similar processes or how it outranks in importance other phonological events like the various vowel lengthenings and diphthongizations we describe throughout this book – has focused upon evidence for the innovation as either a pull or push chain-type phenomenon. Clearly for both models the chronological sequence of events is of the utmost importance, Jespersen (1961: pp. 231–4) settling for a sequence of events where high vowel diphthongization pre-dates the raising of the non-high vowels, so leaving an empty space for the latter to infiltrate. However, despite his statement that 'there is some, to my mind, conclusive evidence that the whole shift began at the upper end' (1961: p. 233) none of the evidence he proposes is entirely convincing, and our observations in section 3.3.2 suggest (with their record of a 'de-sonorization' of non-high vowels) an at least equally early impulse at the 'lower' end of the vowel space.

Luick (1964: pp. 554–60) takes the opposite view from Jespersen, seeing the 'trigger' for the vowel shift in the independent raising of the mid vowels, this in its turn leading to the diphthongal displacement of the [ii] and [uu] segments which, as 'Vokalextremen' he clearly sees as having nowhere else to go. Lass (1980, 1984) basically pursues Luick's *push chain* interpretation of the vowel shift, stressing the interdependence of the entire unitary metareaction upon the behaviour of the mid vowels. To justify his stance, he points to some interesting data from some Northern British English dialects where the vowel shift appears to behave in an 'anomalous' way. In some of these Northumbrian phonologies, while we see diphthongization of the long palatal [ii] segment to [ei/ɛi], *the long labial [uu] remains unaffected by the diphthongization process* and we find lexical items like [huus] '*house*', rather than the 'expected' [haus]. Following Carter (1967), Lass sees the reason for the failure of the [uu] to diphthongize as resting upon the *prior failure of the back high mid [oo] segment to raise*. In the dialects under consideration, we find that [oo] fronts (palatalizes) to [œœ] rather than labialize to [uu] (see Table 3.14). 'No mid vowel raising, no high vowel diphthongization' runs this argument; thus the *English vowel shift* is some kind of *push chain* phenomenon (Lass 1984: p. 128; Donegan 1978: p. 100). But notice that push/pull chain hypotheses are based upon a model which sees the back vowel set as behaving in a way parallel to the front – cf. Dobson (1968: sect. 148, p. 674); where he explicitly states that the 'Raising of ME ǭ to ME ō is an isolative change parallel to that of ME ę to ME ē', while we shall show below that not all vowel shifts need behave in this complementary way at all. Indeed, we shall now go on to state some arguments against seeing the *English vowel shift* as some kind of purely phonologically motivated set of global readjustments reactive to distortions in some notion of a symmetrical vowel space and make some counterproposals of our own.

Yet there can be little doubt that at certain specific historical moments one particularly readily identifiable change or set of changes can affect a whole class of segments in the phonology of a language – a good example of this being the set of mutations to vocalic items we discuss in section. 2.5.3 under the general heading of Old English *palatal vowel harmony*. Although the 'period' we have been reviewing in our present section is hardly chronologically brief, extending as it does over some two hundred or so years, it would appear possible that something 'unitary' is going on, in this instance in relation to the relative height of long vowels, and that this 'meta-process' would obviously seem to involve some kind of cause-and-effect, chain-reaction-type process. Yet not all commentators are happy with such explanations for vowel shifts, seeing them as rather *ad hoc* in the way they characterize phonological constructs themselves and in particular viewing the models of phonological symmetry held up for preservation as being rather parochial in universal phonological terms. We must not assume as do many writers of historical treatises on the English language, that that language is somehow typical or normal. It is certainly far from being universally the case that all languages and dialects exhibit 'neat' height on height, back to front correspondences for the long or short vowel space like that outlined above for some late Middle English dialects. There are documented languages which show long high mid vowels like [ee] and [oo] without any [ii], [uu] matching symmetrical pair (the Wichita instance cited by Crothers 1978) and yet others, like Fox and Shawnee which apparently show a vowel space such that

	FRONT		BACK
HIGH	[i]		EMPTY
MID	[e]		[o]
LOW	EMPTY	[ɑ]	EMPTY

or the Mikasuki vowel system which contains only [i], [o] and [ɑ] (Crothers 1978; Hockett 1955: p. 54; Lass 1984: pp. 134–45). We might argue, therefore, that if such 'off-centre' symmetries are normal events in some languages, attempts to suggest that English historically instigates language change so that it subscribe to some 'canonical' phonological space typology, showing a targeting towards some kind of quadrangular classification where all vowels are seen as matching in height and backness, is at best *ad hoc*.

There is an increasingly popular view that all vowel-shift phenomena can be viewed as context sensitive. That is, the various raisings, lowerings and diphthongizations associated with vowel shifts traditionally seen as the product of chain-reaction effects, are now viewed by many phonologists as the result of *independent phonetic events which can occur both within and outwith global shift type contexts*, events which are independent of any attempt at targeting on some preferred distribution in the phonological space. It is important to bear in mind that not all recorded vowel shifts are 'unidirectional' – if we treat *open syllable lengthening* as a kind of vowel shift, then clearly lowerings as well as raisings of long vowels can occur. Nor do all vowel shifts even involve height changes, some only produce diphthongization, for instance, while we shall see that yet others instigate both diphthongization and height change (like the *English vowel shift*) but in ways which preclude any appeal to either purely pull or push chain effects. Even *open syllable lengthening* processes in some languages are just as likely to produce diphthongal effects as they are lowering and lengthening – cf. Lockwood's (1955: pp. 9–12) description of *open syllable lengthening* in Faroese where we find [æ] segments diphthongized and raised to [ɛa] – ⟨maður⟩ [mɛavur] '*man*'; ⟨lag⟩ [lɛa] '*position*', or even where they have been raised and lengthened to [ee] as in ⟨baoa⟩ [beea] '*to bathe*'; ⟨hagar⟩ [heear] '*over here*'.

Those vowel shifts deemed to be 'context-free' like the *English vowel shift* are fairly common across languages and by no means all of them involve principally raising patterns of the English type. Notably, the vowel-shift characteristic of the Malmö dialect of Modern Swedish clearly shows a process where all the long vowels have the first half of their vowel space systematically *lowered* (in the case of the back vowels, lowered and *fronted*) producing a set of essentially rising diphthongs, as shown (following Bruce 1970: pp. 8 ff; Lass 1984: p. 107) in Figure 4.10. Indeed, many vowel

FIG. 4.10   The Swedish (Malmö) vowel shift

ii → ei	uu → eu
ee → ɛe	oo → eo
ɛɛ → æɛ	ɑɑ → æɑ

shifts do not appear to be 'chain-like' at all. Consider the well attested example of the Dutch vowel shift which occurred over a long historical period between the eleventh and sixteenth centuries (notably in Brabant dialects). Here the long vowels of the Old Low Franconian language undergo various processes of fronting, diphthongization and even raising. Following Schonfeld (1954: pp. 87 ff; Van Loey 1959: pages 70 ff), it seems that the first 'stage' of this vowel shift was the fronting of the long, high back [uu] segment to [üü], as shown in Figure 4.11. Rather than move into

FIG. 4.11   The Dutch vowel shift 1

	Front		Back
High	[ii]	[üü] ←	[empty]
Mid	[ee]		[oo]
Low			[aa]

the 'gap' left by the fronting of [uu], the long high, mid [oo] diphthongized to what was possibly [ou] (despite the orthographic representation ⟨oe⟩, while at the same chronological period [ee] likewise diphthongized to [ei]. At a later historical date, these diphthongized [ei] and [ou] segments themselves raised to [ii] and [uu], while the front [üü] segment diphthongized to [ʌi]. We can represent the process as in Figure 4.12. What is most

FIG. 4.12   The Dutch vowel shift 2

[ii]	[üü]	← [uu]
↑	↓	↑
[ei]	[ʌi]	[ou]
↑		↑
[ee]		[oo]

interesting about this shift is that, while *raising* of the non-high [ee] and [oo] long vowels is involved – as it is in the case of the *English vowel shift* – that raising is, as it were a 'two-step' process; only the first half of the long vowel space is raised in the first 'stage' of the change, while raising across the vowel space's entirety has to wait to be achieved until the second stage of the shift. Clearly a shift of this type does not fit well into any model making appeal to a motivation based upon some kind of knowledge of phonological symmetry.

Can we make a case for suggesting that changes such that [ee] → [ei] and [ei] → [ii] are likely phonetic events in their own right and can occur independently of any phonologically viewed meta-condition on the global vowel space? Notice too how the [üü] of Middle Dutch, while it diphthongizes to [ʌi], does not do so under any condition that as one of the 'Vokalextremen' it has figuratively 'nowhere else to go', since its space has not been encroached upon by any 'pushing' [oo] → [uu] shift in this case. Can we again suggest that changes like [uu] → [üü] → [ʌi] are themselves 'natural' phonetically and are not the product of some pressure to conform to the dictates of some abstract view of the language's vowel space typology?

4.2.2 Vowel shifts as independent phonetic events

Put at its most extreme, the view that vowel shifts are somehow the product of a set of changes dependent upon the language user's desire to preserve some kind of idealized vowel distribution symmetry infers that the possible set of phonological inventories will constrain the possible set of vowel changes. Is it possible to hold to the opposite view that the set of vowel (and consonantal) inventories which we find in natural languages, together with the 'symmetries' into which they pattern, are the result of the possible set of natural *phonetic* processes? Under this model, phonological symmetry is a direct product of possible phonetic change or process type. Such a view is most fully developed in the work of Donegan (especially 1978), Stampe (1979) and Anderson and Jones (1974).

Donegan, for instance, views phonological sets and systems essentially as the direct product of possible types of phonetically motivated operations, themselves subject to constraints and implicational relationships. Her observations and conclusions are complex and we cannot do them full justice here, but one of the major characteristics of her approach is that it sees phonetic change and alternation governed by some kind of principle of *maximization of the phonetic properties of segments*. In the case of vowels, as we are by now familiar, such properties might include *palatalization, labialization,* and *sonority.* To intensify and magnify such features speakers will use a variety of stratagems, especially in the stressed vowel space. The motivation for such a highlighting of these inherent properties of vowels is to maximalize or optimize the *distinctiveness of the acoustic signal.* Donegan isolates a number of situations where there can be such an intensification of the inherent phonetic properties of vocalic segments:

(i) *Increased prominence for 'stronger' properties.* Those segments which are *mixed* or ambivalent as to their phonetic composition will tend to have one quality maximalized at the expense of the suppression of the other. All other things being equal, the more prominent one of the inherent phonetic properties in the mix, the more likely it is to become the dominant or sole property of the vowel space – what Donegan calls 'the rich get richer principle' (1978: pp. 67, 76–7). For example, segments mixed for palatality and sonority (say [e], [ɛ] and [æ]) will tend to be realized with one of these properties to the fore, the more so the greater the presence of that component in the mix (see our discussion in sect. 1.3). Thus, a segment like [e], a complex or mix of palatality and sonority, is likely to be raised, made more palatal, owing to the relative predominance of that characteristic in its complex internal structure. All things being equal, [e] is more likely to become more palatal than is [ɛ], although the latter is more likely to become more palatal than [æ]. But in a system where, for whatever set of reasons, [æ] happens to be palatalized to, say, [ɛ], then there is a strong implication that both [ɛ] and [e] will also themselves be palatalized further.

Again, in a situation where we find elements of relative palatality or labiality linearly juxtaposed, as in the case of diphthongal shapes like [ei] or [ou], there will be a tendency for the phonology to maximalize across the entire vowel space that segment which is closer to the pure palatal or labial form; on the basis of this principle, then, changes like [ei] → [ii] and [ou] → [uu] are likely to occur. It should be clear that such implicational or consequential factors can provide the basis for the establishment of the kinds of vowel shifts we have been discussing above, irrespective of any appeals to vowel space symmetry. Donegan claims that such inter-connected behaviour will also be curtailed by an *avoidance of merger* principle, and that any re-application of a componential maximalization will be rare; thus, she claims, it will be statistically rare for an [ee] segment, itself the product of an earlier palatalization of [ɛɛ], to have the palatalization component in its internal structure further highlighted such that [ii] results. But for some instances of just this phenomenon see section 4.2, although note how severely limited re-application of labialization high-lighting is in the *English vowel shift*, items like [fuul] '*foal*', [guust] '*ghost*' and [hjum]/[huum] '*home*' being rare manifes-tations for those whose vowel space usually only shows an [ɔɔ] → [oo] level of labialization increase (Dobson 1968: sect. 150. p. 676).

(ii) *Dissimilation*. Those segments, especially as we shall see, long vowels which are already heavily 'weighted' for one of the inherent componential properties of vowels, will tend to have one of their parts 'shifted' to another, contrasting property's value. This shifting will result in a polarization in the vowel space between contrasting componential values. The justification for such a polarization, Donegan claims (1978: pp. 74–6), is the maxi-malization of the acoustic properties of the vowel space signal itself. After such a principle, long 'pure' vowel segments like [ii] and [uu] tend to become (*linearly*) 'mixed' by causing one or other of their halves to take on some contrasting inherent vocalic characteristic – say sonority. In this way, we find the creation of diphthongs through independent changes like [ii] → [ei] or [uu] → [au], processes we are familiar enough with from our discussion above of various vowel shift phenomena.

Both the dissimilatory and component maximizing tendencies are most characteristic of vowel space which is in some way (especially durationally) extended or is linearly complex, since Donegan (1978: p. 118) claims:

> The greater the duration of a vowel, the greater the opportunity for heterogeneous articulation, and the greater the possibility that two targets – articulatory and perceptual – will replace one. A vowel which is extended in duration is especially susceptible to changes which affect it over only part of its duration, and to the further dissimilations which follow upon such initial changes.

Perhaps the most important aspect of this approach is that it does not follow the majority of standard accounts of the *English vowel shift* which see it as some 'context free' set of alternations, one triggered not on any independent phonetic grounds but the result of the dictates of the symmetrical shape of some phonological system. Rather, each of the vowel shift manifestations can be viewed as motivated by some *independent phonetically triggered process*. The two counteracting tendencies of (a) maximizing the predominantly present component in either an internal or linearly 'mixed' vowel space and (b) the 'destabalizing' of those pure manifestations of the labiality, palatality or sonority components in durationally extended contexts independently give rise to changes like vowel raisings, lowerings and diphthongizations. It is such independent and 'natural' phonetic properties of the phonology which can give rise to the phonetic inventory itself and the various constraints upon its patterning in a given language.

Let us consider in the light of the above, that version of the *English vowel shift* which Lass (1984: pp. 126–9) cites as evidence for the pull or drag chain 'principle' of *no raising no diphthongization*. Recall that he points to those Northern British English dialects where, although we find an [ii] → [ei] diphthongization, the long back pure labial [uu] undergoes fronting (palatalization) to [üü] rather than the more 'standard' diphthongization to [au]/[ɔu]. This lack of diphthongization, argues Lass, follows from the failure of the high mid [oo] segment to raise to [uu] during the period of the *English vowel shift*. This segment took instead a fronting pathway to [ϕϕ] or [œœ] and so failed to push [uu] 'out of the system' to some diphthongal [ou]. Following the fronting of [oo] to [ϕϕ], the Northumbrian vowel space prior to the operation of the vowel shift, might have appeared as in Figure 4.13. Given the

FIG. 4.13   The Northhumbrian vowel shift 1

Front		Back
[ii]		[uu]
[ee]	[œœ]	
[εε]		[ɔɔ]

'no-raising, no-diphthongization' constraint, the result of the *English vowel shift* upon such a phonological space would be the raising of all the long vowels, and the diphthongization of [ii] only, as in Figure 4.14.

FIG. 4.14   The Northumbrian vowel shift 2

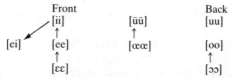

Two other features of the phonology of this dialect are worth noting at this point: the [üü] arising from the raising of [œœ] itself subsequently fronts to [ii] and the undiphthongized [uu] also fronts to [üü] and is eventually shortened. While it is reasonably obvious that changes such as [εε] → [ee] → [ii] can be seen as movements towards a highlighting of a feature of *palatality*, it is no less the case that one involving [oo] → [œœ] → [üü]→[ii] represents just such a palatality targeting as well. Indeed, in this dialect, all segments where there is a low level of sonority present in the vowel space appear to be moving in the direction of ever greater palatality. That from among the back vowels, [oo] rather than [uu] should move first in this palatal direction, accords well with a similar phenomenon we noted for the Old English *palatal vowel harmony* we described above in section 2.5.3. There, it will be recalled, there was a discrepancy between both the readiness of and the extent to which labial vowels palatalized which was a function of their 'height' (or labiality prominence). While [o] → [œ] → [e], [u] tended to restrict its palatal movement only as far as the mixed palatal/labial [ü].

Perhaps we can view the operation of the *English vowel shift* in its Southern dialectal manifestations in the light of the above. On the one hand, we could view its effect on non-high long vowels as one of a targeting to either palatality or labiality or, perhaps more symmetrically, as a movement away from, a suppression of *sonority*. Segments containing a sonority element in their 'mixture', say [ɔɔ] and [ɛɛ] would have it suppressed by the highlighting of their other vocalic component (either labiality or palatality) such that some [oo] or [ee] segment reduced in sonority would be realized. Pure sonorants like [aa] could be 'contaminated' either by increased palatality and so become [ææ] or alternatively (and this would appear to have been the chronologically later pathway for such segments) manifest an addition to their internal structure of a *labiality* component such that a segment like [ɔɔ] might result (see sect. 3.3). Long 'pure' labials/palatals would witness the dehomogenizing of their vowel space by having one of their linear halves contaminated by a sonority characteristic, such that [ii] might become altered to [ai]. Such a set of innovations we might schematically represent as in Table 4.4. For a more detailed description of such a process as well as its possible 'phonetic context', see Anderson and Jones 1974: pp. 78–90; Lass 1984: pp. 279 ff.

Finally, we might tentatively suggest that it is within this kind of framework that a 'vowel shift' like that witnessed in the Swedish Mälmo dialects is best explained. Recall that this phonological event showed long vowels being converted to diphthongs in such a fashion that:

[ii]→[ei]	[uu]→[eu]
[ee]→[ɛe]	[oo]→[ɛo]
[ɛɛ] → [ææ]	[aa]→[æa]

TABLE 4.4 The *English vowel shift*

Pure	Mixed			Pure	Mixed
SONORANT →	SONORANT → PALATAL	PALATAL sonorant	→	PALATAL →	SON.|PAL.
[aa]	[εε]	[ee]		[ii]	[ai]
SONORANT →	SONORANT → LABIAL	LABIAL sonorant	→	LABIAL →	SON.|LAB.
[aa]	[ɔɔ]	[oo]		[uu]	[au]
	Internal Mix				Sequential Mix

The effect of the change upon the 'front' vowel set is not unlike that we noticed for such vowels in the operation of Middle English *open syllable lengthening*. While that thirteenth-century English change brought about a depalatalization of front vowels through a relative sonorancy contamination *across their whole vowel space*, in the Swedish instance that sonority intrusion only affects the first, peak element in the long vowel, thus producing a diphthong rather than a new long, lower vowel. Clearly some kind of partial contamination of the vowel space is also a characteristic of the changes affecting the Swedish back vowel set. However, here the intrusive characteristic is *palatality* as well as *sonority*; those segments which are pure labials or sonorants or mixtures of both components show a move away from these features in the direction of palatalness and sonority; the palatal 'equivalents' of the mixed [o] and the pure [ɑ[segments are [e] and [æ] (again witness the similarity with Old English *palatal umlaut* process). Thus, the behaviour of the first, syllable bearing 'halves' of the vowel space can be characterized as in Figure 4.15. While the *English vowel shift* shows a reduction in sonority levels in its sonority bearing long vowel segments, its Swedish 'counterpart' shows a general tendency to increase the sonority level in the entire vowel space,

FIG. 4.15 The Swedish vowel shift

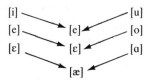

simultaneously reducing labiality in favour of palatality in vowels with labial characteristics. The result of the Swedish vowel shift is the maximization of contrast between the segmental components of the vowel space. For example, a change such as [uu] → [eo] produces a *three-way* opposition in the vowel space, such that palatal, labial and sonority elements are all present in the 'mix', while the [uu] → [au]/[ee] → [ii] changes associated with English version, while they heighten vocalic contrast through component suppression and addition, never achieve anything more complex than a two-way (sonorous/non-sonorous) contrast across the stressed vowel area.

4.3 Vowel diphthongizations and lengthenings: *Breaking* contexts and vocalizations

In this section we shall be especially concerned with an examination, in mainly sixteenth- and seventeenth-century materials, of the stressed vowel space in those contexts (like pre-[x]/[ç] or pre-[l]/[r]) which, as we have already seen in our discussions of both Old and Middle English, appear to bring about innovations involving either increase in vowel length or diphthongization. That such phonetic environments could participate in noticeable, and socially sensitive alternation is very clear from the passage in Shakespeare's *Loves Labours Lost* (c 1597: Act 5, Sc. I, ll. 17–27; David 1956) where the schoolmaster Holofernes in commenting upon the speech habits of Don Adriano de Armando, the 'fantastical Spaniard', observes that:

> He draweth out the thread of his verbosity finer than the staple of his argument. I abhor such fanatical phantasimes, such insociable and point-devise companions; such rackers of orthography, as to speak dout, fine, when he should say doubt; det, when he should pronounce debt – d,e,b,t not d,e,t; he clepeth a calf, cauf; half, hauf; neighbour *vocatur* nebour; neigh abbreviated ne. This is abhominable, which he would call abominable, it insinuateth me of insanie: *ne intellegis domine*? to make frantic, lunatic.

4.3 (1) *Stressed vowels in pre-/ç///x/ fricative and /l/ sonorant contexts*

The implications of the above remarks for us in this section clearly relate to the extent to which in our period post-stressed vowel [l] and [ç]/[x] could be effaced and the effects such an effacement might imply for the stressed vowel space itself. Let us begin by considering, as shown in Table 4.5, what kinds of stressed vowel mutations are associated with the [x]/[ç] fricative contexts in the

TABLE 4.5 Late Middle English *Breaking* and vowel lengthening before [x]/[ç]

	Later Middle English	
12th–15th-centuries	*15th-century*	
(a) 'he bought'		
⟨bowhte⟩		⟨boute⟩
⟨boughte⟩		⟨bowte⟩
⟨bouhte⟩		
⟨bouʒt⟩		
(b) 'night'		
⟨nighte⟩	⟨niiʒte⟩	⟨nyte⟩
⟨niʒte⟩	⟨neyʒte⟩	⟨nite⟩
⟨night⟩	⟨neyʒthe⟩	
1	2	3

period between the late fifteenth and seventeenth centuries, as well as the extent to which those segments themselves have become subject to deletion or effacement. We should remind ourselves at the outset of the types of spelling shapes which can appear from the thirteenth through the fifteenth centuries for items showing respectively a high, back [o] or a pure palatal [i] vowel contiguous with a following voiceless velar and palatal [x] and [ç] fricative. Table 4.5 represents a selection of spelling forms for the items *'he bought'* and *'night'* in that period. Although, as usual, all the spellings there are highly selective, those in column 1 and 2 show innovations to the stressed vowel space of a kind which we have dealt with in some detail in our sections on Middle English *Breaking* and *compensatory lengthening* (cf. sects 3.4–3.4.4 above). Shapes such as ⟨bowhte⟩ and ⟨bouhte⟩ appear to represent a diphthongal (two half) vowel space like [ou] which has been triggered by the post-vowel peak [x], while the ⟨niiʒte⟩ form unambiguously seems to show the durationally extended palatal vowel space associated with a [ç] fricative context. Those in ⟨neyʒt(h)e⟩ suggest some form of pre-[ç] Middle English *Breaking* of an [e] (however arrived at) to a diphthongal [ei]. Even the column 1 ⟨nighte⟩/⟨niʒte⟩ type spellings are likely in fact to represent a durationally extended [ii] vowel space; a conclusion which will have more force in the light of our earlier discussion in section 4.2, where we saw that the late-fifteenth-century representations of this item with a *diphthongal* vowel area infer that it already showed a long stressed vowel in the Middle English period. However, it is the column 3 fifteenth-century shapes (and they are usually more frequent later on in that century) like ⟨boute⟩ and ⟨nyte⟩ which seem to suggest that there has occurred some kind of effacement of the fricative syllable coda subsequent to its effect of 'filling out' the precedent vowel space; alternatively the highly vowel-like fricative has been reinterpreted ('vocalized') as the second (non-syllabic) half of the vowel space proper; for a discussion of both processes, see sections 3.4.1–3.4.3 above.

For most modern dialects of English, it is clear that the most obvious innovation to the column 1 and 2 items in Table 4.5 lies in just such a [ç]/[x] effacement, and in what follows we shall examine both the extent and consequences of that effacement as set out in the observations and phonetic alphabetic representations of some of the major phoneticians and spelling reformers of the sixteenth and seventeenth centuries (Wyld 1936: pp. 304–7; Wyld 1927: pp. 217–18; Dobson 1968: pp. 1985–8; Ekwall 1980: p. 79; Cercignani 1981: pp. 337–43). In general, the kinds of evidence we find in such sources suggest that by the late sixteenth century there existed many sets of alternants showing a contrast between the presence or absence of a post-stressed vowel [ç]/[x] voiceless fricative. Consider the remarks by Edmund Coote in his *English Schoole-maister* of (1596) (Coote 1596: p. 24), an 'Introductory manual for the teaching of English', where he observes of the digraph ⟨gh⟩ that they

> (except in Ghost) are of most men but little sounded, as *might, fight*: pronounced as *mite, fite*: but in the end of a word, some countries sound them fully, others *plow, bou, slou*: Thereupon some with *burrough*, some *borrow*: but the truest is both to write and pronounce them.

Again, in his dialogue in Chapter 6 (p. 33) where 'is set downe an order, how the teacher shall direct his schollars to oppose one another' occurs the exchange:

> Robert: How spell you *might*?
> Iohn: m,i,g,h,t.
> Robert: Why put you in (*gh*) for m,i,t,e spelleth *mite*?
> Iohn: Truth, but with (*gh*) is the truer writing, and it should have a little sound.

Here the suggestion seems to be that the orthographic ⟨gh⟩ representation is for some speakers phonetically redundant, while for others it has the status of whatever is meant by 'a little sound'.

A quarter of a century later in his *Logonomia Anglica* of 1621, Alexander Gil (Gil 1621) almost everywhere suggests by his use of the ⟨ħ⟩ graph that the post-vowel fricative is still produced: ⟨nouħt⟩ '*nought*'; ⟨souħt⟩ '*sought*'; ⟨tauħt⟩ '*taught*'; ⟨thouħt⟩ '*thought*'; ⟨njħt⟩ '*night*'; ⟨rjħt⟩ '*right*', ⟨brjħtnes⟩ '*brightness*', where the ⟨ou⟩ and ⟨j⟩ vowel spellings appear in his system to represent [ou] and [ii] (or the latter perhaps [əi] through the operation of the *English vowel shift* – cf. sect. 4.2); at any rate, the fricatives have triggered some kind of 'complex' vowel space (in the form of a diphthong or durationally long vowel) before them. Only rarely does his phonetic symbol system suggest fricative effacement: ⟨bou⟩ '*bough*'; ⟨nj⟩ '*nigh*' (Jiriczek 1903). Even by the close of the seventeenth century there is strong evidence to show that for such items, fricative-full and fricative-less forms could regularly be produced. In his *English Teacher* of 1687, for instance, Christopher Cooper (1687: p. 105) comments that:

> Some words that are written with useless letters; or that have their sound different from their writing have an arbitrary pronunciation . . . everyone pronounceth them as himself pleaseth . . . So *Fraught*, [loaded, filled, stored with], *Frɑt, Frait, Frӕte*

suggestive of pronunciations such as [frauxt], [frɔɔt] (where the accent ⟨'⟩ with the ⟨ɑ⟩ indicates vowel length), [freit] and [frɛɛt] (Sundby 1953: pp. xxviii–xxix). Yet Cooper appears reluctant to predict the circumstances initiating the fricative loss, arguing that the alternation 'lacks a common measure, and standing rule. Which I have not undertaken to determine'. However, by the mid part of the century it seems to have been the case that in many Southern dialects, both [ç] and [x] fricatives had been effaced in the post-(complex) stressed vowel position, since in his *Tractatus de Loquela* (1653) (Kemp 1972; Lehnert 1936), John Wallis asserts (pp. 30–1):

> *Gh* . . . I believe that this sound used to be pronounced in the English words *light, night, right, daughter*, etc., but nowadays, although the words are still written like this, the sound is almost always omitted. The Northerners, however, and especially the Scots, still have it, or rather they put the *h* sound in its place.

Certainly, by the latter part of the seventeenth century so complete was this fricative effacement in Southern dialects and the ⟨gh⟩ graphic shape so redundant, that those items showing complex stressed vowel space – with diphthongs in [ei]/[əi] derived through the

operation of the *English vowel shift* – were often to be found spelt
with post-vocalic ⟨gh⟩, even though their vowel space characteristics were never the etymological product of pre-fricative
lengthening or diphthongization, thus ⟨delight⟩, ⟨kight⟩ for
Middle English ⟨delit⟩, [deliit], ⟨kite⟩ [kiitə] (Ekwall 1980:
sect. 161; Wyld 1936: pp. 305–6).

Very similar kinds of evidence exist to show that in *Breaking*
produced diphthongal vowel spaces, alternants with or without
their [l] sonorant trigger could surface throughout both the sixteenth and seventeenth centuries. The evidence for a labially
contaminated diphthongal vowel area in pre-[l] environments is
clearly shown by William Salesbury in several of his writings,
notably his *Dictionary of Englysh and Welshe . . .* of 1547 in
which he tells us that "sometimes A has the sound of the diphthong
aw especially when it precedes L or LL, as may clearly be seen in
the words: *balde* bawld moel, *ball* bawl, pel: *wall* wawl gwal'
(Ellis 1871: Part III, sect. 1, p. 775). Salesbury suggests too that
effacement of the diphthong producing [l] sonorant (whether via
vocalization or deletion subsequent to diphthongization we shall
discuss further below) while prevalent, was considered to produce
variants which were stigmatized (Ellis 1869–89: Part III, p. 781):

> L . . . in some districts of England . . . is sounded like *w*, thus
> *bowd* for bold, *bw* for bull; *caw* for call. But this pronunciation is
> merely a provincialism, and not to be imitated unless you want to
> lisp like these lispers

His near contemporary Richard Mulcaster also points to what
appears to be an [l] vocalization phenomenon in his *First Part of the
Elementarie* (1582) (Mulcaster 1582: p. 128):

> *Albe.* which in our ordinarie speche we sound, *aub,* turning the, l,
> into, u, and so we entertain, l, generalie before most of our
> consonants. For thó we write *calm, balm, talk, walk, chalk, calf,*
> *calues, salues*: yet we pronounce them so as if theie had no, l, but
> onelie the duble, w or single, *cawm, bawm, taulk, waulk, chauk,*
> *caulf, cawues, sawues.*

While the 'turning, l, into, u' occurs in all the above items, it would
also appear that the ⟨l⟩ symbol is conventionally retained when
the labial element in the diphthong is graphically represented by
⟨u⟩ rather than ⟨w⟩. By the early years of the following century
it would still seem to be true that both the [l]-full and [l]-effaced
alternants were to be associated with some kinds of extra-linguistic
'formality level' criteria; Gil in his *Logonomia Anglica* (1621),

while recording such variants as ⟨fók⟩/⟨folk⟩, ⟨bâm⟩/
⟨bâlm⟩ and ⟨tâk⟩/⟨tâlk⟩ and admitting that the [l]-less
instances 'licet frequentius dicamus', nevertheless sees the [l]-full
variants to be the perserve of those who are *docti* (Jiriczek 1903:
pp. 15–16). In his *English Teacher* of 1687 Cooper also reflects
the stigmatized character of [l] effacement in such items, stating in
his *Of Consonants* (Sundby 1953: p. 68) that 'L is silent in *Almond,
Calf, Chaldron, Chalk, Half, Halm, Falconer, Mal-kin, Qualm,
Psalm, Sal-mon, Salve, Shalm, Stalk, Walk*'; yet he still records the
two [l]-effaced items ⟨Quawm⟩ *qualm* and ⟨wudst⟩ '*Would'st*' under
the heading '*Of Barbarous Dialects*'.

4.3(2) Stressed vowels in pre-[r] contexts

While so far in this section we have been drawing parallels between
the diphthongization processes triggered by both palatal and velar
fricatives as well as [l] sonorants in data from the sixteenth and
seventeenth centuries and those *Breakings* we found to be such a
characteristic feature of the phonologies of both Old and Middle
English (see sects 2.3 and 3.4 above), it will be obvious that there
is one of these *Breaking* triggers which we have yet to examine
in the later period – post-vocalic [r] either as the coda termination
in a word final syllable or as the first member of a co-articulating
consonantal cluster such as [rd]. We have deliberately separated out
for discussion the effect of [r] segments on their precedent vowel
space since although (as we shall see) there are instances where
they produce the kind of alternation we might by now expect, the
overall effect on the stressed vowel of a contiguous [r] in this later
historical period appears to be at once anomalous and unconnected
with anything we have so far witnessed. Let us begin, however, by
demonstrating that throughout the sixteenth and seventeenth
centuries the effect of a syllable terminal [r] was to produce a
linearly complex vowel space before it; this vowel space was
composed of two contrasting components (usually a palatal and
some non-palatal element). Indeed, the effect of [r] was one of
producing a kind of *Breaking* diphthongization rather similar to
that we have already outlined for the phonology of West Saxon
Old English. There, we will recall, were to be found shapes like
[eorl], ⟨eorl⟩ '*earl*' and [eorθ] ⟨eorþe⟩ '*earth*' cognate with 'simple'
vowel space items such as Old Saxon ⟨erl⟩ and Old High German
⟨erda⟩ respectively. That a process rather like this was operative
in our present historical period is clear from a comparison of the
data represented in Table 4.6 which is gleaned from Gil's
Logonomia Anglica (1621) (Jiriczek 1903). In his fifth chapter on
Dipthongi propriae, Gil states clearly that 'I. cum e, in diphthongam

TABLE 4.6 Seventeenth-century pre-[r] *Breaking*

(a)

[əir]		[əiər]	
⟨hjr⟩		⟨hjer⟩	'hire'
⟨fjr⟩/⟨fir⟩		⟨fjer⟩/⟨faier⟩	'fire'
		⟨attier⟩	'attire'

(b)

[ɛɛr]		[iər]/[iiər]	
⟨hër⟩		⟨hier⟩/⟨hïer⟩	'hear'
⟨dër⟩		⟨dier⟩/⟨dïer⟩	'dear'
⟨nër⟩		⟨nier⟩	'near'

(c)

[ɛɛr]	
⟨bër⟩	'bear'
⟨tërz⟩	'tears'
⟨spër⟩	'spear'
⟨fër⟩	'fear'
⟨fërs⟩	'fierce'

(d)

[iir]		[iər]	
⟨apired⟩		⟨apier⟩	'appear'
⟨appïring⟩		⟨apiereth⟩	

(e)

[aa]	
⟨rär⟩	'rare'
⟨kär⟩	'care'
⟨swär⟩	'he swore'

coalescit in *dier*, dama uel carus: j etiam, in *fjer* ignus, *hjer* merces'
(Jiriczek 1903: p. 301). Gil's spellings listed under (a) in Table 4.6
appear to suggest that subsequent to the diphthongization of the
long pure palatal vowel [ii] to [əi] occasioned by the operation of
the *English vowel shift*, the stressed vowel space comes to be
'contaminated' by some additional component spelt ⟨e⟩ and
traditionally interpreted as some kind of highly sonorant, central [ə]
type vowel, thus ⟨hjer⟩ [həiər]. Again, those items listed under (b)

show that the low front [ɛɛ] represented by Gil's ⟨ë⟩ comes not merely to be de-sonorantized or palatalized ('raised') to [ee] and [ii] by the *English vowel shift*, but once more its new palatal vowel shape becomes contaminated by [ə] addition, thus [hiiər] or [hiər]. However, it should be observed that Gil cites many other instances (represented by those under (c)) where not only do we find lack of [ə] vowel space contamination, but an apparent 'failure' of the *English vowel shift* to 'raise' the items in question further from [ɛɛ] through [ee] to [ii]. Indeed, this *Breaking* diphthongization process in [r] contexts seems, from Gil's evidence, to be constrained to occur mainly when the stressed vowel is predominantly palatal in its composition; internally 'mixed' vowel space heavily weighted for sonority and pure sonorant vowels (as the instances under (e) suggest) are resistant to the process, the significance of which will become more clear below.

But whatever the subtleties of its detailed operation, at least the types of alternations we see in Table 4.6 are those we might expect to appear in pre-[r] vowel space positions, given our earlier observations on Old English *Breaking* outputs. Yet it would appear – superficially at least – that there are other well-documented mutations to stressed vowels in [r] coda contexts which are of a different order from anything we have so far discussed. The principal of these we shall briefly and, given the complexity of the data involved, probably over-simply outline in the remainder of this section. Yet at its conclusion we shall attempt to demonstrate that they too can be characterized in terms of vowel space sonority contamination occasioned by syllable terminating [r] segments. Once more utilizing examples from Gil's *Logonomia Anglica*, let us consider in Table 4.7 the relative behaviour of what were late Middle English [oo], high-mid-back vowels in the early seventeenth century when they occurred in the stressed peak of words showing both non-[r] and [r] syllable terminations. The items under (a) are straightforward enough, witnessing the *English Vowel Shift* loss of sonority, labiality increase associated with the 'raising' of [oo] → [uu], Gil's ⟨ü⟩ spelling. Those under (b) are clearly more complex: they show stressed syllable terminations in [r] and their long [oo] vowels are in some instances (the *'sword'*, *'word'* and *'course'* cases) derived via the effect of the *English vowel shift* on [ɔɔ], a long vowel segment itself produced through the operation of late Old English *homorganic lengthening* (see sect. 2.2.4). Gil's representations for these [oo] shapes are very interesting and are reflected in the works of many of the spelling reformers and phoneticians throughout the sixteenth and especially the seventeenth centuries. The items in column 3 of (b) again show

TABLE 4.7

Late Middle English		Logonomia (1621)		
[oo]		[oo]	[uu]	[əu]
(a)				
[good]	'good'		⟨güd⟩	
[foot]	'foot'		⟨füt⟩	
[tooθ]	'tooth'		⟨tüth⟩	
[doom]	'judgment'		⟨düm⟩	
(b)				
[swoord]	'sword'		⟨swürd⟩	
[woord]	'word'	⟨word⟩	⟨würd⟩	
[koors]	'course'			⟨kours⟩
[joor]	'your'		⟨yür⟩	⟨your⟩
[poor]	'poor'	⟨pör⟩	⟨pür⟩	
[door]	'door'	⟨dör⟩	⟨dürz⟩	
I		2	3	4

what appears to be the regular operation of the *English vowel shift* on [oo] segments, indeed the examples in column 4 suggest that for some of these items Gil's phonology allowed the *English vowel shift* to progress a stage 'further' and diphthongize the [uu] segments to [əu] or [ou] (see sect. 4.2), Gil's ⟨kours⟩ and ⟨your⟩ spellings.

Yet the existence of examples like those in column 2 of (b) point to the possibility that the presence of an [r] syllable termination can *block* the operation of the *English vowel shift* on long peak vowels; 'raising' does not appear to have occurred for such items, and the sonority component of their durationally extended stressed vowel space has not been reduced. Some scholars (notably Dobson 1968: sects 201–9) see in data like that in column 2 evidence for a sequence of events whereby the *English vowel shift* operated normally in items like [poor], realizing as [puur]; the resultant pure labial vowel space was then, they argue, subsequently lowered to [oo] through the influence of the following [r]. However, we wish to claim here that syllable terminating [r] *obstructs* (and perhaps only in a 'patchy' fashion) the de-sonorizing effect of the vowel shift for reasons we shall discuss a little later.

Further evidence for this 'blocking' effect of syllable terminal [r] on vowel shifting of the raising type is also to be found in the extremely valuable lists of words which go to make up Elisha Coles' *The Compleat English Schoolmaster (or the Most Natural and Easie*

Method of Spelling English according to the present proper pronunciation of the Language in Oxford and London) (1674) (Coles 1674). The value of Coles' evidence lies not in any special phonetically orientated orthographic system, but in the fact that he carefully groups together sets of items showing a shared stressed vowel space characteristic. For our immediate purpose we should note the existence in the *Schoolmaster* of two specific subsets within Coles' first word list. One of these, which includes items such as *good, foot, food, book* (pp. 20–1), reflects the 'raising' of Middle English [oo] vowels to [uu] through the *English vowel shift* effect. The other subset, which includes items like *foal, mole, soul, loaf, mope, pope* (pp. 18–19) shows vowel space which is characterized as either [ɔɔ] or [oo]. In this second subset occur (with one exception) all the items with stressed syllable terminations in [r]: *ore, oar, bore, boar, core, door, floor, sore, sour, gore, goar, hore, whore, lore, more, Moor, pore, poor, roar, sore, swore, soar, score, shore, snore, store, tore, yore.* In the first set showing [uu] derived via the 'raising' of [oo], there are no instances of items (with the exception of *Ure* '*your*') showing syllable terminal [r]. The implication to be drawn from this seems to be that post-vocalic [r] inhibited or blocked any tendency to 'raise' [oo] vowels to [uu] via the *English vowel shift* effect. Indeed, Coles' brackets together as homophones items like *more/More* and *pore/poor*, the second of which show 'raising' of [oo] → [uu] in many modern dialects.

Such a 'negative' effect on de-sonorization processes like the *English vowel shift* can again be illustrated from the relative distribution of [ɛɛ], [ee] and [ii] stressed vowels in [r] and non-[r] contexts in sixteenth- and seventeenth-century materials. In his discussion of the possible phonetic realizations of the ⟨ea⟩ diphthongal digraph, Christopher Cooper in his *English Teacher* of 1687 and *Grammatica Linguae Anglicanae* of 1685, remarks that this spelling shape can for him represent at least four distinct phonetic vowel pronunciation types: '*Ea* is put 1. for *e* short. 2. For *e* long. 3. For *ee*. 4. For *a* and *a*' (Sundby 1953: pp. 49–50; Jones 1911: pp. 55–8). A sample of the items he places under these categories can be seen in Table 4.8. Although there is considerable controversy concerning the precise phonetic values to be assigned to Cooper's *e* long and *ee* (Jones 1911: p. 72; Wolfe 1972: pp. 100 ff; Dobson 1968: pp. 644–5), those we have set against Cooper's symbols would seem to have at least a large measure of support. What is perhaps most pertinent to our present discussion from these lists is that Cooper appears to be suggesting the existence in his phonology of some kind of stressed vowel alternation in pre-[r] syllable coda contexts. While the items set out in columns 2 and

TABLE 4.8

e short	e long	ee	a or a
[ɛ]	[ii]	[ii]	[ɛɛ]
⟨bread⟩	⟨appeal⟩	⟨appear⟩	⟨bear⟩
⟨breadth⟩	⟨bead⟩	⟨clear⟩	⟨beard⟩
⟨death⟩	⟨beadle⟩	⟨dear⟩	⟨earl⟩
⟨dread⟩	⟨beaker⟩	⟨ears⟩	⟨earn⟩
⟨Earth⟩	⟨bean⟩	⟨fear⟩	⟨learn⟩
	⟨dream⟩	⟨near⟩	⟨search⟩
	⟨eat⟩	⟨spear⟩	⟨swear⟩
		⟨sear⟩	⟨tear⟩
		⟨sphear⟩	⟨wear⟩
1	2	3	4

3 can be derived from late Middle English sources showing either
[ɛɛ]. (⟨dream⟩; Middle English [drɛɛm]/Old English ⟨dream⟩,
[dræam]) or [ee] (⟨near⟩; Middle English [neer]/Old English ⟨neor⟩,
[neər]) they all appear to attest a palatalization increase to [ii] via the
English vowel shift, even though the column 3 items show syllable
final [r] terminations. The examples in column 4, on the other
hand, mostly derive from Middle English [ɛɛ] through Old
English [æææ] or [æ] and Cooper's identification of them with [ɑ]
seems to suggest that, unlike the late Middle English [ɛɛ] derivatives in columns 2 and 3, they do not always palatalize to [ee]
or [ii] through the operation of the *English vowel shift*. They
seem to represent specific lexical items where the syllable coda
[r] has blocked the operation of increased palatality in the long
stressed vowel space before it. It is interesting to observe in this
respect too that in his *Schoolmaster* (1674) Elisha Coles pairs as
homophones column 4 items like *bear*, *swear*, and *wear* with
pare, *sware* and *ware* respectively in his list of forms showing
unambiguous [ɛɛ] pronunciations (Coles 1674: p. 9.)

The third effect of syllable final [r] on its precedent contiguous
vowel space which we shall discuss in this section relates to what
appears to be an actual vowel lowering when the affected stressed
vowel is short. Such a process was operative from the fifteenth
century, especially in Northern dialectal areas, as can be seen from
a comparison of the items in Table 4.9 (Berndt 1960: p. 70; Jordan
1974: sect. 66). Short vowel segments in [ɛ] (i.e. those with a
predominantly sonorant to palatal internal 'mix') show an increase
in that sonority component (or palatality reduction) such that [æ]

TABLE 4.9

13th-century Middle English	15th-century Middle English
⟨sergeaunt⟩ ⟨sergeant⟩	⟨sargeant⟩ ⟨sargeaunt⟩
⟨serpent⟩	⟨sarpent⟩
⟨sermon⟩	⟨sarmon⟩ ⟨sarmoun⟩
⟨servaunt⟩ ⟨serwand⟩	⟨sarvaunt⟩
⟨certain⟩ ⟨certen⟩	⟨sartan⟩ ⟨sartayn⟩
⟨ferthing⟩ ⟨ferding⟩	⟨farthing⟩ ⟨farding⟩
⟨herte⟩	⟨hart⟩
⟨fer⟩	⟨farre⟩

or [a] results, a process which was initiated even as early as the late fourteenth century. That such an innovation was at least partially productive in the seventeenth century as well can be evidenced from the writings of most spelling reformers and phoneticians during that period, and clearly seen from the spellings used by Gil in his *Logonomia Anglica* set out in Table 4.10.

TABLE 4.10

[εε]/[ε]	[ææ]/[æ]	
⟨hërd⟩	⟨härd⟩	'heard'
⟨swerv⟩	⟨swarv⟩	'swerve'
⟨dezert⟩	⟨dezart⟩	'desert'
	⟨hart⟩	'heart'
	⟨marchants⟩	'merchants'
⟨sertain⟩		
⟨deserve⟩		
⟨erth⟩		
⟨sergant⟩		
⟨personal⟩		

From the sum total of our observations above it would appear that the effect of a syllable terminal [r] on its precedent vowel space is rather a diverse one: we find diphthongization of long pure palatal segments – [iir] → [iiər]; 'blocking' of the raising effect of the *English vowel shift*; increased sonority (lowering) in mixed *sonorant*/palatal (mainly) short vowels – [ɛ] → [æ]. Can we in any way collapse these three apparently disparate effects under any general phonetic process? Clearly, the diphthongization instances show a *sonority* contamination of a vowel space which is (predominantly) palatal – a contamination *which is realized in a linear, side by side vocalic opposition*. The [ɛ(ɛ)] → [æ(æ)] lowerings are also to be seen, at least in the terms of the kind of phonological model we proposed in Chapter 1 (see sect. 1.3), as just such a sonority contamination of the vowel space, only in these cases that contamination in expressed *internally to the segment*; that is a pre-[r] vowel mixture in which sonority and palatality elements are present in equal proportion – [ɛ] – mutates to one where the sonority element comes to be the more prominent – [æ]. The *English vowel shift* blocking effect can also be viewed in this kind of light. Recall that one of the major effects of that vowel shift process was to bring about an overall reduction in the relative sonority of long non pure palatal/labial vowels (i.e. to increase their palatality or labiality), an effect we might characterize as in Figure 4.16.

FIG. 4.16

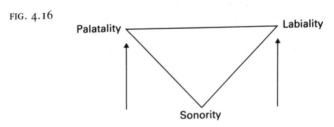

Palatality and labiality characteristics were highlighted at the expense of sonority components; vowels contiguous with [r] syllable codas show this process to be neutralized or reversed – existing levels of sonority are either retained or increased (Cercignani 1891; Valk 1980; Wyld 1936: pp. 212–22).

4.3.1 More *Breaking* stratagems: bi-continuant cluster busting again

We have been proposing that both the diphthongizations as well as the vocalizations which we have outlined above have been manifestations of language users' tendency to highlight or make more prominent any vowel space which is especially 'vowelly'. That particular metaphor we have interpreted as indicative of a situation where a vowel sound shows extended duration qualities or, especially pertinent to our present concerns, where a vowel sound has to its immediate right segments which themselves are highly vocalic in their internal structure. It is the presence of such post-vocalic segments, we have claimed, which provokes the perception of the segmental 'stretch' encompassing the stressed vowel peak and its rightmost syllable boundary as especially highly vowel prominent. We saw in sections 3.2.4 and 3.4.6 above how to some extent in late Old English, but especially in Middle English materials, speakers appear to have had a special perception of those syllables whose consonantal terminations were especially 'vowel-heavy': that is, those which ended in clusters both of whose members were continuant consonants, especially where both consonantal segments were continuant sonorants like [rn], [rm], [rl], [lm] and [ln]. In such contexts we have demonstrated that additional vocalicness was indeed perceived in the overall structure of the lexical items affected, but that unlike *Breaking* diphthongization processes in [rd], [ld] (obstruent terminating) cluster contexts, that heightened vowel-ness was not interpreted as being internal to its original syllable domain, but seen to 'spread' to the right of the item, splitting up the bi-continuant cluster. In this way there was realized a new (but still subordinate to the stressed vowel) vocalic peak or focus in an item which as a result comes to show extra syllabicity. Thus, in Table 3.29 we came across alternations like ⟨darling⟩/⟨dareling⟩ and ⟨erl⟩/⟨eryl⟩ and so on.

In this section we shall try to show that such a process is as well documented a feature of the phonology of sixteenth- and seventeenth-century English as it was for that of the thirteenth through the fifteenth and still is, for many varieties of the modern language. To illustrate this innovation whereby monosyllabic items with complex terminations in [rn], [rl] come to be perceived as bi-syllabic, we shall consider the observations of William Bullokar, especially those set out in his *Booke at Large* of 1580 (Turner 1970) and *A Short Introduction or Guiding, to print, write, and reade Inglish speech . . .* (1580/81) (Danielsson and Alston 1966). Both Bullokar's phonetic writing system and general views on phonological structure are complex and often difficult to interpret (Zachrisson 1913; Funke 1938; Wolfe 1972: pp. 40–4) but of especial interest to us here is his classification of certain segments as '*half vowels*'. Under such a heading Bullokar includes the sonorant continuants [l], [m], [n], and [r] a perception which, of course, very closely resembles the status we have been according these very items throughout this book. As can be seen from the display of vowels, diphthongs and 'half vowels' reproduced from his *Booke*

The amendment of ortography.   44

Diphthongʒ and vowelʒ of ón sound.

ai ay	ab au aw	ei ey	eb ey w	ó oa	oi oy	ow	oy ou ow ꝏw þ u ç ꝏ ꝏ
oi ꝏy	ea eæ e	eb eu b u ew	al ayl	am aym	an ayn	on oyn	uy seldom in vſe.

I boʒow, w, tw mák diphthong after vowelʒ, bóth foʒ hiʒ oꝺ nám and vc, and foʒ that hiʒ new nám iʒ soundꝺ thær-in, and may help in eqiuocy.

Not that, i, y, b, u, and any of the half vowelʒ neuer begin diphthong. Alʃo, b, u, seldom begin any diphthong. Alʃo, e, seldom oʒ neuer beginneth diphthong, except foʒ the help in eqiuocy.

Not that ther iʒ no triphthong in mer english woʒdʒ, thær-foʒ when thʒe vowelʒ com togeðer, deuyd ón of them, and mák the other tvꝏ a diphthong: thær-in nót wel that vowelʒ begin no diphthong (tw spel and sound woʒdʒ the better) excepting that tvꝏ half vowelʒ coming togeðer, and, a, oʒ, o, nert befoʒ them may mák a triphthong (that iʒ) soundꝺ togeðer in ón sillabl: aʒ in caꝺin, hoꝺm.

Now resteth tw know how tw deuyd woʒdʒ intw sillablʒ: foʒ the which, first know your consonantʒ from the vowelʒ, and half vowelʒ and the diphthongʒ afoʒ-said, and then mark the rulʒ folowing: thær-in nót, that eury vowel and half vowel cauʒ a sillabl: except they be in diphthong, and then that diphthong cauʒeth a sillabl: alʃo a vowel and a half vowel coming togeðer mák a diðthong. And a half vowel coming nert after, r, ʒ, iʒ moſt týmʒ in sillabl with the vowel nert befoʒ, r, aʒ in thæʒ woʒdʒ, harm, woʒm, bárn, byrn, churl, márl, but moſt týmʒ eury half vowel iʒ speled by it-ſelf, and yet dependꝺth so vpon the consonant nert befoʒ it in our spech, that it seimeth tw be ioinꝺ in sillabl with that consonant.

Not farder that woʒdʒ which ár mer english ár moſt of them of ón sillabl: except it be a deruiatiu oʒ declinatiu, oʒ compounded: which compoʒitiuʒ, deruiatiuʒ, ꝺ declinatiuʒ, ár æʒily deuydꝺ in speling by the natiu english, that haꝺ la rꝺ, bicauʒ he iʒ acqcintꝺ with the pʒꝺ
mitiu

w. boʒowed tw mák diphthong. Vowelʒ begining no diphthong. No triphthong in mer english woʒdʒ, except, l m: after a, oʒ: o. ꝏw deuyd ſillablʒ in a woʒd caꝺed speling.

moſt english woʒdʒ ár of ón ſillabl: except it be

TABLE 4.11

at Large in Table 4.11, Bullokar represents the last of these types through the special symbols ⟨ɬ⟩, ⟨ṁ⟩ and ⟨ń⟩. If these can be interpreted as some kind of vowel + sonorant combination such as [əl], [əm] and [ən], then they can be used to provide evidence for, among other things, the kind of pre-sonorant diphthongization and sonorant vocalization processes which we described on the basis of other kinds of evidence in sections 4.3(1) and 3.4.4. Consider the data in Table 4.12 which show a selection of items with syllable

TABLE 4.12 Bullokar's *Booke at Large*

-[l]	-[ld]	-[mb]	-[nt]/[nč]	-[ŋg]
⟨baɬ⟩	⟨sowɬd⟩	⟨chaṁber⟩	⟨hańteth⟩	⟨grańg'⟩
⟨smaɬ⟩	⟨faɬt⟩		⟨grańt⟩	⟨chańg'abɬ⟩
⟨caɬ⟩	⟨oɬd⟩/⟨old⟩		⟨brańch⟩	⟨rańg'⟩
⟨aɬso⟩	⟨boɬd⟩			
⟨baɬd⟩	⟨foɬd⟩			
⟨shaɬ⟩	⟨moɬd⟩			
⟨aɬ⟩				
⟨yɬ⟩ 'island'				

final sonorant as well as sonorant initial clusters. Here, *Breaking* produced diphthongal pronunciations such as [baul] (or [baəl]) '*ball*', [bauld] '*bald*' [bould] '*bold*', [fould] '*fold*', [čaumber] '*chamber*' and [graunʒ] '*grange*' are perhaps indicated – cf. the fourteenth-century ⟨bauld⟩, ⟨chaumber⟩, ⟨Graunger⟩ and ⟨braunch⟩ spellings on page 165. But that such additional vocalic contrast within lexical items could also take the form of the manifestation of an additional (but still subordinate) vocalic peak in those cases where the syllable termination was of the bi-continuant ([rn], [rl] etc.) type can clearly be seen from Bullokar's use of the half vowel symbols in the items in Table 4.13. The representations there seem to suggest that for Bullokar stressed vowel peak + syllable termination in bi-continuant cluster combinations were heard as *bi-syllabic*, the highly vowelly double sonorant cluster being 'split' by an epenthetic vowel peak thus, [ferən], [θɔrən], [čærəm], [lærənɪŋg], [hærən], [čurəl], [hɛləm] and so on (compare the data in Table 3.29). The instances in column 4 are particularly interesting in this respect. Bullokar's notation there would suggest that contemporary hearers could accord to the vowel + two sonorant cluster more in the way of vocalic foregrounding or prominence than anything we have so far allowed for. Spelling such as ⟨hoɬṁ⟩, ⟨saɬṁ⟩, ⟨bauɬṁ⟩ and ⟨eɬṁ⟩ would suggest, on the

TABLE 4.13 Bullokar's *Booke at Large*

[rn]	[rm]	[rl]	[lm]
⟨ferń⟩, ⟨barń⟩, ⟨corń⟩, ⟨sterń⟩, ⟨borń⟩, ⟨burń⟩, ⟨hærń⟩, 'heron', ⟨andyrń⟩, 'hand-iron', ⟨brondyrń⟩, 'brand-iron', ⟨thorń⟩, ⟨bourń⟩. ⟨gouerńment⟩, ⟨charḿ⟩, ⟨lærńyng⟩, ⟨coudern⟩, 'cauldron', ⟨mʊrń⟩, 'mourn'	⟨warḿ⟩ ⟨worḿ⟩ ⟨charḿ⟩ ⟨harḿ⟩	⟨churɫ⟩ ⟨cherɫ⟩	⟨reɫm⟩ ⟨heɫm⟩ ⟨elḿ⟩/⟨eɫḿ⟩ ⟨baɫm⟩/⟨baɫḿ⟩ ⟨holḿ⟩/⟨hoɫḿ⟩ ⟨saɫm⟩ 'psalm' ⟨bauɫḿ⟩ 'ointment' ⟨haɫḿ⟩/⟨ham⟩ 'stubble'
1	2	3	4

interpretation we have been using, outputs like [sauləm], [bauləm] [ɛələm] and so on; i.e. not only is the stressed vowel space made more prominent through a diphthongization stratagem, extra syllabicity is also added to its right as well – a combination of the two *Breaking* types we have been discussing throughout this section. Yet evaluation of the data is not always as straightforward as we are suggesting and the existence of dual representations like ⟨elḿ⟩/⟨eɫḿ⟩ and ⟨holḿ⟩/⟨hoɫḿ⟩ might reflect the recognition by Bullokar of some kind of alternative phonetic realization; indeed, at the same time as he proposes representations like ⟨eɫḿ⟩ and ⟨hóɫḿ⟩, he nevertheless comments concerning them 'but the voice doth rather yield in elḿ-tre, and in holḿ' (p. 25), a statement which perhaps suggests vowel prominence reduction at the syllable peak focus.

Yet the issue is even more complex than we are suggesting. Bullokar provides us with a form ⟨haḿ⟩ ([haəm]) – Old English ⟨healm⟩, Middle English ⟨haulm⟩, ⟨halm⟩ – pointing to an *l-vocalization* of a type with which we are now very familiar – recall the ⟨gold⟩, ⟨gould⟩, ⟨goud⟩ alternations in Table 3.24. From his statement seen in Table 4.11 (p. 44 of the *Booke at Large*) it seems that Bullokar saw no possibility for the existence of triphthongs (three member complex vowel spaces) in the English language 'except ɫḿ after *a* or *o*'. A form like ⟨saɫḿ⟩ as we have interpreted it as [sauləm] hardly represents anything that could be described as a triphthongal vowel space, however; we might very tentatively argue (always bearing in mind the difficulty of determining precisely what Bullokar meant by a *triphthong*) that such a spelling actually represents an [l] vocalization. In other words, ⟨sałṁ⟩ is a representation for [sauəm]. It may have been the case that shapes such as [sauləm] were seen as what we might metaphorically refer to as 'too vowelly' – they contravene some phonological constraint upon the maximum canonical amount of vowel prominence which may typify items of certain syllabic lengths. To just such a notion we have already made appeal in our discussion of Middle English *open syllable lengthening*, where the trisyllabic 'shortening' of the stressed vowel space in items like [suuðərnə] *'southern'* to [suðərnə] was justified in terms of such a criterion. So too was the failure of stressed vowel lengthening in the context of a following already heavily vocalic syllable as in items such as ⟨talon⟩, ⟨baril⟩ and ⟨comon⟩; stressed vowel *open syllable lengthening* was blocked in such items because an output like, say, [baarəl] would be perceived as contravening the 'permitted' degree of vowel foregrounding in two syllable items – see sections 3.2.3 and 3.2.4 above.

4.4 Monophthongization processes

Our earlier discussions of monophthongization processes in sections 2.4–2.4.5 produced at least three interesting phenomena. Firstly, there appeared to be occasions where a (sequentially) mixed vowel space (one containing two contrasting, side-by-side, vocalic halves) could come to be realized as a single homogenous vowel. That is, the value of one of the vocalic halves – usually, we observed, the one which bore the syllable beat – was generalized across the entire vowel space, the value of the other being suppressed; what had been a vocalic area where two contrasting vowels existed in a contiguous fashion became one where no vowel quality contrast was apparently evident. Instances of such were to be seen in the 'undoing' of *Breaking* in late Old English where we witnessed a monophthongization of diphthongs like [æa] and [eo] to [æ] and [e] respectively; cf. such instances as [mæaxt] → [mæxt] ⟨meaht⟩/⟨mæht⟩ *'might'* and [feox] → [fex] ⟨feoh⟩/⟨feh⟩ *'cattle'* (see Table 2.31). In these cases the stressed vowel space has clearly come to be interpreted as sequentially non-contrastive, and the 'glide', 'transition' (non-syllabic) element has been effaced. The resultant vowel space manifests only the value of the syllabic first halves [æ] and [e].

But our discussions of this so-called *Smoothing* process showed that other, apparently more complex operations could also be involved in such a simplification of the stressed vowel area. For instance, speakers hearing diphthongs like [æa] and [eo] in pre-fricative [x] or [ç] contexts could interpret them not as [æ] or [e], but as [e] and [i] respectively. That is, there occurred no generalization of the first, syllabic half, but rather the whole vowel space was converted into some raised, more palatal vocalic shape. We pointed to the argument that this monophthongization could, in fact, be seen not as an undoing of the earlier *Breaking* but as an extension of it. We tried to show that in Old English one effect of a velar [x] fricative segment on the preceding stressed vowel space may have been to add labial 'colour' to it – rather than a palatal heavy [æ] or [e] in such an environment, the stressed vowel space came to show an innovatory second half 'transition' which in some way reflected the labiality quality of the contiguous [x] fricative segment – labiality quality was thus added to the vowel space and an overall reduction in palatality ensued. In section 2.4 we suggested the possibility of some independent [x] → [ç] change and for a concomitant increased level of *palatalization* in the [æa], [eo] vowel space contiguous with such a palatal consonantal segment – a mirror image *Breaking* effect. Such an increase in palatalization could, of course, be achieved by the effacement of the non-syllabic labial [u] half of the vowel space; additionally, there could also have resulted some suppression of any non-palatal (in this case *sonority*) characteristics in the remaining syllabic [æ] and [e] half. [æ] and [e] segments are, as we have now on many occasions observed, themselves 'mixed' or complex, composed of simultaneous elements of palatality and sonority to varying degress. A reduction in sonority or increase in palatality innovation would result in such segments being realized as [ɛ]/[e] and [i] respectively, and such late West Saxon spellings in ⟨seh⟩ and ⟨eht⟩ for their 'classical' ⟨seah⟩ [sæax] and ⟨eahta⟩ [æaxta] variants might, we argued, be interpreted as just such a segment internal palatality increase; likewise with the tenth-century Kentish ⟨liht⟩ *'light'* and ⟨niht⟩ *'nearest'* spellings for the West Saxon ⟨lēoht⟩ and ⟨nēahst⟩ (see Table 2.33). Such so-called 'monophthongizations' we might suggest, in fact represent some contextually (pre-[ç]) conditioned *vowel shift* to a palatality target.

Thirdly, we cited in section 2.4.4 some rather interesting twelfth-century, mainly Southern and South Western Middle English examples where the reduction of an earlier diphthongal space produced a monophthong bearing little superficial resemblance to either of the earlier diphthongal vowel space halves. Recall such spelling variants as ⟨eorþe⟩/⟨orthe⟩ *'earth'*, ⟨heorte⟩/⟨horte⟩ *'heart'* and ⟨steorr⟩/⟨storre⟩ *'star'*, where the ⟨o⟩ graph is generally held to represent some durationally long [øø] rounded, half-closed front segment (the labial 'version' of [ee]). Such as [eo] → [øø] change looks very unlike either of the two monophthongization processes we have just been discussing, yet it is a type we shall come to recognize as common in the sixteenth and seventeenth centuries whenever diphthongal vowel space is mutated. We proposed in section 2.4.4 that an [eo] → [øø] innovation represented a different stratagem for showing the palatality/labiality 'mixture' which the side-by-side contrast of [e] and [o] in the diphthong represented. The [eo] diphthong showed a sequentially discrete mixture of those two vowel qualities; in the case of vowels such as [ø], that same mixture of palatality and labiality was still present but the two components are expressed *simultaneously* and there is no temporal contrast in that expression. In the case of [ø], the palatality labiality mix is *segment internal*, there is no side by side precedentially discrete contrast. What we tried to suggest was that an innovation like [eo] → [øø] was not one where one phonetic segment was replaced by another, different one; rather, language users hearing a vowel space sequentially mixed or complex for palatality and liability (i.e. [eo]) interpreted it as non-sequentially – but internally – mixed for the same components and for the same predominance of 'colour' in the mixture. A diphthongal [eo], with a syllable bearing palatality element, is predominantly palatal in colour. Likewise, [ø] exhibits a mix of palatality and labiality where the former is the more heavily weighted (cf. sect. 1.3, Table 1.4; Anderson and Ewen 1987: p. 226). An [eo] → [øø] change can clearly only be seen as a monophthongization in a very special sense – indeed, we might impressionistically see it as some kind of *segment internal diphthongization*. That is, rather than witness a side-by-side vowel quality contrast between labiality and palatality components, *the combined value of both components is spread across the entire vowel space.*

4.4.1 [au] and [ai] diphthongs in the sixteenth and seventeenth centuries

This last type of 'monophthongization' is very typical of some of the innovations which occur to diphthongal vowel space, both lexical and derived, in the historical period which is the subject of this chapter. We shall concentrate our attention here on two diphthongal outputs, both by and large the product of Middle English processes we have outlined earlier; these diphthongs involve a temporal, side-by-side contrast between the pure and relatively pure sonorants [a]/[æ] and the two other manifestations of the primary vocalic characteristics, palatality and labiality, [i] and [u]: [ai]/[æi] and [au]. Consider the display in Table 4.14 of lexical items typical of many late Middle English dialects showing such

TABLE 4.14 Middle English [æi]/[au] diphthongs

Late Middle English [æi]			Late Middle English [au]		
(1)					
⟨dai⟩, ⟨day⟩ [dæi]		*'day'*	⟨claw⟩	[klau]	*'claw'*
⟨kai⟩, ⟨kay⟩ [kæi]		*'key'*	⟨draw⟩	[drau]	*'draw'*
⟨wai⟩, ⟨way⟩ [wæi]		*'way'*	⟨law⟩	[lau]	*'law'*
(2)					
⟨eight⟩	[æiçt]	*'eight'*	⟨naught⟩	[nauxt]	*'not'*
⟨neihbur⟩	[næiçbər]	*'neigh-bour'*	⟨dauhter⟩	[dauxtər]	*'daughter'*
(3)					
			⟨baul⟩	[baul]	*'ball'*
			⟨faul⟩	[faul]	*'fall'*
			⟨sault⟩	[sault]	*'salt'*
(4)					
⟨bailliff⟩	[bæiləf]	*'baillif'*	⟨graunt⟩	[graunt]	*'grant'*
⟨vain⟩	[væin]	*'vain'*	⟨assault⟩	[əsault]	*'assault'*
⟨pay⟩	[pæi]	*'pay'*	⟨fault⟩	[fault]	*'fault'*

[ai]/[æi] and [au] vowel space. The numerical arrangement of the
items in Table 4.14 reflects their 'source of origin' or derivational
pathways: (1) the word final 'vocalization' of [j]/[w] to pure
palatal/labial segments (see sect. 3.4); (2) and (3) represent a
diphthongal vowel space derived through the operation of Middle
English *Breaking* in both pre-[ç]/[x] fricative and sonorant [l]
environments (cf. sects 3.4.1 and 3.4.4); (4) non-derived
diphthongal vowel space in items adopted into English from
Anglo-Norman. A comparison of these late Middle English
diphthongal pronunciations with their modern 'equivalents' is
instructive. In the first place, those with Middle English [au] have
in most modern dialectal versions a 'monophthongal' [ɔ]/[ɔɔ],
[o]/[oo] or [ɑ]/[ɑɑ] vowel space. Those in [æi], while in some
modern British and United States versions showing a monophthongal [e] (or [ɛ]) shape, realize a diphthongal [ei]/[ɛi] output
of that monophthong from the late eighteenth century onwards.
In what follows we shall attempt to show that Middle English
[æi] and [au] diphthongs underwent some kind of what can only
loosely be called 'monophthongization' during the sixteenth and
seventeenth centuries, although we shall see that the original
diphthongal pronunciations persisted for a considerable period of
time and that other, more complex, variations also occurred.

4.4.2 Middle English [au] diphthong developments

Let us begin by considering in more detail in Table 4.15 some of the possible Modern English reflexes of items which in many Middle English dialects would have contained a stressed vowel space in [au]. Some of the items in column (4) we have already discussed in section 3.4.5 above; there we observed that, especially in [ndʒ] and [mb] environments, the [au] diphthong appears to have had its labial [u] element suppressed, the sonorant [a] component spreading across the entire vowel space. In its turn, this [aa] was inputted to the *Middle English vowel shift* (see sects 3.3.1–3.3.2) and was palatalized to [æː]; and even [ɛɛ]/[ee]. The present-day [ei] diphthongs in column (4) items reflect this process. Items in columns (2) and (3) clearly evidence a 'monophthongization' either to a long low mid [ɔɔ] or to some lightly palatal or pure sonorant [æː]/[aa]. Even from the limited data we have set out in Table 4.15 below it would appear that such alternation is at least in part due to the presence of a contiguous nasal element. But observe that the column (3) items with [aa] do not undergo *vowel shift* palatalization to a degree like those of column (4); we do not find *[ɛɛnt], *[dɛɛns] outputs for such items not, at least, in most varieties of British English. Observe too that some lexical items like ⟨vase⟩ appear to have dialectal manifestations showing all three alternations – [vɔɔz], [vaaz]/[væːæz] and [veiz]. Original [au] diphthongal pronunciations have, for the items we have listed, almost everywhere in the modern language been displaced, although cf. such realizations as Southern Scottish [douxtʌr] '*daughter*' (see sect. 3.4.5).

TABLE 4.15 Middle English [au] in Modern English

Late Middle English	Modern English versions		
(1)	(2)	(3)	(4)
[au]	[ɔɔ]	[aa]/[æːæ]/[æ]	[ei]
⟨daughter⟩ ⟨law⟩ ⟨draw⟩ ⟨ball⟩ ⟨fall⟩ etc.	⟨daughter⟩ ⟨slaughter⟩ ⟨law⟩ ⟨ball⟩ ⟨fall⟩	⟨aunt⟩ ⟨dance⟩ ⟨grant⟩ ⟨plant⟩ ⟨command⟩ ⟨laughter⟩	⟨danger⟩ ⟨angel⟩ ⟨Cambridge⟩ ⟨chamber⟩ ⟨safe⟩
	⟨vase⟩	⟨vase⟩	⟨vase⟩

Yet there is little doubt that [au] diphthongal pronunciations for all the items listed in Table 4.15 had survived until late in the seventeenth century. Alongside such pronunciations, and perhaps in a distribution with them conditioned by sociolinguistic and regional dialectal factors, there existed 'monophthongal' realizations as well. This state of affairs is seen as well as anywhere else in Christopher Cooper's *English Teacher* of 1687 (Sundby 1953) and *Grammatica Linguae Anglicanae* of 1685 (Jones 1911). In his definition of the structure of 'true' diphthongs, Cooper gives as an example '*O* in *loss, lost,* joined to *u* we always write *au*; as *audible, audience, auditory*' suggestive of [ɔu] pronunciations for (foreign origin) items which now realize a monophthongal stressed vowel area. Yet in his discussion of 'the Vowel o Gutteral', Cooper observes that 'sometimes we write this sound *a*; as *was, watch*; long *o* as *lost*; *a* chiefly before *ll, lt, all halt*; *aw awl* . . . *au, cause, augh, caught, ough, ought* . . . This sound among the *English* is distinguished neither by name nor character, for distinction sake I shall write it α' (Sundby 1953: A4, sect. 9). This ⟨α⟩ symbol Cooper consistently uses to represent the stressed vowel space in words like *all, chalk, bald, salt,* and *walk,* environments where, as we have observed, derived [au] diphthongs in pre-sonorant contexts would be expected in many late Middle English dialects. This [au] diphthong has apparently in Cooper's time been 'monophthongized' to some kind of 'o Gutteral' vowel, [ɔ] or [ɔɔ].

Some type of monophthongal realization of the Middle English [au] diphthong is suggested by many of the phoneticians, spelling reformers and literary artists writing in the sixteenth and seventeenth centuries although, as usual, the fine detail of its phonetic value is not always possible to determine with any degree of precision. Shakespeare, for instance, has Sir Toby in *Twelfth Night* (Lothian and Craik 1975: Act 1, Sc.3, l. 122) ask: '*Art thou good at these kick-shaws, knight?*', where the ⟨aw⟩ digraph in ⟨kick-shaws⟩ which would historically be associated with a diphthongal [au] type diphthong. However the form ⟨kick-shaws⟩ appears to represent an anglicization of the French *quelque-choses* reflecting a French pronunciation of ⟨choses⟩ in [šɔɔz] predating that of the modern French [šooz], suggesting that ⟨au⟩ type spellings (historically used to represent [au]) are by this date so strongly associated with [ɔɔ] pronunciations that they are even being used to represent that pronunciation in items for which no [au] realization ever existed. (Cercignani 1981: sect. 88, p. 216; Pope 1966: sect. 579). Robinson's *Scale of Vowelles* of 1617 also provides a pointer to such a monophthongal realization of [au]. Robinson regularly spells the vowels in lexical items where we would historically expect an [au] diphthong by his *vowel scale* symbol ⟨*u*⟩. Recall (see Table 4.3) how Robinson perceives long vowels like that represented by ⟨*u*⟩ as 'extended almost to the place of the next short vowel'. His scale shows four non-palatal vowels ⟨*ʔ, S, n, u*⟩ suggesting a progression through positions one to two whereby there is a movement away from labiality (or from pure labiality through sonority) corresponding to the palatality increase we inferred from the movement between his positions three through five. We can represent this diagrammatically as in Table 4.16.

TABLE 4.16 Robinson's vowel positions

Position One		Position Two		Position Three	
Short	Long	Short	Long	Short	Long
⟨*ʔ*⟩	⟨*S*⟩	⟨*n*⟩	⟨*u*⟩	⟨ɛ⟩	⟨3⟩
[ʊ]	[oo]	[o]	[ɔɔ]	[æ]	[ɛɛ]

Thus, if the 'short' vowels in the one to three positions are [ʊ], [o] and [a]/[æ], then the long vowel 'equivalents' of the first two, associated as they are with the articulatory characteristic of the short vowel to their 'right', should respectively be the more sonorant [oo] and [ɔɔ] or [ɒɒ]. Robinson's use of the symbol ⟨*u*⟩ for vowel space historically associated with [au] therefore suggests a 'monophthongization' of that diphthong to [ɔɔ].

Although the evidence is extremely complex, it would therefore appear that during the course of the sixteenth and seventeenth centuries some kind of [au] → [ɔɔ] innovation had occurred in the vowel space of those items in Table 4.14 showing [au] stressed vowels, such that [klau] → [klɔɔ] '*claw*', [drau] → [drɔɔ] '*draw*', [slauxtər] → [slɔɔ(x)tər] '*slaughter*', [waulk] → [wɔɔ(l)k] '*walk*' and so on (Wyld 1927: sects 259–63; Ekwall 1980: sects 35–6; Dobson 1968: sect. 237; Cercignani 1981: sects 64–65; Zachrisson 1913: pp. 190–201; Barber 1976: pp. 301–2). Such a 'monophthongization' would appear to be like the process we detailed above in section 2.4.4 where [eo] → [øø]. An [au] → [ɔɔ] shift is one where the vowel quality of neither of the two contrasting halves is generalized across the stressed vowel area; rather there occurs an internal 'combination' of the sonorant [a] and labial [u] componential halves into a single, internally complex vowel. This complex of sonority and labiality – the former, as syllable peak being the dominant component in the linear 'mix' – is realized internally as a low mid round [ɔɔ] or perhaps [ɒɒ] vowel.

Speakers retain the two half (i.e. peak/glide) structure of the
vowel space but abandon the temporal, side-by-side contrast
between the halves. Although a long vowel results from the original [au] diphthong, the quality of that vowel is the
[SONORITY/labiality] co-mixture of its two previously discrete
halves. However, it has to be stressed again that throughout the
sixteenth and seventeenth centuries (and perhaps even later)
both [au] and [ɔɔ] pronunciations could be heard for all Table
4.14 type items with [au] vowel shapes; as Cooper remarked
'pronunciamus prout *au* vel α *audacious*, *maunder*' (Sundby
1953: p. xxxiii).

4.4.3 Other [au] developments
We have already noted in section 3.4.5 how, during the Middle
English period, those [au] diphthongs to be found in many lexical
items of Anglo-French origin underwent a monophthongization
whereby their 'glide' labial [u] element came to be suppressed,
leaving the syllable peak sonorant [a] half to be generalized across
the whole vowel area; thus [au] → [aa]. We deduced this development
from the characteristics of the stressed vowel space in items like
⟨auncient⟩ and ⟨daunger⟩, where in many Middle English dialects
we find an ⟨a⟩ spelling for the etymological ⟨au⟩, thus ⟨ancient⟩,
⟨danger⟩. That this ⟨a⟩ represents some long monophthongal [aa]
we concluded from its availability as input to the *Middle English
vowel shift*, where it took on increased palatality characteristics
such that, for example, [aanšənt] → [æænšənt] → [ɛɛnšənt];
cf. too such spelling alternants as ⟨change⟩, ⟨chainge⟩,
⟨chaynge⟩ (Jordan 1974: sects 224,270). This [au] → [aa] innovation
some scholars argue to have had a dialectal origin (Ekwall 1980:
sect. 36, footnote; Wyld 1927: sect. 225; Luick 1894) while it may,
at least on occasion, have been the result of its nasal environment.

Cooper, in his *English Teacher* (Cooper 1687), shows by the use
of his ⟨α⟩ symbol an [ɔɔ] pronunciation for the stressed vowel in
items like ⟨chalk⟩, ⟨stalk⟩ and ⟨walk⟩ (historically showing [au]
through the Middle English *Breaking* of [a] in sonorant contexts).
Yet he uses an ⟨á⟩ symbol, connoting [ææ], for items with a
similarly derived stressed vowel space, thus ⟨álmond⟩, ⟨cálf⟩,
⟨hálf⟩ and ⟨psálm⟩ (Sundby 1953: p. xxxiii). Likewise, some
kind of [aa] or [ææ] pronunciation for the stressed vowels in
⟨caught⟩, ⟨daughter⟩, ⟨halter⟩ is perhaps to be inferred from the
fact that they are made to rhyme with ⟨after⟩ by Lear's Fool in
Shakespeare's *King Lear* (1608) Act I, Sc. iv (Muir 1966;
Cercignani 1981: sect. 66):

A fox, when one has caught her,
And such a daughter
Should sure to the slaughter,
If my cap would buy a halter:
So the fool follows after

where the line-end items represent what appear to be the close
to homophonous [kææ(x)tər], [dææ(x)tər], [slææ(x)tər],
[hææ(l)tər], [ææ(f)tər].

Such an [au] → [aa]/[ææ] monophthongization appears to have
been particularly common in contiguity with nasal sonorants which
are themselves the first element in a co-articulating (homorganic)
cluster, the second member of which may be a voiced or voiceless
obstruent or continuant consonant, i.e. [nd], [nt], [ns], [nč], as in
items such as ⟨command⟩, ⟨aunt⟩, ⟨grant⟩, ⟨chance⟩, ⟨dance⟩
and ⟨launch⟩ (Ekwall 1980: sect. 45, p. 24). Again Cooper in his
English Teacher of 1687 observes that in *enhanse, mander, dant,*
and *jant 'a ante n melius forsitan pronunciatur a quam α'* yet he
also gives evidence for [ɔɔ] pronunciations for all these items as well
(Sundby 1953: p. xxxiv). In his *Logonomia Anglica* of 1621,
Alexander Gil (using symbols like ⟨a⟩ for [æ], ⟨ä⟩ for [ææ],
⟨â⟩ for [ɔɔ] and ⟨au⟩ for [au]) records the lexical distribution
for what was historically [au] stressed vowel space as set out in
Table 4.17. Although this display in no way represents the complete
range of Gil's inventory of items with an 'etymological' [au] stressed

TABLE 4.17

⟨a⟩ [æ]	⟨ä⟩ [ææ]	⟨â⟩ [ɔɔ]	⟨ea⟩/⟨ë⟩ [εε]	⟨au⟩ [au]
(1) ⟨angelz⟩	⟨kämbriʒ⟩			
⟨chanʒ⟩	⟨kämbrik⟩		⟨këmbrik⟩	
(2) ⟨chance⟩	⟨chänst⟩			⟨chauns⟩
				⟨aunt⟩
				⟨graunt⟩
				⟨komaund⟩
⟨dans⟩		⟨dâns⟩	⟨deans⟩	
(3) ⟨fal⟩(1)		⟨fâl⟩(6)		
⟨al⟩(2)	⟨äl⟩(2)	⟨âl⟩(54)		
		⟨fât⟩/⟨fâlt⟩		⟨fault⟩
				⟨fâult⟩
(4) ⟨laf⟩				⟨lauħ⟩
				⟨dauħter⟩

vowel space, it still serves to point to a number of facts concerning the early-seventeenth-century realization of this diphthongal form. Firstly, it is interesting to notice how the 'original' diphthongal pronunciations are resisted in [mb], [ndʒ] and [dʒ] environments (those under (1)), the very contexts which we showed had even in Middle English produced a monophthongization of [au] → [aa], and entered the *English vowel shift*; recall the ⟨range⟩, ⟨rainge⟩ and ⟨raynge⟩ spellings above in section 3.4.5. In this context Gil shows the [au] diphthong monophthongized to [aa] or [ææ], with the palatalization to [εε] in ⟨këmbrik⟩ (modern ⟨cambric⟩, '*linen cloth*') a pronunciation folly of those effeminate Mopseys (Jiriczek 1903: p. 33). On the other hand, diphthongal [au] type pronunciation appears by and large to persist in nasal + homorganic obstruent environments (those under (2)), as in ⟨aunt⟩ and ⟨chauns⟩, although even here the occasional lightly palatal [æ] or [ææ] sonorant surfaces. [au] also predominates in pre-fricative contexts; cf. ⟨lauħ⟩ and ⟨dauħter⟩. According to Gil's evidence, the [au] → [ɔɔ] innovation is particularly common in pre-[l] situations, witnessed by the high frequency of ⟨fâl⟩, ⟨âl⟩ and the 'learned' ⟨fâlt⟩ versions, although even here pronunciations with [æ] and [ææ] were also clearly a minor possibility, while it is difficult to know what to make of ⟨fâult⟩. Finally, the [ɔɔ] vowel space in ⟨dâns⟩ is interesting alongside ⟨dans⟩, and also worthy of note is the item's 'Eastern' dialectal pronunciation in ⟨deans⟩, where perhaps some kind of palatalized [εε] is intended (Jiriczek 1903: p. 32).

4.4. Middle English [æi] diphthong developments

We have listed above (see Table 4.14) instances of those items which show a stressed vowel area composed of a sequentially (side-by-side) contrastive relatively pure sonorant/pure palatality 'mix': [æi]. Although many (but not all) dialects of the modern language realize this [æi] vowel space as a diphthongal [ei] or [εi], this is a relatively recent, late-eighteenth – early-nineteenth-century development whereby what was probably an [εε] 'monophthongization' of the Middle English [æi] diphthong itself became split into two contrasting halves, a process we have noted which was likely to occur to durationally long vowels at any historical period (sect. 4.2.2). While the sixteenth- and seventeenth-century 'monophthongization' of [æi] to [εε] is well attested by phoneticians and spelling reformers, the evidence they provide is again difficult to interpret and is often hard to independently support (Dobson 1968: sects 227–30; Ekwall 1980: sects 31–4). Throughout this period diphthongal [æi] pronunciations appeared to have been available, often in the same lexical item, as well as the innovatory [ɛɛ]. Cooper in his *English Teacher* of 1687 describes the existence in his phonology of an [ai]/[æi] diphthong: '*A* in *can, cast,* joined with *i* that is *ee,* makes the Diphthong in *bait, caitiff, ay,* for *I* or *yea,* and *eight* commonly sounded *ait*; which are all I know in our tongue' (Sundby 1953: pp. xxxi–xxxii). His implication is that the [æi] diphthong is confined to an extremely limited, even residual, lexical set of four items only and he goes on to state that this 'etymological' diphthongal pronunciation has been supplanted everywhere else in the lexicon by a long low stressed mid vowel [ɛɛ]: 'For the most part in common Discourse we speak *ai* as *a* simple in *cane*' (Sundby 1953:p. 105), a contention borne out by his alternant rendering of a variant of the epithet ⟨fraught⟩ which he sets out as both ⟨frait⟩, ⟨frɑ́t⟩ and ⟨frâte⟩, suggesting pronunciations like [fræit], [frɔɔt] and [frɛɛt] respectively (Sundby 1953: pp. xxvii–xxx).

It appears that so common was this [æi]/[ɛɛ] alternation in both the sixteenth and seventeenth centuries that ⟨a⟩ and ⟨ai⟩ spelling forms could be used interchangeably in lexical items which 'historically' showed an [æi] diphthongal stressed vowel area. For example, in his *Elementarie* of 1582, Richard Mulcaster tells us that 'Gaie, graie, traie. And maid, said, quaif, English, for coif, quail, sail, rail, mail, onelesse it were better, to write these with the qualyfying, e, quale, sale, rale, male' (Mulcaster 1582: p. 136). Indeed, throughout this period we find many instances where ⟨ai⟩ spellings are used 'unhistorically' in items which had never realized a stressed vowel [æi] space, thus ⟨mail⟩ (Old French ⟨male⟩) and ⟨waist⟩ (Old French ⟨waste⟩).

It is important to note, however, the at first sight paradoxical fact that this 'monophthogization' of [æi] could appear realized, in the sixteenth- and seventeenth-century period, as either [ɛɛ] or [ee]. For instance, John Hart in the phonetic script of his *Orthographie* (1569) (Danielsson (1955–63)) transcribes items showing etymological [æi] as ⟨ē⟩, the same symbol he uses for words with Middle English [ee], thus ⟨sē⟩ '*say*', ⟨mēd⟩ '*maid*', ⟨pēr⟩ '*pair*' (Old French ⟨paire⟩); such a transcription infers a change such that [æi] → [ee]. On the other hand, in his *Art of Pronunciation* Robert Robinson conflates Middle English [æi] diphthongs with those items showing [ææ] in Middle English and which had by his time been *vowel shifted* to [ɛɛ] (Robinson 1617), thus we find him using transcriptions such as ⟨dā⟩/⟨dai⟩ '*day*'; ⟨rāz⟩/⟨raiz⟩ '*raise*'; ⟨fār⟩/⟨fair⟩ '*fair*' where, recall, his ⟨ā⟩ (position three long) symbol on his *Scale of Vowelles* represents [ɛɛ]; cf. Table 4.3. This [ee]/[ɛɛ] discrepancy for the 'monophthongization' of [æi] can perhaps best be explained in terms of 'merger targeting' or some such notion. Although we shall return to such a concept in greater detail below (see sect. 5.2.1), we might suggest here that the monophthongal [ɛɛ] realization of the earlier [æi] diphthong was conflated with, merged with, made equivalent to either (1) that [ɛɛ] which resulted from the *English vowel shift* of [ææ]/[aa] or (2) the lexical [ɛɛ] (produced via the Middle English *open syllable lengthening* of [e]) which itself became raised to [ee] through the operation of the same *vowel shift* (see sect. 4.2(1)). Given that many of the latter palatalized 'as far as' the pure palatal [ii] (thus Old English [metə] '*meat*' → Middle English [mɛɛtə] (*open syllable lengthening*) → [meet(ə)] → [miit] (*English vowel shift*)), it is not surprising that we should find items historically showing stressed [æi] diphthongs, such as ⟨quay⟩ (Old French ⟨quai⟩) and ⟨key⟩ (Middle English [kæi], ⟨kay⟩) realized in the modern language with a pure palatal [ii] vowel space (Dobson 1968: sect. 225; Wyld 1927: pp. 247–9; Luick 1964: sects 515–16; Zachrisson 1913: pp. 197–201).

But it is important to stress yet again that any description of a change like [æi] → [ɛɛ] as 'monophthongization' is clearly very limited. A vowel space which for some speakers was heard as contrastive in two contiguous, sequentially ordered relatively sonorant and palatal halves has come to be interpreted as one where that contrast, now internalized into the complex componential structure of a 'single' vowel, has no longer any temporal manifestation (cf. our discussion of the [au] → [ɔɔ] 'monophthongization' in sect. 4.4.2)

4.5 Syllable shapes and their phonetic consequences

Much of section 3.5 was taken up with a discussion of the proposition that many innovations to the phonology of English up until the fourteenth century could be viewed as the result of speakers' preconceptions of or intuitions concerning what they saw as constituting the 'proper' shape of syllables. Two such intuitions were of particular importance, we argued. In the first place syllables were viewed as having some kind of appropriate or even ideal configuration, with a 'proper' beginning-and-end characteristic as well as showing well-defined features in their peak, or central area. Secondly, the sequence of segments which went to make up individual syllables reflected some kind of crescendo to a climax followed by a decrescendo in the intrinsic vowel-property level of these segments; the edges of syllables tended to be vocalically reduced, those approaching the syllable centre showing increased values for such a vowel-level property. One result of the first of these intuitions concerning syllabic properties was the filling out of those syllables which showed 'empty' spots in the perceived syllable template. For instance we saw in Table 3.34 how onset-less items such as ⟨erthe⟩ '*earth*' were regularly accorded a syllable initiating segment in the form of a glide [j], thus ⟨yerthe⟩. In the same way, we witnessed the addition of minimally vocalic elements at syllable terminations – the ⟨fesan⟩/⟨fesant⟩ type alternations in section 3.5 – both types possibly related, we claimed in section 2.2, to the 'compensatory' filling out by vowel lengthening associated with coda segment loss in such alternants as *[fimβ]/[fiif] '*five*'. The effect of the second perception, we proposed, was the 'devocalization' of segments at the syllable periphery, manifested by the various devoicings and continuant to obstruent consonantal changes exemplified in Tables 3.32 and 3.33.

Yet there was a third implication for phonological preservation and innovation which resulted from language users' tendency to view syllable structures against some ideal template or configuration. We suggested that they tended metaphorically to 'prefer' those segments which appeared at syllable interfaces to be *ambisyllabic*: in this way we characterized the motivation for a variety of apparently disparate phonological processes ranging from consonantal deletion (the ⟨godsib⟩/⟨gosib⟩ alternants) to vowel 'epenthesis' as in the ⟨gosling⟩/⟨goseling⟩ variants – see Table 3.39.

It will be our aim in this section not just to show that innovatory phenomena such as these are also to be found under the same set of phonological conditions in the sixteenth and seventeenth centuries, but to produce instances of yet other novel procedures which we shall claim it is possible to see as motivated by the same kinds of syllable shape related concerns. In particular, we shall look in some detail at the voiceless fricative [h] as it surfaces and is effaced at syllable edges and interfaces, as well as at the ways in which speakers can interpret the nasal segment [n] in syllable interface environments.

4.5.1 [h] dropping and insertion

Most speakers of modern British English are familiar with the (usually socially stigmatized) phenomenon whereby in certain regional dialects, syllable and word initial voiceless fricative [h] can be either deleted or unetymologically inserted. For instance, an item like ⟨Hackney⟩ can, in many varieties of modern London English, be realized as [æknɪ], while, conversely, the same group of speakers will under certain conditions 'introduce' a syllable initial [h]; thus '*I like eels*' may be rendered as [ɑɪ lɑɪ? hiɣz] (Wells 1982: p. 322) where the 'glide' [ɣ] represents the vocalization of the sonorant continuant [l] – see section 3.4.4. Phenomena like these have been widespread throughout the temporal history of English and are certainly clearly attested from the beginning of the thirteenth century, although there is every likelihood that they predate this. In this section we shall first of all present, without attempt at explanation or provision of distributional criteria, some interesting examples of early evidence for both [h] insertion and effacement, followed by a fairly extensive look at some data provided by a rather unusual mid-sixteenth-century source. Our aim will be both to see what kinds of detailed historical evidence can be available for processes like this, at the same time to show how complex is the task of reaching any unified explanation for them and for the constraints upon their occurrence on the basis of such evidence.

Although, as we have already asserted, the phenomenon is very probably of a considerably earlier date (Milroy 1983), we come across a very large number of instances of phonological innovation involving syllable initial [h] in the early-thirteenth-century, South-Western regional, metrical romance known as *Laʒamon's Brut* (Madden 1847; Brooke and Leslie 1963) some of which are set out in Table 4.18. Perhaps it is the three way ⟨ærhscipe⟩/⟨harþscipe⟩/⟨ʒearscipe⟩ '*difficulty*' variable which provides the best clue as to the motivation for such syllable initial [h] adding in the column 4 instances. We have already seen how we could motivate the realization of a new syllable initial [j] as a means of reflecting the speaker's desire to see 'filled out' – by means of some 'compensatory' segment adding process – the onset empty syllable configuration. However, at the syllabic periphery a segment like [h] could also be well motivated. According to the dictates of our model of the syllable as a sequential crescendo⟩descrescendo of vowel prominence, any segment inserted to the left of the vowel peak must show a vowel-level reduction in its internalized structure; [j] and [w] do just that, their relatively constricted vocal tract shapes producing a much reduced level of sonority compared to that of a vowel – yet such 'glides' still tend to maintain, as we have observed, the overall palatal or labial characteristic of the peak vowel whose onset they have become, thus, ⟨ʒerþe⟩ but ⟨woke⟩. The voiceless fricative [h], on the other hand, reflects segment internal vowel reduction in a different way. The constriction in the vocal tract associated with this segment occurs in the laryngeal (pre-oral) region, the oral cavity itself remaining

TABLE 4.18 *Laȝamon's Brut*

[h]-loss			[h]-addition		
'half'	⟨hælf⟩	⟨alf⟩	⟨æhte⟩	⟨hæhte⟩	*'property'*
	⟨half⟩	⟨alue⟩	⟨ahten⟩	⟨hahte⟩	
				⟨heaþte⟩	
'has/had'					
	⟨hafde⟩	⟨aueþ⟩	⟨æld⟩	⟨holde⟩	*'old'*
	⟨hadde⟩	⟨abbeþ⟩	⟨ald⟩	⟨halde⟩	
	⟨haueþ⟩			⟨healde⟩	
'hair'	⟨heer⟩	⟨ere⟩	⟨æm⟩	⟨ham⟩	*'I am'*
'here'	⟨her⟩	⟨ere⟩	⟨and⟩	⟨hand⟩	*'and'*
	⟨hær⟩				
'how'	⟨heu⟩	⟨ou⟩	⟨ært⟩	⟨hart⟩	*'are'*
	⟨hu⟩		⟨eart⟩	⟨har⟩	
			⟨art⟩		
'his'	⟨his⟩	⟨is⟩	⟨is⟩	⟨his⟩	*'it is'*
'him'	⟨hine⟩	⟨ine⟩	⟨ich⟩	⟨hich⟩	*'I'*
			⟨ic⟩		
			⟨ihc⟩		
'health'					
	⟨hele⟩	⟨eale⟩	⟨understonde⟩	⟨honderstonde⟩	
	1	2			*'understand'*
			⟨orchærd⟩	⟨horechard⟩	
					'orchard'
			⟨ærhscipe⟩	⟨harþscipe⟩	
				⟨ȝearscipe⟩	
					'difficulty'
			3	4	

completely *unmodified* for place of articulation characteristic. As a voiceless fricative showing no specification for articulatory place, [h] is thus very suitable as a vowel quality reduced onset to peaks of any palatality, labial or sonority specification. Indeed, [h] is very often treated as merely the voiceless (devocalized) 'equivalent' of the contiguous segment to its right; if that segment is (and it usually is) a vowel, then [h] is best interpreted as a devocalized (vowel content reduced) vowel and as such ideal as a perceived onset to vowel peaks (Pike 1943; Maddieson 1984: pp. 41 and 57).

It is most important to observe that our *Laȝamon's Brut* examples show *both* [h] insertion and deletion; the two apparently contradictory processes, as well shall most clearly see below, appear to go hand in hand. What motivates speakers on some occasions to 'fill out' an empty syllable onset with [h], yet on others to 'deface' the ideal syllable template shape by an [h] effacement? Can we find a set of contexts (and need they all be phonetic) which will enable us to predict [h] placement at syllable boundaries? Let us try to answer these difficult questions by examining a fairly extensive set of data taken from a most interesting and readable mid-sixteenth-century document known as *The Diary of Henry Machin, Citizen and Merchant-Taylor of London* (Nichols 1848). This fascinating account deals with the set of (very often bloody) events relating to both everyday and major political and religious affairs which occurred in the English capital between 1550 and 1563. Machyn's language is often referred to as vulgar and at best 'non-standard', and even his editor notes rather harshly that the diarist was 'of no great scholarship or attainment, as his language and cacography plainly testify, sufficiently prejudiced no doubt, and not capable of any deep views either of religious doctrine or temporal policy' (Nichols 1848: *Preface*, p. v). But since in this book we are concerned more with the possible range of historical phonological variation than with any account of the rise of some self-styled pronunciation norm or standard, Machyn's very personal spelling system is of considerable value to us as a guide to the speech habits of his contemporaries. The following (slightly modified) extract from the diary describes a naval skirmish in 1557 between the English warship *Mary Rose* and a French adversary and provides an excellent example of Machyn's orthographic idiosyncracies (Nichols 1848: pp. 152–3):

> The iij day of August the god shyp callyd the Mare-Rows of
> London, accompanyd with the Maudlyn Dryvers, and a smalle
> crayer of the Whest-contrey, commyng by south chansyd to mette
> with a Frencheman of war of the burden of x skore or ther bowth;
> the wyche Frenche shyp had to the number of ij C. men; and in the
> Mare-Rows xxii men and bowys, the Maudelyn xviij, the barke of
> the West-contrey xij. The Mare-Rows saylyng faster then the French
> man and so in-continent the Frenche shype sett upon the other ij
> shyps, whom seyng the master of the Mare-Rowse cast a-bowtt, and
> set upon the Frence shype, and borded her; and slew to the number
> of C men with the captayn or ever thatt the other came to the
> fyght; ther wher slayne in Mare-Rowse ij men, and on ded a senett
> after, vj hurte wythe the master, whos name was John Couper.
> Then cam the men the Mare-Rowse, and shott on pesse of

ordenanse in to the Frenche schype starne, and gahyng by here
shott arows at the Frenche-men; the Maudelyn dyd no more hurtt;
thye barke nothyng at all. Thus they fought ij owrs; but at the
lengh the Frenche-men wher were of their parts and for-soke
them, nott haveng men to gyde ther sayle.

Perhaps the principal reason for the relative depth of our
discussion in what follows of the evidence provided by Machyn for
the constraints upon [h] placement at syllable edges, is that it will
remind us of the complexity of actual historical data and warn us
against the temptation of too readily accepting 'neat' and
all-embracing solutions for the phonological variation they
provide. With such caveats in mind, let us begin our discussion
by endeavouring to discover whether there are any recurrent
phonetic contexts which, in Machyn's data (all references are to
page of Nichols (1848)) consistently trigger the insertion of an
'unetymological' [h] fricative. The forms in Table 4.19 are
interesting in this respect. All the items there represent verbal
forms where continuity, repetition of activity is indicated, marked
morphologically by the suffixation of an element orthographically
represented in ⟨yng⟩. The most salient difference between the
items in column 1 and those in column 2 lies in the nature of the
interface between that ⟨yng⟩ suffix and the 'head' verbal item to
which it is an accretion. The verbs in column 1 show a 'stem'
syllable termination which is *non-empty* (thus, ⟨spek⟩, ⟨rob⟩,
⟨dwell⟩, etc.); those in column 2 manifest suffix contiguous
syllable codas which on the contrary are *non-full* (as in ⟨ro⟩,

TABLE 4.19 Machyn's Diary

[h]-*less*		[h]-*full*	
⟨syngyng⟩		⟨berehyng⟩	*'burying'*
⟨beryng⟩	*'carrying'*	⟨plah(h)yng⟩	*'playing'*
⟨slanderyng⟩		⟨behyng(e)⟩	*'being'*
⟨kyllyng⟩		⟨carehyng⟩	*'carrying'*
⟨spekyng⟩		⟨dohyng⟩	*'doing'*
⟨proclamyng⟩		⟨blo(g)hyng⟩	*'blowing'*
⟨shutyng⟩	*'shooting'*	⟨gohyng⟩	*'going'*
⟨holdyng⟩		⟨folo(w)hyng⟩	*'following'*
⟨robyng⟩		⟨convehyng⟩	*'conveying'*
⟨dwellyng⟩		⟨tarehyng⟩	*'delaying'*
⟨havyng⟩		⟨rohyng⟩	*'rowing'*
1		2	

⟨tare⟩ and so on). As a result, the column 2 items show a syllable interface between verb 'stem' and suffix which is characterized by the contiguity of two syllable peaks; the syllable to the left of the suffix being coda empty, the suffix itself having no initiating consonantal element. On the other hand, the column 1 items show at the interface between stem and suffix syllable a classical 'overlap' configuration, whereby the syllable terminating segment of the verb can be interpreted as the syllable initiating segment to the suffix syllable, thus:

$$\{_1\text{šu}\{_2\text{t}_1\}\text{ıŋg}_2\} \quad \langle\text{shutyng}\rangle$$

We might argue, therefore, that it is the function of the [h] adding stratagem in the column 2 items to bring about just such an overlap at syllable interface such that:

$$\{_1\text{go}_1\}\{_2\text{ıŋg}_2\} \rightarrow \{_1\text{go}\{_2\text{h}_1\}\text{ıŋg}_2\}$$

given the fact, as we have noted above, that the segment [h] is possibly best interpreted as a devocalized version of any segment with which it is contiguous and could therefore be seen in the example above as the relatively less vocalic 'filling out' element for both syllables. Perhaps further support for notions like this comes from Machyn's rendering of an item like ⟨Underhill⟩ as ⟨Hunderell⟩; the syllable one initiating [h] providing a vowel reduced segment for the otherwise empty syllable onset, while the [h] effacement at the syllable one and two interface can be viewed as a stratagem for activating ambisyllabicity at a point where previously [l] and [r] segments could only be interpreted as uniquely bound to the sphere of their respective syllables, thus:

$$\{_1\text{undər}_1\}\{_2\text{hıl}_2\} \rightarrow \{_1\text{hundə}\{_2\text{r}_1\}\text{ıl}_2\}$$

Certainly such compensatory segment epentheses and effacements brought about through speakers' tendency to map phonetic materials onto perceived 'ideal' template shapes for syllables and their interconnections are a common feature of Machyn's phonology in general. Consider, for example, his widespread use of the innovatory [j] glide as a syllable onset 'filler': ⟨the yerele of Bedford⟩ (178); ⟨the yerlle of Huntingdon⟩ (29 – 30) (although [w] epenthesis in such a context seems rare for him): likewise we come across such syllable interface overlap achieving 'contractions' as ⟨worshefull⟩ 'worshipful' (106); ⟨Pymon⟩ 'Piedmont' (79); ⟨Somesett⟩ 'Somerset' (120); ⟨yrmonger⟩ 'ironmonger' (141); ⟨grenill⟩ 'Greenhill' (113); ⟨senett⟩ 'signet' (151) and ⟨bruderud⟩ 'brotherhood' (166).

But as seductive as such syllable structure governed explanations are for innovatory [j] and [h] shapes and for the deletion of segments at syllable interface, a more detailed study of Machyn's [h] placement quickly shows that matters are much more complex and that the phenomenon is perhaps not open to explanation of a purely phonological kind at all (Milroy 1983). Our examples in Table 4.19 of innovatory [h] adding, while showing that the phenomenon was connected with segment ambisyllabicity, hinted too that it was also linked to verbal *morphology*, a feature of these data perhaps borne out by an example like that at (196): ⟨The furst day of May Ther was . . . gahyng a Mayng⟩ where both *'going'* and *'a Maying'* items show a syllable interface with contiguous vowel elements; [h] adding, however, appears only to be activated in the first, the verbal item, but not with the second, nominal one. Nevertheless, we do find spellings for nominal items like ⟨tryhumph⟩ *'triumph'* (275) and ⟨wyhalles⟩ *'violins'* (282) alongside ⟨laer⟩ *'lawyer'* (309) and ⟨plaers⟩ *'players'* (221). Yet we are still left with the difficulty of the undoubted statistical frequency of the syllable boundary [h] innovations in the verbal morphology contexts.

Matters are made more complex still with the discovery of spellings such as ⟨lyeng⟩ (40), ⟨lyung⟩ (285), ⟨lyeng⟩ (285) *'lying'* and ⟨careng⟩ *'carrying'* (283), verbal forms where we might reasonably expect to find [h] syllable interface insertion to be predominant. Not only this, but [h]-full and [h]-less forms quite commonly appear in extremely close textual proximity, consider: ⟨and on the cart lay on a pycture *lyeing* recheussly with a croun of gold, and a grett coler, and ys septur in ys hand, *lyehyng* in ys robes⟩ (40) showing not only two orthographic versions of *'lying'* but [h] effaced ⟨ys⟩ alongside [h] retained ⟨hand⟩.

But it is when we turn to consider the more general situation as regards [h] placement in Machyn's diary that the true complexity of the phenomenon becomes clear. The data in Table 4.20 show, in column 1, items with 'etymological' syllable initial [h] *which rarely if ever undergo [h] effacement in Machyn*; under column 2 we have lexical items for which the diarist regularly shows syllable initial [h] suppression and under column 3 items in the diary where [h] appears innovatorily inserted. A consideration of the forms in column 2 (especially in a more extended textual context) suggests that their [h] loss is motivated by notions of the kind we have been discussing for the characteristics of segments at syllable (and word) boundaries. For example, [h] deleted shapes like ⟨Doran⟩ *'Durham'* (103), ⟨allalowes⟩ *'all hallows'* (105) and ⟨Whyt-alle⟩ *'Whitehall'* (110) point to an altered perception of originally non-ambisyllabic segments at syllable interface: $\{_1dur_1\}\{_2həm_2\}$

TABLE 4.20

[h] *retention*	[h] *loss*		[h] *adding*		
⟨howsse⟩	⟨ys⟩	⟨hys⟩	⟨here⟩		*'ear'*
⟨hed⟩	⟨ym⟩	⟨hym⟩	⟨hevere⟩ ⟨evere⟩		*'every'*
⟨herse⟩	⟨elmet⟩	⟨helmett⟩	⟨hemages⟩ ⟨emages⟩		*'images'*
⟨hand⟩	⟨alff⟩				
⟨harold⟩	⟨Duram⟩	⟨Dorham⟩	⟨had hordyred⟩		*'ordered'*
⟨hang⟩	⟨alters⟩	⟨halters⟩	⟨haras⟩		*'arras'*
⟨herese⟩	⟨allalowes⟩	⟨allhallows⟩	⟨fasshele⟩		*'falsely'*
⟨hospetal⟩	⟨Whyt-alle⟩		⟨holyff-tre⟩		*'olive'*
⟨Hare⟩	⟨ale-water⟩	⟨halewater⟩	⟨hoathe⟩		*'oath'*
			⟨heythe⟩		*'heath'*
			⟨heth⟩		
			⟨hussers⟩		*'ushers'*
			⟨Hotland⟩		*'Oatland'*
I	2		3		

and $\{_1$ɔl$_1\}\{_1$hælowz$_2\}$; given the unavailability of [rh] and [lh] syllable terminating clusters, these are reinterpreted to project [r] and [l] as simultaneously the codas and onsets to their contiguous syllables. Yet again, a great many of the syllable onset [h] loss items appear in contexts like ⟨toward Bishop Atfield plasse⟩ (120); ⟨qwarell of allf a lb of . . .⟩ (121); ⟨set ard to the wall⟩ (107); ⟨in arnes⟩ (52); ⟨ys elmett⟩ (29) and ⟨all maner of strowhyng erbes⟩ (203). In such cases it is again possible to interpret the [h] loss as a device for bringing into existence an ambisyllabicity condition (here at word boundary interfaces) such that $\{_1$ys$_1\}$ $\{_2$helmet$_2\} \rightarrow \{_1$y$\{_2$s$_1\}$elmet$_2\}$.

But such 'neat' explanations (all be they highly tentative) for Machyn's phonological system of [h] placement are ones which we must still view with considerable scepticism for a variety of reasons. In the first place, we are able to find instances (although admittedly they are not very numerous) where Machyn shows [h] effacement in circumstances where it destroys an extant ambisyllabicity condition; consider instances like ⟨the ale-water stoke⟩ (78) and ⟨in-to one of the olles⟩ (259) where loss of the syllable initial [h] in ⟨hale water⟩ *'holy water'* and ⟨holles⟩ *'holes'* creates a syllable interface of contiguous peak vowel elements, the very context which, we have argued above, [h] deletion was initiated to avoid. Again, the instances of [h] *insertion* in Table 4.20 can appear in contexts which seem to contradict the ambisyllabicity 'goal' of such a consonantal epenthesis: ⟨toke ther hoythe⟩ (268); ⟨they had wyne he-nough for all comers⟩ (141); ⟨the mydwyf haskyd hym how he cold do yt⟩ (242); ⟨the man had ys here naylled⟩ (104); ⟨to have hetten yt there⟩ (74); ⟨did hevere craft⟩ (47); ⟨hanged with ryche haras⟩ (102); ⟨had hordeyned⟩ (99); ⟨masters and hushers⟩ (87). In the not inconsiderable number of instances like these we see the introduction of a consonantal (vowel reduced) onset in items like '*oath*', '*enough*', '*asked*', '*ear*', '*eaten*', '*every*', '*arras*', '*ordained*' and '*ushers*', creating the very syllable domain unique status of syllable finals and initials which we have so strongly hypothesized is ideally 'avoided'.

However the single argument which perhaps militates most strongly against our too readily accepting single solution models for [h] placement in Machyn's data (no matter how phonologically well-motivated they may appear on occasion to be) is provided by the alternation's most obvious characteristic – its 'patchy' nature of application. For instance, the items in column 1 of Table 4.20 are in the main mostly of high occurrence frequency throughout this fairly extensive diary, yet they almost never appear with [h] effacement. The item ⟨harold⟩ '*herald*', for example, occurs in almost every one of Machyn's entries and yet only once appears as ⟨arolds⟩ (160): in the same way, ⟨elmet(t)⟩ '*helmet*' shows less than a dozen [h]-full ⟨helmet⟩ manifestations for an item with a token count running into the hundreds. This 'patchy' or inconsistent application of innovatory phonological processes is one we have commented upon in several places in this book (see, for instance, our discussion of late Old English vowel lengthening in section 2.2.5) and reflects the apparent fact that such innovations are very often *lexical item specific*. That is, even though the general phonetic triggering conditions for its application may be met, a particular innovation may be constrained to occur just with a restricted set of lexical items from the speaker's total inventory; there will remain in his or her lexicon a number of items (even a considerable number of items) which, despite their having all the phonetic pre-requisites which might otherwise bring a particular phonetic innovation into force, remain unaffected and appear as 'exceptions' or 'residuals' in the user's grammer (Wang 1969; Labov 1963; Trudgill 1986: pp. 58–61). This important theory of the mechanism whereby phonological innovations are transmitted through grammars lexical item by lexical item (a process often referred to as *lexical diffusion*), contrasting strongly with those models which suggest that such innovations will always be productive whenever their phonetic triggering conditions are present, will be the subject of further discussion in the next chapter.

Certainly in Machyn's diaries [h] placement seems to be a particularly inconsistent process, [h] deleted/added shapes on very many occasions occurring, as we have already observed, in extremely close textual proximity. Notice, for example, cases like: ⟨that *hevere* man shuld make bone-fyres in *evere* strett⟩ (66);

⟨the woman *h*ad *h*ire *ere* nayled⟩ (64); ⟨was bered . . . my lade *Esley*, wyff of ser Henre *Hesley*⟩ (258) and many more. Perhaps the only conclusion we can safely arrive at might be to suggest that Machyn's materials appear to point to a 'preferred' context for [h] insertion/deletion – i.e. as a stratagem for realizing ambisyllabicity at interface. From such a use [h] insertion appears to have become generalizable to all syllable initial contexts, especially those which are 'etymologically' onset empty. Perhaps from there even greater generalization of this phenomenon was manifested such that [h] could be inserted in any pre-vowel-peak position, as a representative of the next step in the hierarchy of vocalicness reduction to the 'left' of the vowel peak, thus ⟨docthur⟩ '*doctor*' (100); ⟨tawhear⟩ '*tawer*' (208); ⟨towhard⟩ '*toward*' (174); ⟨where⟩ '*were*' (74); ⟨preveshalle⟩ '*privyseal*' (286); ⟨chansheler⟩ '*chancellor*' (74); ⟨fasshele⟩ '*falsely*' (103) and ⟨doshen⟩ '*dozen*' (291), a function perhaps infrequently shared by the glide [w] as in an instance like ⟨lyffwyng⟩ '*clerical living*' (276). But such matters are extremely controversial and require considerably more detailed research.

4.5.2 Nasals at syllable interface

Despite the number and potency of the counter-examples we have just cited and the general rather sporadic nature of the phenomenon, it does appear that the kind of supra-segmental phonology characteristic of the grammar of the mid-sixteenth century was one where syllable-edge contact points were viewed as non-unique and that several different types of stratagem could be employed to achieve the segmental ambisyllabicity that this characteristic demanded. That Machyn had a strong intuition along such lines is evident from the way his spelling system represents items like '*Saint Hellen*' and '*Saint Olaf*' as ⟨was bered at sant tellens⟩ (191) and ⟨sant Towlys⟩ (221, 242). Perhaps even more revealing in this respect is his rendering of the personal name '*Le Strange*' as ⟨Luste Strange⟩ (220). Such spellings seem to unambiguously show that our diarist perceived the [t] and [st] segments as equally part of their preceeding as their following syllable.

However, there is yet another set of contexts not at all unlike these last where we have evidence that at this and earlier periods speakers had intuitions concerning the possibility of an ambisyllabic interpretation for segments at syllable interface. The following late Middle English instances (gleaned from Kurath and Kuhn 1954) involving the item ⟨ok⟩ '*oak*' and its orthographic variants are interesting in this regard:

(1) ⟨The Oke hatte quercus⟩ (1398)
(2) ⟨Mosse of an oke⟩ (1425)
(3) ⟨in a hol hoke⟩ (1404)
(4) ⟨with an hok in hand⟩ (1400)
(5) ⟨Ilex . . . a noke⟩ (1425)
(6) ⟨Thogh he were so stronge as an noke⟩ (1475)

The examples at (3) and (4) might be interpreted as involving [h] insertion as an onset empty 'filling out' device, while the comparison of (2) and (6) suggests that speakers are able to interpret such a determiner + noun construction in terms of two different syllable bracketing configurations, thus

$$\{_1æn_1\}\{_2ok_2\}$$
$$\{_1æ\{_2n_1\}ok_2\}$$

the orthographic presentation in (6) being especially suggestive of the possibility of the latter (ambisyllabic) interpretation. However, the example at (5) would appear to point to the liklehood that such an ambisyllable evaluation could lead (given what we have claimed to be the strength on the *no onset-empty* condition) to speakers interpreting such a structure as if, in fact, it represented that in Figure 4.17. The item '*oak*' may thus be entered into the

FIG. 4.17

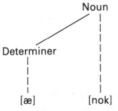

speaker's lexicon as the reinterpreted /nok/; note the personal name examples in ⟨John Nok⟩ (1361) and ⟨Als goode was Jacke Robyn as John at the Noke) *Gregory's Chronicle* (1475) (Kurath and Kuhn 1954: p. 813). Data from Machyn's diary also strongly suggest that a process like this was a very productive one in the mid-sixteenth century. The following are but a small selection from a very large number of instances in Machyn's work:

(1) ⟨Mad an end that day⟩ (200)
(2) ⟨we supposed that the world where at a nend⟩ (265)
(3) ⟨that was never so low a nebe⟩ (167) '*ebb tide*'
(4) ⟨evere on that bare them had a nobe⟩ (62) '*alb*'
(5) ⟨the barber-surgens had on of them to be a notheme at ther halle⟩ (252) '*anatomy*'

(6) ⟨and on off them the surgeons took for a notyme in-to ther halle⟩ (273)

(7) ⟨halffe a noure⟩ (39: 49) 'hour'

(8) ⟨alff a nore⟩ (29) 'hour'

(9) ⟨with a narow shott in the neke⟩ (136)

The instances (2) through (6) would appear to point to 'historically' onset empty items such as ⟨end⟩, ⟨ebba⟩ and ⟨alb⟩ being accorded a new [n] onset due to a reinterpretation of the ambisyllabic determiner + noun construction in, for instance, the configuration {a{n}alb}. In cases like this speakers appear to be utilizing available phonologically suitable material to fulfil the dictates of the *no onset-empty* principle, much in the same fashion as we argued above for the 'syllable-shifted' ⟨yerthe⟩/⟨erthe⟩ alternants (sect. 3.5.1). The examples at (7) and (8) are interesting too in that they appear to involve some lexicalization of the item ⟨hour⟩ as /nuur/. Yet in the light of our deliberations above, we might have expected that a construction like [ə hour] (or however we are to interpret the quality of the stressed vowel space) would have been 'left alone' since it can be interpreted as involving ambisyllabicity at syllable interface, or that one like [ən hour] would show [n] effacement to achieve the same effect. That it is the [h] which is, in fact, suppressed may point to some constraint on the nature of syllable onsets such that they should, where possible, show the maximum available vocalic level contrast with the vowel peak itself. The dental nasal, with its well-defined oral-tract constriction would certainly appear to be more 'consonantal' and further removed from the vocalic 'end' of the sonority hierarchy than any [h] fricative which was contiguous with a vowel. In this way the greater degree of 'devocalization' of the nasal might make it a more suitable shape to appear at the syllable periphery. But note the counter-example at (116): ⟨and mad a nobull haration⟩ 'narration'.

What is important to emphasize, however, is that this [n] insertion into empty syllable onset slots appears to be firmly *syntactically* constrained. Consider the following instances from Machyn's diaries:

(1) ⟨was a nold man set in the pelere . . . the sam old man was set in the pelere⟩ (277–8)

(2) ⟨Was a nold man sett up of the pelere⟩ (136)

(3) ⟨on was a nold voman⟩ (137)

(4) ⟨and nold harlot led the man . . . like a nold hore⟩ (161)

(5) ⟨shott and lost a-nodur game⟩ (132)

(6) ⟨and after on of these whent in-to the pulpytt⟩ (193)

(7) ⟨in evere strett⟩ (66)

Sentences (1) through (5) would appear to point to a relexicalization of the '*old*' item as /nold/ or at least to the fact that the historically syllable final [n] of the indefinite determiner has come to be (equally) associated with the onset to ⟨old⟩, given a syllable bracketing interpretation of the construction as {a{n}old}; indeed, the first ⟨nold⟩ shape in sentence (4) would even seem to suggest that the entire indefinite article had been 'incorporated into' (procliticized to) the following adjectival form. What is especially interesting about the examples in sentences (6) and (7) is that they provide evidence for the fact that [n] syllable re-allocation never operates so as to produce an output like *[ɪ nɛvərɪ stret]. The reasons for such a constraint appear to be of a syntactic rather than a phonological kind and we can only express them briefly and informally here. Only those items which are governed by, fall within the domain of, the same syntactic category 'head' appear to be available for such an [n] placement process as we have been describing above. Thus, for example, a phrase such as ⟨an old man⟩ might be accorded a syntactic configuration such as that in Figure 4.18, where we can see that both the ⟨an⟩ and ⟨old⟩ determiners are controlled by, come within the same defining scope as, a single head or governor of the entire structure – N_1. On the other hand, in a construction like ⟨They found gold in every street⟩, the location specifying item ⟨in⟩ supplies the essential, central information characterizing the relationship of the nominal item ⟨street⟩ to the sentential predicate ⟨found⟩; as such the locational item ⟨in⟩ is itself the head of the ⟨in the street⟩ construction, and clearly does not come under the domain of the noun ⟨street⟩ or its governed

FIG. 4.18

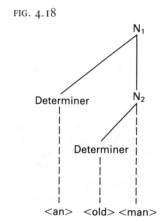
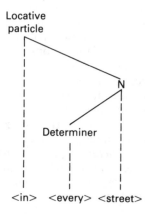

determiner. Yet the kinds of argument we have been proposing for the characteristics of novel [n] placement in Machyn's data must be accepted only with considerable reserve, especially when we find there instances like the following where *bilabial* nasal insertion occurs under syntactic conditions which do not seem to correspond to those we have just set out:

⟨what so *mever* he where that cold bryng forth hym that dyd hang the catt on the galaus⟩ (60)

Our earlier observations on the vagaries of [h] fricative placement should also leave us prepared for the fact that there is evidence to be found for the converse of the 'right shifting' of nasal syllable codas. Although it is not such a widespread phenomenon and appears to be quite severly constrained to occur with a rather limited set of lexical items, it seems to have been the case that by the thirteenth century speakers could occasionally interpret what were etymologically [n] syllable onsets *as if they were the terminations of the preceding coda empty syllables.* Consider the following examples (cited in Kurath and Kuhn 1954) involving the item ⟨napron⟩ (Old French ⟨napron⟩ '*apron*'):

(1) ⟨elnes of new lynnen clothe for an Apron for the Bussop⟩ (1600)
(2) ⟨An aperon worth 4d: 8 haperons, 16.d⟩ (1401)
(3) ⟨Limas: napruns⟩ (1425)
(4) ⟨With her napron feir and white⟩ (1400)

The apparent relexicalization of /napron/ as /apron/ appears to have involved speakers associating its etymological nasal onset with the coda of the terminally empty determiner in the same noun phrase: a type of encliticization perhaps similar to the analysis of [paint] '*pint*' as [painte] ⟨pinta⟩ in many modern British English dialects after the model of the advertising jingle '*Drinka pinta milka day*'; cf. plural formations like ⟨two pintas⟩. Items such as ⟨naddre⟩ '*adder*' (West Saxon Old English ⟨næddre⟩) seem to have been subject to the same kind of process – cf. such fifteenth- and sixteenth-century shapes as ⟨Then he come in neddir likenesse⟩ (1425) and the variants in *Mirk's Festial* of ⟨þe old eddyr⟩/⟨þe old neddyr⟩ (1500) (Luick 1964: sect. 741). But this phenomenon appears limited to a very restricted lexical set and the *Middle English Dictionary* records no [n] effacement in items such as ⟨narowe⟩ '*narrow*'; ⟨narracioun⟩ '*story*'; ⟨nose⟩ '*nose*'; ⟨name⟩ '*name*'; ⟨nede⟩ '*need*'; ⟨neck⟩ '*neck*'; ⟨net⟩ '*net*'; ⟨number⟩ '*number*' and so on.

Chapter 5

The eighteenth century to the present day

5.1 The nature of the data

As in a great many general English language 'histories', our section dealing with materials from the eighteenth and nineteenth centuries will be considerably more brief than the rest. There are many reasons why these two centuries are the Cinderellas of English historical linguistic study. There has always been a suggestion (although it is nowhere made fully explicit), especially among those scholars writing in the first half of the twentieth century, that phonological and syntactic change is only properly observable at a great distance and that somehow the eighteenth, and especially the nineteenth centuries, are 'too close' chronologically for any meaningful observations concerning language change to be made. For some reason it was until quite recently felt that innovations in these parts of the grammar (the stricture not being felt applicable to matters lexical) had a 'pedigree' worth recording only after they could be observed established 'in place' from a respectable temporal distance. On this basis alone materials from the past two hundred or so years have been only sporadically treated by academic historical linguists. As a result, we have no equivalent of the large data surveys such as Dobson (1968), Jordan (1974) or Luick (1964) for this epoch and, in consequence, the range and type of evidence available to us does not fall readily to hand. That there has been relatively such small-scale interest in this later period perhaps also stems from the fact that it is not immediately associatable with any major phonological or syntactic 'event'. It has no innovation equivalent to the *English vowel shift, open syllable lengthening*, or *i-umlaut* with which it can be uniquely identified. Against such a simplistic one to one, period to innovation mapping we have, of course, been arguing throughout this book, and we shall again attempt to show how the eighteenth and nineteenth centuries manifest the same types of phonological processes we have met at earlier historical 'moments'.

While a major research effort is required to bring together and assess the complete range of evidence available for pronunciation habits and the changes they undergo between the early eighteenth century and the invention of voice-recording devices, we must nevertheless not create the impression that no indirect evidence is available or that it has been left completely unresearched. Not only has there been considerable interest in the data provided by poetic end rhymes (Wyld 1923; Gabrielson 1909), but there have been major editions and interpretations of the materials in contemporary foreign-language grammar books, pronouncing dictionaries and handbooks on pronunciation, some of which we shall review in the pages which follow. The fact that interest in the spelling-reform movement was still active during these two most recent centuries means that we have the benefit of some excellent orthoepistic materials. Especially in the nineteenth century, we have a wealth of pamphlets and handbooks dealing with speech and general grammar 'manners', books of 'do's and dont's' for the socially aspiring. At the same time, there is some evidence to be gathered as to contemporary pronunciation habits from the increasingly frequent attempts by literary authors in our era to represent what they intuitively felt was the 'real' speech of their character creations. But, despite recent scholarly interest, full and detailed assessment of this last kind of evidence is still needed.

It is remarkable how recent has been the concern for 'genuine' and ongoing language change. Even until a few decades ago, such study as there was of pronunciation differences between living English speakers was mainly confined to regional dialect scholarship, and many such enterprises – although highly detailed and accurate in their observation and recording techniques – nevertheless showed only a secondary interest in their data as evidence for ongoing phonological change. It is only really with the advent of sociolinguistic research that contemporary language mutation has come to be a major concern for the general linguist. The observation that phonological and syntactic novelty as well as usage could be reflected in a speaker's age, sex, social class, occupation as well as against a whole range of other non-linguistic parameters, has led to a considerable revival in the study of all aspects of temporal language variation. Importantly too, this kind of work has highlighted several central aspects of the ways in which language change is *transmitted* from speaker to speaker and group to group through time, a philosophy of transmission which, in its complexity and apparent heterogeneity, contrasts sharply with the once-and-for-all, everywhere operative sound change 'law' so favoured by the nineteenth- and early-twentieth-century Neogrammarian tradition.

Our knowledge of the mechanisms of temporal linguistic change has been furthered too by the intense study currently devoted to both first- and second-language acquisition, side by side with the important work being undertaken into what, if anything, might constitute phonological and syntactic 'universals' – how alike are phonological systems across language types, and to what extent can they be shown to manifest similar changes to their structures? All the while too, rapid advances in instrumental technology make possible increasingly accurate assessments of the qualitative nature of the sound signal itself, pointing to a range of possible perceptual 'cues' for signal recognition which may in turn suggest constraints upon as well as motivations for mutations in signal processing and production by language users (Ohala 1981).

Important evidence for the nature of language change is also becoming increasingly available from the study of what happens when languages 'die' and when they are 'born'. In both situations, speakers appear to have an 'imperfect' knowledge of a particular language. The types of innovations to the 'full' language brought into being by, for instance, those speakers acquiring it for cross-cultural communication in a multi-lingual context (say, in Pidgin and Creole versions of English) and by those who only partly learn a language which, like Scottish Gaelic, is being swamped by a culturally more powerful type are, apparently, not unlike each other nor untypical of general temporal language change (Todd 1984; Romaine 1988; Dorian 1981).

It would, of course, take all of a book of this size and more even to review the exciting and increasingly productive research being carried out at present into contemporary language change along a temporal axis: we shall have space to examine but a few present-day ongoing innovations in this chapter, selecting in particular those which relate to some of the central historical processes which have been our recurrent concern thus far.

5.2 Vowel length and vowel shifting: the *English vowel shift*

We have in earlier chapters drawn attention to what were apparently large-scale phenomena affecting those stressed vowel segments which had extended durational characteristics. These 'vowel shifts' seem different from many other phonological processes, some argue, in that they can be seen as 'implicational' in their inception and operation. In their case it seemed to be a fact that should an individual long vowel undergo a particular phonological operation, say raising, such an innovation appeared to have a 'knock-on', inferential effect on the rest of the vowel space; all the other long vowels were affected by the 'displacement' to the system occasioned by that first, perhaps independent, change. We outlined the main features of such 'global' operations in our sections dealing with the *English vowel shift* (3.3 and 4.2) and we saw there a situation very approximately outlined in Figure 5.1. Such highly symmetrical representations suppress, of course,

FIG. 5.1

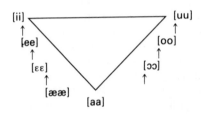

many complex phenomena associated with the processes in question, notably in the case of the *English vowel shift*, the non-raising (de-sonorizing) behaviour of the pure palatal and labial segments [ii] and [uu] which, we recall, are diphthongized to shapes perhaps represented by [əi] and [əu] at the latest by the early sixteenth century. More importantly, perhaps, such configurational representations tempt us into accepting too readily certain theoretical stances concerning both the motivation for and direction of such shifts; our diagram certainly seems to infer that the vowel movements are both symmetrical and 'step-by-step' in nature, assumptions which we have already questioned and to which we shall return in this section.

But before we go on to discuss such theoretical considerations, let us look to see whether we can produce any evidence for some kind of later 're-enactment' of the *English vowel shift*, given that we have laid considerable stress in this book upon the fact that phonological changes often do not appear to be specific to delimited historical periods, but rather can be shown to *recur* or repeat through time. In Table 5.1 we have a very schematic and

TABLE 5.1

13th century	15th century	16th century	18th century
[ee]	[ee] ([ii])	[ii]	[ii]
[ɛɛ]	[ee]	[ee]	[ii]
[ææ]	[ɛɛ]	[ɛɛ]	[ee]

idealistic representation of the historical 'pathways' taken by the long palatal-like vowels in stressed position in items like ⟨meet⟩, ⟨meat⟩ and ⟨mate⟩ as they appear between the thirteenth and eighteenth centuries. The fifteenth-century shapes represent the result of the *English vowel shift* process and show the typical increase in palatality (decrease in sonority) associated with that innovation. Data like these also suggest that all of the outputs of that process could also be available for any subsequent re-enactment it might manifest, the 'new' [ɛɛ], [ee] segments potentially 'raisable' to [ee] and [ii] respectively, the 'new' [ii] a candidate for diphthongization as it gets 'pushed out of the way' of this last [ii] segment. Such a 'copycat' recurrence of this vowel shift could therefore have potentially resulted in a post-seventeenth-century realization for the items in question like Table 5.2. But it is clear from most modern usage that such an [ii]

TABLE 5.2

16th century	Subsequent	
[miit]	*[mɔit]	*'meet'*
[meet]	[miit]	*'meat'*
[mɛɛt]	[meet]	*'mate'*

→ [ɔi] 'displacement' for items like *'meet'* did not, in fact, occur and any palatalization of [ee] → [ii] has not had any expected 'knock-on' effect. Although the phenomenon seems to be attested from as early as the late fifteenth century (cf. such late Middle English spellings as ⟨lif⟩ *'leave'* (Old English ⟨læfan⟩); ⟨diel⟩ *'division'* (Old English ⟨dæl⟩); ⟨riden⟩ *'to advise'* (Old English ⟨ræden⟩)), the first truly reliable evidence for an [ee] → [ii] vowel shift re-enactment are to be found in the writings of grammarians and phoneticians in the early part of the eighteenth century, and perhaps some of the clearest evidence for the phenomenon is to be seen in the *Prononciation de la Langue Angloise* (1740; 1754) by a Paris exiled Jacobite Englishman, Mather Flint (Kökeritz 1944) – a work itself heavily dependent upon the observations of the Frenchman Guy Miege in a work entitled *The English Grammar; or the Grounds, and Genius of the English Tongue* (Miège 1688). In his discussion of contemporary English pronunciation of the sound represented by the digraph ⟨ea⟩, Flint tells us (Kökeritz 1944: p. 25) how 'Le son propre & le plus ordinaire de la diph. *ea* est *î* fr. long' and he cites examples like the following:

meat	*viande*	mît
read	*lire*	rîd
lead	*mener*	lîd
breath	*respirer*	brîʒ

items which, with their Middle English [ɛɛ] source might be expected to have manifested a more palatality-highlighted [ee] shape at least one hundred years before Flint's time, their raising to [ii] in his grammar apparently attesting to a re-application of the *English vowel shift* process in such items. It is important that we stress that the phenomenon may have been strictly limited in its operation in Flint's lifetime to a particular and constrained set of lexical items. Flint is careful to emphasize that although the [ii] pronunciation is current in the items he quotes there is a set of others which, he infers (Kökeritz 1944: p. 25), although they ought also to show just such an [ii] stressed vowel shape, behave in fact exceptionally:

> Voici les mots exceptés, c'est-à-dire où *ea* ne se prononce point *î*:
> *Ea* est *é* fr. long & fermé dans break *rompre*.
> great *grand*. queen *coquine*. sweal *se fondre*.
> bear *porter*. . . .

Such items (and we have already commented upon the irregular vowel shifted nature of some of them above, see sect. 4.2, pp. 210–11) apparently remain 'unshifted' at [ee].

At the same time, Flint's evidence shows clearly that those items which had shown a pure long palatal [ii] vowel space for at least a century previously, failed to be affected by this later vowel shift, and were not 'pushed out of the system' to show diphthongs like [əi]/[ei], as we might have expected had we been operating within the framework of a theory which saw vowel shifts as essentially global vowel space symmetry preserving stratagems. For instance, Flint tells us (Kökeritz 1944: p. 26) that:

EE se prononce tojours e Angl. long, c'est-à-dire *î fr. long*

bee	*abeille*	bı
see	*voir*	sí
beech	*hêtre*	bîtch
bleed	*saigner*	blíd

Both of Flint's observations are crucial for our general interpretation of how vowel shifts work. The failure of the [ii] stressed vowel items like ⟨bee⟩ and ⟨see⟩ to register a 'reaction' to what we have described as an invasion of their area of the global phonological vowel space by the [ee] → [ii] palatalization in the ⟨meat⟩ type items, must cast serious doubt on vowel shift models which adhere to symmetry preserving explanations for their operation. The failure of the ⟨bee⟩ [ii] vowels to 'move out of the way' of those arising from *English vowel shift* re-enactment on [ee] in the early eighteenth century seems to point to the occurrence of what is traditionally referred to as a *phonological merger*. That is, those items manifesting the recently palatalized [ii] are interpreted as if they belonged to the same 'class' of lexical items as those showing the [ii] which had been present in the phonology throughout the previous century. The implication of this kind of view of such an event is that it leaves open the possibility that any subsequent change affecting the 'long standing' [ii] items will apply equally to those which have recently acquired it. But we shall return to this matter below.

The fact that Flint records a 'residue' of items in which the [ee] → [ii] shift has apparently not operated – the ⟨great⟩, ⟨break⟩ and ⟨quean⟩ cases, for instance – has equally important implications. We have on several occasions above commented upon the 'patchy' nature of application of phonological processes, observing that they very often seem to apply one lexical item at a time and can leave areas of the lexicon, which might otherwise be sensitive to their operation, quite unaffected. But such residual [ee] long-vowel items will themselves become conflated, merged with those historically showing [εε] which in the early eighteenth century were vowel shifting to [ee]. This failure of some [ee] bearing items to palatalize to [ii] is well attested in the eighteenth and early nineteenth centuries. Consider the often quoted observation of Samuel

Johnson cited by his biographer, James Boswell, suggesting not only that ⟨great⟩ type items had both [griit] and [greet] variants in his phonology, but that even in 'polite' society there was debate about which form was the more acceptable, although the association of one version with an Irish origin might imply that it was stigmatized:

> When I published the Plan for my Dictionary, Lord Chesterfield told me that the word *great* should be pronounced so as to rhyme to *state*; and Sir William Yonge sent me word that it should be pronounced as to rhyme to *seat*, and that none but an Irishman would pronounce it *grait*. Now here were two men of the highest rank, the one, the best speaker in the House of Lords, the other, the best speaker in the House of Commons, differing entirely.

Even as late as the first years of the nineteenth century we find Thomas Batchelor noting in his *An Orthoëpical Analysis of the English Language* (Zettersten 1974: p. 103) that:

> In Ireland, and in some parts of England, the common diphthong *ea*, as in *treat* (triyt), *compleat* (kompliyt) &c. is pronounced (ey); and this occurs in Bedfordshire, in a few instances; as in *meat* (miyt), and *eat* (iyt), which are sounded (meyt) and (eyt, or et).

Clearly a set of lexical items showing [ee] vowel space has, for a complex of reasons, been left unaffected, an observation confirmed by occasional spellings like the following which surface in various personal letter and other sources throughout the eighteenth century (where we interpret ⟨a⟩ as some kind of [ee] or [ɛɛ] sound): ⟨lave⟩ '*leave*', ⟨spaks⟩ '*speaks*', ⟨say⟩ '*sea*', ⟨spake⟩ '*speak*', ⟨plased⟩ '*pleased*', ⟨incrase⟩ '*increase*', ⟨emadetely⟩ '*immediately*', ⟨percaue⟩ '*perceive*', ⟨plade⟩ '*plead*', ⟨raisonable⟩ '*reasonable*' and ⟨spake⟩ '*speak*' (Matthews 1936b: pp. 52–3). However, that such non-[ii] pronunciations were socially unacceptable is perhaps illustrated by Smart in his *Walker Remodelled: a New Critical Pronouncing Dictionary of the English Language* (1836); in a section dealing with the 'Principles of Remedy for defects of Utterance' (p. xli) providing hints for molifying the effects of the Irish 'brogue', Smart claims that:

> The numerous interchanges that (the speaker) will have to make among the vowels it will be impossible to particularize, – such, for instance, as will convert *plaze* into *please*, *greet* into *great*, *plinty* into *plenty*.

What all this suggests is that there appear to be at least two 'pathways' along which [ee] vowel space could travel at the beginning of the eighteenth century. Firstly, it appears that it could undergo *English vowel shift* re-application and be palatalized to [ii]; secondly, it could remain unaffected by such a process and in its turn see its place in the overall vowel space symmetry come to be 'invaded' by the innovative [ee] segments which result from the palatalization of [ɛɛ] → [ee]. Table 5.3 shows, in a very much

TABLE 5.3 Eighteenth- and nineteenth-century *English vowel shift*

15th century	*17th century*	*18th–19th century*	
[meet]	[miit]	[miit]	'*meet*'
[mɛɛt]	[meet]	[miit]	'*meat*'
[mæææt]	[mɛɛt]	[meet]	'*mate*'

15th century	*17th century*	*18th–19th century*
[meet]	[miit]	[miit]
[mɛɛt]	[meet]	[meet]
[mæææt]	[mɛɛt]	[meet]

simplified form, the general trend of these two possibilities. Both scenarios seem to be characteristic of modern British English regional dialects, many Southern mainland types manifesting the conflation of the ⟨meet⟩/⟨meat⟩ categories, while others – notably North-Western English and many Irish varieties – evidence the 'merging' of the ⟨meat⟩/⟨mate⟩ categories under an [ee] – type vowel, contrasting with the [ii] in ⟨meet⟩ types.

5.2.1 Vowel shifts and mergers

It is the failure of some long vowel segments to 'move out of the way' of others which are 'invading' their area of the global vowel space which has perhaps caused theorists the greatest difficulty with vowel-shift phenomena. If vowel shifts are to be understood in terms of principles like the preservation of overall vowel-space symmetry, then 'collapses' between different vowel-value types like those we have described in the previous section are difficult to explain and must lead at least to some kind of vowel-space restructuring if assymetry is to be avoided. Above all, such 'mergers' would seem to give rise to communicative problems in certain areas of the phonological lexicon; witness the possible homophonous clash they might in various ways provoke among a set like ⟨meet⟩, ⟨meat⟩ and ⟨mate⟩. While many late-Middle English dialects can show a one-to-one mapping of the individual semantic representations of these items onto a unique phonological shape, the result of some of them in 'response' to vowel shifting would seem to leave open the possibility that this mapping could become skewed, and homophony occur. Indeed, we have shown that many scholars see the avoidance of such homonimity as a deep-seated motivation for push-and-pull chain shifts having appeared in the first instance (Samuels 1972: pp. 146 ff). Yet we would hold too simplistic a view of linguistic communicative ability were we to suggest that somehow the transmission of information could be regularly and systematically disrupted through the production of homophonic pairs, no matter how semantically distinct the items in question might be; the speaker/hearer clearly has access to other kinds of linguistic and non-linguistic information to promote his or her processing of 'noisy' materials in the discourse (and these are far from being confined to homophonous lexical items (Edmonson 1981: pp. 152 ff)).

It is of course important to bear in mind that, in our brief description of the *English vowel shift* as it occured in the sixteenth and seventeenth centuries, we stressed the fact that its application was not infrequently asymmetrical. Notably, it seemed that palatalization/labialization increase by more than a single 'step' at a time was not an uncommon phenomenon. We observed, for instance, how Alexander Gil recorded [ii] pronunciations from sources in [ɛɛ], and [ee] realizations for items deriving from 'two-step' apart [ææ] space – recall the [liiv] for [leev] *'leave'* and [keepən] for the 'expected' [kɛɛpən] *'capon'* instances attributed to the *Mopseys* in pp. 220–1 above. Evidence for such a 'leapfrogging' effect could be found too in some of the Middle English *open syllable lengthening* instances where, for instance, we recorded lowerings for the [i] in ⟨wicu⟩ *'week'* which rhyming evidence suggested could be [ee] or [ɛɛ]. Such 'leapfrogging' phenomena clearly make vowel-shift models which are based on the simplest forms of symmetry preservation criteria difficult to accept. But we shall explore this kind of phenomenon further in the next section.

5.2.2 Merger avoiding stratagems

There is even a body of evidence emerging which suggests that observations like those of Flint to the effect that items like ⟨meat⟩, which show [ee] in late Middle English, have come by re-application of the *English vowel shift* to share precisely the same pure palatal area of phonetic space as ⟨bee⟩ and ⟨see⟩ (items which fail to 'divert' from their path), may in fact be the result of poor phonetic observation on his part. There exists a real possibility that at least some of the vowel mergers recorded by our historical sources may be false (Labov, Yaeger and Steiner 1972). In a recent important study relating to the application of ongoing vowel shifting to long stressed vowels in the urban dialect of Belfast, Harris (1985) points to a number of phenomena which can help to illuminate some of the problems we have raised above. In the first place, he highlights the fact (one, remember, first attested by Mather Flint) that in this dialect, the re-enactment of the *English vowel shift* whereby [ee] → [ii] has been extremely sporadic. Citing a mid-nineteenth-century source (Patterson 1860) Harris shows how at that time there appear to have been over one hundred items recorded as showing an [ee] stressed vowel where the modern language shows a 'raising' to [ii] – e.g. ⟨beat⟩, ⟨beak⟩, ⟨leave⟩, ⟨beast⟩, ⟨steal⟩, ⟨speak⟩. In the subsequent period, many items have moved out of this class into that showing [ii] stressed vowels in what seems to have been an item-by-item fashion; certainly there appears to have been left behind a residue of some thirty-five or so items which still show an [ee] pronunciation. With their large number of listed exceptions to the [ee] → [ii] palatalization, Flint's materials similarly suggest a lexical diffusion model for the eighteenth-century innovation as does the fact that even in the previous century we have evidence that [ee] and [ii] pronunciations for items such as ⟨speak⟩, ⟨meat⟩ could exist side by side in the phonology of many speakers (Dobson 1968: sect. 109). 'Transfer' from the [meet] to [miit] class was certainly not a wholesale or everywhere type of operation, rather (and under conditions which we do not fully understand) the re-application of the palatalization increase process to those items showing [ee] in the late seventeenth and early eighteenth centuries appears to have proceeded on a lexical item by lexical item, 'patchy' basis.

But Harris' evidence from contemporary Belfast usage also points to the possibility that we might be premature in assuming that historical phonological mergers took place even to the more limited extent we have been suggesting (Harris 1985: pp. 241–48). Harris brings to light the important fact that close observation of phonetic detail shows that what superficially appear to be phonological mergers producing homophonous pairs may in fact not be such at all. His data show that items such as ⟨meat⟩ and ⟨mate⟩ have a wide variety of pronunciations in the Belfast vernacular including such shapes as [e], [ę], [eə], [ęə], [ɛ] and [iə], where [ę] is a slightly less palatal shape than [e] but less sonorant than [ɛ]: the distribution in his study of such pronunciations for these two tokens is as in Table 5.4. What is striking

TABLE 5.4

	⟨meat⟩	⟨mate⟩
[iə]	0	33
[e], [eə]	20	60
[ẹ], [ẹə]	38	6
[ɛ]	2	0

about these data is that they clearly demonstrate that, for
contemporary speakers in Belfast, there can be no complete
merger between the ⟨meat⟩ and ⟨mate⟩ items at all. The bulk
of the ⟨mate⟩ types occur with [e] or [eə] vowel space; most of
this type are also diphthongal rather than monophthongal in
[e]/[ɛ] and, above all, the ⟨mate⟩ types consistently manifest
pronunciations showing *higher* vowel space characteristics (either
as single vowels or in the first element of diphthongs) – the [iə]
realization being confined, for example, to the ⟨mate⟩ item.
Obviously, the bulk of the tokens appear with [e]/[ẹ] or [eə]/[ẹə]
vowel space, outputs which are phonetically 'very close', so that
in one sense we might talk about a near ⟨meat⟩/⟨mate⟩ merger
in this dialect. But on the whole, the two lexical items are kept
distinct by fine phonetic adjustment, distinctions of a type to
which sixteenth-, seventeenth- and eighteenth-century grammarians may not have been sensitive or for which they were not able
to develop a sufficiently narrow transcription (but see below).
But what is especially interesting about Harris's observations is
the fact that the ⟨mate⟩ types are realized in the vernacular of
Belfast city with an overall *higher* vowel than those of the ⟨meat⟩
type – the reverse of what we would expect from the operation
of the vowel-shift process. The ⟨mate⟩ type have 'leapfrogged'
over those in ⟨meat⟩ – they have undergone a 'double application' of the palatalization increase, much in the same fashion
as Gil's [liiv] for [leev] stigmatized 'Mopsey' pronunciation. Such
a 'leapfrogging' effect might be interpreted as another perceptual
stratagem whereby conflation of whole lexical sets brought about
by the effects of vowel shifting could be avoided (for a similar
phenomenon, see Labov, Yaeger and Steiner 1972).

Yet it is worth bringing to light the fact that the observations of
some of even the early phoneticians are not always devoid of finely
tuned phonetic comment. One quite close observer was William
Tiffin, the creator of one of the first systems of phonetic shorthand,
published in 1757 and entitled *A New Help and Improvement of the
Art of Swift Writing . . . with an* APPENDIX, *containing Characters
and Instructions for the Use of a longer Sett of Vowels, in which*

a philosophical Exactness is farther pursued (Matthews 1936a). In our discussion above, we have readily accepted evidence like that of Flint to the effect that those [ee] stressed vowels (themselves the product of the fifteenth-century *English vowel shift* of [ɛɛ]) were subject in the early eighteenth century to a 'further' palatalization to [ii]; thus [meet]→[miit] '*meat*', [reed]→[riid] '*read*'. In turn, these 'new' [ii] vowels came to be identified with and could therefore be 'merged' with those of the in-place pure palatal [ii]. However, Tiffin's quite close observation of the vowel possibilities of his contemporary phonology suggests that such a view of events is highly over-simple. For instance, in his analysis of his contemporary vowel set (Matthews 1936a: pp. 42–6), he appears to suggest the existence of two quite separate pronunciations for the vowels in the items ⟨see⟩, ⟨eel⟩, ⟨beet⟩, ⟨grief⟩ (derived via the *English vowel shift* of [ee]) and those of ⟨sea⟩, ⟨beat⟩ and ⟨seat⟩ (derived via the operation of the same process on [ɛɛ]): perhaps some type of relatively less palatal [ii̯] sound is intended by the description of his vowel number three:

> 3. Advance the Swelling of the tongue about half Way forward under the Bone of the Roof, and let the Edges press the upper Jaw-Gums a little; and there you meet the Vowel spelt with *ea* in *eat*.

That of his vowel number four perhaps suggests a more raised segment like [ɨi]:

> 4. Bring the Swelling as near as ever you can to the Roof of the Mouth and Fore Gum, hold the Edges of the Tongue somewhat stiff against the upper Jaw-Gums; and so you may pronounce the fourth Vowel, as in *See, seen, Eel,* &c.

A similar observed discrepancy between the two [ii] types can perhaps also be inferred from the following remarks of that close observer of late-eighteenth-century pronunciation, John Walker, in his *A Critical Pronouncing Dictionary and Exposition of the English Language* (1791) who tells us that the sound represented orthographically by ⟨EE⟩:

> in all words except those that end in *r*, has a squeezed sound of long open *e*, formed by a closer application of the tongue to the roof of the mouth than that vowel simple, which is distinguishable to a nice ear, in the different sounds of the verbs, to *flee* and to *meet* and the nouns *flea* and *meat*. This has always been my opinion: but upon consulting some good speakers on the occasion, and in particular Mr. Garrick, who could find no difference in the sounds of these words, I am less confident in giving it to the public.

While, of course, we are not trying to suggest that 'vowel-shift' (and other) phonological processes never give rise to the conflation of previously existing vowel-quality contrasts, historical evidence of the type cited immediately above, together with that provided by some recent phonological studies, perhaps suggest that vowel 'mergers' were less common in the past than the handbooks on English historical phonology would have us believe.

5.3 Diphthongization processes: vowel shifts and diphthongization

One of the most noteworthy features of the later 'development' of the *English vowel shift* lies in the tendency of many modern dialects from the start of the nineteenth century to diphthongize the long mid [ee] and [oo] vowel space to a variety of linearly contrastive vowel oppositions. For instance, the [ee] vowel in items such as ⟨say⟩, ⟨may⟩, ⟨maid⟩ and ⟨pair⟩ comes to be realized as showing increased palatalization *only in its second element*, such that [ee] → [ei]. It is very difficult to date precisely such an innovation and although there is some evidence to suggest it may have its beginnings in the late eighteenth century, the first indisputable manifestation of the process seems to appear in the important grammar book by Thomas Batchelor written in 1809 and called *An Orthoëpical Analysis of the English Language* (Zettersten 1974). Batchelor notes, for instance, that the long equivalents of [o] vowels are not [oo] but some kind of diphthong, perhaps [ou]:

> "*O*, as in *rŏgue, brŏke*, etc. The sound which is here intended, is not similar to that heard in the words *tone, moan*, etc. The latter will be found to be true diphthongs; but the simple sound is heard only in the instances which are given, and a few others, when pronounced short, in the provincial manner."

At the same time, he lists what for some speakers would appear to be a set of homophones which we might interpret as showing an [ee] stressed vowel space; however, he is careful to note (p. 102) that for other (regional) speakers this [ee] vowel could have a diphthongal realization:

> *sale* and *sail, tale* and *tail, male* and *mail, pale* and *pail*, are not distinguished in polite conversation, but they are different sounds in the country; and the persons who would say (a peal face) (*a pale face*) are never heard to say (a *peal* ov *weatur*) for (a *pail of water*).

an observation suggesting that only the first of such pairs could appear with a diphthongal realization (whatever detailed shape it might have had), the other (historically diphthongal!) remaining with a long steady state vowel space. Batchelor goes on to state:

> "By the speech of a native of Lancashire, it appears that the provincial (ea) is very common in that country, in such words as *fail, pail* etc. but, in some cases, the sound of *e* in *met* is pronounced without alteration; as *way* (wey), and *pail* (peyl) are pronounced (we) and (pēl).

The importance of such observations lies in the fact that they are among the first to suggest that at least regionally, and certainly in sociolinguistically stigmatized contexts, a diphthongal innovation was appearing in some items where prestigious speakers only manifested a monophthongal [ee]; certainly Batchelor is pointing to a diphthongal possibility for the vowel space in items like *way* and *pail* (his (wey) and (peyl) perhaps representing [wei] and [peil]) which could exist alongside a monophthongal long vowel alternant.

5.3.1 Long [ee] mid vowel alternants: a case study of a modern dialect

A recent study of the modern English reflexes of the long [ee] monophthong, whose diphthongization to a shape resembling [ei] we have just seen positively observed in the early nineteenth century, will serve to show both how that diphthongization process is manifested in some present-day usage as well as demonstrate how speakers can currently relate such diphthongal and monophthongal variants to extra-linguistic phenomena such as the sex of the speaker. In one of the few detailed examinations of its kind, Kerswill (1983) observed the behaviour of the long high mid vowel [ee] in a speech community in County Durham in the North East of England. Kerswill showed that speakers in that region have available two alternating variables for such a long vowel space; one is monophthongal (usually [ee]) the other comprised of various contrastive vowel segments such as [iə], [eə], [jæ] and several others (Orton 1952). The general distribution of the mono-phthongal/diphthongal variation itself, Kerswill noted, was very much a function of the sex of the speaker. Male speakers tended to maximize diphthongal shapes in items such as ⟨place⟩/[pliəs], ⟨play⟩/[pleə], ⟨face⟩/[fiəs] and so on. Female speakers, on the other hand markedly favoured monophthongal realizations for the vowel space in such items, thus [plee], [fees]. A simplified version of Kerswill's results for this distribution according to the sex of the

FIG. 5.2

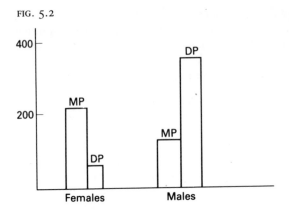

informant is seen in Figure 5.2. A gross percentage count of recorded tokens revealed that females overall used monophthongal variants on no less than 90 per cent of occasions, while male speakers manifested them for a mere 30 per cent of their total use. Diphthongal vowel space in the ⟨play⟩, ⟨face⟩ and ⟨fair⟩ type items can thus be seen to be a clear identifying feature of male linguistic behaviour in this regional dialect.

However, another of Kerswill's conclusions is of equal interest. He noted that there was considerable variety among the kinds of [ei] diphthongs which could be produced in his County Durham community. Although the majority of these were of the 'falling' type – i.e. the first element being relatively more palatal than the second, [eə], [iə], [iɛ], [ɛæ] – much fine phonetic detail could nevertheless be observed in the contrast between the two 'halves' of the stressed vowel space. For instance, there was much diversity in the 'degree of travel' involved in each diphthongal movement; there were measurable levels of contrast between the relative height of the first element and the relative sonority, centrality of the second. The study plotted this degree of 'travel' between the two vowel half elements by mapping it against relative height and centrality parameters shown again in a much simplified form in Figure 5.3. That graph shows clearly that this relative degree of travel between the parameters of height and centrality is overall much greater in a diphthongal shape like [i̞ɛ] than it is, say, for one such as [ɛ̞ə], the latter showing a more 'gradual' movement between its component sections compared with the pronounced 'slope' associated with the former. Monophthongs will, of course, show no degree of travel contrast whatsoever, since being steady state in type, they involve no displacement of relative position of

FIG. 5.3

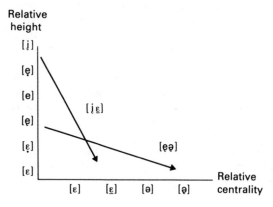

any kind. The total number of monophthongal and diphthongal tokens was counted and plotted on a graph which measured on its vertical axis the number of such recorded tokens set against, on the horizontal axis, the degree of travel (height versus centrality) involved in the production of the two halves of the diphthongal vowel space. Figure 5.4 shows how the data splits up clearly into two groups. (1) where there is no degree of travel involved whatsoever; a high number of monophthongal tokens were recorded here mainly, as we have just observed, from female informants, (2) there is a group of tokens showing varying degrees of vowel travel (measured here on an arbitrary scale of 0 to 5),

FIG. 5.4

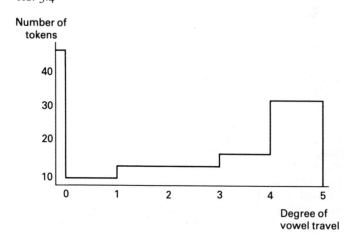

and *in this group the greatest number of tokens is to be found at that end of the spectrum which records the greatest degree of inter-segment travel.* Expressed in its simplest terms, this display shows that speakers choose between a monophthongal or diphthongal realization for the [ee] vowel space in items like ⟨face⟩, ⟨place⟩ and so on; having selected a diphthongal version, they are more liable to realize one where *the phonetic contrast between the two halves is maximalized.* Such an observation accords well with our often repeated assertion that long stressed vowel space tends to be highlighted, foregrounded, made maximally distinct (cf. sect. 4.2.2; cf. sect. 4.2.2; sect. 2.3.1(6)) – in this case this effect is achieved not just by diphthongization, but in the majority of occasions by the selection of a diphthongal contrast showing the maximal height/centrality displacement characteristic between its component parts.

5.3.2 Vocalization and *Breaking*
We have focused much of our attention in this book upon those historical innovations affecting syllable rhymes which are made up of sonorant [r]/[l] and fricative [x]/[ç]/[ʝ]/[ɣ] segment terminations. Two sets of changes were repeatedly observed. Firstly, stressed vowel space in such contexts tended to be foregrounded either through a diphthongization or through a vowel-lengthening stratagem – recall our discussion of the various Old and Middle English vowel lengthening, *Breaking* and vocalization processes in Chapters 2 and 3. In this way, we argued, could come into being such diphthongal innovations as in [calf]/[caulf]/[cauf] *'calf'*, [half]/[haulf]/[hauf] *'half'* as well as such vowel-length contrasts (although these were perhaps more controversial) as [niçt]/[niiçt]/[niit] *'night'*. We shall attempt to show in this section that not only are innovatory phenomena like these typical of the phonology of the English language from the eighteenth century to the present day, but also that during this late period there has come to be established in many regional and social dialects, an important and related mutation affecting the [r] sonorant segment.

That some kind of pre-[r] diphthongization of the [hir]/[hiər] *'here'* variety, which we saw recorded by Gil in the seventeenth century (cf. sect. 4.3), is also an established feature of the phonology of the language more than a century later, can be deduced from the statement of Thomas Batchelor in his *An Orthoëpical Analysis of the English Language* (1809) to the effect that 'When the long *i* (uy) preceded *r* and other sonsonants (*sic*), it is not easily pronounced without dividing the words into two syllables; thus, *shirt* (syurt), would become (syuyrt), and *spirt* (spurt) would be (spuyrt)' (Zettersten 1974: p. 100). Such an observation seems to point to the possibility that some kind of [ɪ] stressed vowel segment had become realized as a diphthongal shape like [ɪə] in the pre-[r] context. But it is Batchelor's remarks a few pages later which perhaps shed the most interesting light on such a pre-sonorant vowel foregrounding (this time provoking stressed vowel length), especially as it relates to (or even results from) the perception by speakers of the relatively high vocalic content of [r] (and [l]) segments in such rhyme terminal positions:

> It will be observed that the long sound. . . .occurs . . . particularly before *l* and *r*; as, in *balm* and *born*. In the former word, the *l* has been gradually softened till it has entirely vanished, and the *a* is sounded long to supply its place. The *u* as in *but*, has always been supposed to maintain one uniform length; but this also appears to be something longer when preceding *r*, as in *burn*, than in other cases. It is difficult, however, to ascertain what portion of the sound belongs to *r*, as both this letter and *l* seem to be but slight alterations or additions to the unaccented *u* in *nostrum*.

Such remarks are especially interesting since they seem to suggest Batchelor's awareness of the possible 'compensatory' lengthening effect on the precedent vowel space brought about by [l] vocalization. At the same time, however, his final sentence seems to hint at his holding a viewpoint similar to the one we have tentatively suggested above (see sect. 3.4.4), whereby the 'additional' perceived vowel-ness of the stressed vowel space in pre-[r]/[l] environments is supplied through the *linear* realization of the inherent vocalic quality which such segments show in their complex internal structure.

Even three-quarters of a century earlier, Walker in his *A Critical Pronouncing Dictionary and Exposition of the English Language* (1791), records such effacement of [l] sonorants in well defined phonetic and morphological and even lexical contexts:

> *L* is mute in *almond, calf, half, calve, halve, chaldron, falcon, folk, yolk* (better written *yelk* with the *l* sounded) *fusil, halser, malmsey, salmon, salve, talbot* (a species of dog).
>
> *L* is mute also between *l* and *k* in the same syllable, as *balk, chalk, talk, stalk, walk*. *L* is silent likewise between *a* and *m* in the same syllable, as *alm, balm, calm, palm, psalm, qualm, shalm*; but when the *m* is detached from the *l* by commencing another syllable, the *l* becomes audible. Thus, though the *l* is mute in *balm, palm* and *psalm*, it is always heard in *bal-my, pal-my, psal-mist, psal-mody*, and *pal-mistry*. . . . But although *l* is mute in the noun *salve*, it is heard in the verb to *salve*, and in *salver* (a kind of plate).

Again, Watts in his *The Art of Reading* (1721: ch. 4, p. 10) reflects a similar state of affairs when, in answer to the question 'When is *l* not pronounced?' comes the response 'The sound of *l* is almost worn out toward the end of a Syllable in many Words; as *Psalm, Half, Fault, Talk, Salmon, Faulcon.*'

[l] effacement or vocalization of this type is, of course, a common feature of several modern English regional and social dialects, notably in the British Isles those of Glasgow and the East End district of the city of London. In such contexts we can find pronunciations like [fio] '*fill*', [fiod] '*field*', [fou], '*fall*' and [piəpo] '*people*'. In many of the London instances, this [l] vocalization in combination with that dialect's tendency to neutralize [ʊ], [u] and [o] segments under [o], has resulted in some items such as ⟨bald⟩, ⟨pulls⟩, ⟨full⟩, ⟨pools⟩ having their stressed vowels 'neutralized', merged under [oo]; thus [bood], [pooz], [foo] where the 'standard' language shows distinct vowel contrasts such as [bɔɔld], [pʊlz], [fʊl] and [puulz] (Wells 1982: pp. 315–16; Trudgill 1986: pp. 46–7).

Yet it is interesting to record too that there exist present-day regional dialects of British English where the stressed vowel space in pre-[r], [l] and [x]/[ç] contexts (the last being still extant there) shows diphthongization of a type and extent almost identical to that we described for Old and Middle English *Breaking* in the same kinds of phonetic environment (sects 2.3.1 and 3.4). Consider the pronunciations in Table 5.5 from the Scottish regional dialect spoken in Dounby, Isle of Orkney (Mather and Speitel 1986: pp. 20–1).

TABLE 5.5 Modern Scottish English *Breaking*

–[r]		–[l]		–[x]/[ç]	
[eə]		[eə]		[ei]	
[beərn]	'*bairn*'	[heəl]	'*hail*'	[dreiç]	'*wet*'
[beər]	'*bear*'	[seəl]	'*sail*'	[eiçt]	'*eight*'
[heər]	'*hear*'	[teəl]	'*tail*'	[streiçt]	'*straight*'
[iə]		[ɛə]		[au]	
[biər]	'*beer*'	[bɛəl]	'*bell*'	[ɪnaux]	'*enough*'
[hiər]	'*hear*'	[ɛəlm]	'*elm*'	[laux]	'*loch*'
		[tɛəl]	'*tell*'	[traux]	'*trough*'
				[raux]	'*rough*'

5.3.3 [r] effacement and vocalization

While we have provided considerable evidence for the fact that speakers appear to be prepared to interpret both the sonorant [l] and the voiced and voiceless palatal and velar fricatives as though they were purely vocalic in nature, we have never suggested that such an interpretation could be afforded to [r] sonorant segments when they appeared post-vocalically in syllable rhymes. While historical data readily attest alternations like [kalf]/[kauf], [niçt]/[niit], [dæj]/[dæi] and [boɤ]/[bou], we have so far produced nothing in the way of evidence to suggest that variants such as, for example, *[ært]/[ææt] – with vocalization, effacement of post-vocalic [r] – could equally commonly surface. Indeed, it seems to be the case that such a phenomenon is extremely uncommon before the sixteenth century and only a very few instances of the process, some of which are recorded in Table 5.6, are noted in the

TABLE 5.6

	15th-century Middle English	
⟨bersel⟩	⟨bessel⟩	'a butt'
	⟨bissele⟩	
⟨hors⟩	⟨hos⟩	'horse'
⟨harsk⟩	⟨haske⟩	'coarse'
⟨morsel⟩	⟨mossel⟩	'mouthful'
	⟨musel⟩	
	⟨moscel⟩	
⟨morther⟩	⟨mother⟩	'murder'
⟨parcel⟩	⟨passel⟩	'portion'
	⟨passelle⟩	
⟨quart⟩	⟨quat⟩	'quart'
⟨dars⟩	⟨dace⟩	'Dace, fish'

handbooks from texts composed before that general date (Luick 1964: sect. 772.a; Dobson 1968: sect. 218). It is only by the early seventeenth century that we begin to see evidence that such a phenomenon was relatively widespread in the phonology of English, one of the earliest important observations to that effect being that of Walker in his *A Critical Pronouncing Dictionary* (1791) where we are told (sect. 419, p. 50) under the discussion headed *R*, that

> In England, and particularly in London, the *r* in *lard, bard, card, regard* &c is pronounced so much in the throat as to be little more than the middle or Italian *a*, lengthened into *baa, baad, caad, regaad*; while in Ireland, the *r*, in these words, is pronounced with so strong a jar of the tongue against the forepart of the palate, and accompanied with such an aspiration or strong breathing at the

beginning of the letter, as to produce that harshness we call the Irish accent. But if the letter is too forcibly pronounced in Ireland, it is often too feebly sounded in England, and particularly in London, where it is sometimes entirely sunk.

Such remarks would seem to point quite unequivocally to some kind of [r] vocalization, especially in those rhymes terminated by an [rd] cluster, producing that vowel-lengthened, post-vocalic [r] deleted configuration which is such a characteristic of much Southern speech in the United Kingdom mainland. Walker's observations are echoed by Watts who, in his *The Art of Reading* (1721: pp. 120–2) records versions like ⟨fust⟩ '*first*', ⟨Nus⟩ '*nurse*' and ⟨Puss⟩ '*purse*'. But it is Walker's other contemporary Mather Flint who, throughout his *Prononciation de la Langue Angloise* (1754), provides us with the most consistent evidence for this effacement of post-vocalic [r], especially when it is the first member of a 'homorganic' consonantal cluster. Flint comments upon the fact that: 'l'*r* devant une consonne est fort adouci, presque muet & rend un peu longue la voyelle qui la precede, *barb, guard, arm, yarn*' (Kökeritz 1944: p. 41). Flint uses the graphic convention of italicization to indicate those lexical items where the effaced, 'adouci' [r] is to be found: 'vous verrez souvent aussi l'*r* en *Italique*, les Anglois l'adoucissant beaucoup plus que les Francois & ne le prononçant que tres foiblement, sur tout lorsqu'il est suivi d'une autre Consonne' (p. 3). Such items with this [r] effacement, he claims, are *hard, regard, retard, third, bird, quart, shirt, flirt, mirth, birth, hearth, arches, urge, serge, girl, harm, barn, warm, born, worms, servant, cork* and a few others (Kökeritz 1944: p. 153).

Although such a process of [r] vocalization was probably firmly established in the phonology of some Southern British dialects by the middle of the nineteenth century, there is some evidence to suggest that its use was considerably stigmatized. For instance, George Jackson writing in 1830 a pamphlet dealing with *Popular Errors of English Grammar, Particularly of Pronunciation*, warns against the vulgarity of such realizations as (cawn) '*corn*', (cuss) '*curse*', (fust) '*first*', (gaal) '*girl*', (hawse) '*horse*', (nuss) '*nurse*', (paason) '*parson*' and (puss) '*purse*'. He also cites several instances of what he clearly regards as the equally non-U habit of 'inserting' unetymological [r] sonorants post-vocalically. These insertions or epentheses seem to occur in response to two different kinds of phonological stimuli. In the first place, Jackson condemns pronunciations such as (darter) '*daughter*', (dorn) '*dawn*' and (sarsepan) '*saucepan*'. Here, we might tentatively suggest, the [r] epenthesis fulfills a similar kind of phonological functions as the [r] which comes to be in post-vocalic position through the operation of *metathesis* (see sect. 3.5.3). That is, it seems possible that speakers are willing to interpret the second half of a long stressed vowel space, perhaps especially when it was relatively low/sonorant in type (which we might expect to surface in the items just cited), as if it were a highly vocalic sonorant [r] consonant. In some sense, we might hypothesize, speakers regard rhymes like, say, [aan] and [arn] as phonologically 'equivalent', the one substitutable for by the other. Certainly, such [r] intrusive long vowel space is relatively well documented from the eighteenth century onwards, instance the ⟨marster⟩ *'master'* and ⟨farther⟩ *'father'* spellings cited by Wyld (1936: pp. 298–9) as well as the frequently occurring spelling of ⟨Blarst!⟩ in popular working-class fiction in the following century (Keating 1973).

5.4 Syllable shapes and their phonetic consequences: [r] at syllable interface

Jackson also provides a second context where such an innovatory (and again, for him, socially unacceptable) instance of [r] epenthesis can occur. He cites instances like (brockler) *'brocolli'*, (drawr) *'draw'*, (duberous) *'dubious'*, (dilemmer) *'dilemma'*, (feller) *'fellow'*, (a meller pear) *'a mellow pear'*, (umbreller) *'umbrella'*, (widder) *'widow'*, (winder) *'window'*, (yeller) *'yellow'* and (pianer) *'piano'*, many of which pronunciations are still to be heard in the speech of many inhabitants of London and the South-East of England. Although Jackson provides no detailed description of the kinds of phonological contexts in which such forms could occur in his language, they are usually associated in handbooks on modern English phonology with 'sandhi' phenomena. That is, they are seen as instances of segment insertion at points of syllable interface where there are two contiguous peak elements. Many present-day Southern British speakers will informally realize forms like [sɪrɪŋ ɪm du ɪt] *'seeing him do it'*; [læst tæŋgər ɪn pærɪs] *'Last Tango in Paris'*; [ɪndɪər ən pækɪstan] *'India and Pakistan'* (Wells 1982: sects 3.2.3, 4.1.4). Such an 'overlap'-achieving stratagem reminds us of the voiceless fricative [h] insertion in just such contexts in the language of Machyn's London speech of some two centuries earlier (cf. Table 4.19 above) – although it clearly leaves unexplained Jackson's (a meller pear) case – and taken together they appear as two possible and perhaps equivalent mechanisms for achieving segment ambisyllabicity at syllable interface.

5.5 Monophthongization processes: monophthongization and merger

The fact that vowel shifts could not only manifest changes in height (palatality/labiality increase) when they affected long vowel segments, but could also achieve greater foregrounding characteristics for such segments through a *diphthongization* stratagem, is one we have commented upon at several places above. We remember from section 4.2 how, for instance, pure palatal [ii] shapes had come to be realized as sequences of contrastive vowel elements like [əi] or [ei] – cf. the *Hymn to the Virgin* spellings such as ⟨kreist⟩, ⟨dein⟩ and ⟨mei⟩ for the earlier ⟨crist⟩, ⟨ðin⟩ and ⟨min⟩. Although we pointed to the possibility that such a diphthongization was a kind of 'merger-avoidance stratagem' to prevent conflation between the in-place [ii] vowel space and that resulting from the *English vowel shift* effect upon [ee], we also left open the possibility that such an innovation was an independent event whose function it was to make more acoustically prominent a vowel space with extended durational characteristics. Perhaps one of the most interesting features of the later, eighteenth-century manifestations of the *English vowel shift* lies in its tendency to use this diphthongization possibility in a way not unlike that we outlined as a feature of the Swedish vowel shift process – cf. Figure 4.15 – and we have just provided evidence to suggest, for example, that by the beginning of the nineteenth century, long vowel segments such as [ee] in items such as ⟨say⟩ and ⟨may⟩, did not show the 'expected' increase in palatalization associated with the vowel shift but, in fact, come to be realized as diphthongs, perhaps [ei].

However, it should be noted that many of the items with long stressed vowels which could be subject to this later diphthongization – items like ⟨say⟩, ⟨sail⟩ and ⟨hail⟩ – were themselves diphthongal in Middle English. Some of these diphthongs arose, as we have seen, via *Breaking*-type processes like those we outlined in section 3.4.2 (cf. thirteenth-century alternants like [dæj]/[dæi] '*day*' and [heej]/[hei] '*hay*' with [j] 'vocalization'/*Breaking*) others were lexical, inherited from the phonology of contact languages like French, as in items such as ⟨bailliff⟩, ⟨jail⟩ and ⟨pay⟩ (Ekwall 1980: sect. 31). We have already shown in section 4.4.4 that there is a considerable but complex body of evidence to suggest that certainly by the mid sixteenth century – and probably even as much as one hundred years before (cf. Dobson's (1968: sect. 227) examples from Hart) – such [æi] diphthongs had come to be interpreted as though they were [ɛɛ] or [ææ] *monophthongs* (Barber 1976: pp. 302–3). The [æi] → [ɛɛ] process very much resembles the [au] → [ɔɔ] monophthongization we described in section 4.4 (recall the [lau]/[lɔɔ] '*law*' variants) in that it seems to show what was originally a *linearly* contrastive sequence of relatively low palatal [æ] to pure palatal [i], reinterpreted as though it were a single vowel segment *whose complex internal structure shows a mixture of just these two elements*: [ɛɛ]. The [æi] → [ææ] change demonstrates, of course, the generalization across the entire vowel space area of the dominant (syllable-bearing) [æ] element.

Most modern commentators suggest that the derived [ææ]/[ɛɛ] monophthongs underwent a classical 'merger' with those [ɛɛ] segments produced via the *English vowel shift* of [ææ] – cf. the stressed vowel development in the thirteenth to fifteenth centuries of the stressed vowels in items such as ⟨name⟩, ⟨face⟩, ⟨safe⟩ and ⟨late⟩. Both sets of items – ⟨day⟩/⟨name⟩ types – show the same subsequent palatalization of [æa]/[ɛɛ] to [ee] and possible later diphthongization to [ei], thus [dei], [neim] (Wells 1982: pp. 192–6), a process we might crudely schematize as in Table 5.7.

TABLE 5.7

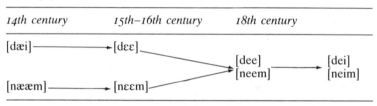

14th century	15th–16th century	18th century	
[dæi]	[dɛɛ]	[dee]	[dei]
[næææm]	[nɛɛm]	[neem]	[neim]

Yet we must take pains to stress that this [æi]/[ææ] 'merger' of the late seventeenth century was by no means an across the board process. On the one hand, Flint in his *Prononciation de la Langue Angloise* (1740) regularly records items which historically show [æi] with the digraph ⟨aï⟩ (Kökeritz 1944: p. 24), as in:

hair	*cheveu*	haïr
stairs	*escaliers*	staïrz
sail	*voile*	saïle
rain	*pluye*	raïne
gay	*gay*	gaï
play	*jeu*	plaï
day	*jour*	daï
way	*chemin*	waï

where such a digraph is identified by Flint as 'l'é Fr. Fermé & long', clearly a monophthong but one which could apparently signify either [εε] or [ee] in the French of that period (Dobson 1968: sect. 230, note). On the other hand, that very careful observer of the first half of the eighteenth century – Dr John Jones – shows clearly in his *Practical Phonography* (1701) (Jones 1701; Ekwall 1907) that such a monophthongization of [æi] to some kind of [ææ] or [εε] type sound was extremely patchy and lexically sporadic. He is prepared only to record a very limited set of items which show a monophthongal pronunciation for the 'historical' diphthong [æi]. Thus, in answer to the question 'When is the sound of *a* written *ai*?', the answer is 'When it may be sounded *ai* as in . . .' and he cites as [æi]/[ææ] alternants 28 items including ⟨pair⟩, ⟨pain⟩, ⟨maid⟩, ⟨fair⟩, ⟨hair⟩, ⟨chair⟩ and ⟨stairs⟩. Likewise [æi]/[εε] variants are ascribed to a limited list of 23 items only. Clearly both diphthongal and monophthongal pronunciations could exist side by side in Jones's phonology, the monophthongizing innovation being non-uniform across the lexicon, perhaps only effective in a 'one lexical item at a time' fashion, leaving behind a residue of unaffected, diphthongal shapes.

Bibliography

ABERCROMBIE, D. (1967) *Elements of General Phonetics*, Chicago: Aldine.

ALSTON, R. C. (1969) (ed.) *John Cheke: De Pronuntiatione Graecae Linguae* (1555), *English Linguistics 1500–1800*, **81**, Menston: The Scolar Press.

ANDERSON, J. M. and C. J. EWEN (1987) *Principles of Dependency Phonology*, Cambridge: Cambridge University Press.

ANDERSON, J. M. and C. JONES (1974) 'Three theses concerning phonological representations', *Journal of Linguistics* **10**, 1–26.

ANDERSON, J. M. and C. JONES (1977) *Phonological Structure and the History of English*, Amsterdam: North Holland.

ANDERSEN, S.R. (1974) *The Organization of Phonology*, London: Academic Press.

——(1980) 'Problems and perspectives in the description of vowel harmony', in R. M. Vago (ed.) *Issues in Vowel Harmony*, Amsterdam, Benjamins: 1–48.

AOKI, H. (1968) 'Towards a typology of vowel harmony', *International Journal of American Linguistics* **34**, 142–5.

ATKINS, J. W. H. (1922) *The Owl and the Nightingale*, New York: Russell and Russell.

BARBER, C. (1976) *Early Modern English*, London: Deutsch.

BENSKIN, M. (1982) 'The letters ⟨þ⟩ and ⟨y⟩ in later Middle English, and some related matters', *Journal of the Society of Archivists* **7**, 13–30.

BERNDT, R. (1960) *Einführung in das Studium des Mittelenglischen*, Halle: Niemeyer.

BLISS, A. J. (1952–3) 'Vowel quantity in Middle English borrowings from Anglo-Norman'. In R. Lass (ed.) *Approaches to English Historical Linguistics*, New York: Holt, Rinehart and Winston (1969) 164–207.

BROOKE, G. L. and R. F. LESLIE (1963) *Laȝamon's Brut*, Early English Text Society, 277, 250.

BRUCE, G. (1970) 'Diphthongization in the Malmö dialect', *University of Lund Phonetics Laboratory Working Papers* **3**, 1–19.

BRUNNER, K. (1952) *Abriss der mittelenglischen Grammatik*, Tübingen: Niemeyer.

BÜLBRING, K. D. (1902) *Altenglisches Elementarbuch I*, Winter, Heidelberg.

CALDER, G. (1917) *Auraicept na n-Éces. The Scholar's Primer*, Edinburgh: Edinburgh University Press.

CAMPBELL, A. (1959) *Old English Grammar*, Oxford: Oxford University Press.

CARTER, R. J. (1967) 'Theoretical implications of the Great Vowel Shift'. Unpublished manuscript.

CERCIGNANI, F. (1981) *Shakespeare's Works and Elizabethan Pronunciation*, Oxford: Oxford University Press.

CLEMENTS, G. N. (1976) 'The autosegmental treatment of vowel harmony'. In W. Dressler (ed.) *Phonologica 1976: Innsbrucker Beiträge zur Sprachwissenschaft* **19**, Innsbruck.

CLEMOES, P. (1952) 'Liturgical influence on punctuation in late Old English and early Middle English manuscripts', *Occasional Papers in Linguistics* **1**, 2–17, Cambridge.

COLES, E. (1674) *The Compleat English Schoolmaster*. In R. C. Alston (ed.) (1967) *English Linguistics 1500–1800*, **26**, Menston: The Scolar Press.

COLGRAVE, B and R. A. B. MYNORE (1969) *Ecclesiastical History of the English People*, Oxford: Oxford University Press.

COOPER, C. (1687) *The English Teacher*. In R. C. Alston (ed.) (1969) *English Linguistics 1500–1800*, **175**. Menston: The Scolar Press.

COOTE, E (1596) *The English Schoole-maister*. In R. C. Alston (ed.) (1968) *English Linguistics 1500–1800*, **98**. Menston: The Scolar Press.

CROTHERS, J. (1978) 'Typology and universals of vowel systems'. In J. Greenberg *et al.* (eds.) *Universals of Human Language*, Vol. 2 Stanford: Stanford University Press.

CUTLER, A. (1980) 'Syllable omission errors in isochrony'. In H. W. Dechert and M. Raupach, *Temporal Variables in Speech*, The Hague: Mouton, 183–90.

DANIELSSON, B. (1955–63) *John Hart's works on English orthography and pronunciation, 1551–1570*, Stockholm Studies in English II, Stockholm: Almqvist and Wiksell.

DANIELSSON, B. and R. C. ALSTON (1966) *The Works of William Bullockar*, Leeds: University of Leeds.

DAUNT, M. (1939) 'Old English sound changes reconsidered in relation to scribal tradition and practice', *Transactions of the Philological Society*, 108–37.

DAVID, R. (ed.) (1956) *Loves Labours Lost*, The Arden Shakespeare, London: Methuen.

DeCHENE, B. (1979), *The Historical Phonology of Vowel Length*, Bloomington, Ind.: Indiana University Linguistics Club.

denOs, E. A. (1983) 'Stressed timed and syllable timed languages', *Progress Report. Institute of Phonetics*, University of Utrecht **8**, 12–23.

DICKENS, B. and R. M. WILSON (1954) *Early Middle English Texts*, Cambridge: Bowes and Bowes.

DOBSON, E. J. (1947) 'Robert Robinson and his phonetic transcripts of early seventeenth century English pronunciation', *Transactions of the Philological Society*, (1947), 25–63.

——(1954) 'The Hymn to the Virgin', *Transactions of the Honourable Society of Cymmrodorion*, 70–124.

—— (1962) 'Middle English lengthening in open syllables', *Transactions of the Philological Society*, 124–48.

—— (1968) *English Pronunciation 1500–1700*, Oxford: Oxford University Press.

DONEGAN, P. (1978) *On the Natural Phonology of Vowels, Working Papers in Linguistics*, **23**, Department of Linguistics, Columbus, Ohio: Ohio State University.

DORIAN, N. (1981) *Language Death: the Life Cycle of a Scottish Gaelic Dialect*, Philadelphia: University of Pennsylvania Press.

DURAND, J. (ed.) (1984) *Dependency and non-Dependency Phonology*, London: Croom Helm.

DURAND, M. (1954) *Voyelles Longues et Voyelles Brèves*, Paris: Klincksieck.

ECKHARDT, E. (1936) 'Die quantität einfacher tonvokale in offenersilbe', *Anglia* **60**, 49–116.

EDMONSON, W. (1981) *Spoken Discourse*, London: Longman.

EDWARDS, A. S. G. (1984) *Middle English Prose: A Critical Guide*, New Bruswick, New Jersey: Rutgers University Press.

EKWALL, E. (1922) *Place Names of Lancashire*, Manchester: Manchester University Press.

——(1980) *A History of Modern English Sounds and Morphology*, Oxford: Blackwell.

—— (ed.) (1907) *Dr. John Jones's Practical Phonography (1701)*, Halle: Niemeyer.

ELERT, C-C. (1964) *Phonologic Studies of Quantity in Swedish*, Uppsala: Monografier utgivna Stockholms Kommunalförvalning.

ELLIS, A. J. (1869–89), *On Early English Pronunciation*, Early English Text Society, 2, 7, 14, 23, 25.

FANT, G. (1956) *The Acoustic Theory of Speech Production*, The Hague: Mouton.

FOLLICK, M. (1975) *The Case for Spelling Reform*, London: Pitman.

FÖRSTER, M. (1926) 'The Welsh Hymn', *Herrigs Archiv* **60**, 187–202.

FUDGE, E. (1969) 'Syllables', *Journal of Linguistics* **3**, 1–36.

FUNKE, O. (1938) 'William Bullockar's *Bref Grammar of English* (1586)', *Anglia* **LXII**, 116–37.

GABRIELSON, A. (1909) *Rime as a Criterion of the Pronunciation of Spenser, Pope, Byron and Coleridge. A Contribution to the History of the Present Day English Stressed Vowels*, Uppsala: Almqvist and Wiksalls.

GIEGERICH, H. J. (1985) *Metrical Phonology and the Phonological Structure of English and German*, Cambridge: Cambridge University Press.

GIL, A. (1621) *Logonomia Anglica*. In R. C. Alston (ed.) (1968) *English Linguistics 1500–1800*, **68**, Menston: The Scolar Press.

GORDON, E. V. (1927) *An Introduction to Old Norse*, Oxford: Oxford University Press.

——(1963) *Pearl*, Oxford: Clarendon.

GRUNDT, A. W. (1974) 'Open syllable lengthening in English'. PhD dissertation, University of Michigan.

HAAS, M. (1969) *The Prehistory of Languages*, The Hague: Mouton.

HAGGARD, M. (1973) 'Abbreviation of consonants in English pre- and post-vocalic clusters', *Journal of Phonetics* **1**, 9–23.

HARLOW, C. G. (1959) 'Punctuation in some manuscripts of Ælfric', *Review of English Studies* **10**, 1–19.

HARRIS, J. (1985) *Phonological Variation and Change: Studies in Hiberno-English*, Cambridge: Cambridge University Press.

HART, J. (1551) *The Opening of the Unreasonable Writing of our English Toung*. In B. Danielsson (ed.) *John Hart's Works*, Part I, Stockholm: Almqvist and Wiksell: (1955–63), 109–64.

HARTUNG, A. E. (1973) *Manual of the Writings in Middle English 1080–1500*, Hamden, Conn.: Connecticut Academy of Arts and Sciences.

HAUGEN, E. (ed.) (1972) *First Grammatical Treatise*, London: Longman.

HEALD, A. R. (1965) 'Some graphic evidence for vowel length in three Old English manuscripts'. PhD Dissertation, Austin: University of Texas.

HECK, C. (1906) 'Die Quantitäten der Accentvokale in ne. offenen Silben mehrsilbiger nicht-germanisher Lehnwörter', *Anglia* **29**, 55–119, 205–55, 347–77.

HERRTAGE, S. J. H. (1880) *Roland and Otuel*, Early English Text Society 39.

HEUSER, W. (1900) 'Die mittelenglischen Entwicklung von *ŭ* in offener Silbe', *Englische Studien* **27**, 353–98.

HOCKETT, C. (1955) *A Manual of Phonology*, Baltimore: Waverly.

HOGG, R. M. (1971) 'Gemination, Breaking and reordering in the synchronic phonology of Old English', *Lingua* **28**, 48–69.

HOLDER, W. (1669) *Elements of Speech: an essay of inquiry into the natural production of letters*. In R. C. Alston (ed.) (1969) *English Linguistics 1500–1800*, **49**, Menston: The Scolar Press.

HOLTHAUSEN, F. (1920) 'The Welsh Hymn', *Herrigs Archiv* **CXL**, 33–42.

HONGMO, R. (1985) 'Linguistically conditioned duration rules in a timing model for Chinese', *UCLA Working Papers in Phonetics* **62**, 34–49.

HOOPER, J.B. (1972) 'The syllable in phonological theory', *Language* **48**, 525–40.

HULME, W. H. (1896) Quantity marks in Old English manuscripts, *Modern Language Notes* **11**, 24–45.

JACKSON, G. (1830) *Popular Errors of English Grammar Particularly of Pronunciation*, London: Effingham Wilson.

JAKOBSEN, R. C., G. M. FANT and M. HALLE (1961) *Preliminaries to Speech Analysis*, Cambridge, Mass: MIT Press.

JEFFERS, R and I. LEHISTE (1979) *Principles and Methods for Historical Linguistics*, Cambridge, Mass. MIT Press.

JESPERSEN, O. (1961) *A Modern English Grammar*, Copenhagen: Monksgaard.

JIRICZEK, O. L. (1903) *Alexander Gil's Logonomia Anglica nach der Ausgabe von 1621*, Strassburg.

JONES, C. (1972) *An Introduction to Middle English*, New York: Holt, Rinehart and Winston.

——(1976) 'Some constraints on medial consonant clusters', *Language*, **52**, 121–30.

—— (1980) 'Some characteristics of sonorant-obstruent metathesis within a dependency framework'. In J. M. Anderson and C. J. Ewen (eds) *Studies in Dependency Phonology*, Ludwigsburg Studies in Language and Linguistics 4, Ludwigsburg 139–55.

——(1984) 'A dependency approach to some well-known features of historical English phonology'. In J. Durand (ed.) *Dependency and Non-Linear Phonology*, London: Croom Helm, 257–68.

JONES, J. (1701) *Practical Phonography*. In R. C. Alston (ed.) (1969) *English Linguistics 1500–1800*, 167, Menston: The Scolar Press.

JONES, J. D. (1911) *Cooper's Grammatica Linguae Anglicanae* (1685), Halle: Niemeyer.

JORDAN, R. (1974) *Handbook of Middle English Grammar*, The Hague: Mouton.

KAISSE, E. M. and SHAW P. A. (1985) 'On the theory of lexical phonology'. In C. J. Ewen and J. M. Anderson (eds.) *Phonology Yearbook 2*, Cambridge: Cambridge University Press.

KEATING, P. (1973) *Working Class Stories in the 1890's*, London: Routledge and Kegan Paul.

KELLER, W. (1920) 'Mittelenglische lange Vokale und die altfranzosische Quantitat', *Englische Studien* 54, 111–16.

KEMP, J. A. (ed.) (1972) *John Wallis' Grammatica Linguae Anglicanae*, London: Longman.

KER, N. R. (1957) *Catalogue of Manuscripts Containing Anglo-Saxon*, Oxford: Oxford University Press.

KERSWILL, P. (1983) 'Social and linguistic aspects of Durham (e:)', *Cambridge Papers in Phonetics and Experimental Linguistics* 2, 3–22.

KIHLBOHM, A. (1926) *A Contribution to the Study of Fifteenth Century English*, Uppsala: University of Uppsala Press.

KING, R. D. (1965) 'Weakly stressed vowels in Old Saxon', *Word* 21, 19–39.

——(1969) *Historical Linguistics and Generative Grammar*, Englewood Cliffs: Prentice Hall.

KIPARSKY, P. (1973) 'How abstract is phonology?' In O. Fujimara (ed.) *Three Dimensions of Linguistic Theory*, Tokyo: TEC Company.

——(1978) 'Issues in phonological theory'. In J. Weinstock (ed.) *The Nordic Languages and Modern Linguistics*, vol. 3 Austin, Tex.: University of Texas Press.

——(1979) 'Metrical structure assignment is cyclic', *Linguistic Inquiry* 10, 421–2.

KLATT, D. H. (1973) 'Interaction between two factors that influence vowel duration', *Journal of the Acoustical Society of America* 54, 1102–4.

——(1976) 'Linguistic uses of segmental duration in English', *Journal of the Acoustical Society of America* 59, 1200–21.

KOEPPEL, E. (1900) 'Zur Frage der Dehnung von ae. ĭ zu me. ē', *Archiv für das Studium der neuren Sprachen* 104, 127–9.

KOHLER, K. (1966) 'Towards a phonological theory', *Lingua* 16, 337–51.

KÖKERITZ, H. (1944) *Mather Flint on Early Eighteenth Century Pronunciation, Skriflev Kungl. Humanistika Vetenskapss amfundet i Uppsala: Uppsala and Leipzig: Almqvist and Winksells*.

—— (1954) *A Guide to Chaucer's Pronunciation*, Stockholm: Almqvist and Wiksell.

KURATH, H. and S. M. KUHN (1952–84) *Middle English Dictionary*, Ann Arbor: University of Michigan Press.

LABOV, W. (1963) 'The social motivation of a sound change', *Word* **19**, 273–309.

——(1966) *The Social Stratification of English in New York City*, Washington, DC: Center for Applied Linguistics.

LABOV, W., M. YAEGER and R. STEINER (1972) *A Quantitative Study of Sound Change in Progress*, Philadelphia: US Regional Study.

LADEFOGED, P. (1971) *Preliminaries to Linguistic Phonetics*, Chicago, Ill.: University of Chicago Press.

LANGHANS, V. (1921) 'Der Reimvokal E bei Chaucer', *Anglia* **45**, 221–239.

LASS, R. (1971) 'Boundaries as obstruents: Old English voicing assimilation and universal strength hierarchies', *Journal of Linguistics*, **7**, 15–30.

——(1980) *On Explaining Language Change*, Cambridge: Cambridge University Press.

——(1984) *Phonology: An Introduction to Basic Concepts*, Cambridge: Cambridge University Press.

LASS, R. and J. M. ANDERSON (1975) *Old English Phonology*, Cambridge: Cambridge University Press.

LEECH, C. (1969) *Two Gentlemen of Verona*, The Arden Shakespeare, London: Methuen.

LEHISTE, I. (1967) *Readings in Acoustic Phonetics*, Cambridge, Mass.: MIT Press.

——(1970) *Suprasegmentals*, Cambridge, Mass.: MIT Press.

LEHNERT, M. (1936) *Die Grammatik des englischen Sprachmeisters John Wallis*, Breslau: Sprach und Kultur der germanischen und romanischen Völker, Anglistische Reihe, Bd 21.

LIBERMAN, A. S. (1966) 'On the history of Middle English *ā* and *a*', *Neuphilologische Mitteilungen*, **67**, 66–71.

LIEBER, R. (1979) 'On Middle English lengthening in open syllables', *Linguistic Analysis* **5**, 1–27.

LOCKWOOD, W. B. (1955) *An Introduction to Modern Faroese*, Copenhagen: Munksgaard.

LOTHIAN, J. M. and T. CRAIK (1975) *Twelfth Night*, The Arden Shakespeare, London: Methuen.

LUICK, K. (1964) *Historische Grammatik der englischen Sprache*, Oxford: Blackwell.

——(1894) 'Beiträge zur englischen Grammatik. II', *Anglia* **16**, 451–511.

LYONS, J. (1967) *Introduction to Theoretical Linguistics*, Cambridge: Cambridge University Press.

MCINTOSH, A., M. L. SAMUELS, M. BENSKIN *et al.* (1986) *A Linguistic Atlas of late Mediaeval English*, Aberdeen: Aberdeen University Press.

MACKENZIE, B. A. (1927) 'A special dialectal development of OE ēa in Middle English', *Englische Studien* **LXI**, 386–92.

MADDEN, F. (1847) *Laȝamon's Brut*, London: Society of Antiquaries of London.

MADDIESON, I. (1984) *Patterns of Sounds*, Cambridge: Cambridge University Press.

MALSCH, D. L. and R. FULCHER (1975) 'Tensing and syllabification in Middle English', *Language* **51**, 303–14.

MARTINET, A. (1955) *Economie des changements phonétiques: Traité de phonologie diachronique*, Berne: Francke.

MATHER, J. Y. and H. SPEITEL. (1986) *The Linguistic Atlas of Scotland: Volume III, Phonology*, London: Croom Helm.

MATTHEWS, W. (1936a) 'William Tiffin, an eighteenth century phonetician', *English Studies* **18**, 97–114.

——(1936b) 'Some eighteenth century phonetic spellings', *English Studies* **12**, 47–60, 177–188.

MAYHEW, A. L. (1908) *The promptorium Parvulorum*, Early English Text Society, Extra Series 102.

MEECH, S. B. (1934) 'John Drury and his English writings', *Speculum* **9**, 70–83.

MIEGE, G. (1688) *The English Grammar*. In R. C. Alston (ed.) (1967) *English Linguistics 1500–1800*, **152**, Menston: The Scolar Press.

MILROY, J. (1983) 'On the sociolinguistic history of /h/ dropping in English'. In M. Davenport *et al*, *Current Topics in English Historical Linguistics*, Odense: Odense University Press, 37– 54.

MINKOVA, D. (1982) 'Middle English final -e from a phonemic point of view,' *Edinburgh University, Department of Phonetics: Work in Progress* **15**, 27–44.

MOORE, S. and A. H. MARCKWARDT (1951) *Historical Outlines of English Sounds and Inflexions*, Ann Arbor: Wahr.

MOORE, S., S. B. MEECH and H. WHITEHALL (1935) *Middle English Dialect Characteristics and Dialect Boundaries*, Ann Arbor: University of Michigan Press.

MORRIS, R. (1868–73) *Old English Homilies and Homiletic Treatises of the Twelfth and Thirteenth Centuries*, London: Early English Text Society, Original Series, **29, 34, 53**.

MOSSÉ, F. (1952) *A Handbook of Middle English*, Baltimore: Johns Hopkins Press.

MUIR, K. (ed.) (1966) *King Lear*, The Arden Shakespeare, London: Methuen.

MULCASTER, R. (1582) *The First Part of the Elementarie*. In R. C. Alston (ed.) (1970) *English Linguistics 1500–1800*, **219**, Menston: The Scolar Press.

MURRAY, J. A. H. (1873) *The Dialect of the Southern Counties of Scotland*, Asher: London.

NAPIER, A. S. (1889) 'A sign used in Old English manuscripts to indicate vowel shortness', *The Academy* **36**.

NICHOLS, J. G. (1848) *The Diary of Henry Machyn, Citizen and Merchant-Taylor of London*, Camden Society 42: London.

NIELSEN, H. F. (1981) *Old English and the Continental Germanic Languages*, Innsbruck: Innsbrucker Beitrage zur Sprachwissenschaft BA. 33.

O CUÍV, B. (1973) 'The linguistic training of the mediaeval Irish poet',
    Celtica **10**, 114–40.
O DOCHARTAIGH, C. (1978) 'Lenition and Dependency Phonology', Eigse
    17, 457– 94.
OGURA, M. (1980) 'The development of Middle English e: a case of lexical
    diffusion', *Studies in English Literature*, 39–58.
OHALA, J. J. (1974) 'Experimental historical phonology'. In J. M.
    Anderson and C. Jones, *Historical Linguistics II*, Amsterdam: North
    Holland, 353–89.
——(1981) 'The listener as a source of sound change'. In C. S. Masek, R. A.
    Hendrick and M. F. Miller (eds) *Papers from the Parasession on
    Language and Behaviour*, Chicago: Chicago Linguistics Society.
    178–203.
OHALA, J. J. and H. KAWASAKI (1984) 'Prosodic phonology and phonetics',
    Phonology Year Book **1**, 113–27, Cambridge: Cambridge University
    Press.
OHALA, J. J. and J. LORENTZ (1977) 'The story of [w]: an exercise in the
    phonetic explanation for sound patterns', *Proceedings of the Third
    Annual Meeting of the Berkeley Linguistics Society*, 577–99.
OHMAN, S. E. G. (1965) 'Coarticulation in VCV utterances:
    Spectrographic measurements,' *Journal of the Acoustical Society of
    America* **39**, 151–68.
O' SHAUGHNESSY, D. (1981) 'A study of French vowel and consonant
    duration', *Journal of Phonetics* **9**, 385–406.
ORTON, H. (1952) 'The isolative treatment in living North-Midland dialects
    of OE ĕ lengthened in open syllables in Middle English', *Leeds Studies
    in English* **7** and **8**, 97–128.
PATTERSON, D. (1860) *The provincialisms of Belfast and the Surrounding
    Districts Pointed Out and Corrected*, Belfast: Mayne.
PAUL, J. (1888) *Principien der Sprachgeschihte*, Tübingen: Niemeyer.
PELLOWE, J., G. NIXON, B. STRANG and V. MCNEARY (1972) 'A dynamic
    modelling of linguistic variation: the urban (Tyneside) linguistic survey',
    Lingua **30**, 1–30.
PELT, J. (1960) 'Vowel shift and open syllable lengthening'. In J. M.
    Anderson and C. J. Ewen, *Studies in Dependency Phonology*,
    Ludwigsburg Studies in Language and Linguistics **4**, Ludwigsburg,
    61–102.
PERKELL, J. S. (1969) *Physiology of Speech Production*, Cambridge, Mass.:
    MIT Press.
PETERSEN, G. E. and I. LEHISTE (1960) 'Duration of syllable nuclei in
    English', *Journal of the Acoustical Society of America* **32**, 693–703.
PICKETT, J. M. (1980) *The Sounds of Speech Communication*, Baltimore:
    University Park Press.
PIKE, K. L. (1943) *Phonetics*, Ann Arbor: University of Michigan Press.
——(1948) *Phonemics*, Ann Arbor: University of Michigan Press.
POPE, M. K. (1966) *From Latin to Modern French*, Manchester: Manchester
    University Press.
PRINS, A. A. (1972) *A History of English Phonemes*, Leiden: Leiden
    University Press.

PROKOSCH, E. (1939) *A Comparative Germanic Grammar*, Baltimore: Linguistic Society of America.

RAPHAEL, L. J. (1972) 'Preceding vowel duration as a cue to the perception of the voicing characteristic of word final consonants in American English', *Journal of the Acoustical Society of America* 51, 1293–1303.

——(1975) 'The physiological control of durational differences between vowels preceding voiced and voiceless consonants in English', *Journal of Phonetics* 3, 25–36.

REIS, H. (1974) *Lauttheorie und Lautgeschichte: Untersuchungen am Biespiel der Dehnung und Kürzungsvorgange im Deutschen*, Munich: Niemeyer.

ROBINS, R. H. (1967) *A Short History of Linguistics*, London: Longman.

ROBINSON, F. N. (1977) *The Works of Geoffrey Chaucer*, Oxford: Oxford University Press.

ROBINSON, I. (1971) *Chaucer's Prosody: A Study of Middle English Verse Tradition*, Cambridge: Cambridge University Press.

ROBINSON, R. (1617) *The Art of Pronunciation*. In R. C. Alston (ed.) (1969) *English Linguistics 1500–1800*, 150, Menston: The Scolar Press.

ROMAINE, S. (1982) *Sociohistorical Linguistics*, Cambridge: Cambridge University Press.

——(1988) *Pidgins and Creoles*, London: Longman.

ROSEBOROUGH, M. M. (1970) *An Ouline of Middle English Grammar*, Greenwood, Connecticut: MacMillan.

ROSS, A. S. C. and E. G. STANLEY (1956) *The Anglo-Saxon Gloss*, Geneva: Urs Graf.

R. R. (1641) *An English Grammar or Plain Exposition of Lilies Grammar in English*. In R. C. Alston (ed.) (1972) *English Linguistics 1500–1800*, 326, Menston: The Scolar Press.

RUBACH, J. (1977) 'Nasalization in Polish', *Journal of Phonetics* 5, 17–25.

RUSS, C. V. J. (1969) 'Die Ausnahmen zur Dehnung der mhd Kurzvokale in offener Silbe', *Zeitschrift für Dialektologie und Linguistik*, 36, 82–8.

——(1982) *Studies in Historical German Phonology*, Bern: Lang.

SALESBURY, W. (1550) *A Brief and Plain Introduction*. In R. C. Alston (ed.) (1969), *English Linguistics 1500–1800*, 179, Menston: The Scolar Press.

——(1547) *A Dictionary of English and Welsh*. In R. C. Alston (ed) 1969, *English Linguistics 1500–1800*, 180, Menston: The Scolar Press.

SAMUELS, M. L. (1952) 'The study of Old English phonology', *Transactions of the Philological Society*, 15–47.

——(1972) *Linguistic Evolution*, Cambridge: Cambridge University Press.

——(1983) 'Chaucer's spelling'. In D. Gray and E. G. Stanley (eds) *Middle English Studies*, Oxford: Oxford University Press, 17–37.

——(1985) 'The great Scandinavian belt'. In R. Eaton (ed.) *Papers from the Fourth International Conference on English Historical Linguistics*, Amsterdam: Benjamins, 269–81.

——and J. J. SMITH (1981) 'The language of Gower', *Neuphilologische Mitteilungen* 82, 295–304.

SCHONFELD, M. (1954) *Historische Grammatica van het Nederlands*, Zutphen: Thieme.

SIEVERS, E. and K. BRUNNER (1941) *Abriss der altenglischen Grammatik*, Halle: Niemeyer.

SIMPSON, P. (1935) *Proof Reading in the Sixteenth, Seventeenth and Eighteenth Centuries*, Oxford: Oxford University Press.

SKEAT, W. W. (1868) *The Lay of Haveloc the Dane*, Early English Text Society, Extra Series iv.

——(1892) *Rime-Index to Troilus and Criseyde*, London: The Chaucer Society.

——(1871-87) *The Four Gospels in Anglo-Saxon, Northumbrian and Old Mercian Versions*, Cambridge: Cambridge University Press.

——(1873) *Piers the Plowman*, Early English Text Society, **54**.

SMART, B. H. (1836) *Walker Remodelled: A New Critical Pronouncing Dictionary of the English Language*, London.

SMITH, A. H. (1964) *The Parker Chronicle 832–900*, London: Methuen.

SMITHERS, G. V. (1948-9) 'A note on Havelock the Dane 2008–2009', *English and Germanic Studies* **2**, 1–9.

STAMPE, D. (1972) 'On the natural history of diphthongs', *Papers from the Eighth Regional Meeting of the Chicago Linguistics Society*, Chicago, 578–90.

——(1979) *A Dissertation on Natural Phonology*, New York: Garland.

STEVENS, K. N. and A. S. HOUSE (1956) 'Development of a quantitative description of vowel articulation', *Journal of the Acoustical Society of America* **27**, 484–93.

STOCKWELL, R. (1961) 'The Middle English 'long close' and 'long open' mid vowels', *Texas Studies in Literature and Language* **2**, 529–38.

SUNDBY, B. (1953) *Christopher Cooper's English Teacher 1684*, Copenhagen: Munksgaard.

SWEET, H. (1885) *Older English Texts*, Oxford: Oxford University Press.

TERAJIMA, M. (1985) *The Trajectory Constraint and 'Irregular' Rhymes in Middle English*, Tokyo: Shinozaki Shorin.

THURESSON, B. (1950) *Middle English Occupational Terms*, Lund Studies in English **19**, Lund.

THURNEYSEN, R. (1946) *Grammar of Old Irish*, Dublin: Institute for Advanced Studies.

TODD, L. (1984) *Modern Englishes: Pidgins and Creoles*, Oxford: Blackwell.

TOPPING, D. (1973) *Chamorro Reference Grammar*, Honolulu: University of Hawaii Press.

TRUDGILL, P. (1986) *Dialects in Contact*, Oxford: Oxford University Press.

TURNER, J. R. (1970) *The Works of William Bullokar: Booke at Large 1580*, Leeds: University of Leeds.

VAGO, R. (1980) *Issues in Vowel Harmony*, Amsterdam: John Benjamins.

VALK, C. Z. (1980) 'The development of the back vowel before [ɹ] in early Modern English'. PhD dissertation, Muncie, Indiana: Ball State University.

VAN BREE, C. (1977) *Leerboek voor de historische grammatica van het Nederlands*, Groningen: Walters-Noordhoff.

VAN LOEY, A. (1959) *Schönfeld's Historische Grammatica van het Nederlands*, Zutphen: Thieme.

VON KIENLE, R. (1960) *Historische Laut- und Formenlehre des Deutschen*, Tübingen: Niemeyer.

WALKER, J. (1791) *A Critical Pronouncing Dictionary and Exposition of the English Language* 1791. In R. C. Alston (ed.) (1968) *English Linguistics 1500–1800*, **117**, Menston: The Scolar Press.

WALLENBERG, J. K. (1923) *The Vocabulary of Dan Michel's Ayenbite of Inwyt*, Uppsala.

WANG, H. S. and B. L. D. ERWING 'More on the English vowel shift: the back vowel question', *Phonology Year Book* **3**, Cambridge: Cambridge University Press.

WANG, W. S-Y. (1969) 'Competing changes as a cause of residue', *Language* **45**, 9–25.

WARDALE, E. E. (1955) *An Introduction to Middle English*, London: Routledge and Kegan Paul.

WATTS, L. (1721) *The Art of Reading and Writing English*, London.

WELLS, J. C. (1982) *Accents of English*, Cambridge: Cambridge University Press.

WELLS, J. E. (1916) *A Manual of the Writings in Middle English 1050–1400*, New Haven: Yale University Press.

WELMERS, W. E. (1962) 'The phonology of Kpelle', *Journal of African Linguistics*, **1**, pp. 69–93.

WIJK, A. (1959) *Regularized English*, Stockholm Studies in English **7**, Stockholm.

WILSON, J. (1926) *The Dialects of Central Scotland*, Oxford: Oxford University Press.

WOLFE, P. M. (1972) *Linguistic Change and the Great Vowel Shift in English*, California: University of California Press.

WRIGHT, J (1917) *Middle High German Primer*, Oxford: Clarendon Press.

——(1925) *Old English Grammar*, Oxford: Oxford University Press.

WRIGHT, J. and E. M. WRIGHT (1973) *An Elementary Middle English Grammar*, Oxford: Oxford University Press.

WYLD, H. C. (1923) *Studies in English Rhymes from Surrey to Pope*, New York: Russell and Russell.

——(1927) *A Short History of English*, London: Murray.

——(1936) *A History of Modern Colloquial English*, Oxford: Blackwell.

YAMADA, N. (1984) 'On characterizing the English Great Vowel Shift', *Lingua* **62**, 43–69.

ZACHRISSON, R. E. (1913) *Pronunciation of English Vowels 1400–1700*, Göteborgs Kungl. Vetenskaps- och vitterhetssamhälks handlingar, 14, no. 2, Göteborg.

——(1918) 'A contribution to the study of early new English pronunciation', *Englische Studien* **52**, 299–326.

ZETTERSTEN, A. (1974) *A Critical Facsimile Edition of Thomas Batchelor* Part 1, Lund: Gleerup.

ZIMMER, K. (1967) 'A note on vowel harmony', *International Journal of American Linguistics* **33**, 166–71.

ZUPITZA, J. (1891) *Guy of Warwick*, Early English Text Society. Extra Series 59.

Index